Wolsey

Through a thematic and broadly chronological approach, *Wolsey* offers a fascinating insight into the life and legacy of a man who was responsible for building Henry VIII's reputation as England's most impressive king.

The book reviews Thomas Wolsey's record as the realm's leading Churchman, Lord Chancellor and political patron and thereby demonstrates how and why Wolsey became central to Henry's government for 20 years. By analysing Wolsey's role in key events such as the Field of Cloth of Gold, the book highlights how significant Wolsey was in directing and conducting England's foreign relations as the king's most trusted advisor. Based on up-to-date research, Richardson not only newly appraises the circumstances of Wolsey's fall but also challenges accusations of treason made against him. This book provides a new appreciation of Wolsey's importance as a cultural and artistic patron, as well as a royal administrator and politician; roles which helped to bring both Henry VIII and England to the forefront of foreign relations in the early-sixteenth century.

Presenting Wolsey in his contemporary and historiographical contexts more fully than any currently available book, *Wolsey* is perfect for students of Tudor England.

Glenn Richardson is Professor of Early Modern History at St Mary's University, Twickenham, UK. He is the author of *The Field of Cloth of Gold* (2014).

ROUTLEDGE HISTORICAL BIOGRAPHIES
Series Editor: Robert Pearce

Routledge Historical Biographies provide engaging, readable and academically credible biographies written from an explicitly historical perspective. These concise and accessible accounts will bring important historical figures to life for students and general readers alike.

In the same series
Bismarck by Edgar Feuchtwanger (second edition)
Calvin by Michael A. Mullett
Oliver Cromwell by Martyn Bennett
Edward IV by Hannes Kleineke
Elizabeth I by Judith M. Richards
Emmeline Pankhurst by Paula Bartley
Franco by Antonio Cazorla-Sanchez
Gladstone by Michael Partridge
Henry V by John Matusiak
Henry VI by David Grummitt
Henry VII by Sean Cunningham
Henry VIII by Lucy Wooding (second edition 2015)
Hitler by Michael Lynch
John F. Kennedy by Peter J. Ling
John Maynard Keynes by Vincent Barnett
Lenin by Christopher Read
Louis XIV by Richard Wilkinson (second edition 2017)
Martin Luther by Michael A. Mullet (second edition 2014)
Martin Luther King Jr. by Peter J. Ling (second edition 2015)
Mao by Michael Lynch (second edition 2017)
Marx by Vincent Barnett
Mary Queen of Scots by Retha M. Warnicke
Mary Tudor by Judith M. Richards
Mussolini by Peter Neville (second edition 2014)
Nehru by Benjamin Zachariah
Neville Chamberlain by Nick Smart
Oliver Cromwell by Martyn Bennett
Queen Victoria by Paula Bartley
Richard III by David Hipshon
Thatcher by Graham Goodlad
Trotsky by Ian Thatcher
Stalin by Christopher Read
Thomas Cranmer by Susan Wabuda
Ho Chi Minh by Peter Neville
Isabella d'Este by Christine Shaw
Charles I by Mark Parry
Wolsey by Glenn Richardson

Wolsey

Glenn Richardson

Routledge
Taylor & Francis Group

LONDON AND NEW YORK

First published 2020
by Routledge
2 Park Square, Milton Park, Abingdon, Oxon OX14 4RN

and by Routledge
52 Vanderbilt Avenue, New York, NY 10017

Routledge is an imprint of the Taylor & Francis Group, an informa business

© 2020 Glenn Richardson

The right of Glenn Richardson to be identified as author of this work
has been asserted by him in accordance with sections 77 and 78 of the
Copyright, Designs and Patents Act 1988.

All rights reserved. No part of this book may be reprinted or reproduced or
utilised in any form or by any electronic, mechanical, or other means, now
known or hereafter invented, including photocopying and recording, or in
any information storage or retrieval system, without permission in writing
from the publishers.

Trademark notice: Product or corporate names may be trademarks or
registered trademarks, and are used only for identification and explanation
without intent to infringe.

British Library Cataloguing-in-Publication Data
A catalogue record for this book is available from the British Library

Library of Congress Cataloging-in-Publication Data
Names: Richardson, Glenn, author.
Title: Wolsey / Glenn Richardson.
Description: Abingdon, Oxon ; New York : Taylor and Francis, 2020. |
  Series: Routledge historical biographies | Includes bibliographical
  references and index.
Identifiers: LCCN 2020012094 (print) | LCCN 2020012095 (ebook)
Subjects: LCSH: Wolsey, Thomas, 1475?–1530. | Great Britain—
  History—Henry VIII, 1509–1547—Biography. | Great Britain—
  Politics and government—1509–1547. | Great Britain—Church
  history—16th century. | Statesmen—Great Britain—Biography. |
  Cardinals—England—Biography.
Classification: LCC DA334.W8 R53 2020 (print) | LCC DA334.W8
  (ebook) | DDC 942.05/2092 [B]—dc23
LC record available at https://lccn.loc.gov/2020012094
LC ebook record available at https://lccn.loc.gov/2020012095

ISBN: 978-0-415-68446-0 (hbk)
ISBN: 978-0-415-68447-7 (pbk)
ISBN: 978-1-003-05626-3 (ebk)

Typeset in Garamond
by Apex CoVantage, LLC

For Christine Melican

Contents

List of illustrations	ix
Acknowledgements	x
Chronology	xii
List of abbreviations	xvi

	Introduction: Wolsey and the historians	1
1	From Ipswich to Hampton Court: Wolsey's rise to power	16
2	Cloth of Gold: Wolsey's 'Universal' Peace	42
3	Chief executive: Wolsey in council and court	74
4	Cardinal legate: Wolsey and the English Church	115
5	Cardinal benefactor: Wolsey's cultural and educational patronage	154
6	'Cardinalis pacificus': Wolsey's 'Eternal Peace'	192
7	The Cardinal's greatest matter: Wolsey and the annulment	219

viii *Contents*

8 The turn of Fortune's wheel: Wolsey's fall 252

Conclusion: the Cardinal's legacy 288

Suggestions for further reading 301
Index 309

Illustrations

2.1	Cardinal Wolsey's Arms in terracotta, Hampton Court Palace	52
3.1	Cardinal Wolsey's procession, from the 1578 edition of Cavendish's *Life and Death of Cardinal Wolsey*	80
5.1	Cardinal Wolsey by Sampson Strong, c. 1610, Christ Church, Oxford	179
7.1	'Me and My King' by Sir John Gilbert RA c. 1886	233
9.1	David Annand's statue of Wolsey at Ipswich	299

Acknowledgements

The scholarly debts I owe to the many historians whose work has inspired and guided my own will be clear from the endnotes and Further Reading. A number of colleagues and friends offered useful advice in the course of helpful discussions and collaborations over the years on Wolsey, on cardinals, and on Henry VIII's kingship. I would like to thank Jennifer DeSilva, Brett Dolman, Susan Doran, Alasdair Hawkyard, Mary Hollingsworth and Julian Munby. I would also like to thank Alden Gregory at Historic Royal Palaces Agency who shared his expertise and allowed me access to a number of items associated with Wolsey as we worked together on the Field of Cloth of Gold anniversary exhibition at Hampton Court Palace in 2019–20.

I am grateful to St Mary's University and the Strawberry Hill Trust for hosting the 2015 conference I convened on Renaissance Cardinals. That was of great assistance in better understanding Wolsey in his international context. I would like to thank Ellie Woodacre for offering a special edition of the *Royal Studies Journal* in 2017 for the papers from the conference, and for her assistance in editing that volume.

I am grateful to Judith Curthoys, Archivist of Christ Church Oxford, and her colleagues in the Library, who offered advice on Wolsey's educational foundation and gave me access and advice on the archival collections in their care.

I would like to thank Tony Claydon, Alden Gregory, Brian Kendall, Simon Lambe, Scott Lewis, Diarmaid MacCulloch, Nicky McKenna, John Murphy, Stephanie Saunders and Tim Schroder for reading draft chapters and for their helpful and constructive

Acknowledgements xi

comments. David Starkey kindly read several chapters and helped me formulate my approach to the subject. George Bernard read a full draft and offered many helpful comments and suggestions, for which I am grateful.

My approach to writing a biography of Wolsey has been informed by conversations with my students at St Mary's University, and my inaugural lecture as Professor of Early Modern History at St Mary's enabled me to explore some ideas about Wolsey and Henry VIII. I would also like to thank Christine Jackson, David Beard and Shirley Fawdrey at the Oxford University Department for Continuing Education for the opportunity to offer study-day lectures and summer school classes on Wolsey. The enthusiastic engagement of students at these events has been encouraging and helpful. I am particularly grateful to my colleagues in History at St Mary's for their support in this project.

I thank Robert Pearce for commissioning the book for this series, for carefully reading the final draft, and for his patience. My particular thanks go to my Editor, Laura Pilsworth, and her team at Routledge for their encouragement and assistance. I am also grateful to the publisher's anonymous readers who gave helpful advice on the initial proposal for the book and on the final draft.

Chronology

1470–1	(but 1472–3 is also possible) Thomas Wolsey is born in Ipswich, Suffolk
1491	Prince Henry, the second son of Henry VII and Elizabeth of York, is born
1497	Wolsey obtains MA; continues studies in Theology, Magdalen College, Oxford
1498	Ordained priest
1500	Obtains the living of Limington, Somerset, under the patronage of Thomas Grey, Marquis of Dorset
1501	Becomes a chaplain to William Deane, Archbishop of Canterbury
1502	Prince Arthur dies, and Henry becomes Prince of Wales and heir to the throne
1503	Wolsey becomes a chaplain to Sir Richard Nanfan, Deputy of Calais
1504	Pope Julius II issues a dispensation to allow Henry to marry Katherine of Aragon
1507	Wolsey becomes a chaplain in the household of Henry VII
1509	Made Dean of Lincoln cathedral under Henry VII Henry VIII accedes to the throne; marries Katherine of Aragon Wolsey is made almoner to the new king
1510	Presumed year of birth of a son, Thomas, to Joan Larke and Wolsey
1511	Made a canon of St George's Chapel, Windsor Birth of Prince Henry in January; dies early February Wolsey begins regular attendance at royal council meetings

Chronology xiii

1512	Superintends preparation of an English army sent to Guienne
	Daughter named Dorothy born
1513	Acts as quarter-master general for Henry VIII's invasion of France and accompanies the king on campaign; Tournai is captured
	Election of Pope Leo X
	Wolsey is made Bishop of Tournai
1514	Made Bishop of Lincoln
	Made Archbishop of York in succession to Cardinal Bainbridge
	Negotiates the Treaty of London with France
	Obtains the manor house Hampton Court; lease finalised early the following year
1515	Accession of Francis I of France
	Wolsey is made Cardinal Saint Cecilia beyond Tiber by Leo X
	Henry VIII makes Wolsey Lord Chancellor of England
1516	Charles of Habsburg becomes king of Aragon; regent for his mother in Castile; Princess Mary is born
1517	Martin Luther publishes his 95 Theses; 'Evil May Day' riots in London
1518	Wolsey made a papal legate *a latere* by Leo X
	Negotiates Treaty of Universal Peace, signed in October
1519	Charles of Spain is elected Holy Roman Emperor in June
1520	Field of Cloth of Gold in June
1521	War begins between Francis I and Charles V
	Duke of Buckingham is executed for treason
	Wolsey presides over burning of Luther's books at St Paul's Cathedral
	Henry VIII publishes *Assertio Septem Sacramentorum*; granted the title of Defender of the Faith by Leo X
	Wolsey convenes the Calais conference
	Concludes the secret Treaty of Bruges with Charles V
	Death of Leo X
1522	Election of Pope Adrian VI
	Charles V visits England; Wolsey entertains him at Hampton Court

xiv   *Chronology*

	Wolsey orders 'general proscription'; assessments of wealth for parliamentary taxation and loans levied in 1522–3
	Establishes Legatine 'Court of Audience'
1523	Parliament votes subsidy taxation for Henry's war in France
	English army invades northern France
	Election of Pope Clement VII
1524	Wolsey made cardinal legate *a latere* for life by Clement VII
	Clement approves foundation of Cardinal College, Oxford
	Francis invades Milan for the second time
	Work begins on Wolsey's tomb
1525	Defeat of Francis I at Battle of Pavia; he is taken prisoner to Spain
	Henry licences establishment of Cardinal College; building there already begun
	Failure of the Amicable Grant
	Treaty of The More ends war with France
1526	Promulgation of the Eltham Ordinances
	Wolsey presides over second censure of Luther's works and public recantation of heretics at St Paul's
	Francis I returns to France from captivity in Spain
	Wolsey begins new programme of building at Hampton Court
1527	First secret legatine enquiry into Henry's marriage to Katherine
	Treaty of Westminster; alliance with France agreed
	Sack of Rome
	Wolsey travels to France, negotiates Treaty of Amiens or 'Eternal Peace' with Francis I
	French embassy entertained at Hampton Court
1528	Wolsey given authority to create new dioceses
	Royal licence given for establishment of St Mary's College, Ipswich
1529	Legatine trial at Blackfriars (June–July)
	Wolsey sees Henry for the last time at Grafton (September)
	Charged with *praemunire* (October)

Chronology xv

Deprived of the Lord Chancellorship and his English ecclesiastical titles; surrenders the Great Seal and moves from York Place to Esher

Submits to *praemunire* charge and is privately pardoned by the king

1530   Restored to his ecclesiastical titles, but not all of his income (February)

Begins journey north to York on 5 April

Reaches Cawood near York in October

Warrant for Wolsey's arrest issued on 1 November

Arrested for treason at Cawood on 4 November

Reaches Leicester Abbey on his way back to London on 26 November

Wolsey dies on 29 November

Abbreviations

AN	Archives Nationales de France, Paris
Bernard,	*King's Reformation*
	G. W. Bernard, *The King's Reformation: Henry VIII and the Remaking of the English Church* (New Haven and London, 2005)
Bodl.	Bodleian Library, Oxford
BL	British Library, London
BNF	Bibliothèque Nationale de France, Paris
Cavendish	George Cavendish, *The Life and Death of Cardinal Wolsey* in *Two Early Tudor Lives*, ed. R. S. Sylvester and D. P. Harding (New Haven and London, 1962)
Chronicle of Calais	*The Chronicle of Calais, in the reigns of Henry VII and Henry VIII, to the year 1540*, ed. John Gough Nichols (London, 1846)
Colvin	*The History of the King's Works*, ed. H. M. Colvin (6 vols; London, 1933–82)
CSP Sp.	*Calendar of State Papers Spanish*, ed. P. de Gayangos, G. Mattingly, M. A. S. Hume and R. Tyler (15 vols in 20; London, 1862–1954)
CSPV	*Calendar of State Papers and Manuscripts Relating to English Affairs, Existing in the Archives and Collections of Venice etc.*, ed. R. Brown, C. Bentinck and H. Brown (9 vols; London, 1864–98)

Abbreviations xvii

Du Bellay	*Mémoires de Martin et Guillaume Du Bellay,* ed. V. L. Bourrilly and F. Vindry (4 vols; Paris, 1908–18)
EHR	*English Historical Review*
Fiddes	R. Fiddes, *The Life of Cardinal Wolsey* (2nd ed, London, 1726)
Fox, *Letters*	P. S. Allen and H. M. Allen (eds), *Letters of Richard Fox, 1486–1527* (Oxford, 1929)
Foxe	John Foxe, *Acts and Monuments*, ed. S. R. Cattley and G. Townsend (8 vols; 1837–41)
Gunn	S. J. Gunn and P. G. Lindley (eds), *Cardinal Wolsey: Church, State and Art* (Cambridge, 1991)
Gwyn	P. Gwyn, *The King's Cardinal: The Rise and Fall of Thomas Wolsey* (London, 1990)
Hall	*The Union of the Two Noble and Illustre Famelies of York and Lancastre* (1809 edn)
HJ	*The Historical Journal*
LP	*Letters and Papers, Foreign and Domestic of the Reign of Henry VIII, 1509–1547*, ed. J. S. Brewer, J. Gairdner and R. H. Brodie (21 vols and addenda; London, 1862–1932)
ODNB	*Oxford Dictionary of National Biography* (online edn: Oxford, 2004)
Pollard	A. F. Pollard *Wolsey* (1965 edn; London, 1929)
Rawdon-Brown	*Four Years at the Court of Henry VIII. Selection of despatches written by the Venetian ambassador Sebastian Giustinian . . . 1515 to 1519*, translated by L. Rawdon Brown (2 vols; London, 1854)
Rutland Papers	*Original Documents illustrative of the Courts and Times of Henry VII and Henry VIII from the private archives of the Duke of Rutland*, selected by W. Jerdan, Camden Society (London, 1842)
Rymer	*Foedera, Litterae, Conventiones . . .* ed. T. Rymer (20 vols; London, 1727–35)

xviii *Abbreviations*

Scarisbrick	J. J. Scarisbrick, *Henry VIII* (London, 1968)
SCJ	*Sixteenth Century Journal*
STC	*A short-title catalogue of books printed in England, Scotland and Ireland, and of English books printed abroad 1475–1640.* Second edition, revised and enlarged, begun by W. A. Jackson and F. S. Ferguson, completed by K. F. Pantzer. London: Vol. I (A–H). 1986. Pp. 620. Vol. II (I–Z). 1976. Pp. 504. Vol. III (Indexes, addenda, corrigenda). 1991
SR	*Statues of the Realm*, ed. A. Luders et al. (11 vols; London, 1810–28)
St. P.	*State Papers Published under the Authority of his Majesty's Commission, King Henry VIII* (11 vols; London, 1830–52)
TNA	The National Archives, Kew
TRHS	*Transactions of the Royal Historical Society*
Vergil	Polydore Vergil, *Anglica Historia* (1555 version): a hypertext Critical edition, ed. D. F. Sutton, Book 27 www.philological.bham.ac.uk/polverg/27eng.html

Introduction

Wolsey and the historians

> *There was also borne before him first the Great Seal of England, and then his Cardinal's hat by a nobleman or some worthy gentleman right solemnly, bareheaded . . . thus passing forth with two great crosses of silver borne before him, with also two great pillars of silver, and his sergeant at arms with a great mace of silver gilt. Then his gentlemen ushers cried and said 'On my lords and masters, make way for my lord's grace'.*[1]

Cardinal Thomas Wolsey is one of the great figures of late-medieval English history. We know a great deal about what he did and how he did it. As the opening description shows, we also know something about the manner in which he did many things in his public life. Yet about the man Thomas Wolsey we know very little for certain. Even in his own lifetime, Wolsey was something of an enigma. He came from comparatively obscure origins but helped to shape the life of the most famous and compelling king in English history. One cannot properly understand Henry VIII without Wolsey, and one certainly cannot explain Wolsey without Henry VIII.

From very early in their long working relationship Henry saw Wolsey as 'his' cardinal. He made him, as Lord Chancellor and Archbishop of York, a key figure in his regime. He supported Wolsey being made a cardinal and a papal legate, the meaning of which will be explored in what follows. The two men worked well together, imaginatively, enjoyably and above all very effectively in the governance of early sixteenth-century England. In establishing this relationship, Wolsey deployed the intellectual and rhetorical

2 Introduction

skills developed through his education and what might today be called his 'emotional intelligence'. He communicated with Henry in ways that intrigued the young king and first engaged Henry's own considerable intelligence and charm. From the start, Wolsey made sure that for the king he was stimulating company and easy to work with. He undertook the most onerous tasks of royal administration, freeing Henry to explore the more glamorous and creative aspects of monarchy. With Wolsey, Henry was never wrong – merely sometimes yet to see the full picture. When he did, it was usually Wolsey who showed it to him. Wolsey also soothed when required, reassuring the king that his royal authority was paramount in all things, especially when exercised by his cardinal. Henry could not only enjoy the sporting and leisurely pastimes for which his early reign in particular is now famous, but also the pomp and circumstance of opening Parliament, receiving ambassadors, signing treaties and the like, in which he was always the centre of attention. He could also get serious about his place in Europe, pursue his passion for hunting, for archery and all the sports of the tournament field. He could develop his interests, artillery, maps, technology and architecture, and devote such time as he chose to his music, poetry and of course to theology – his favourite intellectual hobby. Wolsey's imaginative political thought and capacity for hard work, which endeared him so early and for so long to Henry, may have disconcerted other people, but reassured the king. With Wolsey minding the shop, as it were, all would be well. And so it was for nigh on 20 years, until suddenly it wasn't.

Throughout his time in the service of his king, Wolsey played a double game. He used his legatine authority to extend his control over the Church in England, assuring successive popes that he did so to serve the needs of the Church universal. At the same time, he assured Henry that he used delegated papal authority in England, and internationally, always in the king's service and for his honour and renown alone. The inherent contradictions of this position became clear over Henry's wish to have his marriage to Katherine of Aragon annulled. Then, Wolsey was finally caught between the irreconcilable expectations of the pope and the king and could do nothing satisfactory for either. In the aftermath of that failure, Wolsey fell from power. Afterwards, his wealth and often-haughty demeanour, alluded to in the opening description, resulted in

Introduction 3

Wolsey being labelled ambitious, arrogant and self-serving. His fall was divine reproof of his vaunting ambition. That, at least, was the view of many of his contemporaries. How else could 'a man like that', from such humble origins, have risen to such heights of power? It is a very good question indeed but one that has, more often than not, been answered in derogation of Wolsey's reputation. It has also distorted the memory and the memorialisation of Wolsey who, perhaps because he said so little about himself, was posthumously made to stand for all that Henry no longer wanted himself or his kingdom to be. In the nearly five centuries since his death, many commentators and historians have proved distinctly ambivalent, and often directly hostile, towards Wolsey.

Against and for the cardinal

The criticism of Wolsey as a flawed and failed royal servant first found dramatic expression in January 1531, only a few months after his death, in a play whose subject was the cardinal being dragged down to Hell. It was commissioned by Thomas Boleyn, Earl of Wiltshire, the father of Anne, and Thomas Howard, Duke of Norfolk. Evidently a piece of mocking satire, it did not please the French ambassador La Guiche in whose presence it was first performed. It was apparently enjoyed by Henry when played before him some time later. No copy is extant, and we know it only from the report of the Imperial ambassador Eustace Chapuys.[2] The play almost certainly drew on contemporary satires of Wolsey. In 1521–2 the poet John Skelton had penned *Speke, Parott* and *Why Come Ye nat to Court* in which he attacked Wolsey's pretentions and accused him of arrogance, criminality and even physical malady and deformity. Skelton's relationship with the real and the literary cardinal he created has since been shown to have been far more complex than the satirical poems suggest, but they have offered Wolsey's critics a rich seam of ideas and allusions to mine. The critical literary tradition thus begun was picked up by William Tyndale who attacked Wolsey in his tract *The Practice of Prelates*, first published in 1530. Throughout it, Tyndale, the most important English Protestant writer of Henry's reign, knowingly misspelled the cardinal's name as 'Wolfsee' – a play on the popular Lutheran trope of bishops and cardinals as wolves attacking the sheep of Christ's

4 *Introduction*

flock. He characterised Wolsey as proud, avaricious and corrupt, the embodiment of the Church as a whole.[3] The attack was amplified by the two major chroniclers of England writing in Henry's reign. The first was by Polydore Vergil, an Italian papal official who was in England from 1502 to 1515 as a deputy tax-collector, working for Adriano Castellesi (of whom more later). He was back in England between 1517 and 1533. Vergil was a well-regarded humanist whom Henry VII had commissioned to write a history of England. The resulting *Anglica Historia*, written in part at least from a journal he kept from his arrival in England, first appeared in 1534. It went through several editions and only in the last, of 1555, does Wolsey appear. Vergil's relations with Wolsey were quickly hostile. In his history, he portrayed the cardinal as a clever upstart, ruthlessly ambitious and conniving. Wolsey, Vergil says, deployed his considerable rhetorical powers to monopolise the king's favour, thereby to enrich himself, to overturn the accepted order and to displace the nobility as the king's true advisors. He had nothing good, directly at least, to say for Wolsey. Yet he makes some interesting observations which will be referred to in what follows, and his animus does not necessarily invalidate all his observations about the cardinal. A man's enemies do not necessarily speak less truly of him than do his friends.

Edward Hall was the author of *The Union of the Two Noble and Illustre Famelies of Lancastre and Yorke*, first published in 1548 and known usually as Hall's *Chronicle*. A second edition followed in 1550 after Hall's death with additions by its editor and printer, Richard Grafton, and it is accepted as the most complete contemporary account of Henry VIII's reign. Hall, a London lawyer and sometime Member of Parliament, was about 33 years of age at Wolsey's death and is unlikely to have known him well, if at all. Hall echoes Vergil's account of Wolsey's arrogance and is as hostile towards him as both are unashamedly adulatory towards Henry. He was evangelical in outlook, anti-clerical, intensely Francophobic and presents Wolsey as arrogantly presuming to run England's foreign affairs to the advantage of France and his own benefit. He also locates the reasons for Wolsey's final disgrace in his mismanagement of Henry's international relations and consequent intriguing abroad. For Hall, as for Tyndale and generations of Protestant writers after him, Wolsey was the embodiment of the worldly, arrogant

Introduction 5

and corrupt prelate of a Church of which England had been well rid by 'Henry the Great'.

It was nearly 30 years after Wolsey's death before the first sympathetic account of his life was written by George Cavendish. Born in Suffolk like Wolsey, Cavendish was the genteel son of an Exchequer official. He became a Gentleman Usher, or personal attendant, to Wolsey in 1522 when he was himself around 22 years of age. His book *The Life and Death of Cardinal Wolsey* first appeared in about 1556–8. It was not a biography in a modern sense but a structured reminiscence, full of incident, combining the great set-piece moments in Wolsey's later years with observations of daily life as Cavendish experienced it in the cardinal's household. Cavendish was angered at the posthumous vilification of Wolsey by Vergil, Hall and others. His Wolsey is the star of a medieval moralising tale of Fortune, by whose wheel his subject had been brought up from naught and just as surely taken down again, showing the folly of worldly ambition. He is also something of the repentant sinner who finally makes a good Catholic death. For Cavendish, Anne Boleyn and her family played a major part in the cardinal's undoing, but the accuracy of this view will be considered in what follows. Cavendish's recollection of his subject was inevitably somewhat distorted by the passage of time, and he is not always accurate on the sequence of events. He is, however, a companionable interpreter for the modern reader of Wolsey's milieu, and his vivid pen portrait is drawn from close personal observation and from an evident sense of admiration and loyalty for his former master. His wish to correct the record publicly was almost certainly prompted by what he rightly hoped was the more receptive atmosphere of Mary I's reign. It also helps to explain his work's carefully implicit, never explicit, criticism of what he saw as Henry's ingratitude towards Wolsey in his last days. He wrote in the final years of his own life, itself no longer than Wolsey's.

In his *Acts and Monuments*, John Foxe, the Protestant martyrologist, continued the critical view of Wolsey, which Cavendish had tried to debunk, into the later sixteenth century. His account owed much to the satires of Skelton's and Hall's accounts. In the 1570 and subsequent editions, Foxe castigated Wolsey as the embodiment of the 'vainglorious church of Rome' whose body, at the end of his life, was literally corrupt and decaying from within. He contrasts

6   *Introduction*

Wolsey's life with that of Thomas Cromwell, whose providential existence 'was nothing else but a continual care and travail how to advance and further the right knowledge of the gospel and reform of the house of God'.[4] Yet there were also some supporters who derived much of their assessment from Cavendish. Raphael Holinshed's 1577 *Chronicles of England, Scotland and Ireland* endorses a view of Wolsey first expressed by the Jesuit Edmund Campion, that while he had his faults and was overbearing, the cardinal was also talented, high-minded and particularly honourable in his ambition to promote education. This is echoed in the 1587 edition even if Hall's influence is also detectable, resulting in a rather more ambiguous picture of Wolsey. This found its way into the character of Wolsey in Shakespeare's 1613 play of *All Is True* known as *Henry VIII*, co-written with John Fletcher, together with some incidents drawn directly from Cavendish. In a play that works dramatically towards a celebration of the birth of Elizabeth I, Wolsey appears as the grand prelate and has about the same number of lines as the king. He is not an entirely negative character. He is solicitous for friends and possessed of a sense of humour and fun. He entertains the king but still lords it over nobles like Buckingham. Henry enters the second scene leaning on Wolsey's shoulder, an obvious visual allusion to the king's dependence on his advisor. Wolsey's responsibility for initiating the annulment case is questioned. He dies repentant of his former grandeur, and his reputation is somewhat eulogised in a speech given to one of Katherine's servants that ends with the line that she knew he had 'died fearing God'. In the eighteenth and early nineteenth centuries, a series of leading actors, including Colley Cibber, Charles Kean in 1855 (wearing Wolsey's supposed hat acquired from Horace Walpole's collection at Strawberry Hill) and Henry Irving all incarnated Shakespeare's Wolsey with portrayals variously sympathetic and otherwise.

The first account of Wolsey written with something like modern historical method, with an emphasis on a considerable number of primary sources, was published in 1724. Richard Fiddes's *The Life of Cardinal Wolsey* echoes Cavendish's account in more than just its title. He was determined to rescue Wolsey's reputation from the afflictions it had suffered after Cavendish's death from Catholic and Protestant polemicists alike. As an Oxford man himself, Fiddes praised Wolsey's patronage of learning within the university

Introduction 7

and beyond and took a more benign view of the cardinal's foreign policy, even if he had an understandable tendency to try to squeeze Wolsey into eighteenth-century notions of a royal 'Prime Minister'. In 1888, Mandell Creighton, himself a clergyman, wrote a very positive and appreciative biography of Wolsey, crediting him with exceptional statecraft and personal authority and seeing the cardinal's leadership of England's ecclesiastical and secular life as beneficial to both. This stood in some contrast to the prevailing Whig view of history, which chronicled the supposedly inexorable triumph of secular, liberal, and particularly Parliamentary, democracy over medieval princely and ecclesiastical autocracy.[5]

The start of the twentieth century saw Wolsey become a rather more complex character even if still puzzlingly medieval to historians. This was due in large measure to the great project of collecting, collating and publishing the *State Papers* and the *Letters and Papers* of Henry VIII's reign, together with various series of diplomatic documents drawn from Continental archives, which offered a fuller picture of Wolsey's role in Henry's regime, especially foreign affairs. Until that time, knowledge of Wolsey had been very largely based on literary sources, such as Hall, Cavendish, Foxe and so on. The views of contemporaries, especially ambassadors, could also be brought into consideration. The detailed reports of the Venetian ambassadors in particular are among the best sources of information on the early years of Henry VIII's reign and Wolsey's prominence during them. The publication of these primary sources enabled a new appreciation of the complexity of Wolsey's roles and the sheer range of domestic issues in which he was involved as Chancellor and cardinal legate. A number of the editors of the various state papers series, such as J. S. Brewer and J. Gairdner, offered new appreciations of Wolsey in their introductions to them and, in Gairdner's case, important reassessments of the complexity of the annulment proceedings. The publication project also confirmed that virtually nothing of what might today be called Wolsey's private correspondence or personal literary artefacts survived in public and royal archives. Nevertheless, there are still many glimpses of Wolsey the man in them, and we can see how his mind works in particular contexts through them.

A. F. Pollard's account of Wolsey's life and career, published in 1929, was the first to be drawn directly from this range of

8   *Introduction*

published archival sources. It considered him thematically as well as chronologically. It presented Wolsey as a man driven primarily by a desire to align England with the papacy in order that he might himself one day become pope. It finds little consistent or laudable in Wolsey's personality or his record domestically and casts him as an authoritarian but essentially shallow man whose downfall was largely the product of his own vaunting ambition and 'essential for the preservation of the institutions of the English church and state and to their further development'.[6]

This view was largely reinforced by G. R. Elton, who again cast Wolsey as pompous, egotistical and although possessed of considerable talent, unable to direct it where it could do most good in the evolution of English government. Elton considered that Wolsey would barely scrape into the top ten list of English statesmen of the past, and when he called Wolsey 'so thoroughly medieval a figure' who had presided over 'the last years of truly medieval government', it was not a compliment. Wolsey's foreign policy, Elton admitted, was successful in deriving some measure of glory for his king, but he took on too much domestically and focused on administration, consequently having no time for the constitutional changes that Elton considered necessary to have been done in the sixteenth century. Wolsey had little understanding of economics and was a shameless pluralist. None of this is, strictly speaking, untrue, but Elton had little interest in explaining Wolsey in his own context and the constraints under which he operated. Like Foxe, Elton saw Wolsey as conservative, almost reactionary, and unable to transcend his own age in a way that demonstrated true greatness. That distinction, for Elton (as for Foxe for different reasons), belonged alone to Thomas Cromwell, the far-sighted reformer who presided over the 'Tudor Revolution' in government of Elton's imagining and who supposedly put England on the long and sometimes difficult road towards becoming the core of the modern British state.[7]

Elton's student Jack Scarisbrick saw Wolsey rather more sympathetically. In his biography of Henry VIII, he portrays the cardinal as a talented man, in his personal style no worse than many other prelates of his day and one whose imaginative intelligence was brought to bear decisively upon the king's foreign policy, to Henry's advantage. Scarisbrick rejected completely Pollard's view of Wolsey's supposed ambition for the papacy. He saw him as genuinely, even a touch naively, committed to international peace and motivated by Erasmian ideals (which also drove his educational patronage). He saw him as a sophisticated administrator and planner who worked prodigiously hard to manage the range of his responsibilities in church and state. While championing Wolsey's energy and skills, Scarisbrick argued that the cardinal was ultimately defeated by the complex theological contradictions of Henry's annulment case (to which, despite some criticisms, he remains the best guide) and of papal politics.[8]

In the last 40 years or so, led by John Guy's investigation of Wolsey's work in the court of Chancery and George Bernard's on Wolsey and taxation and Henry's kingship, historians have portrayed Wolsey as a more effective and somewhat less isolated figure than previously. They have seen him as dominant over the Henrician regime certainly, but also working with its prominent members in order to run the kingdom for Henry. Before he was any kind of administrator or legal reformer, Wolsey was a consummate courtier and politician. In his writing on the Henrician court and council and on Anne Boleyn since the mid-1980s, David Starkey has, surely rightly, emphasised Wolsey's personality, his genuine friendship with the king and his extraordinary capacity to influence, interpret and execute Henry's wishes in a way that no one else ever did as well and for so long, including the secular-sainted Cromwell.

Peter Gwyn's *The King's Cardinal: The Rise and Fall of Thomas Wolsey*, which appeared in 1990, took up Wolsey's cause as never before. At over 650 pages, it is a monumental work of remarkable scholarship, unapologetically supportive of its subject. Gwyn described his book as a 'political biography' rather than a personal one and 'a major work of restoration'. A bold claim, but one justified perhaps in its almost archaeological approach to the subject. No other author has drilled down into the minutiae of Wolsey's administration across the whole range of his responsibilities as Gwyn did. He brought to light a myriad of details about how Wolsey worked in particular instances as Chancellor, as legate and as the Henrician equivalent of secretary of state for foreign affairs. Written over some 11 years, it is the most thoroughgoing exposition of Wolsey's public career ever written. Its depth of detail and idiosyncratic structure, however, make the book hard to navigate at times and thus limits its accessibility for many readers. Like Fiddes before him, Gwyn

10   *Introduction*

wrote in direct refutation of the most recent critical historical tradition as far forward as Pollard and Elton. He contested the claims of virtually all the prominent Tudor historians since them as well, including Guy, Starkey and Bernard. He also went as far back as the ambassadors Chapuys and Giustinian, rejecting any notion that Wolsey was ever the 'alter rex' of those diplomats' imaginations. For Gwyn, the king led at every turn, and Wolsey's policies were rather less ideologically coherent than has often been supposed. He saw rather a pragmatic and short-term approach in most spheres of Wolsey's responsibilities. There is much to commend in this construction, but Gwyn's Wolsey is almost too entirely the king's creature and has little sense of himself as a prince of the Church, as the embodiment of the English administrative state, as well as, to be sure, Henry's cardinal. Gwyn's contention that Wolsey would have followed Henry into schism to save his own career cannot easily be substantiated in the face of Wolsey's own reflections on their relationship as recorded by Cavendish, and a serious disjuncture between them evident from the summer of 1527.

In 1991 Steven Gunn and Peter Lindley presented *Cardinal Wolsey: Church, state and art*, a volume of essays concentrating on his cultural, artistic and architectural patronage. Such a multidisciplinary study was long overdue and remedied the default in Gwyn's account, and virtually all others that preceded it. Gwyn contended that the record of such patronage could tell us little about Wolsey himself, a decidedly anachronistic attitude to biography and material history even at the time he wrote. The essays in that volume brought a wealth of detail to bear on the range of Wolsey's possessions, their deployment in his international roles especially and his significance as a cultural patron. These insights were incorporated into Sybil M. Jack's 2012 entry for Thomas Wolsey in the *Oxford Dictionary of National Biography*.[9] In that entry, and in Stella Fletcher's 2009 account, Wolsey was also presented more fully and comparatively than ever before as a European cardinal, not just an English one.[10] This was something Wolsey himself always tried to do, conscious as he was of his status in the wider Church. This recent trend to see Wolsey in his international context continued in the special issue of the *Royal Studies Journal* on 'Renaissance Cardinals' published in 2017.[11] In a post-modern vein, in 2019 J. Patrick Hornbeck II offered an engaging appraisal of the literary, material,

Introduction   11

cinematic and televisual representations of Wolsey from Edward Hall to *Wolf Hall*.[12]

Given the foregoing review, the question may be asked why another book on Wolsey is thought necessary, or at any rate willingly undertaken. The first reason is that Wolsey remains comparatively neglected. Only ten book length studies have appeared in English since 1900, most of which have just been noted. This compares with more than 100 of Henry and at least 30 of Anne Boleyn. This book cannot satisfactorily resolve the enigma of Wolsey any more than those that have preceded it. It can, however, engage once more with that same enigma for a new generation of readers in ways that accord with contemporary ideas and concerns, while giving due attention to the insights of past generations. That kind of dialogue between the present and the past is the principal meaning of history after all. The book's broadly interdisciplinary perspective draws on recent scholarship and the author's own research on Wolsey's role in foreign relations. In that light, it concentrates on three broad themes. The first is Wolsey's management of Henry's relations with his two principal European contemporaries. The second is Wolsey's role in the governance, secular and sacred, of Henry's kingdom. The third is Wolsey's role as a political, cultural and educational patron during the first half of Henry's reign.

International relations were the sphere in which Wolsey most invested his energies and which, in turn, energised him more than any other, and so it bulks large in this account of his life and career. A very large proportion of his correspondence calendared in *Letters and Papers* relates to the conduct of relations with the rest of Europe. Wolsey was ambitious for Henry and clever in his conduct of the king's international relations, especially with his two chief rivals, Francis I of France and the Holy Roman Emperor Charles V, and with the papacy. To that end, it will be argued, Wolsey first convinced Henry that peace-making (and ideally genuine peace) could be done magnificently and as an alternative to the kind of 'magnificent' warfare to which the youthful king was naturally disposed. This led to a series of detailed and complex alliances and to events such as the Field of Cloth of Gold in 1520. Wolsey never ruled out war when circumstances appeared to favour it. He superintended two attacks against France in 1512–13 and 1523, but always kept peace-making to the fore, as a way of avoiding costly

12   *Introduction*

conflicts when necessary or making the best of the threat of them, in Henry's interests. During Wolsey's time England was a force to be reckoned with, and Henry used the lessons of the 1520s as he began to take a far more active role in his own diplomacy after Wolsey's fall.[13]

As Lord Chancellor, Wolsey sought to make the legal system as efficient as it could be and to ensure that the king's writ ran throughout the land. He wanted to ensure that everyone in the kingdom, particularly the high-born, understood that royal authority was paramount and to be respected. To this end, in Chancery and the other law courts over which he presided, he took on a number of vested interests. He does seem to have accelerated the demand for speedier justice with innovations such as the court of poor man's requests, but demand quickly overran any capacity to meet it. The range of administrative and legal issues Wolsey investigated with a view to reform, including parliamentary taxation and enclosures, was impressive. Yet his effectiveness in all areas is questionable. His ambitions to do the best for the king as he saw it often outran the several administrative systems' capacities. From the limited evidence that survives, fundamental reforms did occur to him, but he seems never to have had sufficient time, amidst his other myriad responsibilities, to bring them to fruition. Here, Elton's emphasis on the contrasting record of Cromwell as a focused and determined reformer is well founded.

It was a similar story in Wolsey's governance of the Church, where he never sought wholesale restructuring but fully appreciated the need for reform in certain areas. Being a cardinal legate meant a very great deal to Wolsey. When combined with the Archbishopric of York, it gave him a status and authority in the Church in England virtually unparalleled in its history. He first wanted to use that legatine status to do things for his king internationally, but he also sought to safeguard the Church from heresy and saw education and good discipline among the clergy as the best way forward. Although his authority was great, it was not uncontested, and he often faced accusations of disregarding the rights of other episcopal jurisdictions, not least that of Canterbury. In whatever sphere, sacred or secular, Wolsey tended to act as 'the king's cardinal' rather than the pope's, with important consequences for England and for himself. He did much to augment and improve the operation of royal authority and in so doing enhanced Henry's already strong sense of his kingship and the respect due to it in England – and beyond.

Wolsey's cultural patronage is only now being appreciated fully. He was a man of genuine intelligence, one shaped by his education and the physical environment into which his ambitions and talent led him. Although humble in origins, Wolsey daily lived at the highest echelons of the kingdom, its academia, the judiciary and administration, the Church and the royal court itself. As his career progressed he rapidly adapted to these environments, adopting the mores and habits of his patrons, quickly becoming one himself. His own patronage of others was concentrated on his household as cardinal and in educational provision through the school he founded at Ipswich and Cardinal College, Oxford. Both foundations were based on earlier traditions of episcopal patronage of learning but, as with everything that Wolsey did, intended on a vast scale. His building and renovating at these locations, at Hampton Court, York Place and elsewhere, was similarly grand. He was a patron of book collection and publishing, of music and textile production, especially tapestry and much else. The sheer range of things with which he furnished his own houses to provide an environment for himself and others that he saw as consistent with his international status as a cardinal was extraordinary for the time and more than matched the king's during the 1520s.

Across its narrative, this biography seeks to elucidate these key aspects of Wolsey's public career, to give an account of his fall and to assess the validity of the charges of treason levelled against him in the last months of his life. Where possible it offers information on his personal life and tastes. It also seeks to make sense of him according to criteria which, so far as we can tell, would have made sense to him and to his contemporaries; to unstitch him from the tapestries of Protestant, Catholic, Whig and Administrative history commentators alike. The narrative is not uncritical of him, but tries to present him as a talented and ambitious man in himself, and one more typical of men of his background than is often realised. The Wolsey presented here is in many respects less the pompous arch-administrator or 'prime minister' of previous imaginings. He is more the courtier and political 'fixer', at times even the 'spin doctor', whose personality (so far as it can be remembered and reconstructed through sources) was well adapted

14   *Introduction*

to the politics of his own day, as is true of any successful politician in any age. There was a great deal of the charmer and the actor about Wolsey, as there was about the king whom he served. He understood very well the milieu of the English and Continental elites into which he was drawn and with whose key figures he dealt routinely. With his 'filed tongue', as Cavendish called it, that is, his gift for language, rich with classical allusion, spiritual verities or chivalric glories as occasion demanded, Wolsey was a formidable and energetic presence in the England of the young Henry VIII. Magisterial he was, but all his power and status came entirely from Henry. For that reason, Wolsey also remains something of a remote, tragic and enigmatic figure because so soon after Henry no longer wanted him as his chief advisor, this compelling person literally ceased to exist. Scarcely anything of that once vibrant public persona was permitted to survive by the powerful force that helped to fashion it. That makes it difficult, though not impossible, to get a sense of Wolsey the man and his significance in English history. As Edward Hall observed of him, grudgingly perhaps but respectfully, 'to write the life and doings of this cardinal, it were a great work, but whatsoever he did, God forgive his soul his body's misdeeds'.[14] Wolsey may not have been a 'Man for All Seasons' like the sainted Sir Thomas More, but he was *the* man for quite a few of them. What is your view of him?

Notes

1 Cavendish, p. 25.

2 *CSP Sp.* IV ii, 615.

3 W. Tyndale, *The Practice of Prelates*, ed. H. Walter for the Parker Society, 1850. (Reprinted, London, 2016), pp. 22 ff.

4 Foxe, V, p. 384; see also G. Walker, *John Skelton and the Politics of the 1520s* (Cambridge, 1988).

5 M. Creighton, *Cardinal Wolsey* (New York, 1888).

6 Pollard, p. 370.

7 G. R. Elton, *The Tudor Revolution in Government* (Cambridge, 1969), pp. 36–65.

8 Scarisbrick, pp. 74–96 et seq.

9 S. Jack (2012, January 5). Wolsey, Thomas (1470/71–1530), royal minister, archbishop of York, and cardinal. *Oxford Dictionary of National Biography*.

10 S. Fletcher, *Cardinal Wolsey: A Life in Renaissance Europe* (London, 2009); D. Matusiak, *Wolsey: The Life of King Henry VIII's Cardinal* (Stroud, 2014) is in the older narrowly critical tradition and has little positive to say for its subject.

11 G. Richardson, 'Princes of the Church: Renaissance Cardinals and Kings' in 'Renaissance Cardinals: Diplomats and Patrons in the Early Modern World', *Royal Studies Journal*, Special Edition 4 (2) (2017): 1–11.

12 J. Patrick Hornbeck II, *Remembering Wolsey: A History of Commemorations and Representations* (New York, 2019).

13 G. Richardson, *The Field of Cloth of Gold* (New Haven & London, 2013).

14 Hall, p. 774.

1 From Ipswich to Hampton Court

Wolsey's rise to power

In whom the king conceived such a loving fancy, especially for that he was most earnest and readiest among all the council to advance the king's only will and pleasure without any respect to the case.[1]

Nobody knows exactly when Thomas Wolsey was born. The man whose eventual fall from power and subsequent death would reverberate across Europe appeared with little trace. He was, in the words of his first biographer, an 'honest poor man's son, born in Ipswich' who rose from obscurity, as Cavendish tells us, through his willingness to 'advance the king's only will and pleasure'.

Much ink has been spilled on trying to narrow the range of possible dates of his mother's presumed happy event to some time between late 1470 and early 1474. The Venetian ambassador Sebastian Giustinian estimated him to be about 46 in 1519, so born around 1473. On the other hand, Cavendish, who knew him well towards the end of his life, tells us that at Peterborough at Easter 1530, as Archbishop of York, Wolsey washed the feet of 59 poor men; one for every year of his age. If this is accurate, then the likely date of his birth is the early part of 1471, possibly March, a date first suggested by Richard Fiddes in the eighteenth century and followed by Creighton and Sybil Jack. Based on traceable Maundy practice, however, Pollard argued that 59 men meant one for every year in which the benefactor had lived, incomplete as well as complete, making 1472–3 more likely. In that case, by April 1530, Wolsey had been alive during 59 years, although he would only have been aged 57 years and 11 months. Cavendish's modern editors

From Ipswich to Hampton Court   17

and Gwyn both favour 1472–3. Perhaps an exact date doesn't matter very much. It certainly doesn't seem to have mattered to Wolsey who, almost uniquely among his contemporaries, did not wish to dwell on the precise details of his origins. His enemies harped on them constantly, calling him the 'butcher's cur' and a man of no social standing whatsoever.[2]

Childhood, education and early career

The basis of this insult was that Thomas's father, Robert Wolsey, or Wulcy, as it was also spelt, carried out a butchery business in Ipswich, kept and grazed livestock and did a spot of beer selling and inn-keeping on the side. Of humble stock he may have been, but Robert was not literally poor in either the Tudor or the modern senses of the word. Even Polydore Vergil, Wolsey's sternest critic, later said of him that, 'he had a father who was an upright man, but a butcher, which he [Wolsey] did not like to remember, as something unworthy of his station'.[3] Robert owned his own premises with dwellings, as well as tenements and a tavern in the parish of St Mary at the Elms. He was evidently a man on the make, and sometimes fell foul of local regulations governing brewing, ale-house-keeping and public health. He made an advantageous marriage to Joan Daundy who came from an East Anglian yeomanry family. Her brother, Edmund, was an Ipswich merchant of standing, a town burgess and a sometime MP. Robert and Joan had four children, of whom Thomas was the eldest. The 'Mr Wulcy' later listed as an attendant in the royal household is likely to have been one of those brothers. Robert Wolsey died in 1496, a comparatively wealthy man who left ten marks (£6 10s) for masses for the repose of his soul, to be said, he instructed in his will, by his son if Thomas was in holy orders within 12 months of his death. Wolsey was not in fact ordained until March 1498 at the age of 27 (if a birth date of 1471 is accurate). His mother remarried and died in 1509. On 21 February 1510, Edmund Daundy obtained a licence to found a chantry chapel in the town with masses to be said for the souls of the family, including Robert and Joan Wolsey.

Thomas was born in the family home, but while he was still very young his parents moved to a somewhat more central location in the busy port town, just down from the Cornhill, near St Peter's

18   *From Ipswich to Hampton Court*

church. From an early age he was, according to Cavendish, 'very apt to learning'. A boy from his background is likely to have attended a local guild or 'petty' school where he would have been taught his alphabet, reading, writing and arithmetic, all skills which would be used in helping his father's business and in which he doubtless first showed his native intelligence. It is likely that his maternal uncle, Edmund Daundy, took the lead in developing that promise in the education of his nephew, having greater resources and social standing than Robert his brother-in-law. Probably under his auspices, Wolsey went to the local grammar school established in 1476 near the neighbouring Dominican church. He would have learnt Latin and perhaps some Greek, but he was not there long before, as Cavendish tells us, 'his parents or his good friends and masters conveyed him to the University of Oxford'. Thomas did indeed go to Oxford, to Magdalen College School there, possibly on one of four scholarships for bright boys in the gift of James Goldwell, the Bishop of Norwich.[4] After a fairly short interval there, and presumably continuing to show that promise of which Cavendish later wrote, Wolsey enrolled as an undergraduate at the College of St Mary Magdalen, not long before founded by William Waynflete, Bishop of Winchester. There, in short order, 'the butcher's cur' became 'the boy bachelor'. In or about 1486, at the age of 15 by his own account, he graduated BA 'which was a rare thing and seldom seen'. Gwyn believed that Wolsey was more likely to have enrolled at 15 and finished about four years later. The university's records are silent on the subject, but, then as now, the Bachelor's degree was only the first rung on the academic ladder. Wolsey gained his MA in 1497 and thereafter proceeded in Theology. He would have been taught the techniques of the scholastic tradition, including logical thought and disputation, complex oratory and participation in discussions on divinity and moral theology. Magdalen had been founded for the teaching of the last two subjects particularly. He may have encountered in lectures some of the great English figures in what was becoming the fashionable curriculum of biblical humanism, focusing on Greek and the new exegesis of classical and biblical texts. For example, William Grocyn and John Colet gave lectures in the university while Wolsey was there. He would later become a generous patron of such learning at Oxford. Wolsey continued his studies in theology with some continued distinction, but

From Ipswich to Hampton Court 19

had not fully completed them by the time he left Oxford in 1501–2. He evidently had an aptitude for languages and while at university became proficient not just in Latin but also French, which he seems to have spoken fluently. As ambassadors would later attest, he also spoke some Italian and perhaps a little Spanish. Wolsey's choice of theology as his principal study probably reflected his personal interests and talents, although he never wrote publicly with any authority on the subject. His own education was formally completed in 1510 when the university admitted him, despite incomplete studies, to the degrees of Bachelor and Doctor of Theology.[5]

Like many talented boys of his background and generation, the university and the Church provided the next steps forward. Wolsey was made a Fellow of Magdalen in 1497 and the following year was ordained priest in the parish church of St Peter at Marlborough. In 1498 he also became the junior bursar of his college and at some time in 1499–1500 became its senior one. He also became briefly the master of Magdalen College School, the beginning, we may suppose, of his life-long commitment to educational provision.

As bursar, Wolsey was in charge of the on-going building works at Magdalen. There is a college tradition that he was accused of misallocating monies for the completion of its great tower and that he was consequently forced to resign. Perhaps he took short cuts with the work, or overspent in getting it finished? Perhaps the accounts were not as fully auditable as they ought to have been? His resignation of his fellowship has often been cited as retrospective evidence of this financial indiscretion. There is, however, no documentation to support the story, and Wolsey's departure is more likely to have been due to the college's statutory requirement that any Fellow who obtained a benefice above the value of £8 per year had to give up his place. This was exactly Wolsey's situation. In October 1500, he obtained just such a living (worth £21 annually) in Limington, Somerset, within the diocese of Bath and Wells.[6]

While he was Master of Magdalen School, he had overseen the education of the three sons of Thomas Grey, first Marquis of Dorset. Grey was the eldest son of Elizabeth Woodville, Edward IV's queen, by her first marriage. It was he who presented Wolsey to the living at Limington, but the appointee may not have spent much time there or even resided at all. The idea that Wolsey ever did so rests principally on yet another of those anecdotes that punctuate

Cavendish's life of the cardinal. This was that while in Grey's service, an anti-social (probably drunk) Wolsey was put in the stocks at a fair in Limington by the local sheriff, Sir Amias Paulet. Wolsey is alleged to have had his revenge some twenty years later by confining Paulet to the Middle Temple (whose Treasurer the latter then was) at the royal council's pleasure. Paulet may have had lodgings there and been prevented from leaving the London area without permission of the council – a genteel form of Tudor open detention. He is supposed to have made amends by embellishing the Temple's gatehouse with Wolsey's coat of arms and other symbols. The truth of the story is impossible to establish, but it is used by Cavendish in his narrative to emphasise the impermanence of power, not least Wolsey's, in the circle of Fortune.[7] In fact, barely had the Somerset benefice been settled on Wolsey than Grey died, and the ambitious churchman bade farewell to the first of his major patrons.

Towards the end of 1501, Wolsey became a chaplain to William Deane, the Archbishop of Canterbury and Chancellor of England, whom he may have first met when in Grey's service. Wolsey obtained the vicarage of Lydd in Kent, with a papal dispensation to be absent from his existing benefice and to hold another. It was with Deane that Wolsey got his first experience of the demands of civic administration, of diplomacy and dynastic politics – and his evident taste for its pomp and circumstance. The archbishop was involved in negotiating the treaty for the marriage of Katherine of Aragon to Arthur, Prince of Wales. He then conducted their wedding ceremony at St Paul's in November 1501. Deane was also involved in negotiations with James IV which culminated in a peace treaty sealed by the king of Scots' betrothal to Henry VII's eldest daughter, Margaret. A chaplain like Wolsey would have acted as secretary, messenger and perhaps confidant to Deane in these discussions, and also would have played a conspicuous ceremonial role in the archbishop's suite. Doubtless he did his best to learn as much as he could and to impress all observers. Deane died in February 1503, and after a seemly pause as chief mourner (and possibly executor), Wolsey became a chaplain in the household of Sir Richard Nanfan, the Lieutenant of Calais, then acting as the Deputy (or governor) of the territory in the prolonged absence of Giles, Lord Daubeney.

According to Cavendish, on the strength of Wolsey's 'wit, gravity and just behaviour', Nanfan, who was an important figure in

From Ipswich to Hampton Court 21

the conciliar circle of Henry VII, entrusted him with the 'whole charge' of his own office at Calais. This assertion cannot literally be true and was largely an intimation in Cavendish's narrative of Wolsey's extraordinary capacities and the future they would bring him. During this time, however, Nanfan was certainly very busy in discussions with the Burgundian Netherlands, Saxony and Riga, negotiating over trade and the security of the Tudor regime, seeking to apprehend members of the Yorkist affinity, chiefly Richard de la Pole. He may well have relied on Wolsey to a considerable extent in the day-to-day administration of the Calais garrison, giving his chaplain valuable experience in military organisation and logistics that was to stand him in good stead. He evidently esteemed Wolsey and may have been responsible for his appointment as vicar of Redgrave in Suffolk in 1506. He certainly recommended his chaplain to the king. At Nanfan's death in January 1507, Wolsey, who was co-executor of the old knight's will, was appointed to the royal household as a chaplain. There he worked closely with Sir Thomas Lovell, the President of the royal council, and with the man who was his greatest patron and mentor to date, Richard Fox, the Bishop of Winchester since 1501.

Fox was an early supporter of Henry VII. Keeper of the king's privy seal (and thus effectively in charge of the business of the royal council) from 1487 and a close counsellor to the king, Fox was also an important diplomat who would negotiate the betrothal of Princess Mary to Charles of Castile and the treaty for the marriage of Katherine of Aragon to Henry, Prince of Wales in 1508.[8] Fox was that rare thing in Henry VII's regime, a true royal confidant. He sought assiduously to guard his influence with the king and to deny the same to others. The founder of Corpus Christi College Oxford, he was, as Bishop of Winchester, the official 'Visitor' (the ultimate authority) at Magdalen, and this is probably where he first met Thomas Wolsey. A relatively recent convert to the humanist 'new learning' himself, Fox may also have been influential on the new royal chaplain's interest in this developing intellectual fashion.

Whatever his own theological interests, Wolsey seems principally to have assisted Fox in the conduct of Henry VII's diplomacy. He was entrusted with a message from the king to James IV of Scotland in April 1508. He was also sent as an envoy to the Holy Roman Emperor Maximilian, probably on some aspect

22   *From Ipswich to Hampton Court*

of Henry VII's continuing hopes for a marriage between himself and Maximilian's daughter, Margaret of Savoy, the emperor's representative in the Netherlands, and regent there for her nephew, the future emperor Charles V. Seeing his chaplain still apparently hanging around some days later, a rather annoyed king demanded to know why Wolsey had not yet set out as instructed. He was astonished to learn that his envoy had already been, delivered the message, furthered the negotiations with the emperor on his own initiative and returned, in three and a half days – or so Wolsey told Cavendish years afterwards. How, when and over what period of time Wolsey actually conducted this mission cannot precisely be dated. He probably exaggerated the speed for effect, but his capacity for hard work and his stamina suggests that if anyone could have pulled off this astonishing feat of early-modern shuttle diplomacy, it was Wolsey. Again, for Cavendish, this story was an intimation of the greatness to come. On 2 February 1509, at the king's behest, came Wolsey's first significant ecclesiastical appointment. He was made Dean of Lincoln Cathedral and prebend of Welton Brinkhall in the same place, but exchanged it barely two months later for that of Stow Magna and resigned his first benefice at Limington. By then Henry VII had died, and Wolsey farewelled the last of that string of patrons whose short-lived favour he had enjoyed.[9]

Henry VIII became king of England on 21 April 1509. His advent was greeted with spontaneous public rejoicing and with highly choreographed royal ritual. Within weeks, the 18-year-old king had buried his father and married his brother's widow. Henry and Katherine were crowned together on 24 June 1509. The king's youth seemed to rejuvenate the elite of the whole kingdom, and his apparent royal virtues garnered praise from subjects high and low. Henry was 6' 2" tall, physically strong and considered a prince handsome beyond compare. His accession seemed to promise good times for all, in contrast to the last years of his miserly father. Everyone did their best to encourage this hope in grand coronation ceremonies and the banquets, masked dances, called 'disguisings', and other entertainments to celebrate his advent. The accession and the marriage of this new king, which Wolsey viewed from afar as a minor servant of the old one, would change his life completely.[10] At first this season of 'pastyme with good company', whose virtues Henry praised in song, seemed to hold little for the former royal chaplain. Approaching

From Ipswich to Hampton Court   23

forty, Wolsey was not a member of that generation of gilded youth that now flocked to the court to surround the new king. Contrary to popular belief, Wolsey was not even immediately taken into Henry VIII's service. Yet, due to his friends and doubtless making the best of any opportunity he may have had to impress Henry personally, he did not have to wait too long. In October 1509, the king gave Wolsey the first of the very many gifts he would eventually bestow upon him. This was some property in the parish of St Bride's in London owned by Richard Empson, one of Henry VII's financial ministers who was arrested within hours of Henry VIII's accession. It consisted of a garden on which Empson had taken a long lease from the Knights of St John of Jerusalem, together with the adjacent rectory house of St Bride's located by the river Fleet near its confluence with the Thames.[11] This autumnal gift signalled a new spring in Wolsey's career with his acceptance into royal service. In November, Wolsey was formally appointed the royal almoner, although he may have been exercising the function as early as September – hence the provision of a London residence.

The office of royal almoner was an ancient one, dating from at least the early twelfth century, with responsibility for royal charity in general, and the distribution of alms to the poor. The almoner stood outside the royal court's ecclesiastical establishment, the Chapel Royal, and answered to the king directly. Under his supervision, alms to an amount of 37s 11d per week were distributed from the revenues controlled by the Treasurer of the Chamber. Other alms were also distributed from the king's private expenses revenue, known as the Privy Purse.[12] Because of its financial and spiritual functions, the office of almoner also conveyed membership of the royal council. Wolsey thus became not only a notional servant of the new king's spiritual needs, as he had been of the old, but a member of his political regime. Once in post, Wolsey promptly resumed that acquisition of offices, livings and other income that he had begun under Henry VII. On 27 April 1510, he became the Registrar of the Order of the Garter, responsible for maintaining its records. In July the same year he added the prebendary of Pratum Minus in Hereford Cathedral to his collection. In November 1510, he obtained the living of the parish of Torrington in Devonshire, and on 17 February 1511, he was made a canon and prebendary of St George's Chapel, Windsor.

24   *From Ipswich to Hampton Court*

Wolsey was an orthodox and conventional Catholic of his time. Later, as a cardinal-archbishop, he had his own chapel within his household that maintained the full observance of the Church's calendar, with daily Masses and the solemnities of high days and holy days throughout the year, administering to the needs of his large household. Cavendish says he had 16 chaplains to say Masses for him in his private 'closet' or oratory. Of his personal religious life or spirituality, however, there is little direct evidence. Devotion to a particular saint or saints might be expected of him, but no one object of veneration stands out in what little is known about his personal religious patronage. Like thousands of others of his time, he made a pilgrimage to the shrine of Our Lady of Walsingham in 1517, possibly to give thanks after a bout of illness. As a priest, he would have said or heard Mass at least once daily. As Cavendish reminds us, he also followed the daily Office of readings at least from Matins to Vespers 'as he was accustomed to do', even after an extremely long day of fraught correspondence when he was in France in 1527.[13] This commitment to his formal priestly devotions is perhaps characteristic of a man who seems always to have had the energy to do all that his many responsibilities required of him. He was a man for details and strictures, but his dedication also suggests that he drew some at least of his personal strength from his spiritual observance. It certainly had to come from somewhere. At some point during his rise to public authority, and probably from the time he became Archbishop of York, Wolsey adopted the personal motto of *Dominus mihi adjutor*, 'the Lord is my Guide'. It thereafter appeared everywhere, often with his coat of arms. It was woven on tapestries, engraved on plate, sculpted in stone and depicted in the margins and frontispieces of books he owned. This motto was no doubt a conventional expression of Christian piety, of a kind expected in a senior ecclesiastic. What it meant to Wolsey personally we can never know, but it may well have expressed how he saw his life's path being led by the Almighty. Whatever it may have meant spiritually, and wittingly or otherwise, it certainly articulated the nature of his relationship with his earthly, human, 'Lord' the king, whose ambitions and demands were Wolsey's guide in virtually all he did.

At the same time, it is reasonably clear that while Wolsey's priestly status was a genuine aspect of his public and personal identity and meant a great deal to him, he did not have a compelling vocation to work as a priest as such. In this he was not alone among the many ordained civil servants who served the English and many European crowns. His priesthood was always for him an important means for some things (but was never allowed to stand in the way of others) that he wanted. Vergil said that Wolsey 'was a witty fellow who would often cast aside his priestly personage, abandon his gravity, and strum the lute, dance, indulge in pleasant conversation, smile, joke, and play'.[14] Although this was probably intended as a critical, even mocking, characterisation of a priest, Vergil concedes he had the capacity to charm when he wanted to. It was vital in securing Henry's favour, and presumably that of others before him. Contrary to the caricature of him perpetrated by his enemies as insufferably arrogant and remote, Wolsey could evidently be a likeable man. He was liked, and even loved. By the time he became the royal almoner, Wolsey had formed a relationship with one Joan, or Jane, Larke, the daughter of a Thetford tavern-keeper. We have no idea how or when they met, but Joan had two brothers who had entered the Church, and it is probable that Wolsey met her through one or other of them. They both eventually entered royal service under Wolsey's auspices. Thomas Larke was another Suffolk man on the make and, like Wolsey, one of considerable intelligence and charm, to which Erasmus himself testified. Larke was for a time a royal chaplain, and by the early 1520s, he was Master of Trinity Hall, Cambridge. He eventually became Wolsey's confessor, dying a year after his de facto brother-in-law, if he may be so described. Joan's other brother, Peter, was for a time a servant to John Kite, Bishop of Carlisle, and was then in Wolsey's household and received a modest French pension while there. He eventually worked for Stephen Gardiner after the latter succeeded Wolsey as bishop of Winchester.

Joan is usually described as Wolsey's mistress, and still sometimes rather prissily as his concubine. She is better described these days as his companion or partner, and she presumably shared her family's intelligence and ambition. What she saw in him may be what the king also saw, and it is hard to imagine a man of Wolsey's complex character forming a serious relationship with Joan just because she was the Thetford equivalent of the girl next door. Living with her broke canon law, but in this Wolsey was unexceptional among

26 *From Ipswich to Hampton Court*

many clergymen. What is more, there is no suggestion at the time that their long-standing relationship was thought scandalous, and it seems to have been one of fidelity and harmony. The poet Skelton once alluded to 'lusty Larke' as Wolsey's bedfellow, but given that his critics usually seized upon anything to disparage Wolsey, their silence on the relationship during its continuance speaks of its acceptability at least. Joan may have been some years younger than Wolsey, and they were together for about 15 years before, presumably with his assistance, she married George Legh of Adlington in Cheshire with whom she had four children. Wolsey's involvement in a complicated land transaction, apparently to provide her with part of a dowry, eventually led to a Chancery case involving Legh and Sir John Stanley in which the Chancellor was accused at the time of his fall of partiality, and from which some details of Joan's life after Wolsey are derived.[15]

Wolsey and Joan had a daughter, Dorothy, born in 1512. As the child of a cleric, she could not be raised in her father's household. Dorothy was adopted by one John Clansey and later became a nun in a convent for well-to-do ladies in Shaftesbury. She received a pension from Cromwell when the house was eventually dissolved. They also had a son, Thomas, whose birth date is unknown (although some have suggested 1510). Like many of his fellow Renaissance cardinals, Wolsey was happy to acknowledge his son as his 'nephew'. He was named Thomas Wynter or Winter (a clue perhaps to the time of his conception or birth?). Wynter was not adopted out but spent his early years in what might be called a foster home with a family before following his father into academia and the priesthood. In 1526 he arrived in Paris where he studied Latin, Greek and French with the Scots humanist Florens Volunzenus. The English ambassador Dr John Taylor helped him to settle into accommodation found for him in the university quarter. In May 1528, Wynter was at the French court at Poissy, apparently wanting to meet the high-ranking nobleman Anne de Montmorency. John Clerk, the English ambassador, wrote to Wolsey that his son, by then about 18 or 19, had 'grown much in body and mind, and gives himself well to learning'. He was taller than when Wolsey had last seen him 'and beginneth to grow in breadth to a very good and a comely man's stature and fashion'.[16]

Master almoner

Back at the office, so to speak, from 1510 Wolsey began to give intermittent attendance on the royal council as and when required. He watched and listened. During the first two years of Henry's reign, it was still dominated by his father's men, led by Fox. It met routinely at Westminster Palace, usually in the king's absence. Henry had inherited a kingdom at peace. Although he sacrificed Richard Empson and Edmund Dudley, Henry VII's financial councillors, in order to distance himself from his father's unpopularity, Henry benefitted directly from their work. His father's regime had stilled, if not entirely settled, the restive English nobility in the aftermath of the Wars of the Roses. Henry VII had ruled the kingdom effectively enough and rebuilt the wealth of the monarchy, much diminished during the years of civil strife. The king's annual income at his death has been most recently estimated as between £100,000 and £113,000.[17] This wealth had been amassed through the vigorous assertion of the fiscal powers of the royal prerogative, in fines on recalcitrant nobles and gentry and, in significant part, by Henry's financially successful diplomacy with France.[18] Henry avoided expensive wars against French kings while allying against them with Ferdinand of Aragon and the emperor Maximilian. Under the 1492 treaty of Étaples, he accepted Charles VIII's effective control of Brittany, and in return the French king withdrew his support for the Yorkist imposter Perkin Warbeck. He was also to receive 742,000 crowns, payable at 50,000 crowns per annum. Peace at home and abroad, personal wealth, and a sufficiently secure international status, constituted Henry VII's bequest to his son, and the old guard were determined that the new king should not only accept, but appreciate and enhance it.

Henry VIII's attitude to his legacy was rather different. He was brought up on chivalric romances and on the history of the heroic deeds of his ancestors Edward III, Edward the Black Prince and Henry V in the Hundred Years War against France. They represented an ideal of heroic kingship that appealed strongly to him and which he was determined to emulate. Henry made no secret of his ambition to have the realm of France. His coronation procession displayed his territorial claims there more explicitly than had those of his father or Richard III before him. The Venetian and

Spanish ambassadors who came to congratulate him on his accession were impressed with his personal attributes and his ambitions to renew the Hundred Years War against France.[19]

The first clear indication that Henry would pursue this ambition was his marriage to Katherine of Aragon. Historians have never accepted the story that Henry told Margaret of Savoy at the time (and that he and his propagandists would later tell the whole world), that he had married on his deceased father's orders. Even his most sympathetic chronicler, Edward Hall, gives a different story. He emphasises Henry's adolescence, allowing him retrospectively to justify the subsequent demand for an annulment when, after twenty years of marriage, Henry still had no male heir. As Hall puts it:

> the king was moved by some of his council that it should be honourable and profitable to his realm, to take to wife the lady Katherine . . . by reason of which motion, *the king being young* and not understanding the law of God espoused the said lady Katherine, the third day of June, the which marriage was dispensed with by Pope Julius at the request of her father, King Ferdinand, contrary to the opinion of all the cardinals of Rome being divines.[20]

In fact, the decision was entirely Henry's. Theirs was evidently a truly loving relationship that evolved during the last years of his father's reign after Henry VII had repudiated Ferdinand of Aragon and treated Katherine rather shabbily. Even if 'he were still free', Henry told his father-in-law after the marriage, 'he would choose her in preference to all others'.[21] A personal decision it was then, made for love, but not one made without the political calculations inevitable in a royal marriage. One of the few depictions of Katherine as queen shows her surrounded by her ladies, dutifully watching her husband jousting at a tournament held in January 1511 to celebrate the birth of their first son, Prince Henry. Sadly for the royal couple, the prince died within six weeks of his birth. Their inability to secure a male heir together after him had profound consequences for their marriage, and with it the career of Thomas Wolsey. In the short term, Henry consoled his distraught wife as best he could and distracted himself (gladly enough we may imagine) with the possibility of a real war which had increased markedly by the end of February that year.

According to Polydore Vergil, Wolsey had first owed his place on the royal council to Fox's need of assistance to counterbalance the influence there of Thomas Howard, Earl of Surrey. He may well have been right. Like most of the English nobility, Surrey was heartened by Henry's accession and hoped that it meant the overthrow of men like Empson and Dudley and the return to real political power of the noble elite. With his son, and with Charles Brandon, the king's friend and alter-ego on the tournament field, with Edward Neville and like members of the new generation, Surrey supported Henry's militaristic ambitions to the full. This threatened the peace that Fox and his acolytes, including Wolsey, were apparently determined to preserve. By the summer of 1511, theirs was an increasingly difficult task.[22]

Louis XII of France had become embroiled in a dispute with Pope Julius II over various territorial claims in Italy, resulting in his calling a General Council of the Church at Pisa to depose the pope. To this, Julius had responded by excommunicating Louis and declaring his kingdom forfeit. He looked for allies to punish the 'heretical' king of France, including Henry, to whom he wrote in July 1511. As a loyal son of the Church, Henry suddenly faced an opportunity, and indeed an international expectation, to support the pope's punishment of France. His moment had come. Yet most of his clerical councillors hesitated. Most, but not all.

Wolsey had initially been an occasional figure at the council board, present as and when its agenda demanded. Two years into his appointment, however, he was in regular attendance on the council and, crucially, in his role as almoner, on the king at court – in a way that Fox was not. This is evident from the earliest extant letter in Wolsey's hand between them, dated at Windsor on 30 September 1511 and addressed to the bishop of Winchester by his 'true and humble priest'. It gives Fox the gist of the council's diplomatic business, the king's proposed movements and the rumour that Queen Katherine was again pregnant. It also relates how Surrey 'was so discountenanced' with his recent reception by the king at court that he had departed the following day. Wolsey boldly expressed the view that Surrey should be 'utterly excluded' from the Council and pressed Fox to return to court where Surrey's

30   *From Ipswich to Hampton Court*

son was urging the king to war with Scotland. Wolsey also related how, of his own accord, he had advised Henry to support the emperor's preferred candidate for the papacy, one Cardinal Adriano Castellesi, who had been, for 20 years, representing English interests before the Holy See.[23]

Written in a highly confidential tone, the letter well demonstrates the close relationship between Wolsey and Fox. Equally important perhaps, it shows Wolsey's early political acumen and self-confidence as a royal councillor. While his deference to Fox appears genuine, Wolsey justified rather than apologised for advising the king of his own volition, albeit on a matter on which he and Fox probably agreed. His letter shows that same instinct and gumption to act on his own initiative that he had first demonstrated in his mission to the emperor a few years earlier. It also shows Wolsey's early and acute awareness of the need for proximity to the king for political security. This would become his watchword for the rest of his career in Henry's service. Twice in his letter he urged Fox to come to court to ensure a happy outcome of their business. His remarks on Surrey also gave an intimation of the ruthless streak necessary to get ahead in politics in any age. However dutiful its tone, the letter could not have left its recipient in any doubt that Fox's protégé was rapidly becoming his own man in relations with the king.

Vergil ascribed Wolsey's subsequent rise less to his being a supporter of Fox against others, than to his capacity, by personal charm and efficiency, to persuade the young Henry VIII that:

> the government of the realm would be more safely entrusted to one than to many, and that it was permissible to commit it to somebody other than himself until he attained maturity of years, when he himself could manage things.[24]

Fox himself, according to the Italian, was one of the early victims (if that is the right word) of Wolsey's rise. Cavendish's description of how the relationship between Wolsey and Henry VIII developed at this time somewhat supports Vergil's and may even be derived from it. He says that the 'king was young and lusty, disposed all to mirth and pleasure and to follow his desire and appetite, nothing minding to travail in the busy affairs of this realm'. This royal

From Ipswich to Hampton Court 31

disposition Wolsey quickly understood and, as quoted at the outset of this chapter, showed himself to be 'the most earnest and readiest among all the council to advance the king's only will and pleasure without any respect to the case'. The affect upon Henry was profound and immediate. As Cavendish goes on:

> The king therefore perceived him to be a meet instrument for the accomplishment of his devised will and pleasure, called him more near unto him, and esteemed him so highly that his estimation and favour put all other ancient counsellors out of their accustomed favour that they were in before.[25]

The phenomenon Cavendish describes was evident by late 1511. While, as we have seen, assuring Fox of his voice as one for peace and stability, Wolsey was by then confident enough of his relationship with the king to have, secretly at first, broken from Fox, Warham and others of the peace party, and he became an earnest advocate of war – because he really appreciated, in a way they did not, what it meant for Henry.

In accounting for Wolsey's rise, both Vergil and Cavendish emphasise Henry's youth. This emphasis alerts us to the fact that, although a king in full sovereignty, Henry was still an inexperienced ruler and a young man in a patriarchal society that esteemed sufficient age and experience as the essential pre-requisites of masculine authority. Edward Hall, too, celebrated Henry's youth at his accession but also frequently referred to its negative side, usually in explaining and excusing the king's immature behaviour during these early years, specifically in 1511, when he could not apparently see that he was being fleeced in gambling by French and Italian merchants at his court. As we have seen, Hall deals with Henry's decision to marry Katherine of Aragon in the same manner.[26] Cavendish and Vergil both emphasise how Wolsey sought to monopolise the king's favour by encouraging him to enjoy himself, and to leave the business of government to him. The inference that Wolsey took advantage of the king's youth to sideline Henry is often drawn. Yet it is mistaken. Wolsey never underestimated Henry's acute sense of his own sovereignty. He sought, rather, to increase his influence by putting Henry's youthful ambitions centre-stage in a way that the conservative councillors had hitherto tried desperately to avoid.

He made a virtue of the king's inexperience, which the peace party on the council had used to reason against war in the summer of 1511. Over the following year, their argument was turned on its head. War was presented by Henry and Wolsey, working together, as a necessary part of his education in kingship. Vergil's account of Henry (not Wolsey) standing up to the council on the issue of his personally going to war in 1513 has him explaining himself in exactly these terms:

> it behoved [benefitted] him to enter upon his first military experience in so important and difficult a war in order that he might, by a signal start to his martial knowledge, create such a fine opinion about his valour among all men that they would clearly understand that his ambition was not merely to equal but indeed exceed the glorious deeds of his ancestors.

How could any royal councillor gainsay an ambition cast in such terms? Its agreement was finally secured with an assurance that the proposed 'educational' campaign would be conducted jointly with Emperor Maximilian, a man superior in years, experience and international status to the young king of England. Vergil goes on to tell us that:

> Learning this, all went over to the opinion first stated by Henry thinking that, since at his young age he needed to learn the art of war, he could not do so more happily under any teacher other than Maximilian, a veteran commander. So war was decreed by vote of the Council.[27]

Henry's youth was thus transformed from a monarchical problem into a royal opportunity. Behind this outcome we may detect the 'filed tongue', the eloquence and intellectual suppleness of Wolsey. Putting the proposed war on educational grounds allowed the king to express his ambition, while apparently respecting his elders' well-intentioned concerns over his inexperience. For their part, the councillors, seeing first in 1512 that without Wolsey's support the fight for peace was lost, were given a face-saving way of acceding to the royal will and supporting the very action they had so long opposed. From that moment in the council Henry and Wolsey were

From Ipswich to Hampton Court 33

as one. All observers, contemporary and modern, have emphasised that Wolsey's switch to supporting war against France was the making of him, but Wolsey really built the rest of his career on the trust Henry placed in him because he first took Henry seriously as a young man in his own right, and not just as a king.

Quarter-master general

Henry entered the Holy League against Louis in October 1511 less than a month after Charles Somerset, Earl of Worcester, had written to the French king assuring him that Henry would be faithful to their amity, whatever reports he might hear to the contrary. By February 1512 the French were expecting an English attack. In March, Julius II excommunicated Louis and spoke privately of crowning Henry personally in Paris if he could defeat the French monarch. This pitch of ambition and consequent activity led to an abortive English attack on Guienne, supposedly with Ferdinand of Aragon's support. In fact, Henry's father-in-law used English funds and troops to seize the kingdom of Navarre. He then did nothing to assist the English campaign in Guienne, and Henry's army was forced to withdraw by a French force nominally under the command of the earl of Angoulême, the future King Francis I of France. These events led to a serious breakdown in Henry's relationship with Ferdinand, Queen Katherine's efforts to prevent it notwithstanding.

Wolsey's second surviving letter to Fox in the summer of 1512, written in the aftermath of the Guienne debacle, shows how far and how fast he had come in as little as eight months. This time Wolsey made little more than a pretence of subservience. After an apology for not having written before, he related the news of the campaign and a naval battle with the French off Brest in which Sir Thomas Knyvett and Sir John Carew had been killed and one of Henry's ships, *The Regent*, had been destroyed by the French. To be privy to this sensitive information (which he asked Fox to keep confidential), Wolsey had to have been at the forefront of planning and decision-making in the war, in a way that Fox was not, although he remained in high office. Wolsey enclosed letters from various English ambassadors in Italy which Fox was entitled to see. It is clear from that exchange of letters that Wolsey now operated effectively as Henry's quarter-master general in full charge of the preparations and logistics of the war in France.[28]

The opening months of 1513 were busy ones for the royal almoner. He became Dean of York, having already succeeded the deceased Dean Harrington as prebend of Bugthorpe there. He was also made Dean of St Stephen's Westminster. This appointment more or less coincided with the election of the new pope, the Florentine Giovanni de' Medici who took the name Leo X. Although still only one of a number of councillors directly charged with preparations for the next stage of the war, Wolsey had the lion's share of the work; a fact acknowledged by Fox in a series of letters between them. Fox worked on preparing an English fleet at Portsmouth, sent in April 1513 to clear French shipping from the waters of the Narrow Sea. Meanwhile, Wolsey worked with John Daunce, the Treasurer of the Wars, in arranging the victualing of Calais for the planned land invasion. By the end of the month he was hearing fears for the safety of Jersey from its governor, Sir Hugh Vaughan, and in early May came the dramatic news of the death of the Lord Admiral Edward Howard in a naval battle with the French in April.[29] Wolsey assisted with preparations in Southampton of a second fleet, under the command of Howard's brother Thomas, to go to Brittany to provide cover for the invasion fleet crossing to Calais.[30] By mid-May Wolsey was receiving progress reports on this, and on musters of men for the royal land army. He received reports from spies in France, sent by Sir Gilbert Talbot, joint-Deputy of Calais, and, among other signifiers of his rising profile, a gift of venison from the earl of Arundel. During June, his attention was focused on the logistics of the royal army's crossing to Calais.[31]

Henry's enthusiasm for battle at the end of June 1513 is noteworthy. He landed at Calais with an army estimated to be 30,000 strong, dressed in a fine suit of armour with a mantle of cloth of gold embroidered with the cross of St George. On his hat he wore a brooch engraved with an image of the saint. He made an offering at St Nicholas's church and prayed for success. The king was accompanied by his entire household, and for the following three weeks he supervised preparations, liaised with allies and enthusiastically showed off his martial talents, notably archery, to his commanders.[32] Tight discipline, good camp hygiene and the correct handling of prisoners were the main tenets of a reformed military

From Ipswich to Hampton Court 35

code Henry published for that campaign as part of his effort to be seen as a chivalric royal warrior on a holy mission in defence of the pope, supported by the English Church and people.[33]

Wolsey travelled in the king's, or middle, ward of the army with 200 attendants, twice the number that escorted the bishops of Durham and Winchester who also accompanied the king. His accommodation was spacious to say the least; some 1,700 square feet of tented pavilions, the largest of which was known as the 'Inflamed House' presumably on account of its decoration, were set up for the almoner and his large suite. He was also one of only five household officers for whom a 'close stool', that is, a personal lavatory, was provided. Wolsey oversaw the movement of supplies with the army as it besieged successively the town of Thérouanne and the city of Tournai. During July, Wolsey disbursed further funds for espionage behind enemy lines. On the morning of 16 August, during the siege of Thérouanne, Henry's forces won the only recognised battle of the campaign, a cavalry skirmish at Guinegatte, known as the 'Battle of the Spurs'. In September, Wolsey was part of the English delegation that brokered the surrender of Tournai to Henry, as 'king of France'. He then oversaw plans for the English occupation of the city and was made, at Henry's gift, its new bishop.

Henry returned to England in October 1513 accompanied by the new bishop of Tournai. Even before he reached England with the king, Wolsey had been charged with strengthening the alliance with Maximilian. Henry soon ratified a treaty for the marriage of his sister Mary to Charles of Burgundy, the emperor's grandson. This was to take place the following May. He was greeted at home as the heroic conqueror of Tournai. He also cheerfully took the credit for England's victory over Scotland at the Battle of Flodden on 14 September, although it was very much the work of Queen Katherine and her commander in the field, Thomas Howard, the Lord Treasurer and Earl of Surrey. In a ceremony at Lambeth Palace in February 1514, Henry rewarded Howard with the restoration of the dukedom of Norfolk, while Howard's son, Thomas (the Admiral since 1513), succeeded to the earldom of Surrey. At the same ceremony, Henry's friend Charles Brandon, Earl of Lincoln, was made Duke of Suffolk. Just over a month later, on 26 March, there was another ceremony at Lambeth at which Thomas Wolsey was consecrated Bishop of Lincoln, in succession to William

36 *From Ipswich to Hampton Court*

Smith who had died in January 1514. Brandon and Wolsey had little in common save their regional association, but their meteoric rises that year indicated the heights to which Henry's favour might carry a man whom he trusted and liked. Brandon's comparatively lowly gentry origins made his rapid elevation to the height of the aristocracy truly exceptional. Wolsey's rise, to this point at least, less so. Although his yeoman origins were later mocked, he was quite typical of English bishops in the reign of Henry VIII, nearly all of whom were from the same background. Perhaps the best example, apart from Wolsey himself, was John Fisher, a protégé of Lady Margaret Beaufort and later Bishop of Rochester, who was executed in 1535 for his opposition to the break with Rome.[34] Polydore Vergil supposed Wolsey and Brandon to be 'harmonious in thought and word', principally against the Howards. As so often, Vergil misconstrued the situation, but Wolsey not long after certainly sought to put Brandon in his debt, and perhaps make an ally of him, in circumstances neither could have predicted at the time of their promotions in early 1514.

Wolsey's possession of two senior ecclesiastical appointments required papal dispensation from canon law bans on pluralism. Leo X was happy enough to oblige Henry, who had nominated Wolsey to both, and this was easy enough to do in respect of Lincoln – although Wolsey was required to relinquish his office of royal almoner. He was succeeded by Richard Rawlins, then Master of Merton College, Oxford. It was a rather different matter at Tournai where Wolsey faced determined opposition to his appointment by a rival candidate, Louis Galliard, whom Leo had appointed in June 1513. He was the 21-year-old son of a high-ranking royal judge and had the support of Louis XII. His age technically barred his appointment to the benefice, something Wolsey unhesitatingly pointed out. Yet just as Wolsey could be dispensed from the canon law requirements in respect of his multiple, and increasingly lucrative, appointments, so Gaillard could be in respect of his age. He could hold the bulls of office but had to remain bishop-elect until his 27th year. This problem was eventually 'solved' by Leo appointing Wolsey as in effect care-taker bishop until Galliard reached the required age. The young cleric refused, however, to swear an oath of loyalty to Henry as 'king of France'. Most of the diocese was outside English-controlled territory anyway, so Wolsey could never get hold of its sizeable revenues. Wolsey fought hard for Tournai long after he really needed to, principally as a way of supporting Henry's claim to be sovereign over Tournai as part of 'his' kingdom of France. In the end, however, Wolsey agreed to surrender all claims to the bishopric in return for a papal pension.[35]

Within months of his appointment at Lincoln came news of the death in Rome in July 1514 of Cardinal Christopher Bainbridge, Archbishop of York. Bainbridge was one of two leading representatives of English interests at the Vatican. The other was Cardinal Silvestro Gigli, titular Bishop of Worcester and Cardinal-Protector of England. The two had long been at odds. One of Gigli's servants soon confessed to poisoning Bainbridge on his master's orders. Doubtless eager to avoid a prolonged scandal, Leo X rapidly acceded to English pressure and absolved Gigli from any blame in his rival's demise. Wolsey was appointed in succession to Bainbridge and received the temporalities of the see of York as early as August 1514. His translation was formally approved in Rome a month later.

Archbishop of York

Wolsey now occupied one of the ten wealthiest sees in Christendom with numerous manor houses and several episcopal palaces. The most prestigious of these was York Place on the north bank of the Thames not far from the Palace of Westminster. Its location is no longer easily identifiable but was roughly in the area of Whitehall presently bounded to the north-east by Whitehall Place, on land now occupied by Inigo Jones's Banqueting House and the Ministry of Defence buildings. Wolsey also had a house on the opposite bank of the Thames, Bridge House, at Battersea and the use at times of the royal palace at Eltham, where Henry had spent much of his childhood. York Place required renovation at considerable expense, and as an archbishop and ecclesiastical peer, Wolsey needed a suitably magnificent household and suite. It has been estimated that by early 1515 the combined revenues of Lincoln and York alone gave him a net income of over £5,000, easily as much as that of the highest-ranking peers, Buckingham and Norfolk. His household would have numbered around 160 persons by this time.

38   *From Ipswich to Hampton Court*

As his ecclesiastical status and responsibilities in the royal regime increased, Wolsey also needed houses that were reasonably close to Henry's palaces. Since a fire at Westminster Palace in 1512 had destroyed virtually all its accommodation space, Henry had no royal residence in the political capital of his kingdom. Instead he lived mainly at Greenwich Palace and 'commuted' up and down the Thames as and when his presence at Westminster was required. At all other times everyone, including Wolsey, went to him. Henry also spent significant amounts of time, particularly during the hunting seasons, at Windsor and at the royal palace of Richmond, which had been substantially rebuilt by his father. The king's presence there is likely to have prompted Wolsey to make his first property acquisition as archbishop, a house on the banks of the Thames at Surrey about seven miles upriver from Richmond, at Hampton.

In less than a decade, Thomas Wolsey had gone from being a talented clerical administrator and chaplain to being the most important member of Henry VIII's regime. Yet we have no reliable likeness of the man himself. The best-known image of Wolsey was made by an anonymous artist of the 'English school' after his death. Now in the National Portrait Gallery, the painting in oil on oak panel depicts him in profile, a staff in his right hand and scrip of paper in his left. The jowly face and ample trunk under red clerical vestments are a product of critical contemporary views of him as a fat man, intended to disparage him as pompous, over-indulged and gluttonous. There is little reliable evidence of Wolsey's eating habits, and that which does survive tends to suggest that he was more than capable of abstaining from food and drink in accordance with religious injunction or contemporary customs of entertaining guests. Yet the portrait became the basis to a greater or lesser extent of every subsequent image of the cardinal in a variety of media. Of these, perhaps the best known is that by the Dutch artist Sampson Strong (1550–1611) which now hangs in the Hall at Christ Church, Oxford (see Figure 5.1). It dates from around 1610 and features a version of the Portrait Gallery Wolsey with his right hand raised in blessing a background depiction of the college at the time it was painted and before the appearance of Wren's Tom Tower. On close examination, it is a surprisingly rough-and-ready depiction; the fingers of the right hand remain unfinished. Most subsequent depictions of Wolsey in nineteenth-century painting

From Ipswich to Hampton Court   39

and on film and television owe much to this portrait type, perhaps most famously that of Orson Welles in *A Man for All Seasons* in 1966, and Anthony Quale in *Anne of The Thousand Days* three years later. Such images contrast sharply with the admittedly anachronistic rendition of a bearded and rather slimmer Wolsey in two illustrations for the 1578 edition of Cavendish's biography (see Figure 3.1).

The only other near contemporary image of Wolsey in existence is in a collection known as 'The 'Receuil d'Arras', now in the civic library of Arras in France. It identifies him in French as 'the cardinal of York' and 'author of the schism'. The drawing was owned, and possibly made, by one Jacques le Boucq, a mid-sixteenth-century Flemish herald. It shows Wolsey in clerical dress and cap, with a clean-shaven face slightly turned from the viewer. He is still a substantial figure but hardly obese, with a strong nose and smallish mouth. The face is open, placid and still somewhat youthful, the eyes fixed on the middle distance. Although the collection in which it appears dates from about 1567, the portrait is of a man in early middle age, evoking perhaps the Wolsey of the later 1510s, during his first decade in service to Henry VIII.

Whatever he looked like, in Wolsey, the king had found a servant of extraordinary skill, application and dedication whose personality suited Henry's. In the king, Wolsey found a young man who valued his native intelligence, wit and imagination and appreciated those aptitudes he had been acquiring and improving upon since his boyhood. He also found a patron and master who could reward him as no other before him and whose ambition in all aspects of kingship made the most of the skills Wolsey had to offer. By then, Wolsey had entered what seems to have been a happy personal relationship which we may assume in the absence of evidence to the contrary sustained him as he rose in power, responsibility and status in the kingdom. He had also acquired serious wealth and the capacity for the first time in his life of 40 or more years to become a significant patron of architecture, a love of which, like the king, he had developed in his youth. The work that Wolsey now undertook at what became Hampton Court Palace will be examined in more detail later, but as he began extending and renovating his new manor house, Wolsey was conscious of creating a splendid residence that rivalled those of the greatest nobles of the realm, whose ranks, as an

40   *From Ipswich to Hampton Court*

ecclesiastical peer, he had now joined and which befitted his status as the Primate of England. The work had not progressed very far, however, before Hampton Court would be required to have yet larger dimensions, literally and metaphorically, as the palace of a Prince of the Church.

Notes

1 Cavendish, p. 12.
2 Pollard, pp. 11–12 and p. 276 n.1; S. M. Jack, 'Wolsey (1470/71–1530)', *ODNB* [accessed October 2019].
3 Vergil, Book 27, section 11.
4 Matusiak, pp. 13–14.
5 Gwyn, p. 2; Boase, *Register of the University of Oxford* I, pp. 67, 296. http://archive.org/stream/registerofuniver01univuoft/registerofuniver01univuoft_djvu.txt
6 Gwyn, p. 2.
7 Cavendish, pp. 5–6; S. Lambe, '"Towards God Religious, towards Us Most Faithful": The Paulet Family and the Gentry of Early Tudor Somerset 1485–1547', (Unpublished University of Surrey PhD thesis, 2016), pp. 64–6.
8 C. S. L. Davies, 'Fox, Richard (1447/8–1528)', *ODNB* [accessed September 2018].
9 *Letters and Papers Illustrative of the Reigns of Richard III and Henry VII*, ed. J. Gairdner (2 vols; London, 1861–3), vol. II, pp. 426–52; Cavendish, pp. 7–10. Most authors date the mission of which Wolsey spoke to about August 1508.
10 D. Carlson, 'Royal Tutors in the Reign of Henry VII', *SCJ* 22 (2) (1991): 253–79; D. Starkey, *Henry: Virtuous Prince* (London, 2008), pp. 67–73; 118–35; 172–83.
11 *LP* I i, 257 (31).
12 L. Tanner, 'Lord High Almoners and Sub-Almoners', *Journal of the British Archaeological Association* 20–1 (1957–8), pp. 72–82.
13 Cavendish, p. 62.
14 Vergil, Book 27, section 11.
15 Gwyn, p. 324.
16 *LP* IV ii, 4294 Clerk to Wolsey, Poissy, 24 May 1528.
17 R. Hoyle, 'War and the Public Finance', in D. MacCulloch (ed.), *The Reign of Henry VIII: Politics, Policy and Piety* (Basingstoke, 1995), pp. 75–99 at p. 77.
18 Rymer, XII, p. 493.
19 *CSPV* II, 52; Rymer, XIII, p. 271.
20 Hall, p. 507. My italics.
21 *LP* I i, 119 Henry VIII to Ferdinand of Aragon, Greenwich, 26 July 1509.

22 Vergil, Book 27, section 11.
23 *LP* I i, 880 Wolsey to Bishop of Winchester, 30 September 1511; T. F. Mayer, 'Castellesi, Adriano (*c.*1461–1521)', *ODNB* [accessed 18 June 2018].
24 Vergil, Book 27, section 11.
25 Cavendish, pp. 12–13.
26 Hall, p. 520.
27 Vergil, Book 27, section 12.
28 *LP* I i, 1356 Wolsey to Fox, Farnham, 26 August 1512.
29 Ibid., 1827 William Sabin to Wolsey, 30 April 1513; 1829 Vaughan to Wolsey, the same date.
30 Ibid., 1844 report on the naval battle off Brest dated 5 May 1513; Hall, p. 537.
31 Ibid., 1795, 1853, 1859, 1874, 1906.
32 Hall, pp. 539–40; *LP* I i, 2391 John Taylor's diary of the war.
33 *STC,* 9333, *Certeyn Statutes and Ordenaunces of Warre Made by King Henry Viii.* Printed by Richard Pynson (London, c. 15 May 1513).
34 A. Chibi, 'The Social and Religious Origins of the Henrician Episcopacy', *SCJ* 29 (1998): 955–73.
35 C. G. Cruickshank, *The English Occupation of Tournai 1513–1519* (Oxford, 1971), pp. 143–87.

2   Cloth of Gold

Wolsey's 'Universal' Peace

Thus in great honour, triumph, and glory he reigned a long season, ruling all thing within this realm appertaining to the King by his wisdom, and also all other weighty matters of foreign regions with whom the King and this realm had any occasion to intermeddle. All ambassadors of foreign potentates were dispatched by his discretion, to whom they had always access for their dispatch.[1]

Within two months of Henry's arrival back in England in the autumn of 1513, preparations began for his return to continue the war in France the following year. After his successful organisation of the military campaign, Wolsey was now Henry's principal advisor on foreign relations. As Cavendish tells us, it became a position of trust and responsibility that he maintained for the next 15 years. He wanted to ensure that Henry secured the gains of the war and was in a position to capitalise on them further, ideally with another campaign in the summer of 1514. Yet by then the international context for continuing the war had changed significantly. In March 1513 Giovanni de' Medici had been elected as Pope Leo X. The second son of Lorenzo the Magnificent, Leo was every bit as much a dynast as his predecessor, but he determined upon a very different record and reputation as pontiff from Julius II. He sought simultaneously to enhance his Florentine family's interests and the international status of the papacy by making peace between Christian princes.

Even as the English war against France had begun, Leo had been reconciled with Louis. While he could do nothing to prevent

Cloth of Gold 43

Henry's invasion, Leo's election deprived Henry of the prospect of any further papal support against France. Louis promptly also made peace with Ferdinand of Aragon and Emperor Maximilian, both of whom had long since wanted to dissolve their alliance against him. This they did without consulting Henry or Wolsey, leaving both aggrieved.[2] What then should Wolsey advise Henry in this new and uncomfortable situation?

In May 1514, Leo flattered the English king with the gift of a 'cap of maintenance' (the red, ermine-trimmed lining for the metal circlet of a crown) accompanied by a request for him to be reconciled with Louis. The French king played his part, offering Henry a new, financially advantageous settlement, such as his predecessors had agreed with Henry VII and Edward IV before him. He went further and offered Henry a Franco–English alliance. Never had the two ancient enemies been allied before. Suddenly, Wolsey saw a very different way forward for his sovereign. Such an alliance would entirely turn the tables on Ferdinand and Maximilian who had patronised Henry since his accession and disrespected his wishes in coming to peace with Louis behind his back. It was Wolsey's view, which the king came to accept, that peace with France might be acceptable if it was made in a way that kept as many of his options in Europe open for the time being, limited though they might be. Above all, however, a peace and alliance treaty had to demonstrate Henry's status internationally as at least the equal of that of the French monarch. After some wrangling over the early summer, Henry eventually agreed to negotiate with Louis.[3]

What had happened to Wolsey the warmonger of 1512, and why did Henry consider peace when he had returned from France so determined to continue the war? Was it, as Scarisbrick suggested, from his desire to be revenged upon Ferdinand for betraying him and to show Maximilian that he was a force to be reckoned with in diplomacy as well as on the battlefield? Or, was it his 'simple idea, of using the French as a lever to exert maximum influence on the other powers of Europe', as Peter Gwyn suggests?[4] The answer is perhaps both these things, but neither of them alone. It seems to have dawned on Wolsey that to stay as the king's most trusted foreign policy advisor, he would have to be just as imaginative and counter intuitive as Louis and Leo had been. He had secured his place with Henry by telling the king he could have what he wanted

44   *Cloth of Gold*

and then giving it to him. Now, in order to maintain his influence, Wolsey had to give the king, not what he wanted, but what he needed and to provide it for him.

Henry himself afterwards declared that nobody had worked harder for the peace finally agreed in the summer of 1514 than Wolsey. Historians have also noted Wolsey's hint to Leo that it was not only his supporters, but also his enemies in the king's council, who saw him as the prime mover of the peace negotiations with France. Certainly, the pope identified Wolsey and Richard Fox as his allies in the cause, but even as he began negotiations, Henry was still hoping that the Swiss could be levered into action against the French. Wolsey supported this plan as well, but increasingly he saw peace as a more viable alternative in the short term at least because, as he saw, there was then no prospect of allies against France anyway, and Henry had run out of money. Wolsey therefore worked hard on the king to get him to see the potential advantages of peace and an alliance with France in the circumstances. After all, the prospect of peace in 1514 was not easy for Henry to contemplate. It required him completely to renounce that which, until then, he had seen as his most effective means of achieving international prominence. Yet, it was in these circumstances that Henry first showed sufficient imagination to realise that, as Wolsey was now suggesting, something might be salvaged, some time and renown gained, by accepting an alliance with France when the pope was in favour of it. But it would have to be based on the right kind of peace.

Louis d'Orléans, the duke of Longueville, had been captured at the Battle of the Spurs in 1513 and was still a prisoner in England. He had now been instructed by Louis to initiate peace with England. Henry sent Wolsey a letter describing the audience he gave the duke, noting with evident satisfaction, that when the duke began, he 'was as ill afraid as ever he was in his life, lest no good effect should come to pass'. The king made clear to the French nobleman that his master had publicly to acknowledge Henry's claim to the French crown by paying him a yearly compensation or 'tribute' of 100,000 crowns for it. Three times Henry repeated that he could not, his 'honour saved', accept anything less.[5] At this point, he handed negotiations over to Wolsey, and it paid off handsomely. In the end, Louis agreed to pay Henry one million *écus* as well as offering to put a Tudor on the throne of France,

Cloth of Gold   45

albeit as queen-consort. Louis's wife, Anne of Brittany, had died earlier that year, and so the French king offered his own hand in marriage to Henry's younger sister, Mary. The Treaty of London, as the peace and alliance agreement became known, was proclaimed on 6 August 1514. It was an astonishing turnaround from the previous year. A week later, Mary and Louis were betrothed by proxy, Longueville standing in for the king in the ceremony. Louis sent frequent letters to Mary and Henry, assuring them of his good intentions towards peace and said that he expected his fiancée to be with him by October at the latest.[6]

The 1514 treaty was the first real investment by Henry in staking a place in Europe without resorting to open warfare. It was an auspicious first step down this new path along which he was guided by Wolsey, who first saw the advantages to Henry of an ostentatious peace and alliance. Mary was after all the first English princess ever to marry a reigning French monarch, and she was the only English woman ever crowned queen of France. Henry instructed the duke of Norfolk, the leader of the embassy escorting Mary to France, to remind Louis that their alliance would cause other princes 'so to regard them and envy of them that the state of Christendom shall be in condition of better peace and restfulness than it hath been these many years'.[7] In other words, Henry said that he made peace from a position of strength, not weakness.

The man responsible for preparing the embassy was, predictably, the newly promoted Archbishop of York. As Louis acknowledged, Wolsey organised things quickly and efficiently, and Mary was ready within about five weeks of her betrothal. Wolsey was involved down to the smallest details of preparations. On 14 September, Nicholas de Neufville, one of Louis's personal secretaries, arrived with letters and gifts for Mary, including a large diamond subsequently known as the 'Mirror of Naples'.[8] Wolsey consulted him and a French court artist, Jean Perréal, who had come to paint a portrait of the bride, on even minor aspects of Mary's dress. He saw that it was important for her to look right and be dressed on arrival in France in French *haute couture*. In an undated draft of a letter possibly sent to Mary's chamberlain, Lord Berners, Wolsey wrote that a French envoy had brought 'certain accoutrements for her [Mary's] head after the French fashion', following a request from Wolsey approved by Louis.[9] There is also circumstantial evidence

46   *Cloth of Gold*

suggesting that some of Mary's jewels may have been supplied and perhaps set by French craftsmen brought over to England for that purpose by Wolsey. In late September 1514, Henry paid £811 3s 8d to 'Jacques Langeloys, Jeweller of France upon a bill of master Compton his hand'.[10] At least some of this expense may have been for Mary, whose dowry of 400,000 crowns was to be sent in plate, jewellery, tapestries and clothes, all of which were inventoried at Abbeville on 9 October.[11]

Mary's wedding to Louis took place in the collegiate church of St Wulfran in Abbeville on 8 October 1514. The town had been preparing for some months for her arrival. Mary's presentation, that Wolsey had supervised, evidently impressed French and foreign observers with the wealth and sophistication of the English king and his court. In a culture where the deliberate display of wealth bespoke power and commanded respect, the French had no option but to focus their competitive energies on presenting themselves as even more gracious and magnanimous hosts. The spirit of competition in this encounter was noted by a contemporary observer, probably Venetian, who reported:

> In truth the pomp of the English was as grand and costly as words can express; and the princes and nobles of France, and the ladies likewise vied with them for the whole French court sparkles with jewels, gold and brocades.[12]

The marriage embassy set the tone for several important encounters between the English and French regimes over the course of the following decade. In striking a dramatic new bargain with France, Henry, aided closely by Wolsey, not only demonstrated political versatility but an ability to reinterpret and perhaps even re-invent traditional ideas of how royal power should be demonstrated. The benefits of this new alliance manifested themselves not only in the prospect of war against Ferdinand, but also in a sizeably increased French pension and Henry's first direct exposure to the French court's expertise in the sophisticated presentation of royalty.

Wolsey reaped the rewards of this success, primarily in his promotion to York after the death of Cardinal Bainbridge. Thereafter the maintenance of good relations with France as and when advantageous to Henry (and himself) became an essential item of his political agenda. Yet the hopes that Henry and Wolsey had begun to build upon the new alliance appeared to be dashed in the first few days of 1515 when the news reached England that the king of France was dead.

A new rival and new cardinal

On the morning of 1 January 1515, Louis XII was succeeded by Francis, Duke of Valois and Earl of Angoulême, who reigned as Francis I. The new king was 20 years old. He was tall, reputedly handsome and full of chivalric ambition to go to war. He had first properly come to Wolsey's attention only a few months beforehand as he was leading the French court's reception of Mary. Norfolk had written of him to Wolsey: 'Here is nothing done but the said duke is made privy and doer thereof by the French king's commandment . . . My lord, I assure you this prince can speak well and wisely'.[13] Francis's accession was greeted by the members of the French nobility rather as their English counterparts had welcomed Henry's in England six years earlier. Like Henry, Francis inherited a relatively stable and prosperous kingdom. He, too, was determined to be ruler in fact as well as name.[14] This had serious implications for Wolsey because Francis's youth and ambition immediately engaged Henry in what became an intense and life-long rivalry between them. How should Henry best respond to this new king of France who was determined to stake his own claim to pre-eminence among European princes? The first thing to do was to renew the Anglo-French peace.

As was customary, Henry sent an embassy, led by Charles Brandon, Duke of Suffolk, to congratulate Francis on his accession, and to escort home Mary Tudor, now Louis's widow and forever afterwards called 'The French Queen' by the English. On or about 10 February, Francis first notified the English ambassadors that he wished to have the city of Tournai, conquered by Henry in 1513, returned to him. Henry's attitude to his conquest remained constant until 1518. 'His' city would only be returned to France, if at all, on his own terms. There was, however, evidently a range of views about Tournai in the council, and it seems that Wolsey at least was willing to consider the possibility of a return if it could be advantageous for Henry and also because it was already proving

48 *Cloth of Gold*

very costly to maintain. On 21 February the ambassadors sought instructions on how to respond to the French king's demands about Tournai, 'if your good lordships and other lords of the council be minded *as we suppose ye be* considering the great charge of it and the little profit that comes thereof'. Henry and Wolsey were clear. As the ambassadors themselves recognised, Tournai could be re-purchased by Francis but only after he renewed the restrictive alliance and undertook Louis's monetary obligations to Henry. He could not bargain for it as the price of renewing the peace. Only after that was secured would the city's return then 'be put in execution as if it were then our deed for the entire love and affection between them'.[15]

No one understood this better than Francis. He therefore tried to force Henry into returning the city in response to an equally magnanimous gesture of his own. The details of the duke of Suffolk's secret marriage to Mary in early 1515 are reasonably well known. In February, Francis discovered the truth from Mary herself about her relationship with Suffolk and their secret marriage. He was entitled to take it as an insult to him for, as dowager queen of France, Mary was one of Francis's subjects, and she owed him respect and obedience in succession to Louis. Suffolk, of course, was Henry's subject who had no permission to marry the king's sister while she was still in France. Instead, Francis accepted the reality of their relationship, told the duke that he was aware of it and offered to intercede on his behalf with Henry.[16] Francis knew this intervention would both embarrass and obligate Suffolk and Henry to him. But he went further still. He wrote to Henry, and thereafter strongly intimated to Suffolk, that this gentlemanly and royal obligation to him over the marriage should be met through an equally prompt and cooperative return of Tournai. He told Suffolk he wanted him to handle the negotiations over the city, and the duke's ambassadorial colleagues told Wolsey that Francis 'would daily call upon my lord of Suffolk to know what answer he may have from the king's grace'.[17]

Wolsey was quickly drawn into the growing scandal and took control. He was genuinely alarmed and angry at Suffolk's unauthorised marriage to Mary because it compromised Henry's attempts to check Francis through a speedily renewed peace, a peace Wolsey had worked so hard to secure the previous year. It also jeopardised

Cloth of Gold 49

the chances of getting back the considerable dowry paid on Mary's behalf and the jewels and other gifts she had been given by her husband. But Wolsey also saw that, the deed having been done, there were advantages in securing the gratitude of such a potentially powerful couple. He already had the trust of Mary, who had praised his adroit handling of her marriage preparations and told Henry she wished Wolsey had been part of her entourage in France. As Wolsey did not hesitate to remind Suffolk at this moment (apparently without a trace of irony about his own status), he, the duke, was a relative outsider and 'of low degree'. Suffolk's meteoric rise based on the king's personal favour was rivalled only by Wolsey's. It made sense for the trio to work together. There is no doubt that Wolsey spoke on the couple's behalf to the king, even as he also made sure that Suffolk and Mary felt the king's displeasure as keenly as possible and portrayed himself to them as their only friend on the council. Suffolk was fortunate that his new wife had her brother's mettle in equal measure and was acting, as she reminded the king, on a promise apparently given by Henry at her departure to France, that after Louis's death she could marry whomever she wanted. He was also fortunate that, as a young man at least, Henry could forgive much in his favourites. Acting on Wolsey's advice, as well as instinctual self-preservation, Suffolk admitted his fault in marrying Mary and threw himself upon the mercy of he 'who is my sovereign lord and master and he that has brought me up of nought'.[18] The couple were forced to hand over a substantial amount of cash, and Mary surrendered some at least of her jewels and plate to her brother. They were first received by Wolsey, and then the king, on their return to England in May. They married publicly at the Greyfriars convent at Greenwich, although the Venetian ambassadors in England noted that this was to such evident disapproval at court that they were in a quandary as to whether or not they should offer the couple the congratulations of the Signory.[19] They finally regained royal favour through Wolsey, a fact which the duke acknowledged while he laid low until the fuss died down. Thereafter, he and Wolsey established a reasonably good working relationship, but one day Suffolk would have another conversation with Francis that would play its part in ending Wolsey's career (see Chapter 8).

Francis must have realised by mid-March that his effort to capitalise on an English royal family squabble had backfired, and he

50   *Cloth of Gold*

dropped the whole issue of Tournai. A general peace treaty negotiated by Wolsey was eventually signed at Westminster in April 1515 which the English hoped might still give them some leverage over Francis. He agreed to pay the arrears of one million *écus* owed by Louis and to avoid interference in Scottish affairs. Francis also recognised, as had Louis before him, that Wolsey was a force to be reckoned with and had to be kept on side as far as possible. As well as annual payments to Henry, Francis confirmed an annual pension of 1,750 *livres tournois* (approximately £175) for Wolsey, alongside ten other English courtiers, including the dukes of Norfolk and Suffolk. By 1525, Wolsey's pension had risen to over 2,000 *livres* (£200) a year. Although he faced accusations of being pro French throughout his career, there is no evidence that it was these relatively modest payments that made him so. He and others also received pensions and gifts from other foreign powers as part of international diplomacy. Wolsey's 'pro-French' policy, if that was what it was, was prompted by his concern to keep Henry always at the forefront of European affairs. With a strong king like Francis I, France was inevitably a major part of Wolsey's calculus in doing so.[20]

Having been rebuffed by Henry, Francis now turned his hand, as the English king had done two years earlier, to that time-honoured method of status enhancement – warfare and conquest. In practice this meant, first and foremost, taking the duchy of Milan, whose Orléanist ruler Francis claimed to be both in his own right and as Louis's successor. In July 1515 a Holy League was formed between Pope Leo, Ferdinand of Aragon, Emperor Maximilian and Duke Massimilano Sforza of Milan to defend the Italian states from the ambitious young French king. Aware as he was, in turn, of the forces ranged against him, Francis wasted no time. He marched a huge army over the Alps, and at the battle of Marignano on 14 September 1515, the king led his mounted heavy cavalry, the *gendarmerie*, to victory over a mercenary Swiss army hired by Sforza to defend his duchy. A few days later, Francis entered Milan as its victorious conqueror and new duke.

Henry was horrified by the speed and panache of Francis's success. During the spring of that year, he and Wolsey had been full of proud boasts to the Venetians and others that Francis could do nothing without their leave. Henry had lost no opportunity to

Cloth of Gold 51

impress foreign observers with his personal qualities and skills. Thus, as the Venetian ambassadors reported, on May Day 1515, Henry jousted very strenuously in front of a large audience 'more particularly on account of Pasqualigo (who is returning to France today), that he may be able to tell King Francis what he has seen in England, and especially with regard to his Majesty's own prowess'.[21]

Francis's actions gave the lie to Henry's boastful words. By the end of the year, the coalition against him had disintegrated, and Leo met the French king at Bologna, there to agree a Concordat (formally confirmed the following year) recognising Francis as duke of Milan.[22] Wolsey was also alarmed by this turn of events. Only a few years earlier he had helped Henry to become the papal champion in war. Now it seemed like a return to the bad old days of isolation before 1512. Henry looked to him to do something – anything!

So, for the next 18 months, that is what Wolsey did – anything and everything that might get Henry noticed, using his own recently enhanced international ecclesiastical status to the fullest extent. The discussions about the possibility of Wolsey becoming a cardinal had already begun in secret in February 1514 and became more pressing with the death of Bainbridge in the summer of that year. Polydore Vergil, whose account of Wolsey's rise we have already noted, returned to Rome after serving for a dozen years as the collector of papal revenues in England. He took with him a request that Wolsey not only be made a cardinal but a cardinal legate *a latere*. The implications for him of being a papal legate will be discussed later (see Chapter 4). Suffice it to say that it gave him the status of one who had come from the pope's side and made him, in effect, a papal plenipotentiary in England. During the latter half of 1514, as Wolsey negotiated the Treaty of London, English supporters in Rome busied themselves getting expensively acquired support in the Curia for Wolsey to become a cardinal. Wolsey made it plain that he had the king's support. He wrote to the English agent in Rome,

> I cannot express how desirous the king is to have me advanced to the said honour to the intent that not only men might thereby perceive how much the pope favoureth the king, and such as he entirely loveth, but also that thereby I should be the more able to do his grace service and execute his commandments.[23]

52   *Cloth of Gold*

Wolsey reminded him that his immediate predecessors had secured large sums of money from French kings in return for peace. The statement was intended to impress upon the pope Henry's authority in England and to put himself forward as the papacy's best means of securing the king's support, but it also stands as a testament to how Wolsey viewed the plan to become, indeed, the king's cardinal.

By early 1515, Leo was very keen to encourage exactly the sort of cooperation from England that Wolsey promised and principally against France. Still he hesitated, but with further insistent prompting by English agents, Leo finally called Wolsey to a place in the Sacred College. On 10 September that year, only days before Francis's victory at Marignano, Wolsey was made Cardinal-Priest of the church of Santa Cecilia beyond Tiber. The church, one of the oldest in the Trastevere district of Rome, not far from the Vatican, had formerly been held by Cardinal Carlo Domenico del Carretto and had been, in the fourteenth century, the seat of another Englishman, Cardinal Adam Easton. The cardinal's hat became the distinguishing feature of his coat of arms. Wolsey was not, however, immediately made a legate *a latere* as he had requested.

Figure 2.1 Cardinal Wolsey's Arms in terracotta, Hampton Court Palace

The cardinal enthroned

Wolsey was delighted to have been made a cardinal, the pinnacle of his clerical ambition to date. Henry was also pleased. A new cardinal for England betokened his own high international status and equality with his brother monarchs in the Church's eyes. Wolsey also seems to have been determined that Henry's subjects should appreciate anew the significance of having a cardinal among them. After all, there had not been a resident cardinal in England since Morton in the previous reign.

Instinctively conscious of the importance of symbols and ceremony in the echelons of society at which he now lived, Wolsey was particularly keen to obtain his *galero*. This was the red, wide-brimmed, clerical hat with its pendant tassels, or *fiocchi*, 15 on either side. Worn only once at investiture, it was the public symbol of a cardinal, 'a worthy jewel of his honour, dignity, and authority', as Cavendish calls it. The hat eventually arrived in England in early November 1515. When Wolsey heard that the papal protonotary, Cardinal Gambara, had landed, apparently rather modestly attired and carrying it in little more than a post bag, he was *not* pleased. He immediately insisted that Gambara wait until he could be outfitted in expensive silk robes as 'seemed decent for such an high ambassador'. Wolsey then arranged for receptions for the hat (and its bearer) at Blackheath, where Continental envoys were usually greeted when they reached the outskirts of London, and at subsequent stages on its route through London to the royal capital of Westminster. On Sunday 18 November 1515, the great and good of the whole realm, led by the king and queen, were assembled at Westminster Abbey to witness the consecration and investiture of the new cardinal. During High Mass, before the bishops and abbots of the kingdom, all in their finest vestments and mitres, William Warham, Archbishop of Canterbury, placed the *galero* on Wolsey's bowed head. His new title and style were proclaimed and read out in full. Dean Colet of St Paul's, England's foremost humanist scholar of Greek, preached the sermon, reminding his audience what a cardinal was, and the newly consecrated cardinal that he must treat all people, high and low, equally and justly. Trumpets blared, the organ of the abbey church roared, and drums sounded to the heights of its vaulted stone ceiling. The whole ceremony was,

54   *Cloth of Gold*

in Cavendish's words conducted as if it 'had been at the coronation of a mighty prince or king'. Afterwards the dukes of Norfolk and Suffolk led Wolsey's escort to an unusually splendid celebratory banquet at York Place.[24]

Historians down to the present day have often treated the reception of the *galero* in England as evidence of Wolsey's personal conceit, but there was more to it than that. Doubtless he immensely enjoyed the whole experience of his investiture. For a man of humble origins, to be lauded and honoured in that way by the whole realm must have been wonderful. Doubtless, too, Wolsey was acutely conscious of the personal kudos inherent in the appointment as cardinal. As his critic Vergil said of him, 'all day long he would think about what he was, not where he had come from'.[25] Yet the red hat was received in the reverential way it had been not only because of the personal choice of Wolsey, but because he was now, in Cavendish's words, a 'mighty prince' – of the Church. He had joined the elite of what the French called 'the first estate' and was superior in rank in England to all secular nobles, save the monarch and his immediate family. Wolsey's elevation certainly honoured Henry and his realm as much as the man himself.

A cardinal's hat, without its tassels, reputed to be Wolsey's, and apparently discovered in the Royal Wardrobe in the seventeenth century, was owned by the antiquarian Horace Walpole. He displayed it at his house at Strawberry Hill in a specially designed 'gothic' case. The hat was subsequently purchased by the nineteenth-century actor Charles Keane and used in his several performances of the role of Wolsey in Shakespeare's *Henry VIII*. In 1898 it was acquired by Christ Church (originally Cardinal College) Oxford, and it is kept there on display, still in its gothic case, in the library. Radiocarbon dating has determined that the hat is made of Italian rabbit felt and dates from Wolsey's time. It might well be his, and it is hard to imagine otherwise how such an object ended up in the royal collection, but there is no definite proof that it is Wolsey's *galero*.

The ceremony and celebrations over, Wolsey and his king got back to work on trying to find a way to stop Francis aggrandising himself any further. The French king had already acted to take advantage of his opponents' disarray. By November 1516 he had safeguarded France from the threat of the Swiss through the

Perpetual Peace of Fribourg. In March 1517, he agreed the treaty of Cambrai with Charles and with Maximilian by which they all promised to assist each other if any one of them were attacked. Once more, Henry was left isolated. Following the failure of various anti-French schemes, on 5 July 1517, Henry finally agreed a league between himself, Charles and Maximilian designed to nullify the Cambrai league. It was celebrated with tournaments and extravagant banquets.[26]

The 1518 Treaty of Universal Peace

So far, not so good – but, by late 1517, Wolsey had been informed of Pope Leo's plans for an international truce as a prelude to a crusade. This was a tried and tested mode of papal leadership dating back to Urban II. In 1095 he had proclaimed the First Crusade against the Seljuk Turks, who had not long conquered the holy city of Jerusalem. For Leo, five centuries later, it was the Ottomans who were the enemy. In 1453, they had taken Constantinople and since then had also conquered much of the Middle East and North Africa, and they now threatened Christendom in the Balkans. He proposed to appoint Cardinal Lorenzo Campeggio as his legate *a latere* to England, alongside legates sent to France, the Holy Roman Empire and other states, to call for the international truce. Henry initially expressed apparent disquiet about this, asserting that England did not usually admit such legates. He responded (presumably at Wolsey's suggestion) that only if the Cardinal of York were also made a legate would Campeggio be admitted. It was highly unusual, though not unprecedented, for popes to appoint a native of the country where the legateship was to be exercised. Yet this is what Wolsey, and more importantly Henry, now insisted upon, and eventually they got their way. In May 1518, Wolsey was duly appointed Leo's legate *a latere* in England jointly with Campeggio.

Wolsey saw immediately that an international peace and league between Christian princes might be a more effective way of restraining Francis than relying on a short-lived truce, or an alliance with the ever-unreliable Habsburgs. As early as November 1517, he told Leo that Henry and he were both convinced that rather than a truce, the defence of Christendom was best secured by a 'universal peace'.[27] Henry's *de facto* leadership of an international league would take him once more to the heart of European affairs and make Francis seem, by comparison, a king who had undermined Christian peace with his conquest of Milan. Wolsey was further prompted in this direction from March 1518, when the birth of the dauphin François had been announced at the English court. By a promise he had made to Leo in 1516, the king of France was thereby committed to war against the Ottomans.[28] Wolsey's view was that, unlikely though such a prospect was, Francis must never be allowed to champion such a magnificent undertaking. That was Henry's job. Therefore, bringing Europe together under his own master's aegis, as a prelude to action against the Ottomans, was the focus in Wolsey's conduct of England's international relations. Ever politic, Giustinian, still the Venetian ambassador in England, praised Wolsey for this outcome. The cardinal, who could never resist boasting to the Venetians it seems, assured him that he would unite England and France once more. In response, Giustinian:

> lauded this excellent project, and told him he could do nothing more glorious in the world, or that could add greater splendour to his eminent qualities than in the midst of such great strife amongst princes to prove himself the *lapis angularis* [corner stone] which joined the two detached walls of the temple.[29]

Francis still wanted Tournai back and knew that he would only get it by treaty, so negotiations soon began for a new Anglo-French alliance secured by the marriage of the dauphin to Henry's two-year-old daughter, Princess Mary.[30] A renewed alliance was concluded, subject to final royal approval, by 22 July 1518.[31] Among other things, it provided that Francis and Henry should meet personally. Francis had at first given only limited and conventional support to the idea of an international peace agreement. Yet, as negotiations continued in England and as the scale of the project became clearer, he had changed his view radically. On the one hand an alliance with England and the return of Tournai were both welcome to him, but on the other a dramatic restructuring of alliances threatened to disturb the 1517 status quo, which was so much in his favour. Why, then, did he support the alliance?

By 1518, the French king had agreements with the archbishops of Trier and Mainz, two of the electors of the Holy Roman Empire,

Cloth of Gold 57

that, when Emperor Maximilian died, they would vote for Francis to succeed him and become the ruler of the German peoples. In June 1517 the margrave of Brandenburg gave a similar undertaking and the Elector-Palatine likewise. Consequently, Francis believed (or at least hoped) he had a good chance of becoming emperor, displacing Charles of Spain as the most likely successor. A prominent role in creating a Christian peace, of the kind Wolsey was offering him, therefore suited Francis nicely and seemed to show that he was serious in his commitment to lead a papal crusade as he had promised Leo he would. In August, even as negotiations with Wolsey were underway, came news from the Diet of Augsburg that the Emperor Maximilian had secured the promises of five electors for his grandson Charles.[32] Francis hoped that Henry's support (as the price for his own inclusion in the universal peace) might prove useful. Papal approval might also be secured, and an international peace would also prevent Henry from creating any new and separate alliance with the Habsburgs. Accordingly, Francis instructed his ambassadors to co-operate fully with Wolsey and to assure the cardinal of his trust.[33] He assembled a large and impressive embassy to be sent to England for the treaty signing. William Sandys, the governor of Calais, received this embassy in the town as it made its way to England. He told Wolsey that he thought 'the very purpose and intent of their coming is for good . . . and as goodly and well appointed company they be as I think ever was sent to any prince'. Prominent within it was a group of Francis's close friends and attendants who held the court office of *gentilhomme de la chambre du roi*. Sending them was ostensibly a very personal gesture of trust and regard for Henry by Francis.[34]

Over the following month, attended frequently by Wolsey, Henry displayed to the large group of French ambassadors the kind of ostentatious and self-regarding generosity which quickly became the hallmark of his dealings with Francis. Meanwhile Wolsey busied himself with final negotiations and assisting in the entertainment of the French visitors. On 2 October, the Treaty of London, which became better known as the Treaty of Universal Peace, was sworn to by its French signatories and the Anglo-French alliance followed suit in the days after. One of the key terms of the treaty was that the two kings would meet personally to affirm their alliance. The alliance and the international peace were sanctified and spiritually inaugurated during High Mass celebrated by Wolsey with all possible solemnity on 3 October. The royal secretary, Richard Pace, delivered an oration which was afterwards published by the king's printer Richard Pynson.[35] Pace was no pacifist Francophile, and the choice of him as orator was almost certainly Wolsey's. He had spent two of the three previous years engaged in complex negotiations with potential allies for Henry that had come to nothing because of broken promises and unfulfilled commitments. At one level, his oration appears to be a rather conventional Christian humanist praise of peace, of a kind that Erasmus would have endorsed. On closer reading, however, it is really a lecture to the French in general and Francis in particular about the roles of peace and war within effective and honourable kingship and the keeping of good faith between kings.[36] Pace spends some time praising Henry as a victorious warrior, saying how he was physically and mentally a born chivalric soldier who had defeated his French enemy in 1513. Yet he now chose peace. This was also an expression of his knightly and royal virtue. Pace set out in order of importance the three things being sworn to at the Mass. These were:

To the treaty, that it shall be entered into in holiness;
To faith, that it shall be sincere and inviolable;
To peace, that it shall be perpetual – that is, not only shall all war be removed but suspicion of any war shall totally be taken away.[37]

In other words, peace was not an abstract ideal in itself. It was, first and foremost, the fortunate consequence of honouring treaties. At heart, Pace's oration is a forceful assertion of Henry's personal and moral superiority over Francis and, incidentally, of Wolsey's view of peace-making. Thanks to Wolsey, the king was now where his virtue demanded he should be – at the head of the international community. If Francis broke the treaty, Henry's universally acknowledged intelligence and military capability would allow him to punish France again, just as he had done in 1513. It is a warning to the French against discounting the significance of the Treaty of Universal Peace and challenging the new status quo. The dauphin was betrothed to Princess Mary on Tuesday, 5 October, and this was celebrated two days later with a tournament and a

Cloth of Gold 59

banquet at Greenwich. The centre-piece of the entertainment was a pageant presentation of Henry's greatness as the protector of the Universal Peace.[38]

Wolsey understood that for this model of knightly or 'chivalric' peace to work, one thing was essential. Each king had to feel that his status had at least been protected and even enhanced by it. Despite the idealistic and somewhat abstract rhetoric with which it was enacted, peace-making between princes was never done for its own sake. It had always to result in peace 'with honour' or advantage. A successful peace treaty made room for each participant to assert his own status and power in activities other than war between them. Under the treaty, Francis was able to re-purchase the city of Tournai lost to the English in war in 1513. Henry secured increased annual payments from Francis that he regarded as 'tribute' for 'his' kingdom of France. Thus, each monarch gained something from the other that strengthened his status among his fellow princes and the nobles of his own realm. Assured of his own status, each king could join with the other in an enterprise whereby they displayed their power to the rest of the world.

At the end of 1518, the English prepared to send the second great embassy of Henry's reign to France to receive Francis's ratification of the Treaty of Universal Peace and the new alliance with England. Wolsey knew that it had to be as splendid as the one sent to England in the autumn. Once again, he took care of every detail of its composition and arrangement. Henry insisted that a number of his younger companions known as his 'minions' were included, to reciprocate Francis sending the French *gentilshommes de la chambre* to England. Wolsey finally agreed but was evidently unsettled by their inclusion, perhaps unsure how Francis would respond. The ostentatious entertainment of the English ambassadors began as soon as they arrived in France. It was calculated to outdo that which Henry had given their French equivalents earlier that autumn. It culminated in a magnificent banquet at the Bastille on the night of the winter solstice which celebrated the Universal Peace and Francis's power as conqueror of Milan and Europe's foremost military leader – a direct answer to the boastful celebrations staged by Henry in England.

After the festivities, and as the English prepared to leave Paris, the preparations for the return of Tournai got underway. Henry

60   *Cloth of Gold*

was to hold a number of French courtiers, including *gentilshommes de la chambre du roi*, at his court as hostages for the full payment due for the city. In January 1519, Henry heard rumours that the proposed hostages were in fact 'not of his [Francis's] chamber before now but only the one and also that they were not personages that the French king favoured greatly'.[39] He therefore refused to accept them. Wolsey ordered the English ambassadors in France immediately to obtain the best hostages possible. He explained why this was important:

> For to this point all other princes take special regard; whereupon, and [not] only, depends the surety of the conventions, but also the stopping of the dishonourable bruits [rumours] which, by the acceptation of insufficient hostages might be spread all over; which is more to be pondered than the importance of Tournai, or any other thing thereupon depending.[40]

Wolsey's statement focuses directly on the personal nature of international politics, particularly between Henry and Francis. It makes Henry's credibility a matter of greater significance than his acquisition or ceding of conquered territory. Moreover, the 'any other thing thereupon depending' to which Wolsey referred was the recently signed treaty and, consequently, the universal peace for which he had striven, and upon which his hopes for Henry rested. These instructions show that Wolsey really did regard the maintenance of the king's honour as central to Henry's success in international affairs. Eventually Francis agreed to send Henry six hostages who were his close courtiers. Once this issue had been resolved, the transfer of Tournai proceeded, albeit not without further disputes about precedence on the day it was handed back to the French.[41]

While all this was going on, news reached England of the death of the Emperor Maximilian. This triggered the Imperial election for which Francis had long been planning. He now looked to Henry for his support as the quid pro quo for his recent cooperation with the English. This, Henry was reluctant to offer because, while publicly expressing diffidence about the possibility, he too had allowed his own name to go forward. With Charles of Spain as the main contender, it became a three horse race. Wolsey had to manage Francis's expectation of public support without putting his master in the embarrassing position of declaring for the French king while contesting the election himself. In the end, Charles was elected as the 'German-Roman King' in June 1519 and was known thereafter as the Holy Roman Emperor Charles V. On hearing the news, Henry pretended to the French ambassador and the hostages then in England that he was disappointed that Francis had not been elected.

The difficult circumstances of the Imperial election and the provisions in the Anglo-French treaty specifying that Henry and Francis would meet personally required very delicate handling by Wolsey. He was keen to foster trust and good personal relations between the two rivals. Partly in order to do this, he oversaw a major innovation in the conduct of England's relations with France. In 1519, the two kings exchanged resident ambassadors for the first time. Until then English and French sovereigns had sent and received ambassadors on very specific missions which might well involve prolonged, but finite, stays. They might also on special occasions send embassies of high-ranking nobles, as had happened the previous year, but had not appointed permanent representatives in each other's courts. Under Wolsey's guidance, this now changed. The first resident English ambassador in France was Sir Thomas Boleyn, the father of a famous daughter. His counterpart in England was Olivier de La Vernade, seigneur de La Bastie. Boleyn handled the negotiations necessitated by the sovereigns' competing claims during the Imperial election reasonably well. He also began the planning required for the proposed meeting of the two kings. These were eventually completed by his successor Sir Richard Wingfield, who received conspicuously favourable treatment during his time at the French court.[42]

The Field of Cloth of Gold

Henry and Francis did finally meet, on 7 June 1520, the Feast of Corpus Christi, during an event that has become known as the Field of Cloth of Gold. The Field was, before all else, a tournament held to inaugurate the Anglo-French alliance agreed in 1518. As the sovereigns and as leaders of their respective national orders of chivalry, the two kings jointly hosted the celebrations in order to demonstrate that peace could be a perfectly acceptable alternative

62   *Cloth of Gold*

to war, provided that it, too, had a chivalric and ennobling quality about it. Who better to organise the event than the man who had brought about the peace between these two kings, Thomas Wolsey.

In February 1520, the cardinal drew up a treaty for both kings to ratify, which set out the prospective arrangements for their meeting where they would come together and prepare 'to do some fair feat of arms, as well on foot as on horseback against all comers'. Henry was to be at his town of Guînes within the Pale of Calais, with Katherine and his sister Mary, Duchess of Suffolk, by the end of May. Francis was to be at his town of Ardres with Queen Claude and his mother Louise of Savoy within four days of the end of May. A copy of Wolsey's proclamation was sent to France.[43] Lists of those attending and their prescribed entourages were drawn up to ensure that sufficient shipping was organised and that all could be accommodated and fed once they arrived at the event. Each king would bring with him an entourage of approximately 6,000 people. Transporting, accommodating, ordering, feeding and watering, protecting and entertaining this vast concourse of people was certainly akin to organising a royal military campaign, and Wolsey had of course done just that in 1512–13. The Deputy of Calais, Sir John Peche, warned Wolsey of the need to provide sufficient food and fuel to cater for such a huge number of participants. A team of commissioners was sent to Calais to organise the English accommodation in Guînes castle, a temporary banqueting house, and in a tented encampment near its walls. A French team of commissioners supervised preparations for Francis's participation, centred on Ardres and its surroundings.

During the spring of 1520, hundreds of artisans and labourers on both sides prepared the site of the meeting. While supervising the whole event, Wolsey was also concerned about his own participation and accommodation. Part of an undated set of instructions issued by Wolsey to one 'Waren', presumably Richard Waren, one of his gentlemen ushers, seems to have anticipated or responded to these concerns. Waren was to confer with Sir John about a house, possibly 'Mrs Baynam's' for Wolsey at Calais. He was also to 'take his opinion of purveyance', and the relative costs of commodities and whether all that was needed could be had in the area, especially whether 'beer be as cheap, good and plentiful there as in England'. Waren was then to go to Guînes and arrange that Wolsey's tents

Cloth of Gold 63

were set up in a 'dry and convenient place'.[44] Perhaps predictably, the number of Wolsey's personal attendants as Cardinal and papal legate exceeded even those of the dukes. He was able to bring 50 gentlemen, 12 chaplains and 237 servants; that is, 299 men in total and 150 horses.[45]

As activities proceeded apace in the early spring, Wolsey began to get word that the Emperor Charles V, who had first been alerted to the realistic prospect of an Anglo-French summit in February, wanted to meet with Henry before the event. Charles was preparing to leave Spain to return to his native Flanders after his election as emperor. Should he agree, Henry would have the honour of being the first European monarch to meet Charles since his election. Wolsey seems to have seen this as a good opportunity both to reassure Charles but also to impress upon him how committed Henry was to the new international peace, which had serious implications for Charles's ambitions. It has usually been inferred it was Henry's intention to deceive Francis and that he met Charles before the Field in order to stitch up a deal that would nullify any commitments that might be made to the king of France. This was certainly what Charles wanted, but Wolsey did his best to prevent it. He wanted Henry to meet Francis without any prior commitments to Charles in order to act in good faith under the terms of the Universal Peace. The most Henry finally agreed with Charles was that he would meet with him again immediately after the Field. Dynastic and diplomatic protocol urged the meeting as well, and it was finally agreed that as he travelled from Spain in May, Charles would put into Dover and meet Henry and his aunt Katherine. The emperor duly arrived, and he and the king spent Whitsun at St Augustine's Abbey at Canterbury, amidst a mixture of religious observance and extravagant celebrations of the family connections between them. This meeting disconcerted the French, but also reminded them of Henry's powerful allies beyond France and, Wolsey hoped, impressed upon them that he must be taken seriously as a major political and military force.[46]

On Friday, 31 May 1520, Wolsey escorted Charles to Sandwich from where the emperor crossed to Flanders and Wolsey embarked for Calais. The following day Wolsey set out from there to meet the king of France for the first time and to complete the final negotiations prior to the personal encounter between the two sovereigns.

64   *Cloth of Gold*

Escorted by an impressive guard of more than 100 men, the cardinal, dressed in scarlet silk and velvet robes, rode a mule richly caparisoned in gold and crimson. A second mule was led before him, together with his *galero*. Before him also proceeded six of the eight English bishops who had come to France.[47] When Wolsey entered French territory, he was met by the dukes of Alençon, Bourbon and Vendôme, by Marshal Châtillon, the seigneur de La Trémoïlle and other gentlemen, together with 50 mounted archers of the French royal guard. As he arrived at Ardres, he was greeted with an artillery salute from the battlements of the town. Francis, escorted by more archers, came through the gates to meet Wolsey. They embraced, and Wolsey removed his hat as a mark of respect for Francis but deferred no further, nor did he dismount. The king of France escorted him through the town, and at the royal lodgings, he and Wolsey embraced again.[48]

Wolsey's splendid procession and his manner of meeting Francis have often been mocked by historians as examples of that arrogance which his critics scorned in him. As with the reception of his cardinal's hat, his behaviour has rarely been seen in its proper context. This was that his journey to Ardres that day was the first time Wolsey had left English sovereign territory and appeared internationally as cardinal legate *a latere* and Chancellor of England. He met Francis as no ordinary ambassador, however exalted. He came as the personal representative of the pope himself and, just as importantly for him, of a king whose international status he was charged with maintaining at the meeting. Just as Henry would do a few days later when he met the French king, Wolsey had to look the part. For six years previously he had been receiving and negotiating with French and other national ambassadors. They, like their Venetian counterparts at the English court, had sent home detailed, if sometimes equivocal, accounts of him. Wolsey wanted to impress and persuade Francis and his entourage of nobles with the power and dignity of his several high offices and his personal influence with Henry, hence his entourage and behaviour at first meeting the king of France.

Wolsey remained at Ardres negotiating for two days before returning to Guînes to report to Henry. Seeking to dispense with both the French and English councils and negotiate directly between the two kings, Wolsey requested plenipotentiary power from his sovereign. This being granted, Wolsey then went back to Ardres and demanded the same from Francis; a papal legate would perhaps not have expected less, and Francis had little choice but to grant Wolsey equivalent power. But no sooner had it been offered than Wolsey scrupulously refused to accept it unless and until he had Henry's express permission to do so. In effect Wolsey allowed Henry to arbitrate on Francis's decision to delegate his own sovereign power to him. He therefore made his own master the one whose final consent was required for Wolsey to exercise both royal *and* papal authority. Wolsey did so in order to reassure Henry of his fidelity and good service. After all, as Wolsey understood, Henry was the king upon whose favour his own career entirely depended.

Of the negotiations Wolsey conducted at Ardres with this ample power, we have no record. The various disputes between Francis and Charles V were probably involved. Anglo-Scottish disputes and the French role in, or response to, them evidently were discussed. The resultant treaty of 6 June confirmed a total French debt to Henry of one million crowns, to be paid in six monthly instalments of 50,000 crowns, and acknowledged that some of this had already been paid by the French. It effectively recognised the return of Tournai as completed. Its conclusion was followed by the prompt despatch to England directly from the Field of a small delegation sent to greet Princess Mary in the name of the dauphin. In return for all this, Louise of Savoy, who was a powerful figure in her son's regime and a strong advocate of peace, was to work directly with Wolsey on resolving Anglo-Scottish disputes. This mediation never really got off the ground before the war that broke out between Charles and Francis rendered them apparently irrelevant.[49]

Wolsey was next with Francis on 7 June, the day the two kings met for the first time. He rode once more to Ardres at mid-morning and dined with the French king as a final gesture of reassurance and goodwill, for tension remained very high. Wolsey then returned to Guînes at about 3.00PM to join his own sovereign's procession to the meeting point. At about 5.00PM, three cannon salvos were fired from Guînes, answered by three from Ardres, which signalled that each king had set off towards the appointed place, about a mile east of Guînes in a location named the Val d'Or or 'golden valley'. Wolsey rode on Henry's left as he is shown doing in the famous painting of the event at Hampton Court Palace.

But whereas in that painting he is depicted in a monkish grey or brown habit and is scarcely visible alongside a golden Henry, Wolsey was in fact splendidly arrayed in crimson satin as cardinal, riding a large, magnificently caparisoned mule surrounded by his own immense entourage and preceded again by his two crosses.[50] When they arrived at the appointed meeting place, the two kings detached themselves from their entourages and, with a few close attendants, approached each other to within a hundred yards or so. Wolsey rode to this point with Henry, together with the Marquis of Dorset, bearing the sword of State, Sir Henry Guildford and Sir Richard Wingfield, the king's ambassador in France. He watched the two kings greet each other with dramatic flourishing of bonnets and attempted embraces while still on horseback. He then joined Henry and Francis, and they all entered a richly decorated tent for refreshment. Here Wolsey chaired the first personal discussion between the two kings at which they essentially affirmed that they would honour the alliance between them and were happy for the tournament to proceed. Their meeting went on for much longer than planned, and as dusk drew on, Wolsey became concerned for the safe end of the encounter and urged them to part for that day at least.

As an ecclesiastic, even the highest-ranked one at the event, Wolsey is not recorded as ever formally attending the jousting or other competitions in the tournament that occupied the next ten days. That would have been thought unseemly. It is, nevertheless, hard to imagine him not taking an interest in how the kings and the teams of mixed English and Frenchmen they led were doing in the competitions. Most of his time seems to have been occupied with being, as usual, Henry's chief executive. Wolsey kept a watchful eye over the court officers and, through them, on the continuous provision of the food and drink needed for the several splendid banquets the king and queen gave to their French guests during the fortnight. He also oversaw the general running, feeding and watering of the English entourage. Meanwhile, he kept tabs on the movements of the emperor in Flanders and corresponded with the royal council at home and the English representatives in Rome, so as to keep the pope informed of events at the Field.

Wolsey ran the event from Guînes castle, from his tented pavilion and from a suite of rooms in the famous temporary palace that

Cloth of Gold 67

Henry had built for the Field. These were described as 'two halls and a chamber' in lodgings which extended from the gate house around the angle of the building and about half way along the left side wing. Wolsey's apartments connected to the king's slightly larger suite. According to one observer, they were decorated with 'silken tapestry without gold, of astounding beauty'.[51] In these rooms, he gave three formal dinners to high-ranking French ecclesiastics when they accompanied their king to Guînes, including one on the first Sunday of the event. On the second, he and Queen Katherine hosted Louise of Savoy and the ladies of her household in his apartments.

Wolsey's last big moment at the Field came when, as cardinal legate *a latere* and the most senior churchman present, he presided at High Mass sung on Saturday, 23 June, the eve of St John's and Midsummer Day. The night beforehand, the tiltyard between Guînes and Ardres had been transformed into a public stage for the Mass. A temporary open timber chapel was built on wooden posts, and the viewing galleries were turned into temporary oratories for members of the royal parties, senior nobles from both nations and the many ambassadors of other realms present at the meeting. The chapel was hung with rich hangings and tapestries, and the altar was adorned with ten large silver gilt images, two golden candlesticks and a large jewelled crucifix. From a bishop's throne under a canopy to the right of the high altar and dressed in full pontifical vestments, with jewelled sandals on his feet, Wolsey presided at the Mass of the Trinity. Cardinal de Boisy, the papal legate to France, sat opposite him under a canopy to the left of the altar but one step down. Over 20 prelates from England and France were arranged before him while the bishops of Armagh and Durham assisted directly in the liturgy of the Mass. As the celebrating priest, the cardinal ritually washed his hands at three points in the Mass, assisted successively by three barons, three earls and finally by the earl of Northumberland and the dukes of Suffolk and Buckingham. At the moment of the elevation of the Host, the most sacred moment of the Mass (or just afterwards according to one source), there appeared above the altar a 'flying dragon'. This seems to have been one of the elaborate kite fireworks often used in celebrating the eve of St John's day. The dragon was made by the English, and it may have represented the dragon of Wales, thus Henry. It might,

68 *Cloth of Gold*

alternatively, have been intended to be a dragon-like salamander, the personal emblem of Francis.[52] It caused quite a stir, and Wolsey might not have been entirely pleased at its unexpected appearance during his big moment at the Mass. The following day, amidst an exchange of expensive presents between the highest ranked members of the two national entourages (including Wolsey), the two kings parted. Despite promises to the contrary, they were not to see each other again for another 12 years, by which time Wolsey was dead.

In May it had been agreed that Henry and Charles V would meet again on Imperial territory at Gravelines on Wednesday, 4 July. The king was to be entertained by Charles for three days, and then the emperor was to return with him to Calais on 7 July for a further three days. Henry duly arrived back in Calais from Guînes on 25 June to reports that the Imperial court had suggested that the Anglo–Imperial encounter should now take place at Bruges. 'They had proposed Bruges as more commodious; Gravelines is not sufficient for the company'.[53] The real reason for this seems to have been partly that Charles was then busy receiving a large number of his Flemish and German nobles. In effect, he was asking for a delay to the meeting, and there was no suggestion that he would not eventually come to Calais, but he was also saying, deliberately or otherwise, that he considered his current business to be more important than meeting with Henry, according to the terms of the agreement made in May.

Wolsey rejected the suggestion out of hand and countered that if Charles persisted in this demand, Henry would leave for England within four days. He was not having the king of England trot meekly after Charles as if he were some minor Netherlandish princeling. A day later it became clear that, however occupied Charles was at Bruges, the main reason for requesting a delay was so that the emperor might first send his Chancellor, Mercurino Gattinara, and Guillaume de Croy, the marquess of Aerschot, for private talks with Wolsey. Charles and his advisors were evidently worried by a letter sent on 13 June by the Imperial ambassador at the papal court, Juan Manuel, who wrote that Wolsey had boasted to a papal official with the court at Guînes of his power to 'conclude an alliance between the King of England, him [the emperor] and the King of France'. What the emperor wanted is clear from the

Cloth of Gold 69

Chancellor's marginal note on Juan Manuel's letter, indicating that the ambassador in Rome need not fret about this prospect, as 'we are about to conclude a treaty with the King of England'. Other correspondence from the papal court indicates that this was to be an offensive alliance between Leo X, Henry and Charles against Francis in support of Charles's attempt to wrest Milan from French hands; exactly the sort of alliance that Francis feared.[54] The pope so favoured an anti-French alliance that he expressed a willingness to 'make the Cardinal his legate in England' (actually to renew his existing and, at that stage, temporary legateship) if Wolsey could bring it about. Leo conferred the see of Badajoz in Spain on Wolsey at this time. Charles had first asked the pope to give Wolsey this rich living in May.

It seems clear in the light of this that the delay to the emperor's arrival was engineered to allow time for his ministers to talk with Wolsey and at the very least ensure that Charles would not be confronted with a demand to join any tri-partite alliance *with* France. No record of the discussions between Wolsey and the Imperial representatives survives, but it is evident from subsequent events that Wolsey did not shift his position, despite the obvious inducements from Leo to do so.[55] Henry and Charles did finally meet on 10 July at Gravelines. The following day, the emperor was escorted to Calais and lodged at the Staple. Although a treaty was signed at Calais, nothing in it contravened the pre-existing Anglo-French agreement for Mary's marriage to the dauphin. They agreed to maintain all existing treaties between them and to send special representatives to Calais within two years to work towards increased co-operation between them. In the meantime, resident ambassadors were to be exchanged for the first time, in emulation of existing practice between England and France.[56] There was, in other words, no grand anti-French alliance of the sort Charles hoped for and which some historians have laboured to detect in this agreement, and to which they imply Henry was already committed by May 1520. At Gravelines, Wolsey and Henry asserted the English king's potential as an arbiter of European peace, whatever the status of the emperor, as firmly upon Charles as they had on Francis. Only time would tell whether or not Henry really had the means to fulfil that potential as well as Wolsey hoped he would.

Universal peace?

In 1511–12, Wolsey had made his name on Henry's royal council as the de facto leader of the war party. He had done so because at that time it served his own interests best and raised the international profile and importance of the king he served. His organisation of Henry's first military campaign had cemented his place as foremost royal advisor. Wolsey was never, however, committed to war for its own sake. He could, at the very least, see the danger the Ottomans might potentially pose and the advantages to Christendom of unity. He probably had genuine sympathy with the humanist views of Erasmus and others on the importance of peace and certainly deployed the rhetoric of chivalric Christian peace very readily. One thing, however, had not changed in his thinking. Henry had to be returned to the forefront of international affairs in the wake of Louis XII's death and the accession of Francis I. If a magnificent, compelling and knightly peace could do that, then peace it was. Wolsey transformed the 1517 papal plan for a truce among Christian princes into Europe's first multilateral non-aggression compact and in 1518 made London, not Rome, the centre of international attention. The Universal Peace to which most European states were sworn that year was inaugurated at the Field of Cloth of Gold. As Wolsey made clear to Charles's representatives directly after the Field, the emperor needed Henry's help against Francis more than Henry then needed his. Henry's support could not be assumed by anyone and would have to be earned by everyone. An English monarch was once again a Continental force to be reckoned with, in a way not seen since the time of the Hundred Years War. Charles's preponderant power did begin to turn relations with Henry to his favour – but that was only some two years later, when the situation had radically changed. By then, Wolsey had established a reputation as a powerful and skilled negotiator. He may not have in fact established a 'universal peace' in Christendom, but he had definitely secured an Anglo-French peace that proclaimed Henry's strength. As it had been from the outset, securing and maintaining the king's high international status remained central to the rest of Wolsey's career in the service of Henry VIII.

Cloth of Gold 71

Notes

1 Cavendish, p. 26.
2 *LP* I ii, 2611 Fox and Wolsey to Bishop of Worcester in Rome, February 1514.
3 Scarisbrick, pp. 46–56.
4 Gwyn, p.15.
5 BL, Cotton MS Caligula D VI, fo. 121r [*LP* I ii, 2956] Henry to Wolsey, May 1514.
6 Ibid., fo. 139; LP I ii, 3155] Longueville to Mary Tudor, 16 August 1514; Vitellius CXI, fo. 155v; Bohier to Wolsey, 28 August 1514 [*LP* I ii, 3201].
7 SP1/230, fo. 247 [*LP* I ii, 3294] Instructions to the English embassy to France.
8 *LP* I ii, 3239 Credence for Neufville.
9 TNA, SP1/230, fo. 244; E36/215 fo. 169; Rymer, XIII, p. 456 [*LP* I ii, 3323] Louis to Wolsey, September 1514.
10 TNA, E36/215, fo.169.
11 Rymer, XIII, pp. 423–8. TNA, PRO 31/8/137, fos. 71–9.
12 BNF, IMP. Lb 29.50 *Entree de La Royne a Ableville*. Anonymous. Published in 1514 or 1515; *CSPV* I, 510, 511.
13 BL, Cotton MS Caligula B II, fo. 36 [*LP* I ii, 3342], Norfolk to Wolsey, Montreuil 7 October 1514.
14 R. J. Knecht, *Renaissance Warrior and Patron: The Reign of Francis I* (Cambridge, 1994), pp. 41–61.
15 BL, Cotton MS Caligula D VI, fos. 218–19 [*LP* II i, 175]. Suffolk and the ambassadors in France to Wolsey, Paris, 18 February 1515. My italics.
16 BL, Cotton MS Caligula D VI, fos. 176–7 [*LP* II i, 106]; S. J. Gunn, *Charles Brandon, Duke of Suffolk 1485–1545* (Oxford, 1988), pp. 35–8; Gwyn, pp. 570–1.
17 Ibid., fos. 219 [*LP* II i, 175] Suffolk and the ambassadors in France to Wolsey, Paris, 18 February 1515.
18 BL, Cotton MS Vespasian F XIII, fo. 153 [*LP* II i, 367] Suffolk to Henry, Montreuil, 22 April 1515.
19 *CPSV* II, 618 Andrea Badoer and Giustinian to the Signory, London, 15 May 1515.
20 AN, KK 349, fos. 263–78 List of English payees, November 1521; see also LP IV I, 3619; C. Giry-Deloison, 'Money and Early Tudor Diplomacy: The English Pensioners of the French Kings, 1475–1547', *Medieval History* 3 (1994): 128–46.
21 Rawdon Brown, I, pp. 76, 79–81, see also pp. 84–7.
22 Knecht, pp. 62–87.

72   *Cloth of Gold*

23 *LP* I ii, 3497 Wolsey to Silvestro Gigli, undated draft but from context November 1514.

24 Cavendish, p. 17; J. Arnold, 'John Colet, Preaching and Reform at St Paul's' Cathedral, 1505–19', *Historical Research* 76 (194) (November 2003): 450–68.

25 Vergil, Book 27, section 11.

26 *LP* II ii, 2965, 2968, 3437; Scarisbrick, pp. 57–69.

27 *LP* II ii, 3812/3, Letters between Wolsey to Silvestro Gigli in Rome, November 1517; G. Mattingly, 'An Early Nonagression Pact', *HJ* 10 (1) (1938): 1–30; see also his *Renaissance Diplomacy* (New York, 1955).

28 BNF, MS français 2964, fo. 6 Francis I to Pope Leo X, Paris, 2 February [1518].

29 Rawdon Brown, II, p. 177.

30 BL Cotton MS Caligula D VII, fo. 2 [*LP* II ii, 4046] Instructions to ambassadors Jean Gobelin, the Bishop of Paris's secretary and Nicholas de Neufville, seigneur de Villeroy.

31 Ibid., fos. 9–17 [*LP* II ii, 4303]; Rymer, p. 609 [*LP* II ii, 4293, 4304]; *CAF* I, 864, 868 Villeroy's commission for the alliance, Angers, 3 July 1518.

32 Knecht, pp. 170ff.

33 BL, Cotton MS Caligula D VII, fos. 2, 8 [*LP* II ii, 4064, 4166]; MS Caligula E I, fo. 124ff [*LP* II ii, 4254–5].

34 TNA, SP1/17, fos. 61–2 [*LP* II ii, 4432].

35 R. Pace, *Oratio Ricardii Pacei in Pace Nuperrime Composita* (London, 1518), translated from the Latin by D. A. Russell in J. G. Russell, *Peacemaking in the Renaissance* (London, 1986), pp. 234–41. *STC* 19081A; BL, *Printed Books Catalogue*, no. 33. b. 39.

36 Pace, fo. A ii v [Russell, p. 235].

37 Ibid., fo. B ii v [Russell, p. 240].

38 Hall, p. 595; TNA E36/216, fo. 21v, Richard Gibson was paid £230 4s. 4d. for costumes and scenery for this and other pageants in October 1518.

39 BL, Cotton MS Titus B I, fo. 308 [*LP* III i, 141] An undated letter from the duke of Suffolk to Wolsey (my redaction of Suffolk's idiosyncratic spelling in the original).

40 J. Strype, *Ecclesiastical Memorials Relating to Religion and the Reformation of It etc.* (3 vols; London, 1822), vol. I, part i, pp. 32–4; BL, Cotton MS Caligula E I, fo. 209 [*LP* III i, 15] Wolsey to West, dated c. 12 January 1519.

41 BL, Cotton MS Caligula D VII, fos. 83–4, 78–9 [*LP* III i, 13]; Gwyn, pp. 93–4, 98–103.

42 Ibid., fos. 88–90 [*LP* III i, 57, 69] Inferred from these letters from Boleyn and Francis to Wolsey dated 2 and 9 February.

43 BNF MS français, 5761, 39r–42r 'Articles pour l'entrevue du roy et du roy d'angleterre faicte à ardre'. For the formal treaty agreeing to these articles see Rymer VI, pp. 180–1.

Cloth of Gold 73

44 Richardson, *Field*, p. 95.

45 Hall, p. 602; see Richardson, *Field*, Appendix A for the list of those who accompanied Henry and Katherine.

46 *LP* III i, 551 Charles V to the Bishop of Elna, 12 December 1519; *CSP Sp.* II, 274 [*LP* III i, 740–1] Treaty documents dated London, 11 April 1520; 279 Juan Manuel, Imperial ambassador in Rome to Charles V, 12 May 1520.

47 *LP* III i, 869; *CSPV* III, 58, 59.

48 Hall, p. 607. The book to which Hall refers is probably *L'ordonnance et ordre du tournoy* summarised in *LP* III i, 870.

49 Hall, pp. 607–8; Rymer, XIII, 719–20 [*LP* III i, 861].

50 *CSPV* III, 67 Anonymous letter to the Signory; 68 Letter to Pietro Montemerlo, 7 June 1520.

51 T. P. Campbell, *Henry VIII and the Art of Majesty: Tapestries at the Tudor Court* (New Haven & London, 2007), pp. 149–55.

52 *CSPV* III, 93; Richardson, *Field*, pp. 171–4.

53 *LP* III i, 883, 885 Spinelly to Wolsey, Brussels, 27 and 28 June 1520; 888 Charles V to Wolsey, Brussels, 30 June 1520.

54 *CSP Sp.* II, 281 Juan Manuel, Imperial ambassador in Rome to the emperor, 13 June 1520; 288 Juan Manuel to the emperor, Rome, 22 July 1520, reporting news heard in earlier in the month.

55 *LP* III i, 866 Spinelly to Wolsey, Ghent, 8 June 1520; *CSP Sp.* II, 283, 286, Juan Manuel to Guillaume de Croy, seigneur de Chièvres, Rome, 5 July, and the same to the emperor 13 July 1520.

56 *CSP Sp.* II, 287 Treaty between Charles V and Henry VIII dated 14 July 1520; see also *LP* III i, 908, 914.

3 Chief executive

Wolsey in council and court

And there [Westminster Hall] lighted and went after this manner up through the hall into the Chancery. Howbeit, he would most commonly stay a while at a bar made for him a little beneath the Chancery and there commune sometime with the judges and sometime with other persons. And that done he would repair into the Chancery, and sitting there until eleven of the clock, hearing suitors and determining of divers matters. And from thence he would divers times go into the Star Chamber, as occasion did serve, where he spared neither high nor low, but judged every estate according to their merits and deserts.[1]

Thus, Cavendish described Thomas Wolsey arriving at Westminster Hall, the place he spent most of his time during the legal terms of the year. Having begun his career as the king's almoner in 1509, he had become, as we have seen, Archbishop of York in 1514, a cardinal in 1515 and a papal legate *a latere* in 1518. Being the highest member of England's clerical hierarchy by virtue of his legateship was, however, but one half of Wolsey's public responsibility and authority in the kingdom of Henry VIII. On Christmas Eve 1515, just six weeks after he had formally received his cardinal's hat, Wolsey was made the Lord Chancellor of England. In contrast to that grand public occasion, he took the oath of office as Chancellor and received the Great Seal of England privately from Henry at Westminster. Wolsey was now the realm's highest judicial and administrative official, the chief executive officer of the Crown, whose status on the royal council was second only to that of the ruler himself.

Chief executive 75

Wolsey's personal arms, granted to him by Thomas Wriothesley, Garter King of Arms, and Thomas Benolt, Clarencieux herald, in August 1525, allude clearly to the dual nature of his authority from 1515. They are described heraldically as 'Sable, on a cross engrailed argent a lion passant gules between four leopards' faces azure; on a chief Or a rose gules barbed vert and seeded or between two Cornish choughs proper'.[2] There are several surviving versions and depictions of these arms (see Figure 2.1). All are surmounted by a cardinal's *galero*. The 'chief' or main band across the top of the shield is gold and has at its centre a red rose with a gold centre and points. This symbolises Wolsey's king, Henry VIII, at the place of highest honour on the shield. The choughs on either side are Cornish birds of the crow family, often symbols of Thomas à Becket. They here allude to Wolsey's first name and perhaps his high status within the Church, although Becket was of course Archbishop of Canterbury, not York. Below the chief, set within a silver cross on a black background are four, blue leopards' faces. The silver cross is derived from the arms of the Ufford earls of Suffolk, and the leopards from the De la Pole earls and dukes of Suffolk, Wolsey being a native of that county. At the centre of the cross is a red (gules) lion standing on its legs, facing left or *passant*. This is sometimes wrongly regarded as a reference to Henry as king. The three lions of England are gold, not red, and are facing forward with a forepaw raised, *passant guardant*. The red lion is thus better understood as a visual pun alluding to Pope Leo X who made Wolsey a cardinal and legate. Depictions of the arms are usually supplemented by the two crosses that the cardinal always had carried before him; one for York and the other for his legateship, and usually two pillars, sometimes referred to as maces, also symbolising his status as cardinal legate. The arms ably reference the two sources of authority that Wolsey sought to exercise harmoniously, but it is the red rose, not the lion, that dominates the coat of arms.

For nearly three years prior to his appointment as Lord Chancellor, Wolsey had been, as we have seen, the strongest force on the royal council. He had organised war and 'magnificent' peace for his master and raised Henry's international profile to new heights. During those years, Wolsey had gradually taken more and more of Henry's administration into his own hands. Giving him the Chancellorship in succession to William Warham, who retired from

76   *Chief executive*

office voluntarily but perhaps, it is often suggested, under pressure from Wolsey and even the king himself, effectively formalised his position. The appointment was, however, primarily intended to allow the king and the cardinal the greatest possible freedom in their co-ordinated exercise of royal power.

Wolsey and the law

The Chancellor was essentially responsible for authenticating the king's formal written communications, agreements, commands and grants, giving them full legal authority under the Great Seal of the Realm, recording them and putting them into effect. In practice, well before Henry's reign, royal administration had become far more complex than the remit of the Chancery. In 1509, most of the king's responses to personal requests for patronage were issued through a rather cumbersome administrative process whereby his signature, giving assent to a written request or petition, was eventually turned into a 'signed, sealed and delivered' document. This process, known as 'the course of the seals', was supervised by the royal council and the Keeper of the Privy Seal (in the early years Richard Fox, Wolsey's mentor). To make a grant, Henry usually signed a 'bill' or petition addressed to him as king. His signature on it acted as an order to his secretary to draw up a 'warrant' under the king's 'signet', or personal seal, addressed to the Keeper of the Privy Seal. The secretary then kept the original bill or petition as his authority. The Keeper oversaw the receipt of these signet warrants. One of his (ordinarily) four clerks then drew up a second 'warrant', this time sealed with the Privy Seal, retaining the secretary's warrant to him as his authority. This Privy Seal warrant was then sent to the Chancellor as his authority to draw up Letters Patent (or Close) as appropriate, giving legal effect to the grant, under the Great Seal, and it was entered on the Chancery's records, kept by the Master of the Rolls. This whole process was intended to ensure proper conciliar scrutiny of royal decisions. Not surprisingly perhaps, the young and inexperienced Henry found it complicated, time-consuming and decidedly irksome.[3] It is probably the first thing Wolsey noticed about Henry as he began working with the king as one of his councillors.

As early as 1511, Wolsey had begun assisting Henry to side-step the full process, telling the Chancellor (then Archbishop Warham)

Chief executive 77

that the king's signature or 'sign manual' on a bill was now his 'sufficient warrant' as an authenticating instrument to have a grant made under the Great Seal. Warham registered his objection to this novel and peremptory instruction. He recognised Wolsey's close working relationship with the king, however, and complied with the new order. While much of the business of routine grants and administrative orders, to which the king was largely indifferent, continued to pass through the prescribed process, decisions on important grants, or matters in which he took a particular interest for any reason, no longer routinely did. This direct communication of the royal will to the Chancellor is perhaps the best indication why, four years later when Warham retired, Wolsey himself was appointed as his successor. It made it much easier for Henry and Wolsey to direct the king's patronage towards those whom he favoured and thereby to extend and consolidate the network of royal clients upon whom his regime effectively depended. This would certainly have important implications for the conduct of royal government and the personal politics of Henry's reign throughout Wolsey's years in power – and well beyond.[4]

As was typical of the man, Wolsey was determined from the outset to be an active and effective Lord Chancellor. Although not technically numbered among England's judges, the Chancellor exercised a judicial function and was responsible for the operation of the legal system. He also superintended the proceedings of the House of Lords, and Parliament generally. These roles gave Wolsey ample scope to assert his authority, but it was in the court of Chancery where he really made his mark. Chancery had been established by the end of the fourteenth century to handle petitions and complaints addressed to the king. It was principally charged with the resolution of legal matters that stood outside the scope of the common law. It heard suits about real property, contracts, debts, wills, inheritances and the like. However, its decisions were reached according to 'equity', or 'conscience' (in our terms 'fairness'), on the merits of the case. Litigants before it did not use the hide-bound Latin 'forms of action' used to sue at common law. Defendants in such common law cases could often frustrate their opponent by pointing out a small factual error in the claim against them and counter-suing in the Court of King's Bench, or simply not showing up for the case – effectively bringing the plaintiff's case

78 *Chief executive*

to a halt. Chancery's writ of subpoena could compel respondents more effectively to attend. Its procedures could get more readily to the facts and to a decision based on equity, often a compromise, on the claims of litigants, based on its determination as to the respective merits of their cases. It could resolve issues of land inheritance by will and enforce contracts between parties rather than simply imposing damages on one party or the other, that being the preserve and method of the common law. Chancery had a range of injunctions and other 'remedies' for cases before it, which supplemented the available outcomes at common law. Chancery could also revoke cases to itself from lower jurisdictions, overturning or revising decisions on appeal. Not surprisingly, by Wolsey's time, Chancery had become a popular court in both its appellant and original jurisdictions. Just under 70% of its cases concerned land ownership and inheritance, many of them on appeal from lower courts. It has been estimated that some 7,526 cases were brought before him in Chancery, averaging out at about 500 per year. The number of cases per annum certainly increased somewhat under him but had already been doing so under his predecessors Morton and Warham.[5]

To resolve those legal cases that particularly concerned the run of the king's writ and peace, the Chancellor also presided over the royal council when it sat at Westminster in its judicial guise, in 'Star Chamber' (so called because of the ceiling decoration in the room off Westminster Hall where it met). These cases had, in general, to involve a breach of the king's peace, public disorder, riot or similar, and it had both civil and criminal jurisdictions. Its supervision was important in helping the monarchy to increase its control in the localities through conciliar interventions and arbitration of disputes. It being a time-honoured principle that royal justice should be swift justice, Star Chamber also held an appeal for clients in certain types of cases. As John Guy observed, 'Wolsey imposed on the council courts his conviction that the availability of conciliar justice in suits between party and party was a great public benefit'.[6] It was comparatively easy for allegations to be made of obstruction of justice in order to get a case before the council in its judicial guise. Similarly, fictional allegations of violence might be made by parties to a civil dispute (and sometimes actual breaches of the peace arranged between them) in order to get a case before Star Chamber.

Chief executive 79

Under Wolsey, the number of cases rose more significantly than in Chancery, from an average of 12.5 to 120 per year; that is ten a month or between two and three a week. Approximately 40% of these cases concerned title to land. Wolsey's intention was that Star Chamber should also be comparatively inexpensive and therefore theoretically open to many people down the social scale, even if that sometimes meant he made access to the court too easy, requiring adjustments from More and later Chancellors to reduce the flow of cases. To his credit, in modern eyes at least, it has been estimated that about one third of litigants in Star Chamber were husbandmen or yeoman and one third were gentlemen. After Wolsey, upper gentry and noblemen brought the bulk of cases in Star Chamber, but partly in response to the success of equity, as the century progressed, litigation in other courts became comparatively less expensive and perhaps more effective than it had been in Wolsey's time.[7]

As his critics did not hesitate to point out, Wolsey was not himself a lawyer, but this did not prevent him from making judgements in Chancery and Star Chamber cases where notions of common sense and equitable outcomes informed decisions rather than the elaborate technicalities of the common law, in which he had no expertise. He may not, however, have entirely lacked legal experience. As bursar at Magdalen, as chaplain to Henry VII, almoner to Henry VIII and a member of the latter's council, Wolsey would certainly have been involved in dozens of legal matters over his career to this point. As almoner he had general legal supervision over 'poor men's causes' heard by royal judges. He was also responsible legally for money obtained from the sale of the goods of felons and that made from the sale of objects that had been the immediate cause of a person's death. The money raised would then be applied to charitable causes.[8] Moreover, he had ample judicial expertise around him on which to call. Cavendish's description of Wolsey carrying out his role as Chancellor, quoted at the outset of this chapter, alludes to his doing exactly this. After processing to Westminster Hall (see Figure 3.1), he would first confer with the judges of the King's Bench. Ensuring that equity 'fulfilled' the common law, rather than undermining it, was a live issue among royal judges in Wolsey's day, and such consultations helped to finesse its operation in principle and in particular cases.

80　*Chief executive*

Figure 3.1 Cardinal Wolsey's procession, from the 1578 edition of Cavendish's *Life and Death of Cardinal Wolsey*

Faced with evidence (incomplete though it is due to a lack of surviving council records) of increasing appeals to Chancery and Star Chamber, historians have argued about the extent to which the Chancellor advocated, and even encouraged, their use. John Guy saw the court of Star Chamber as becoming 'the Cardinal's court' under Wolsey. He argued that Wolsey used the tribunal to increase the appeal of royal justice, probably out of a genuine ambition to improve its quality and reach, but also as a way of securing a tighter grip on law enforcement.[9] There is some near-contemporary support for this view. The Elizabethan commentator Sir Thomas Smith later said of Star Chamber that it:

> took great augmentation and authority at that time that Cardinal Wolsey Archbishop of York was Chancellor of England; who of some was thought to have first devised the court because that he after some intermission by negligence of time, augmented the authority of it.[10]

In other words, Wolsey increased and highlighted the importance of the court. Peter Gwyn was somewhat sceptical and attributed the rise in cases to a longer-term decrease in the appeal of common law practices, and a concomitant increase in the appeal of those of the equity and conciliar courts. Lawyers treated the Chancellor's two courts of Chancery and Star Chamber as simply alternative potential tribunals in which to plead, depending upon the particulars of their clients' cases. Gwyn was also insistent that while the workloads of these courts certainly increased under him, Wolsey did not significantly alter the scope of their jurisdiction, and on balance, the admittedly incomplete surviving evidence supports this view. That may be so, but the increase in cases under him to record levels indicates that Wolsey advertised the merits of the equity and conciliar courts. This in turn assisted the enforcement of crown authority through its tribunals, officials and the control of powerful individuals at regional and local level through arbitration of disputes and punishment of malpractice. The more effective their remedies were, the more people used these courts and the more involved royal officials became in the orderly oversight of legal matters centrally and at local level, generally to the credit of Wolsey and, as he would have said, to the upholding of the king's justice and honour.[11]

In 1520, as part of his apparent commitment to justice for all, Wolsey drew together a number of 'under-courts' established to hear poor people's causes into what eventually came to be called 'the king's most honourable Council in his Court of Requests'. Here, poor (and, as it turned out, not so poor) petitioners could bring cases in order to avoid the onerous fees charged by common-law lawyers. According to his critics, principally these same lawyers of course, Wolsey boasted that he could deal with all the cases this policy generated, but in reality, he could not. By the mid-1520s the Chancery and Star Chamber, as well as the Court of Requests, were all overburdened with unresolved cases, undermining their original appeal as sources of speedy justice. In his effort to provide this, Wolsey also used arbitration at a local level, conducted by a range of appointees, including local Justices of the Peace, lawyers and clergy, acting under the authority of Star Chamber in an attempt to resolve cases which would otherwise have to be heard formally.

82 *Chief executive*

Four commissions were also established to hear them, and Wolsey had cases listed before the royal council returned to the regional councils – that of the Marches of Wales under the titular headship of Princess Mary and the Council in the North under the duke of Richmond. He pressed his fellow councillors, most of them not specialist lawyers but gentry and noblemen, to work even harder. From 1517, Wolsey sat personally in Star Chamber on Monday, Tuesday, Thursday and Saturday with 12 to 15 royal counsellors, leaving the king only a remnant of advisors in his personal entourage – to the latter's apparent frustration at times. So great was the workload, however, that by 1528 he was forced to limit the number of suits with which Requests could deal.

As Lord Chancellor, Wolsey was also responsible for running the House of Lords, presenting and piloting government legislation through both houses of Parliament and ensuring its correct and timely conduct more generally. It was in his management of Parliament and reforms to the taxation system that Wolsey made his most significant contribution to the Tudor crown's ability to tap the realm's wealth and economic output to fund national defence and administration. The traditional form of parliamentary taxation was of 'fifteenths and tenths' of wealth in goods and property. Over time, these had become fixed quotas that no longer reflected the true wealth of the country, and attempts to supplement them with other forms of taxation had not been very successful. From as early as 1512, Wolsey began working to introduce a scheme of directly assessed tax levies or 'subsidies'. These were based not on fifteenths and tenths but on the value of individuals' property and moveable goods. Between 1512 and 1515 successive parliamentary sessions passed subsidy acts based on assessments of incomes and goods and even a poll tax of 4d on anyone over the age of 15 not otherwise taxed. Their introduction was a response to the need to secure and enhance Crown revenues given the amount of wealth Henry had disbursed in land grants, annuities and offices after his accession, and on his first war against France in 1512–13. These Acts had been passed through careful but assertive management of parliament by Wolsey, including an Act of Resumption in 1515 which brought back crown lands into its possession, netted the government between £5,000 and £10,000, and was intended to show the Commons that it was committed to fiscal responsibility. Yet these measures did not raise as much revenue as had been anticipated. In the spring and summer of 1522, faced with the need to finance Henry's imminent war against France (see Chapter 6) and anticipatory action on the border with Scotland, Wolsey returned to the issue of subsidies and their assessment. Under his revised scheme, those eligible to pay tax were individually assessed by a 'general proscription'. Commissioners were appointed before whom those liable to tax appeared on oath as to the true value of their wealth. Wolsey bullied and hectored Parliament until a subsidy was voted in 1523, collectable in 1524–5. This subsidy was more successful in raising the amount of revenue expected. Rates of tax were flexible, and there was a minimum income threshold, below which no tax was payable at all. A very sizeable proportion of the population was exempt altogether, and the burden of taxation fell more on the rich, so that Wolsey's assessment system was both progressive and efficient.[12] For the first time in nearly two centuries, the crown had a mechanism that allowed it, theoretically at least, to tax its subjects based on more accurate assessments of their wealth. Wolsey more than doubled the yield of parliamentary taxation to the crown in subsidies between 1512 and his fall. As we shall see, however, in the circumstances of 1525, all this money was still not enough, and demands for more, for which Wolsey was blamed, provoked widespread opposition.[13]

Wolsey and the king's authority

In the various tribunals he oversaw as well as his supervision of Parliament, Wolsey very consciously deployed the language of impartial and effective justice and equality before the law. It became a kind of 'mission statement' for his role as Chancellor. For example, in 1517 the so-called Evil May Day riot against foreigners in the City of London broke out among apprentices and some tradesmen. After some days, the Mayor and the aldermen, aided by the retinues of some nobles, put the unrest down, and Henry determined to make an example of those found guilty of breaking the peace and inflicting damage on the city and foreign traders. Wolsey attended the king in Westminster Hall when many men and boys convicted of rioting were paraded before him, already condemned to death and wearing halters around their necks. In a highly choreographed

84   *Chief executive*

ceremony, they cried out for mercy. They were pardoned by Henry at the urgent request of the lords. Wolsey then lectured them on their misbehaviour and the rigour of the law which had to be upheld, but also the king's mercy towards them, 'to the great gladness of all the hearers'.[14]

Giustinian was persuaded of Wolsey's sincerity and efforts in the law, praising him on his return to Venice in 1519: 'He favoured the people exceedingly, and especially the poor, hearing their suits, and seeking to despatch them instantly. He also made the lawyers plead gratis for all poor men'.[15] Cavendish echoed this language in his portrayal of the cardinal. This was partly because he wanted to locate his subject within the conventions of good Christian government. As John Colet, the Dean of St Paul's, urged Wolsey at the Mass inaugurating him as cardinal in 1515, 'My Lord cardinal, be glad and enforce yourself always to do and execute righteousness to rich and poor, and mercy with truth'.[16] This was something Wolsey prided himself on doing in the various judicial bodies over which he presided.

There was another view. Wolsey frequently used Star Chamber as Henry VII had done with its defunct equivalent 'the Council Learned in the Law', to enforce the obedience of those who thought themselves above the law and who had raised disorder or disturbances in the counties, or who had tried to subvert justice at a local level. One instance of this was the long-running dispute over lands and wardships between Thomas Grey, Marquis of Dorset, on the one hand and Sir Richard Sacheverell and Lord Hastings on the other. Beginning in 1516, accusations of illegal retaining, intimidating juries and other 'enormities' against Crown justice were traded between the parties over the course of a decade, and all were hauled before Star Chamber at times to account for themselves and accept enforced arbitration of their disputes.[17] Similar accusations were made in 1517 over an affray between the servants of Thomas Pygot, a sergeant-at-law, and Sir Andrew Windsor, himself a royal councillor and keeper of the Great Wardrobe. This case prompted Wolsey's famous letter to Henry in which he wrote about teaching these two the 'new law' of Star Chamber which, he trusted, would set them straight about how the king's authority was paramount and to be respected. This rhetorical flourish underscored Wolsey's real aim, which was not so much to innovate as to ensure proper

Chief executive 85

enforcement of the existing laws of the realm.[18] Writing later in the century, Sir Thomas Smith seemed to accept this view of Wolsey's use of Star Chamber. After noting that it had been 'augmented' under him, he went on:

> which was at that time marvellous necessary to do, to repress the insolency of the noble men and gentlemen of the North parts of England, who being far off from the King and the seat of justice made almost as it were an ordinary war among themselves, and made their force their Law, banding themselves with their tenants and servants to do or revenge injurie one against another as they listed [liked].

This enforcement, Smith continued, enabled Henry to make his subjects 'to understand that they had a Prince who would rule his subjects by his laws and obedience'.[19] The upholding of royal authority, the maintenance of royal justice and military preparedness beyond the south and east of the kingdom were perennial issues for Wolsey and Henry, particularly in the three 'Marches' of the north along the border with Scotland. In 1524 special commissioners were appointed to enquire into the administration of this area and into rivalry between the local magnates, the earls of Northumberland and the crown representative Lord Dacre of the North. Dacre was called to Westminster and charged with negligence in failing to tackle the 'reavers' or cross border raiders and maintaining patronage connections with some who undermined law and order at a local level. He admitted the charge and was for a time imprisoned. Despite various control strategies deployed subsequently, the area remained 'bandit' country with incursions on both sides of the border.[20]

Wolsey also used the Star Chamber in areas where law enforcement intersected with what today might be called social or economic policy, and here again his chief targets were often wealthy landowners. The Chancellor called before him those accused of enclosing common land illegally, using fences, hedges and ditches. This practice prevented rights of common grazing and was done in order to increase the amount of land on which a private individual could run sheep in the hope of increasing the yield of wool. Naturally, those most prone to this malpractice were those who

86   *Chief executive*

had large estates, the wealthier gentry and some noblemen. Wolsey launched an enquiry into enclosures in 1517–18 to see how much common land had been taken, or 'engrossed' in contemporary language, within private estates, and its economic effects. Numerous prosecutions resulted, some followed with attention by Wolsey and even the king himself. These efforts against enclosure were followed in 1519 by proposals for further enforcement of laws, the fixing of prices of basic foodstuffs and related matters. Probably, however, because they were prompted more by Wolsey's political concerns at the time than by a thorough-going reconsideration of existing processes, they were never implemented – something Elton justifiably noted in his critique of Wolsey.

The use of Star Chamber and Wolsey's own grandiloquence about law enforcement did not endear him to powerful individuals among the land-owning elite, any more than did his efforts in the Court of Requests and Chancery among common-law lawyers. In *Why Come ye nat to Courte?* John Skelton provided a vivid pen-portrait of their view of Wolsey:

> Thus royally he doth deal
> Under the king's broad seal;
> And in Checker he them checks
> In the Star Chamber he nods and becks
> And beareth him so stout
> That no man dare rout;
> Duke, earl, baron nor lord
> But to his sentence must accord.
> Whether he be knight or squire
> All men must follow his desire.[21]

Wolsey may not have been entirely displeased by Skelton's lines. Albeit in a mocking vein, they focus precisely on the Chancellor's intentions as law enforcer – namely to ensure that 'no man dare rout [complain]' and that the nobility and gentry obeyed 'his sentence'. At least everyone understood that the king's law was in Wolsey's hands, not theirs. Far from being offended, Wolsey probably read this as a back-handed compliment. In the longer term, however, the resentment which Skelton's satire articulates caught up with the cardinal. It was not finally his capacity to control the Chancery or the law courts that undid him, but his inability to govern the council and the royal court beyond Westminster.

An insight into Wolsey's apparent ambitions and the limits of his effectiveness as a judicial reformer has been gained by a study of the County Palatinate of Chester, an area with considerable institutional autonomy. Whereas Henry VII, like most of his immediate predecessors, had sought to make the palatinate work for him as earl of Chester, his son's regime in the person of Wolsey brought its administration further into line with the rest of the kingdom. From the mid-1510s, and despite the fact that Cheshire was not generally more violent than any other part of England, there were increased prosecutions of Cheshire criminal cases at Westminster. As Tim Thornton has suggested, this enthusiasm to hear Chester cases may have been less about Wolsey trying to subject the palatinate and its gentry to his personal control, as used to be the view of everything he did, as about demonstrating that someone from semi-autonomous Cheshire could get as speedy retribution (or redress) in his courts as anyone from elsewhere. Nowhere within the king's dominions, whatever its privileges, lay beyond the reach of royal justice. Yet, as we have also seen, Wolsey's courts could not cope with the total workload well, and on 21 June 1521, he ordered 'all matters of Cheshire depending here remitted to the Council in the Marches of Wales'. As Thornton notes, 'Wolsey was interested in a few high-profile targets in the short term, not in changing the constitutional position of the palatinate'.[22] This approach seems to be broadly typical of Wolsey in whatever area of the country he was dealing, and the response to his encouragement to bring cases before him outran even his considerable energy and capacity for work, and certainly that of the royal councillors who worked with him.

Wolsey as king's counsellor

The royal council's role in quasi-political matters such as enclosures and prices, reminds us that it was as much an advisory body as a judicial one, and Wolsey was aware of the implications for him of its membership in its various roles. For the majority of the time that Wolsey served Henry, they formed a two-man team. No other royal councillor (except, perhaps, Sir Thomas More, who was also the

88 *Chief executive*

king's secretary for a time) enjoyed anything like the same favour with Henry. In one way, this suited Wolsey very well. That was, after all, how he had gained power in the first place, shielding Henry from the demands of the council while ensuring that the king's will prevailed by taking all its business into his own capable hands. By first so doing, Wolsey had, in Cavendish's memorable phrase, 'put all other ancient counsellors out of their accustomed favour that they were in before'.[23] The general pattern was that Wolsey and Henry first devised policy between them and then presented it to the council for wider consultation and debate before taking the final decision.

Yet Wolsey could not always be with his master and faced demands for more involvement of the nobility in advising the king. During the early 1520s, his workload in Chancery and Star Chamber kept him at Westminster for most of the week. There was then no working royal residence at Westminster due to a fire there in 1512 (although areas of the palace that had survived the fire were used by the king on special occasions). Henry's nearest residence was down the Thames at Greenwich Palace upon which he had spent lavishly and was the principal site of royal display and hospitality. The Chancellor ran the business week from York Place and Westminster Hall, being in the exercise of his responsibilities, according to Giustinian in his final report, 'learned, extremely eloquent, of vast ability, and indefatigable. He transacted alone the same business as that which occupied all the magistracies, offices, and councils of Venice, both civil and criminal; and all state affairs were managed by him'. Wolsey would keep ambassadors and 'all the lords and barons of England' waiting, perhaps genuinely because of pressure of business, or probably to make them better appreciate the significance of meeting him. If it was the latter, he was hardly unique among statesmen of his time, or since.[24] The one person whom Wolsey never ordinarily kept waiting or uninformed was the king. He communicated with Henry almost daily by letter and personal messengers, who were often other council members. For this reason, a very large number of his letters to Henry survive and show how Wolsey kept his sovereign informed of decisions taken and sought mandates for future action. In 1525, stung by the Imperial ambassador de Praet's assertion that Wolsey's authority was such that it was hard to get anything from the king directly, the cardinal gave a concise view of how his relationship with Henry worked, stating:

> that His Grace is a Prince of such great wisdom, knowledge and experience in his affairs that I, whom His Highness does put in so singular trust and special confidence, would be loath to say or do anything in so great matters as this be, before I had first well and substantially known the mind and pleasure of his Grace and been by the same commanded so to do; nor I may or will of myself take upon me without the authority, knowledge and express commandment of his highness either to do or undo.[25]

Some of this is a rhetorical slap-down to an envoy who had impugned the correct order of things in England, yet the words encapsulate Wolsey's mode of operation. He exercised royal authority amply but always under strict guidelines. They suggest strongly that he did not see himself as the 'alter' or 'ipse' rex of the realm in the way others did. This is further supported by his actions and how he addressed the king. In his letters, many of which he wrote himself in a fine, neat hand, Wolsey used the expected reverential forms of address. He normally called the king 'Sir' or 'Sire'. Given the rhetorical conventions of the time, of which he was a master, Wolsey usually wrote in a reasonably direct voice and tone. Those conventions allowed him to emphasise how hard he was working for Henry to uphold his authority and high reputation at home and abroad. His letters were often quite detailed, explaining the issue at hand fully and in a manner that he understood the king expected. This was the case even when they came with instructions to the bearer to report orally to Henry. Wolsey usually explained his course of action to date in whatever matter was to hand. He then surveyed the available options as he saw them. He suggested or argued for his preferred one and then remitted the final decision to Henry. He usually signed himself, even at the height of his power and status, as 'Your humble chaplain'.

Most of Henry's hundreds of letters to Wolsey were dictated to secretaries and signed by him, but a few autograph letters do survive. All readily demonstrate the ease of communication and trust between the two men. In June 1518, Henry responded to what

90   *Chief executive*

seems to have been a series of questions or points of clarification sought by Wolsey. Because in response they 'ask long writing', that is, were complicated, Henry responds by his secretary, but confides in his own hand the news 'which be so secret' that he believes Katherine to be again pregnant, after the birth of Princess Mary two years earlier. This news, he knows, will be 'comfortable' to Wolsey.[26] The letters also show the plenitude of power Wolsey enjoyed until the last years of his career. In two undated letters, probably written in 1520 or early 1521, Henry addressed Wolsey as 'mine own good cardinal' to whom he re-entrusts or, 'recommends', himself 'with all my heart'. In the first, the king acknowledges Wolsey's work for him and in the second explains his brevity by reason of the fact that he finds writing 'somewhat tedious and painful'. Both letters concern actions, or decisions, evidently previously discussed, about which Wolsey has sought further instruction. We will return to the contents of the second letter shortly. In the first, the king declares that Wolsey has so well looked after the realm's affairs at home and abroad that he can 'add nothing'. To Wolsey's evident request for instructions in one specific matter, Henry replies that he is 'well content with what order so ever you do take in it'. Nevertheless, because the cardinal has asked for it, he gives his opinion in a verbal message to be conveyed by the bearer of the letter. Both letters conclude with the words 'written with the hand of your loving master, Henry'.[27] The king also gave indirect testament as to how he worked with Wolsey and his view of his work for him. In June 1518, the royal secretary Richard Pace wrote to Wolsey in response to the cardinal's recent letters which the king had 'read, and diligently pondered everything comprised therein particularly'. Pace was to commend Wolsey 'for the intolerable [labour] ye do sustain daily there for the administration of good justice, which thing, as [his] grace saith, doth not only appertain [to] his honour but also to the commonwealth and of all this his realm'.[28] What greater expression of approval and support could any royal minister have desired from his master?

Henry expected Wolsey to assist him in maintaining his power as well as his authority as the deputy-head of his regime and not just formally as his Chancellor. He trusted nobody else as he did Wolsey, and for so long. At some point before mid-1521, Henry wrote another of those rare autograph letters to him. This one was darker

in tone, giving written instructions that Henry did not think right
to disclose to the bearer, 'nor none other but you'. The cardinal was
to keep a close watch on five named nobles, including the king's
brother-in-law, Charles Brandon, Duke of Suffolk, and Edward
Stafford, Duke of Buckingham, 'and others whom you think suspect'.[29] Was it a serious suspected plot for which Wolsey was to keep
these prominent men under close watch? It seems highly unlikely
given the evidence of reasonable contentment with the king among
the nobility at the time. Was it, then, some other matter, more
annoying or troublesome than threatening, that the king wanted
Wolsey to keep an eye on? Did Wolsey share the king's concerns,
or did the instruction come as a complete surprise to him? Historians have speculated that the letter may have something to do with
the fall of Buckingham, but the precise circumstances of its writing
remain unknown. Whatever those were, it certainly shows the king's
reliance on Wolsey in the early 1520s as his primary confidant, and
enforcer, even against the highest-ranked in the land.

Buckingham was an aristocrat with at least as much royal blood
in his veins as Henry, a fact of which both men were very conscious.
He was descended on his father's side from Thomas of Woodstock
and Edward III. His mother was Katherine Woodville, sister of
Edward IV's queen Elizabeth. His wife was Eleanor Percy, daughter of the fourth earl of Northumberland. His only son, Henry,
was married to Ursula Pole, daughter of Margaret Plantagenet,
Countess of Salisbury and thus of the house of York. Contemporary descriptions of Buckingham all agree that he was vehemently
proud of his ancestry and his familial links across the highest ech-
elon of the English nobility. His wealth was exceptional, displayed
in his personal adornment and his luxurious homes at Thornbury
Castle in Gloucestershire and at Penshurst Place in Kent, where
he entertained the king and the French hostages in the summer of
1519. It was there that Henry learned that Charles of Spain had
been elected emperor and pretended to the hostages that he was
displeased that Francis had not been elected. Buckingham's relations with Henry seem generally to have been cordial rather than
warm, and they had clashed early in the reign over Buckingham's
objection to the king's relationship with his sister Anne.

It was Polydore Vergil, and to a lesser extent John Skelton, who
cast Wolsey as the ruthless operator at the centre of an elaborate

92   *Chief executive*

plot to bring the great man down because of his alleged hatred for him.[30] In fact there is no substantive evidence of this claim, and reports of the duke's animosity towards Wolsey seem exaggerated. They centre on an episode in which he had supposedly objected to the cardinal washing his hands in a basin after the king had washed his. The infuriated duke apparently emptied it onto the cardinal's shoes. Clash they may have done at times. Buckingham may well have shared his fellow nobles' distaste for Wolsey's some-times pretentious manner. The duke had more than a few cases in Star Chamber, not all of which went his own way. But there is no evidence that he disputed their outcome or accused Wolsey of injustice in these cases. Ambassadors certainly reported that Buck-ingham headed an aristocratic group opposed to Wolsey's foreign policy and peace with France. Although he had taken a full and grand part in the Field of Cloth of Gold in 1520, the duke had spo-ken disparagingly of the event as a waste of time and money. But there is no real evidence of bad blood between them, or of Wolsey using cases deliberately to do Buckingham down. As with Suffolk and Thomas Howard, Duke of Norfolk, Buckingham worked with Wolsey as and when required, and the marriage of the duke's son, Henry, was contracted at Wolsey's suggestion.

Yet Wolsey needed no ill-feeling with the duke, nor an ulterior motive, to take seriously credible reports of Buckingham speculat-ing about the timing and consequences for him of Henry's death. To speak in that way was bound to cause alarm, and Anne Boleyn was to die in part for allegedly doing the same thing. Other reports suggested that he had threatened to kill the king, and his personal demeanour when first confronted had reinforced rather than allayed such fears. He was summoned to London and there arrested. He faced trial before his peers on 13 May 1521, a trial in which Wolsey was not involved directly. Perhaps inevitably, he was convicted and was executed on Tower Hill three days later. Edward Hall, who never missed an opportunity to criticise Wolsey, and who wrote the longest and largely sympathetic account of the duke's fall upon which historians now rely, blames Buckingham entirely for his own demise. He also notes a curious incident suggesting that the duke's view of Wolsey was not entirely hostile either.

As Buckingham was being conveyed by river to London to face questioning, and while still a free man, he suddenly ordered his

Chief executive 93

barge to put in at York Place and there demanded to see Wolsey. When told the cardinal was ill, he nevertheless demanded a drink; 'yet will I drink my lord's wine or [before] I pass'. Why did he do that? Was it yet another example of his lordly arrogance? Had he come there to have it out with Wolsey, whom he blamed for his predicament, and in anger at being refused a meeting decided to help himself to the cardinal's wine? It is possible. Or had he come to seek the help of a man whose judgements in Star Chamber he may have grudged at but abided by, and one whose influence with Henry, he knew, weighed more heavily at that moment than his own exalted ducal status?

Buckingham's demand for a drink betokened an expectation of hospitality at least and, perhaps more importantly, recognition of him even as he was being rapidly disowned by all around him – as he said himself. Having a drink was also playing for time; time in which Wolsey might yet agree to meet him and help him. Hall notes that the duke was taken 'with much reverence' to the cellar and there served with wine, but 'when he saw and perceived no cheer to him was made, he changed colour and so departed to his barge'. Buckingham had evidently expected, or at least hoped, for help at York Place. A desperate hope it may have been, but not one, surely, he reposed in one whom he knew to be his sworn enemy? It was too late for Wolsey to help in any case. Perhaps the duke knew that too. Having left York place, Buckingham's barge was intercepted a short way down the river towards London by Sir Henry Marney, Captain of the king's guard, who boarded it and arrested him of high treason.[31] He never saw the king or Wolsey again.

Buckingham was attainted posthumously in 1523, but its repercussions for his family were comparatively light, and none of them were physically harmed. His fellow dukes, of Norfolk and Suffolk, gleefully shared some of the spoils not retained by the crown. Wolsey gained nothing personally from the overthrow of England's pre-eminent aristocrat, but Buckingham's fall was confirmation of the power of the Tudor king whose 'chief executive' he was. Doubtless, Wolsey hoped, it had reminded the peers of England of their duty to their sovereign lord, even if the regrettable episode had won him no friends among them. The cardinal contemplated all this in his heart and thereafter made securing personal access to Henry, and

94   *Chief executive*

restricting that of others if possible, the watchword in his conduct of relations with his master.

Wolsey and the royal court

By the time of Buckingham's fall, Wolsey's omni-competence suggests, at first sight, that he was steadily reducing and restricting the nobles' capacity to advise the king. This was certainly the accusation later made by his critics. In fact, Wolsey was by then working the nobility as royal advisors harder than ever before. With him, sitting at times up to six days a week, was the royal council at Westminster staffed by noblemen as well as legal administrators. So much so that Henry sometimes felt bereft of royal councillors about him, and when he did, he grumbled about it to his Chancellor. Wolsey was confident of his capacity personally to deal with any issue the king might put to him, and to persuade him of his own view of it. Yet he fretted about those who were with Henry, almost from the outset. At the royal court could be found men and women of noble and gentry rank whose personal access to the king may not have threatened his position but nevertheless disconcerted him. In addition to communicating by letters and instructions to the royal secretaries, therefore, he strove to see the king as often as possible.

Cavendish describes how, during the legal terms, Wolsey would often visit Henry at Greenwich on Sundays. He travelled by barge to just west of London Bridge, then through the city on a mule to avoid the turbulent 'races' under the bridge, and then took his barge again from Billingsgate to Greenwich. Arriving with his usual array of servants and the symbols of his authority borne before him, the Lord Chancellor would brief the king on the main items of business and clarify with him future initiatives or decisions. He would also take care to demonstrate to all those surrounding Henry in the royal entourage his closeness to the king and the status that proximity gave him in the realm.[32] Wolsey usually met the king in private for discussions, although they also frequently conversed in public, but apart from company, often by a window. Polydore Vergil described a technique apparently adopted by Wolsey whenever he wanted to get the king's attention:

> he would bring some little present, such as a dish of fine workmanship, or a jewel, or a ring, or something of the kind, and

while the king closely examined and admired it, he would art-fully bring up what he had in mind.[33]

How Vergil knew this we do not know, but it sounds about right. Henry loved all kinds of gadgets and trinkets, cameos, figurines, astrolabes, clocks, compasses and so on. Wolsey's technique might have worked well to distract the king's attention while he slid over the details of some complicated matter in such a way as to secure royal assent to his dealing with it as he thought best. Such skill doubtless provoked wonder and jealousy in equal measure among those that witnessed it in action.

Wolsey had to ensure that he had as many as possible of the most experienced councillors working with him at Westminster, in order to ensure that the king's justice was being done, and being seen to be done, effectively while also allowing the king a sufficiently large 'council attendant'. Summers were often a worrying time for him. True, he was freed from his duties at Westminster Hall as formal government business stopped, but this reduced Wolsey's opportunities to be with Henry. As Hall observed of the year 1526, 'all this summer the king took his pastime in hunting and nothing happened worthy to be written of'.[34] Wolsey remained on duty (more or less) at Hampton Court, or The More, superintending the realm while the king went off hunting and showing himself to his people on his nearly annual progresses – and with whomever he chose.

To ensure that at such times Wolsey was always well informed, he tried to provide the king with councillors from among men whom he trusted. First, the nobleman Thomas Neville, then Sir Thomas More, John Clerk and Stephen Gardiner were sequentially responsible for handling council-related business at court. Their proper status and salaries as royal secretaries were eventually sorted out, and More in particular, alongside Richard Pace, became an intermediary between the king and Wolsey. Henry appears to have been reasonably pleased, initially at least, but for Wolsey this was but half the job done. What about those at court who were not royal councillors but who still had opinions they were only too willing to share with the king? The last thing he wanted was for Henry to be advised informally and in ways that contradicted his own views and decisions.[35] By 1517, chief among these courtiers was a group of the king's friends, his jousting and dancing companions, known as

96   *Chief executive*

his 'minions', led by Francis Bryan and Nicholas Carew. They had emerged, and indeed made something of a deliberate public debut in July that year, during entertainments for a visiting Imperial embassy. Unlike other courtiers, these young men enjoyed access to the king throughout the day in the most private apartments of the court, the department of the Privy Chamber. Most people only saw Henry when he was formally 'in public'. This gave them unequalled opportunities to request favours for themselves and their friends or to try to influence him to their own advantage – that at least was what Wolsey finally accused them of doing. His first attempt to get some control over these courtiers came in 1519.

As David Starkey first showed, it was in September 1518 that these young men had first been called 'gentlemen of the king's Privy Chamber', in emulation of an equivalent French court office invented by Francis I for his own young companions. As we saw, several of the young English gentlemen of the Privy Chamber were sent to France in 1518 as part of the reciprocal English embassy to receive Francis's ratification of the Treaty of Universal Peace (see Chapter 2). They had been treated exceptionally favourably and honourably by Francis because he understood them to be the very close companions of Henry. Flattered by this attention, some of them had apparently returned to the English court brimming with new-found enthusiasm for all things French, including the relative informality of the French court. According to Hall, when in the king's company these men 'were so familiar and homely with him, and played such light touches with him that they forgot themselves'. This behaviour so offended the royal council as derogating Henry's honour that a number of them were dismissed from their posts. According to the Venetian ambassador Giustinian, the French ambassador La Bastie took offence at these dismissals, believing that they resulted 'either from a distrust of France or at the instigation of Cardinal Wolsey who has apprehended that these young men might oust him from the government'.[36]

Despite some scepticism among historians on this point, there is ample evidence that Wolsey *was* involved in these dismissals and was probably their instigator. This was not because he genuinely believed that the young courtiers had been contemptuous of Henry, or had been suborned by Francis, and certainly not because they were even remotely likely to 'oust him from the government', as Giustinian reported. This move was not a preconceived attack against Wolsey's true rivals – those men, like Norfolk, were too powerful. The young gentlemen posed no real threat to him, but they disconcerted Wolsey nevertheless, and he took the opportunity to nip in the bud any pretensions they may have had to influence the king over matters of patronage that he saw as under his control. In other words, he tried to assert his authority over the court using their apparent misdemeanours as a reason to do so.

As part of this strike, Wolsey also recalled to England two other young courtiers, Percival Hart and Anthony Browne, then guests at the French court. Perhaps they were intended as replacements for some of the gentlemen of the Privy Chamber who had been dismissed. This recall inevitably came to the attention of Francis, who chose to see it, and the dismissals in England, as a calculated snub to himself. He demanded an explanation from Henry's resident ambassador with him, Sir Thomas Boleyn, as to why men whom he had treated so well out of regard for Henry had been so dishonourably treated on their return. The dismissals in England were even reported to Francis's representative at the Imperial court, with a note that Wolsey was believed to have instigated them.

Whoever was in fact responsible for the dismissals, Wolsey certainly made the most of them. The dismissed 'minions' were replaced by four somewhat older men who were given the new title of 'Knights of the Body in the Privy Chamber'. They were not, as Giustinian imagined, 'creatures of the cardinal', but they were men of experience who had served (and would continue immediately to serve) as ambassadors, as soldiers and, crucially from Wolsey's point of view, as royal counsellors. They were, in short, the sort of men with whom Wolsey was more comfortable and upon whom he could more naturally rely to support the policies and decisions which he advocated.[37]

The so-called 'expulsion of the minions' proved to be a rather brief episode at Henry's court. The council's point having been made, the young favourites quickly mended their francophile ways. They showed themselves willing to do a decent day's work in royal service in Calais and elsewhere and were soon enough recalled to the king's presence. They did not displace the new Knights of the Body in the Privy Chamber but simply augmented the numbers of 'honourable attendants' around the king, to his

98   *Chief executive*

evident satisfaction and presumably Wolsey's chagrin. He had tried to remove potential interference by heightening the importance of the conciliar status of those around the king, linking it to his own power base and excluding the king's young favourites as unsuitable for such status. In the process, however, he had not only furthered the institutionalisation of the council attendant, but also of the Privy Chamber with important unforeseen consequences.[38]

Wolsey was always keen that his own influence over Henry should be unimpeded and that, as far as possible, the two men should be of one mind on any subject – ideally, his own. Yet the friendly letters and commendations from Henry we noted earlier do not tell the whole story of Wolsey's working relationship with the king. Although he routinely did so, Henry did not always give his cardinal leave to take 'whatsoever order' he chose to do in every matter. Inevitably, they disagreed at times over issues, usually when Henry saw, or suspected, some deliberate or negligent derogation of his own authority. We shall never know how many times they did disagree as the evidence is rare on paper at least. Ever scrupulous in the public display of respect of Henry's royal authority (as in his rebuke to the Imperial ambassador), Wolsey ensured as far as he could that no word of frustration or conflict between himself and the king ever got out.

Sometimes, however, it did, and there were always those around the court, and beyond, who seized on any evidence of friction or disagreement to attack Wolsey, whom they accused simultaneously of over-weening ambition and being what would today be called a 'control freak', and of incompetence. One example of an argument comes from the autumn of 1521 when the king and the cardinal disagreed as to whether English vessels should, as accustomed, sail to Bordeaux to ship the wines of that year's vintage. The issue arose while Wolsey was in Calais ostensibly mediating a dispute between Charles V and Francis I under the terms of the Treaty of Universal Peace (see Chapter 6). Having been asked his advice on the matter by Henry, Wolsey replied that he thought they should. He was worried that not sending the wine fleet might provoke French distrust just as he was posing as the impartial arbiter in the Franco–Imperial dispute. Henry did not like this advice at all, suspecting some malign French action on the high seas. Doubtless frustrated,

Wolsey replied that if Henry could not show better faith in Francis, then he did not know what was to be done. Highly displeased by the tone of that letter, Henry (now writing through his secretary, Pace) shot back that *he* did not lack faith, that it was Wolsey who was deceived, and that his advice was misleading, if not disingenuous. To all this Wolsey replied at some length and so particularly that just as suddenly as Henry had raised them, he dropped his objections.[39]

Henry also expressed disquiet at the length of time Wolsey was taking in Calais, having with him the Great Seal of England, the mainspring of formal royal administration. Pace informed the cardinal that the king would prefer him to return if no resolution of the dispute seemed likely. He was very anxious to have Wolsey home, and if an immediate conclusion was not in prospect, then he was to return 'considering that he hath great need of you here, as well for the ministration of justice as the ordering of his realm otherwise'.[40] At the very least Wolsey should send home the Great Seal with Thomas Ruthall, the Bishop of Durham, who was assisting Wolsey in the negotiations. Towards the end of the month Pace again wrote to Wolsey that the king wanted his return as soon as possible. Even against the background of a disagreement, there could hardly be a clearer statement of Henry's reliance on him as his chief administrative servant for much of the day-to-day running of government.

In drawing attention to these episodes, Greg Walker argued persuasively that John Skelton's satire *Speke Parott*, begun in September 1521, alluded to Henry's frustration with Wolsey at this time. Evidently aware of it through sources peripheral to the court, but misunderstanding its true nature, Skelton seized on Wolsey's mission to Calais and his taking the Great Seal there. He satirised his apparently incompetent handling of the king's affairs. The poem is perhaps best seen as a very misguided attempt to court royal favour, and popularity in London circles, rather than the start of a determined satirical campaign against the cardinal. Skelton clearly overestimated the extent of the rift between the king and his chief minister. Nevertheless, it suggests that people beyond the court were aware that Wolsey and Henry did not always work in seamless union, in the way Wolsey would have preferred them to believe.[41]

Wolsey and the royal affinity

As had monarchs since at least the time of Richard II, Henry sought to increase the numbers of reliable administrators and officials who worked for him, rather than relying entirely on comparatively few high-ranking nobles to represent the crown in the counties. During the course of the fifteenth century in England, as elsewhere in Europe, the royal court had become the focus for contact between the monarch and his or her ruling elites and a brokering-house for royal political patronage. This trend intensified under the young Henry VIII, who was at first almost too generous with his grants – hence the course of the seals. The focus of these appointments was the king's Chamber, the ceremonial heart of the court if, by Henry's time, no longer its political one. Clients were often appointed to largely supernumerary positions in the royal household, such as knights and esquires of the king's body, ushers, yeoman, grooms and the like. These positions did, however, give their holders the opportunity to seek further patronage for themselves and their families and friends. They became 'sworn men' of the king who were appointed as local officials, such as stewards, escheators and receivers in the counties, as well as receiving rewards in cash and kind. They might be used alongside local nobles and upper gentry as Justices of the Peace and commissioners of peace as the eyes and ears of the crown in the localities. They constituted a crown following or 'affinity' that enabled it to supplement if not necessarily displace local nobles as the primary political patrons in most counties of England and Wales.[42]

As was true of all senior royal administrators in the early-modern period, much of Wolsey's capacity to garner any support for his policies and to have decisions carried out in the country beyond Westminster depended upon his also maintaining a personal following among these same nobles and gentlemen at the local level which linked into and extended the royal affinity. As Wolsey reminded Henry in 1519, in order to ensure that the crown's power remained preponderant, the king had 'to put himself in strength with his most trusty servants in every shire for the surety of his royal person and succession'.[43] As Lord Chancellor, and as England's most senior ecclesiastic by virtue of his legatine powers from 1518, and most of all because of the favour with Henry which he enjoyed, Wolsey quickly attracted the interest of individuals and families who sought the offices and rewards he could offer. These came not from his personal resources but from the revenues he gained in royal and Church service. As a result, Wolsey quickly gathered about him clients whose ranks fed into crown political patronage, developing and enhancing royal influence and power across the realm. Through his household and wider circle of administrative servants, he developed his capacity to govern the kingdom effectively in Henry's name. Wolsey's household had representatives within it of virtually every county of England, and some members also worked at various times of the year in the royal household.[44]

In the central and southern shires of England, one of the important ways in which he used such servants in the localities was to appoint them to judicial and administrative commissions of peace. Provided they were considered a 'fit and proper' person and had at least sufficient education and aptitude for the role, such local gentlemen would be named JPs and meet in courts of quarter-sessions in each county. As Chancellor, Wolsey was responsible for these appointments and the operation of these sessions and appointed those upon whom he knew he could rely. For example, Sir William Gascoigne, Treasurer of Wolsey's household, was named to the bench of his local Bedfordshire. Recent research on the Tudor gentry of Somerset has shown that Wolsey worked towards creating a broad group of local gentry and lawyers known to him, instead of relying on a single nobleman as representative of the county. In Somerset, Henry VII's government had looked very largely to Giles, Lord Daubeney, the king's Lord Chamberlain, as chief nobleman and the predominant power broker in the county. Wolsey's differing approach drew in a rather wider group of local, reliable gentry focused on Sir Amias Paulet – the same man, incidentally, then the local sheriff, who is supposed once to have put the young Wolsey in the stocks at Limington. Under two generations of the Paulet family, the extended royal affinity in the county very largely supplanted that of the local magnate, Lord Daubeney.[45]

Another example of this phenomenon comes from Cheshire and the rise there of William Brereton, son of the Chamberlain of Chester. In the opening decade of Henry's reign, Sir Ralf Egerton had been the 'king's man' in the locality, a champion jouster and royal standard bearer. Brereton was at court by 1521 and progressively

102   *Chief executive*

used his position of proximity to the king (he was a groom of the Privy Chamber by 1526), acquiring numerous grants, offices and substantial lands in Chester and North Wales (many grants facilitated by Wolsey), enabling Brereton eventually, successfully to challenge the power of Egerton. His power in the locality became all pervasive and not always to good effect. When he was implicated in Anne Boleyn's fall and executed for treason, his many properties, offices and other sources of income were widely distributed by the crown among potential clients to widen its direct contacts in the area that Brereton had so dominated.[46]

In Yorkshire, an area of the country where Wolsey's influence was significant as the Archbishop, he adopted a somewhat different approach. While he did use his own nominees on commissions of peace in Yorkshire as elsewhere, from 1525 royal control of the county and indeed of Cumbria and Northumberland was exercised primarily through the establishment of the Council of the North under the titular headship of Henry's natural son, Henry Fitzroy, Duke of Richmond. This took over a jurisdiction never entirely successfully exercised by Lord Dacre. The council had supervisory powers over all aspects of law and order within its jurisdiction. Its effectiveness was limited however. Towards the end of Wolsey's time, the sixth earl of Northumberland was appointed to oversee the area but with similarly disappointing results. It remains true that in Wolsey's period, and indeed Cromwell's after him, ministerial efforts to secure a 'crown-controlled magistracy' in all the localities, and particularly in the north, were only ever partially successful.[47]

One reasonably fruitful patronage relationship Wolsey maintained was with the city of York itself. The corporation often appealed to Wolsey to protect its interests and autonomy and to secure privileges. It was not always successful in these requests, but in 1523 Wolsey was able to secure, for an apparently cash-strapped city, a monopoly on the shipping of Yorkshire wool fells – wool-bearing skins – in overseas trade. The city's corporation and individual merchants clearly saw Wolsey as their man with the king. In return, it offered civic offices to members of the cardinal's household. Those whom Wolsey appointed became intermediaries for the city and his spokesmen to it. The office of recorder, the city's legal counsel and representative in London and Westminster, was

Chief executive   103

successively held between 1519 and Wolsey's fall by Sir Richard Rokeby, comptroller of Wolsey's household; Sir William Gascoigne, the treasurer; and finally Sir Richard Page, the cardinal's Chamberlain. Page was also elected as MP for York in September 1527. Wolsey's patronage relationship with York was mirrored in London, at least until the mid-1520s when the shortcomings of his capacity to secure the cooperation of nobles, gentry and town corporations in negotiating conformity to the Crown's will were tested almost to destruction, chiefly in London and the south-east.[48]

The affinity in crisis? The Amicable Grant

In 1525, Wolsey was faced with a nationwide open rebellion against the so-called 'Amicable Grant'. This occasioned a very public disjuncture between himself and the king and the Chancellor's first effort to ground his actions publicly on conciliar government and collective responsibility, rather than on the king's favour towards him. The subsidy taxation system Wolsey had developed between 1512 and 1522 was far from perfect and had barely gotten into its stride when, in 1522, Wolsey demanded several forced 'loans' from the City of London and other areas to support preparations for war and to pay for the visit that year of Henry's ally Charles V (see Chapter 6). They were based on the assessments of wealth carried out by royal commissioners during that year, even though these had been made ostensibly for future taxation purposes. The loans were eventually made but not without significant complaints, not least about the assessment methods. This first loan had not been repaid before a second was demanded. By the summer of 1523 approximately £260,000 had been raised from laymen and from the clergy, which was a remarkable achievement. Then, in the parliament of 1523, Wolsey demanded subsidy taxation of £800,000, probably knowing he would never get anywhere near that much. He even tried to get wealthier people to pay in advance of the due date for payment in the subsidy act. It was eventually based on fresh and lower evaluations to make it more palatable, but finally proved insufficient. In the middle of the military campaign, during appalling wet weather, the armies could not be sufficiently well supplied by Henry's ally. More money had to be found to maintain the campaign.[49]

104   *Chief executive*

In response, but as if to add insult to injury, in March 1525 Wolsey demanded a non-parliamentary levy, the so-called 'Amicable Grant'. This proposed grant was intended to assist Henry's planned personal invasion of France, suddenly decided upon in the wake of Francis I's defeat at Pavia in February that year (see Chapter 6). Wolsey knew that a further recourse to Parliament for taxation was out of the question, but, as Henry apparently planned at that stage to lead his army in person, he could rely on an ancient feudal tradition (nothing more) of a 'benevolence', whereby a king could ask the direct financial help of his subjects when he went to war. Benevolences of the 1525 kind were within the constitutional framework, but a grant depended entirely upon consent and could not be enforced, legally at least. The proceeds of the 1525 grant were to be based on the valuations for the 1523 subsidy made in 1522, but this was quite a different proposition from the loans of three years earlier (that had in any case still not yet been repaid). The crown's initial demand for a sixth of income from at least the wealthiest (the records are unclear) was communicated by specially appointed commissioners in late March. During April and early May, they tried to persuade the great and the good of the counties, both lay and clerical, to take up the cause of the grant and press people to contribute, on a sliding scale of incomes, according to Hall's account of Wolsey's address to the Mayor and Aldermen of London. Broadly speaking, he requested 3s 4d in the pound from all those of £50 income and over; 2s 8d on those with between £20 and £50; and 1s in the pound from those with lower incomes.

At this demand Wolsey's audience was 'astonished', and some commoners whom the Chancellor later summoned before him to repeat the request expressed themselves so trenchantly that they ended up temporarily imprisoned. 'In conclusion', said Hall, 'all cursed the Cardinal'. This resentment and a reluctance to pay boiled into an open rebellion. The grant had not been voted for in parliament and came so soon after the 1522 forced loans and the 1523 subsidy that people at all social levels simply refused to pay it. The City of London's merchants and lawyers quickly and vociferously cried out against it. There were serious disturbances in East Anglia where 10,000 men marched on Lavenham. Faced with this opposition, Henry denied all knowledge of the grant (almost certainly a lie) and presented himself as ameliorating the original

Chief executive 105

demand put by Wolsey. Henry instructed Wolsey to tell the mayor and aldermen of London and all commissioners that he, Wolsey, had in effect misled them as to the royal will. It had never been his intention, Henry now said, that his subjects should be impoverished by the grant and that at his instruction 'ways of moderation' to the original demand were being implemented. A twelfth rather than a sixth was suggested, but even this met stiff resistance. Henry's regime still wanted at least some money from the exercise, but its rapidly altering demands were communicated at different speeds in different parts of the country, and there was general confusion. In the end, when he addressed the London authorities on 26 April, Wolsey presented himself as having been their advocate before the king, who now 'at my desire and petition' was content to revoke the request for the grant. He would now not specify any amount and only ask for a benevolence of whatever people wanted to pay out of good will towards him. Even this was refused, the people saying 'that they had paid enough before, with many evil words', according to Hall.[50]

Henry's distancing himself from an unpopular and unsuccessful government policy is hardly surprising, and it doubtless suited him to allow Wolsey to deal with the public relations disaster. Historians have frequently and even recently followed Hall's lead, interpreting it as evidence simultaneously of Wolsey's ambition and his incompetence. Some have argued, though not finally convincingly, that he actually wanted the grant to fail as a way of disabling the king from pursuing a military campaign which he did not support and as a way of discrediting his aristocratic rivals who did.[51] It is nevertheless clear, from correspondence between Henry, Wolsey and the principal commissioners for the grant, that, as ever, the cardinal was in charge of an operation developed between himself and the king. He had, nevertheless, also acted with the advice and consent of other members of the royal council even if the measure was agreed upon at short notice and with a sense of urgency, if not emergency.

As part of his customary vilification of Wolsey, Hall, a Londoner himself of course, claimed that Wolsey had been acting unconstitutionally. The demands were indeed rejected as against the 'common weal' insofar as the grant was an extra-Parliamentary impost. Wolsey was told flatly and correctly by the London authorities' lawyer that a benevolence was contrary to a statute made in the

106   *Chief executive*

reign of Richard III. In fact, the most frequently voiced objection beyond London was not that it was unconstitutional but that the people were simply unable to pay the grant – coming as it did hard on the heels of the two loan demands of 1522 and the subsidy of 1523. The evidence from commissioners, such as the dukes of Norfolk and Suffolk, the marquess of Dorset and Bishop West in East Anglia, was that a good deal of informal pressure was put on leading members of gentry families by the king's men in the counties to secure consent first to a grant, then subsequently a benevolence. They were subjected to pleas, remonstrations and rebukes in equal measure during the spring of 1525, but most seem to have understood implicitly the government's weak position. For the most part, resistance was passive rather than actively rebellious and perhaps all the more effective for it. The more Wolsey, his commissioners, and his men at local level blustered and threatened, the more people quietly dug their heels in and continued to plead poverty.[52]

The demand for any grant or gift whatsoever was eventually abandoned in mid-May 1525. Wolsey answered publicly, and correctly, that although he was blamed by all (including the king) for demanding the grant, it had been the decision of the whole council. He would put up with the opprobrium heaped upon him, he said, 'but the eternal God knoweth all'.[53] In the weeks that followed, the appearance of efficient government maintaining law and order was played out quite deliberately. Those of any standing in local communities who had resisted demands with any sort of affray were brought before Wolsey in Star Chamber. They were often as not then elaborately and publicly pardoned, the Chancellor even paying some of them their travel expenses home. No further parliamentary taxation was demanded for the remainder of Wolsey's time in power, although further subsidy assessments were carried out in 1527. Yet the principle of relatively regular taxation, based on accurate assessments of wealth introduced by Wolsey, was gradually accepted and later built upon further by Thomas Cromwell.[54]

A house in order: the Eltham Ordinances

Wolsey may have successfully linked his own affinity into the royal one, but he was never the only great patron of the realm. As we have seen, from at least the fall of Buckingham, and as Henry matured as a king, he gradually wanted advice from more than one source. The issue of the role of the nobility in his government became more pressing. Wolsey's insistence during the Amicable Grant that he had acted with the advice of the whole council was designed to protect himself from precisely the charge of being individually too powerful and out of an appreciation, for once, of the advantages of 'collective responsibility'. Yet that played into the hands of his aristocratic rivals who eagerly agreed that the king ought well to have the benefit of their advice, given as of right, on the way forward for the country. This only added to Wolsey's continuing discomfort about the informal access to Henry enjoyed by them and also the king's young friends, most of whom had close family connections into all levels of the nobility.

In 1526 Wolsey reasserted himself. The troubles over the Amicable Grant were in good part remedied by his negotiation in August 1525 of a financially advantageous peace with France, the Treaty of the More (see Chapter 6). Money would soon start flowing again from France, and crucially, the kingdom was once more at peace. Now, Wolsey decided, was the time to take a much more concerted approach to the issues of Henry's wish for a council attendant and his own wish to limit the influence with the king of those who were not his own appointees. In January that year, the Chancellor promulgated a new set of royal household regulations, known as the Eltham Ordinances. With typical grandeur these were presented as a major programme of court reform to suit Henry's new, honourable and above all profitable peace with France, upon which Wolsey was then endeavouring to build. Following the model of the 'Black Book' of Edward IV, the household regulations prescribed the staffing and daily conduct of the household, the numbers of attendants to which those gentlemen and ladies attending court were entitled, together with what meals they could take at the king's expense. There were regulations improving cleanliness of staff and spaces in court, such as banning all but ladies' lap dogs from the precincts, and much more besides. Consequently, there were some retrenchments among supernumerary servants, and these must have been put into action as Hall took the opportunity to attack Wolsey for making people redundant and reducing them to poverty and crime. Wolsey's regulations did not introduce any major structural innovations in household organisation or its operation as such, but they

108   *Chief executive*

did establish the council attendant on the king as the pre-eminent council and one from which most of the former 'minions' were excluded. Its establishment is best seen as Wolsey's response to a challenge from the nobility with whom he always had distinctly ambivalent relations.[55]

In a move which Wolsey intended would control the minions further, their function at court was also formalised with the definitive establishment of the office of 'Gentleman of the King's Privy Chamber'. Emphasising that the private space of the king should be 'reserved secret, at the pleasure of his Grace, without repair of any great multitude thereunto', the Ordinances provided that only a specified group of men had the privilege of entering that space unbidden. That privilege, however, entailed duties, responsibilities and restrictions. For a start, they should learn restraint and discretion. Their service to the king in the Privy Chamber was to be 'humble, reverent, and lowly', and they were expressly forbidden from 'pressing his Grace, nor advancing themselves'. They were enjoined further not to 'intermeddle of any causes or matters whatsoever they be'. They were to keep strictly private any discussions with the king they had or might hear (including his own presumably), 'keeping secret all such things as shall be done or said in the same, without disclosing any part thereof to any person not being for the time present in the said Chamber'. Any breaches of this and other rules were to be reported to the king and the Council, over which Wolsey presided of course. On the other hand, if they proved themselves capable, they might be trusted with special responsibilities as ambassadors. Their status and personal qualities made them, as the Ordinances put it, 'meet and able to be sent on familiar messages or otherwise, to outward princes, when the case shall require'. After all, the Chancellor may have quipped to himself, they liked being flattered in France, so why not send them there – and elsewhere. Acting under his direct instructions as ambassadors abroad, they could make less mischief at home. Thus, Wolsey hoped, the young men would trade enhanced status and genuine responsibility for increased compliance with his view of how government worked.[56]

In retrospect, such hopes of resolving the contradictions inherent in his powerful yet vulnerable position, dependant as it was entirely on the king's favour, seem fanciful. The ordinances dealing with the

Chief executive 109

Privy Chamber more reflect his own expectations and experience of personal service in his own household than any realistic hope of shaping how Henry's relationship with his noble and gentry intimates worked. They may well have improved standards of attendance, order and cleanliness in the royal palaces, at least among the lower household servants, but they signally failed to give him anything more than the illusion of control over the court and the king's gentry and noble friends. In the process he had also created an important element in his own eventual downfall. For it was from the families represented among the ranks of the Gentlemen of the Privy Chamber, whose status and proximity to the king could not now be gainsaid – by Wolsey's own regulations – that, barely a year later, there came the first real, and final, challenge to his relationship with Henry.

That courtiers could sometimes insist on their own way was proven to Wolsey in quite personal terms in 1528 in the matter of the appointment of the abbess of the Benedictine priory at Wilton, in Wiltshire. Wolsey was effectively acting bishop of Worcester in the absence of Ghinucci and, with the agreement of the majority of nuns at Wilton, nominated Dame Isabel Jordan to the position. Yet a minority of nuns favoured Dame Eleanor Carey, the sister of William Carey, a Gentleman of the king's Privy Chamber. He was the husband of Mary Boleyn, the king's former mistress and the sister of Anne. One or other of these people, and most likely Anne, evidently secured Henry's attention and gained his support for Eleanor Carey. Glad in the difficult circumstances of the summer of 1528 to do this favour for Anne, Henry indicated that Eleanor should be appointed. Wolsey objected to her because she admitted that a long time previously, she had had two children by different priests. Once Henry knew of this, he, too, dropped his support for Eleanor, but directed that both candidates should be set aside and a third woman chosen. This instruction Wolsey ignored, pretending not to have received it, and confirmed Isabel Jordan as prioress. He seems genuinely to have believed that she was the right woman to reform the community there along the lines he favoured. She was finally confirmed, with Henry's approval, but not before he gave Wolsey an extraordinary reprimand in one of those rare handwritten letters. His real objection was to Wolsey's pretence of not

110 *Chief executive*

having comprehended his instructions. Writing in a highly indignant tone, the king tells Wolsey:

> My Lord, it is a double offence both to do ill and cover it too, but with men that have wit, it cannot be accepted so, wherefore good my lord use no more that way with me for there is no man living that more hateth it.[57]

Strong words indeed, of a kind Henry did not normally direct towards his cardinal. Throughout, Henry emphasises his expectations of someone whom he calls his 'trusty loving friend and servant' and his 'best beloved servant and friend'. The king also calls himself Wolsey's 'master and friend'. He praises Wolsey's virtuous way of life, the continuance of which was to his honour, acceptable to God, 'nor more desired of your friends, amongst the which I reckon not myself the least'. Henry signed the letter 'with the hand of him that is and shall be your loving sovereign, lord, and friend'. Wolsey made quick amends and was rapidly assured by Henry in another 'rude [unrefined] yet loving letter' written shortly afterwards, that there remained 'no spark of displeasure towards you in my heart'. The two had argued before, and Wolsey knew that, with the right answer, Henry's anger could be assuaged as easily as it was aroused. The king concluded his letter in a cheerful tone, reassuring Wolsey that he and those around him were well at Ampthill.[58]

The letter's many pointed references to Wolsey as the king's friend were intended primarily to remind its recipient of his duty. Yet, although full of angry sarcasm in the moment, Henry deployed them sincerely, and the letter may plausibly be read as evidence that he really did genuinely think of Wolsey as his friend, as well as his servant, and in a way very different from almost anyone else. Diplomacy with Francis I aside, the only other person whom Henry is recorded as calling his friend, on paper at least, was Anne Boleyn.

The cardinal-courtier?

As Scarisbrick memorably observed, Henry was a difficult man for Wolsey to serve: 'Now glad to release all into his minister's hands, now irrupting suddenly and decisively into affairs both big and small, now in enthusiastic partnership with his servant, now

Chief executive 111

equally unpredictably, lapsing into lazy indifference to public business'.[59] In order to work for a master such as Henry, Wolsey tried to make himself as useful as possible in every area of government, from chairing the royal council as a political body to guiding its decisions as a judicial one. He had always to contend with the sheer range of matters entrusted to him, while anticipating every detailed question the king might ask should he suddenly want clarification or disagree on some point. Wolsey had to bring as many people as needed into royal service to assist him in the business of government at central and local levels, thereby to demonstrate his authority to the realm while also assuring himself that they would carry out his instructions properly. That would demonstrate his capacity as a patron and his effective use of the ample powers delegated to him by the king and affirm the need for his service. To this end he had the royal council work harder than it had ever done in its existence as an institution, both at Westminster and in its attendance upon the king. During his career as Chancellor and 'chief executive', he wrote thousands of letters to men all over the country, insisting upon adherence to settled policy, if possible, in whatever matters arose, or a variation to it when needed in particular cases, consistent with the affirmation of royal authority. Yet this was not enough. He had also to ensure that men and women of higher gentry and noble rank whose company his gregarious king enjoyed, indeed demanded, did not also use their proximity to him to persuade Henry to take decisions in matters both small and great that ran contrary to Wolsey's best interests. It must often have been frustrating and always exhausting. Little wonder then, that he was frequently impatient, bombastic and sometimes arrogant. Nevertheless, an arrogant demeanour in the exercise of that authority, upon which virtually all sources, even Cavendish, are agreed, may well have sprung from some sense of personal insecurity. Unknowingly echoing what would become Machiavelli's famous dictum, Polydore Vergil said that Wolsey, being 'ignorant of the true path of glory, appeared to prefer being feared by the great men of the land rather than being loved by them'.[60] That may be so, but it was unlikely that the nobility of England would ever have loved Wolsey. While they had to work with him, there were those among them who always looked for a way to reduce, or better still, completely undermine the cardinal's influence upon the king. The appearance

112   *Chief executive*

of the king's other friend, Anne Boleyn, and Henry's love for her, would play a crucial part in turning an endemic, residual resentment of Wolsey into a focused and sharpened opposition to him.

Notes

1 Cavendish, p. 25.

2 'Armorial', in *An Inventory of the Historical Monuments in the City of Oxford* (London, 1939), pp. 189–192. *British History Online.* http://www.british-history.ac.uk/rchme/oxon/pp189-192.

3 Pollard, p. 15. In the latter years of Henry VIII's reign, the 'Dry Stamp', effectively a facsimile of the king's signature, under the control of the Chief Gentleman of the Privy Chamber, was used frequently in place of the king's actual sign manual.

4 Elton, *Tudor Revolution*, pp. 10–19.

5 J. Guy, *The Cardinal's Court: The Impact of Thomas Wolsey in Star Chamber* (Totowa, NJ, 1977), pp. 51–78; Gwyn, p. 114.

6 Guy, p. 26.

7 S. J. Gunn, *Early Tudor Government* (Basingstoke, 1995), pp. 84–92.

8 Tanner, 'High Almoners', p. 72.

9 Guy, pp. 119–31.

10 T. Smith, *De Republica Anglorum* (London, 1583) online edition. www.constitution.org/eng/repang.htm Book 3: Chapter 4. 'Of the court of starre chamber'.

11 Gwyn, pp. 121–2ff.

12 J. J. Goring, 'The General Proscription of 1522', *English Historical Review* 341 (1971): 681–705.

13 Hoyle, 'War and the Public Finance, pp. 75–99.

14 Hall, pp. 588–90.

15 *CSPV* II, 1287 Giustinian's report to the Venetian Senate, September/October 1519.

16 J. H. Lupton, *A Life of John Colet: With an Appendix of Some of His English Writings* (London, 1887), p. 197.

17 Guy, pp. 60–1.

18 *LP* II Appendix, 38; Wolsey to Henry VIII, August 1517; Gwyn, pp. 106–17.

19 Smith, *De Republica Anglorum*, in the same place.

20 S. G. Ellis, 'A Border Baron and the Tudor State: The Rise and Fall of Lord Dacre of the North', *HJ* 35 (2) (1992): 253–77.

21 J. Skelton, *Why Come Ye Nat to Courte?* lines 333–58, www.exclassics.com/skelton/skel065.htm; Walker, pp. 100–23 for a discussion of the context and meaning of the poem.

22 T. Thornton, *Cheshire and the Tudor State, 1480–1560* (Woodbridge, 2000), esp. pp. 187–95.

23 Cavendish, p. 12.

24 *CSPV* II, 1287 Giustinian's report to the Venetian Senate, September/October 1519.

25 *St. P* VI, pp. 395–6 (*LP* IV i, 1083).

26 BL, Cotton MS Vespasian F iii, fo. 73 [*LP* III i, 4279] Henry to Wolsey, undated but from context June 1518.

27 BL, Cotton MS Vespasian F xiii, fo. 138 Henry to Wolsey undated but from context c.1520.

28 BL, Additional MS Vitellius B xx fo. 89 [*LP* III i, 4257] Pace to Wolsey, 24 June 1518.

29 BL, Additional MS 19,398, fo. 44 [*LP* III i, 1] Henry to Wolsey, calendared at 1 January 1519 but date undetermined.

30 Vergil, Book 27, para 29.

31 Hall, pp. 622–3.

32 Cavendish, p. 26.

33 Vergil, Book 27, para, 25.

34 Hall, p. 712.

35 D. R. Starkey, 'Court, Council and Nobility in Tudor England', in R. G. Asch and A. M. Birke (eds.), *Princes, Patronage and the Nobility: The Court at the Beginning of the Modern Age, c. 1450–1650* (Oxford, 1991), pp. 175–203.

36 Hall, p. 598; BL, Cotton MS Caligula, D VII, fos. 121–2 [*LP* III i, 246] Boleyn to Wolsey, Poissy, 20 May 1519.

37 G. Richardson, '"Most Highly to be Regarded": The Privy Chamber of Henry VIII and Anglo-French Relations, 1515–1520', *The Court Historian* 4 (2) (August 1999): 119–40, for a fuller discussion of this episode and its consequences.

38 Starkey, 'Court and Council', pp. 184–5.

39 *St. P.* I, pp. 33–47 for the correspondence on this dispute.

40 Ibid., pp. 42, 46 Pace to Wolsey 9 and 27 October 1521.

41 Walker, pp. 73–89. But see A. Fox, *Politics and Literature in the Reigns of Henry VII and Henry VIII* (Oxford, 1989), pp. 131–205 for a different view of Skelton and Wolsey.

42 C. Given-Wilson, *The Royal Household and the King's Affinity: Service, Politics and Finance in England, 1360–1413* (New Haven & London: Yale University Press, 1986), pp. 203–57; J. Guy, 'Thomas Wolsey, Thomas Cromwell and the Reform of Henrician Government', in D. MacCulloch, *The Reign of Henry*, pp. 35–57.

43 TNA, E36/130, fos. 165–231 [*LP* III i 576 (3)], cited in J. Guy, 'Wolsey and the Tudor Polity', in Gunn and Lindley, pp. 54–75 at p. 67.

44 Guy, 'Wolsey and the Tudor Polity', pp. 69–70ff.

114 *Chief executive*

45 S. Lambe, 'The Paulet Family and the Gentry of Early Tudor Somerset, 1485–1547', (Unpublished PhD thesis, University of Surrey, 2016), esp. pp. 44–72; see also D. J. Ashton, 'The Tudor State and County Politics: The Greater Gentry of Somerset, c. 1509–1558' (Unpublished DPhil thesis, University of Oxford, 1998).

46 E. W. Ives, 'Patronage at the Court of Henry VIII: The Case of Sir Ralph Egerton of Ridley', *Bulletin of the John Rylands Library* 52 (2) (1970): 346–74; and see also his 'Court and County Palatinate in the Reign of Henry VIII: The Career of William Brereton of Malpas', *Transactions of the Historical Society of Lancashire and Cheshire* 123 (1972): 1–38.

47 Ellis, 'A Border Baron and the Tudor State', pp. 269ff.

48 N. Lewycky, 'Cardinal Thomas Wolsey and the City of York, 1514–1529', *Northern History* 46 (1): 43–60; see also her 'Serving God and King: Cardinal Thomas Wolsey's Patronage Networks and Early Tudor Government, 1514–1529, with Special Reference to the Diocese of York' (unpublished University of York PhD dissertation, 2008).

49 G. W. Bernard, *War, Taxation and Rebellion in Early Tudor England: Henry VIII, Wolsey and the Amicable Grant of 1525* (Brighton, 1986), pp. 119–23.

50 Hall, pp. 696–8; Bernard, *War, Taxation and Rebellion*, pp. 60–6.

51 R. L. Woods, 'Politics and Precedent: Wolsey's Parliament of 1523', *Huntingdon Library Quarterly* 40 (4) (August 1977): 297–312.

52 Bernard, *War, Taxation and Rebellion*, pp. 150–7.

53 Hall, pp. 697–700.

54 Guy, 'Thomas Wolsey, Thomas Cromwell and the Reform of Henrician Government', pp. 35–57.

55 *A Collection of Ordinances and Regulations for the Government of the Royal Household Made in Diverse Reigns*, published by the Society of Antiquaries (London, 1790); Hall, p. 707.

56 Ibid., pp. 154–5; Starkey, 'Court and Council', pp. 188–9.

57 Fiddes, *Collections* (primary source material included separately in his 1726 biography of Wolsey), p. 139 [*LP* IV, 4507, 4509].

58 Ibid.

59 Scarisbrick, p. 228.

60 Vergil, Book 27, para 27.

4 Cardinal legate

Wolsey and the English Church

And York, perceiving the obedience that Canterbury claimed to have of York, intended to provide some such means that he would rather be superior in dignity to Canterbury than to be either obedient or equal to him. Wherefore he obtained first to be made priest cardinal and legatus de latere *unto whom the Pope sent a cardinal's hat with certain bulls for his authority in that behalf.*[1]

So it was that Wolsey's first biographer characterised his subject's motives in obtaining the status of cardinal legate *a latere* in England. The true origins of Cardinal Wolsey's jurisdiction over the Church as the pope's personal representative in England lay not in domestic ecclesiastical power struggles, but in the international papal politics of the period (see Chapter 2). For A. J. Pollard, England's various changes in alliance in the 1520s were then determined by Wolsey's ardent support for papal policy as legate *a latere*, whatever it was, pursuant to his ambition ultimately to wear the shoes of the fisherman himself.[2] Later historians, especially Gwyn, have instead emphasised Wolsey's ingrained sense that his legateship was to be used first and foremost in the service of his king, rather than the pope, and that view is affirmed in what follows. As often, Cavendish may be wrong on the details, but his instincts were right. Issues of jurisdiction and his authority in the Church relative to a host of others were to the fore throughout Wolsey's career from 1514. Other contemporaries certainly understood how important legatine status was to Wolsey. Ten years after his appointment as

116   *Cardinal legate*

cardinal legate, his fellow legate Campeggio observed of him that 'all his grandeur is connected with the Apostolic See'.[3]

Wolsey as legate *a latere*

In the early sixteenth century there were two kinds of papal legate. The *legatus natus* was a resident of high ecclesiastical authority, usually a bishop, and usually a native of the country in which he was appointed. He was given a delegated general jurisdiction from the papacy to administer canon law within the realm, usually his diocese. Wolsey had, for example, become a *legatus natus* in 1514 as Archbishop of York and Primate of England. Archbishop Warham of Canterbury also had this kind of legateship exercised through the Court of Arches, which had an extensive jurisdiction over marriage, probate, defamation, church property and good behaviour among the clergy and laity.

A papal *legatus a latere* was rather different. He was endowed with the status of one who had come from the pope's side – as in lateral, hence the title. He represented the pontiff personally and was, in effect, a papal plenipotentiary. He was sent usually for specific diplomatic negotiations or equipped with amply delegated jurisdiction to carry out specific tasks in ecclesiastical governance or reform. He was usually a foreigner in the country to which he was sent. Yet, coming directly from the pope, a legate *a latere* outranked for the time of his legacy all in the local ecclesiastical hierarchy, including fellow cardinals and even the highest archbishops. The conciliar movement of the later fourteenth century had seen national churches, often supported by rulers, seek to limit notions of papal supremacy to assert the binding authority of Church councils and of cardinals as representatives of the Church and the electors of popes. From the mid-fifteenth century, however, following the Council of Basel in the early 1430s, the pendulum began to swing back the other way. Successive popes sent legates *a latere* to princes and republican states throughout Europe, often as part of reasserting papal influence and to open direct dialogue with rulers. The appointment of such legates shortened and straightened lines of communication between themselves and monarchs and gave them their own man on the ground, as it were, who could ensure that papal interests and demands were represented in whatever business

Cardinal legate 117

they were delegated to conduct, sometimes against the wishes of local bishops and monasteries. For rulers, too, it might be useful to have a legate appointed for a time insofar as he could do things, take decisions and make arrangements locally that rulers favoured and that might otherwise have to be dealt with through the complex and time-consuming processes and bureaucracies of the papal Consistory (council of cardinals) and the Curia (secretariat/administration). From the outset, acquiring legatine status was key to all Wolsey had wanted to achieve as cardinal for Henry and himself because it made him the surest link between crown and papacy. Or so he thought. He pursued his campaign to secure a legateship for life, itself almost unprecedented, relentlessly and ultimately successfully, although it took more than six years to achieve.

In 1518, Pope Leo's need for just this sort of direct communication and cooperation from Henry over his plans for an international truce led him to send a legate to England for the purpose. Wolsey suggested that for this to happen, he, too, would have to be made a legate, as 'foreign' legates had not traditionally been accepted in England. Yet royal support for a resident legate, of the kind he was proposing, was also virtually unknown in England. The only precedent had not been a particularly happy one. In December 1417, Henry Beaufort, the bishop of Winchester, had been made a cardinal and legate by Pope Martin V, who also granted him exemption from the jurisdiction of the archbishop of Canterbury. The archbishop, Henry Chichele, portrayed the presence of a legate *a latere* in the realm as a danger to Henry V's authority and his people and pointed out the conflict of interest Beaufort inevitably faced in serving pope and king. Beaufort was very wealthy, and Hall and Shakespeare later cast him as the precursor to Wolsey as the avaricious, ambitious churchman. Wolsey's position was, however, different from Beaufort's in at least two important respects. Firstly, from the outset, Wolsey had his king's support in his request for legatine power precisely because it was said to enhance, not undermine, royal authority. He was also already a cardinal, Lord Chancellor of England and the king's leading advisor at the time of his appointment as legate. Secondly, unlike Beaufort, Wolsey had no family of consequence for whose political interests he was working. Nor did he have Beaufort's independent wealth, and he owed everything he had to Henry. Wolsey's position as a papal legate *a latere* actively

118   *Cardinal legate*

working over an extended period for the crown and the papacy, with the trust of both, remains unique in English history.[4]

Insofar as Wolsey always insisted that his own enhanced supervision of the Church was consonant with strengthening royal authority and, to a significant extent, its control over the clergy, he had a nearer and closer predecessor than Beaufort. This was Cardinal John Morton. Morton had served both Henry VI and Edward IV, acquiring, as Wolsey would do in turn, a plethora of lucrative benefices, although unlike Wolsey and Beaufort, he never acquired a reputation for personal aggrandisement. He fled the regime of Richard III and played a vital role in securing Innocent VIII's support for Henry Tudor's claim to the English throne. As king, Henry nominated Morton Archbishop of Canterbury in October 1486, Chancellor the following year, and he became a cardinal in 1493. Although he was never a legate *a latere*, Morton worked closely with Henry to increase the Church's compliance in matters of clerical taxation. He used his power to reform clerical malpractice and clashed with several orders of monks exempted from episcopal supervision. He placed restrictions on the benefit of clergy and limited the rights of sanctuary. As legate and Morton's *de facto* successor, Wolsey tackled those same issues, and others besides, with at least as much vigour as Morton and, again, with the support of his king.[5]

As a cardinal and prince of the Church, Wolsey might have chosen to go to Rome, to be installed personally in his titular church of Santa-Cecilia in Trastevere, and there to reside and represent the interests of his king and the English Church with the consistory and the Curia, as well as to carry out any role to which the pope might appoint him. His immediate predecessor as cardinal of England and Archbishop of York, Christopher Bainbridge, had done just that. He voted in the conclave that chose Leo X in March 1513, the first English cardinal to have participated in a papal election for more than 140 years. Although he was never made a legate to England, Bainbridge worked hard for Henry VIII's interests at Rome, drawing together a team of young assistants among whom were the future royal secretary Richard Pace and the future bishop and diplomat John Clerk. There were differences of opinion and approach in doing this between himself and his English colleagues, not least the up-and-coming Wolsey. Wolsey might also have gone to Rome to participate in the several conclaves for the election of the pope that took place during his lifetime. This is, after all, still the principle and most solemn duty of cardinals.[6] Of course, he did none of these things. He never went further into continental Europe than the French towns of Amiens and Compiègne in 1527. As Chancellor it was impossible for him to have done otherwise. Even when he left England for a few months for the Calais peace conference he called in the summer of 1521, much of English government ground to a halt. Yet he was far from unique. By the middle of the fifteenth century, and despite the revived power of the papacy re-established in Rome, some cardinals were being appointed with the understanding that in ordinary circumstances, they would act as papal agents in their native countries rather than servants in Rome. Most of these appointees were of the great European noble houses. Several were, like Wolsey, also leading statesmen in their homelands – not least Cardinal Morton. Mention has already been made of Georges D'Amboise, the cardinal-chancellor of France under Louis XII and Wolsey's nearest point of comparison. Wolsey's actual French contemporary, Cardinal Antoine Duprat, was also Chancellor of France but not a resident *legate a latere*.[7]

Wolsey's situation did, however, leave the king with a problem. Unlike his continental counterparts who had perhaps three or four cardinals to their name, Henry had only one, and he was resident in England. Who, then, would represent royal interests and those of the national Church at the highest levels in Rome as Bainbridge had done till his death in 1514? Happily, and characteristically perhaps, Henry VII had provided a solution to this administrative and diplomatic difficulty. He appreciated how vital it was to have close and dependable allies in Rome and good communication with them. Accordingly, in 1492 Henry appointed Francesco Piccolomini, the Cardinal of Siena as the first 'Cardinal Protector' of England. His principal task was to give a voice to England in the Consistory. There he had supported or sponsored Henry's preferred candidates for major benefices in England – something he did with remarkable success. He also oversaw the defence of cases in the papal Rota (the appeal court) and secured a series of papal indulgences for religious foundations in England, particularly those under the patronage of Queen Elizabeth of York. He was supported by Giovanni Gigli, who was made absentee bishop of Worcester

120　*Cardinal legate*

in 1497 and was succeeded in the diocese the following year by his nephew Silvestro, both of whom then acted as resident English ambassadors in Rome. By 1500 they had been joined by another curial insider, Adriano Castellesi. He had acted as papal tax collector in England in the 1490s. In 1502, he was made absentee Bishop of Hereford and a cardinal a year later. In 1503 the English cardinal protector was elected as Pope Pius III, whose pontificate was one of the shortest in papal history. In 1504 Cardinal Castellesi was made absentee Bishop of Bath and Wells and continued to act as informal 'protector' of England during the pontificate of Julius II until Bainbridge took on direct representation of his nation with his own elevation to the cardinalate in 1511.[8]

Henry's early relations with the papacy therefore echoed those of his father, and he, too, seems to have appreciated the need for high level and effective representation in Rome. With Wolsey's appointment in succession to Bainbridge, that representation was necessarily left to Italian cardinals, but Wolsey and Henry scored a real coup by securing as successor to Piccolomini as cardinal protector none other than the pope's cousin, Giulio de' Medici, the vice-chancellor of the Church. He appears, together with Cardinal Luigi de' Rossi, in Raphael's famous 1519 portrait of Leo X. The painting alludes strongly to Leo's closeness, even dependence, on Giulio. At first glance, he seems the best-placed cardinal to defend England's interests in the Curia. Unfortunately for Henry perhaps, that very prominence attracted a range of competitors for the cardinal's assistance. A little over a year after Giulio de' Medici had become cardinal protector of England, he also became cardinal protector of France. This was largely prompted by Francis I's reconquest of Milan in September 1515, which brought immense French military power and political influence back into northern Italy, the borders of the papal states and the Medici pope's native city of Florence. The inevitable conflict of interests between the ambitions of the English king and his professed support for the papacy, and the power of Francis I, recognised by Leo as legitimate duke of Milan in the Concordat of Bologna in 1516, severely compromised Giulio de' Medici's capacity to act entirely in England's interests. Consequently, relations between himself and Wolsey and Henry were friendly but often strained. Giulio could offer no real help, for example, in Consistory in the long-running dispute between Wolsey and a French-backed potential incumbent over the possession of the bishopric of Tournai, to which Wolsey had been appointed following Henry's conquest of the city in 1513.

In these circumstances, Wolsey continued to work closely with Silvestro Gigli in Rome, who did not himself, however, work at all well with Castellesi, the other English advocate in the Curia. Castellesi had done his best to undermine Gigli's reputation as English representative, countenancing allegations that the Bishop of Worcester had been involved in the suspected poisoning of Cardinal Bainbridge, a charge of which Gigli was formally acquitted. Perhaps fortunately for Wolsey, another Italian was to hand to assist in English affairs. This was Lorenzo Campeggio, a native of Bologna, the papal nuncio to the Emperor Maximilian, at whose request he was made a cardinal in 1517 and cardinal protector of the German lands. An ally of Giulio de' Medici, he was, as we have noted, nominated a *legate a latere* to England in March 1518 for the organisation of the pope's five-year truce among Christian princes.

Wolsey had no trust in Castellesi and was determined to use Campeggio's coming to England in July 1518 as the means to ensure his dismissal from the bishopric of Bath and Wells. Accordingly, Campeggio was refused permission to come from Calais to Dover until Leo had agreed and Castellesi's deprivation had been announced. This finally took place in Consistory on 5 July, news of it being sent the same day to Henry by Cardinal de' Medici. At Henry's request, the pope also made Wolsey Bishop of Bath and Wells *in commendam* with York, thereby placing in the hands of the king's closest advisor one of the kingdom's wealthier bishoprics. Only then was Campeggio allowed to sail to England.[9]

This outcome and his cardinal's new appointment affirmed Henry's sense of his power and authority over the Church in England, to the consolidation of which Wolsey was by then committed. Yet, as Wolsey realised, other important people in England were less impressed with, even indifferent to, his being made a legate. Campeggio's formal reception into the kingdom was therefore minutely stage-managed by Wolsey in order to highlight his own status as the cardinal legate *of* England. Hall informs us that at Campeggio's arrival in Deal on 23 July 1518, his meagre entourage was newly outfitted by Wolsey and his baggage train of 8 sumpter mules supplemented by 12 more. This was mocked by Hall and

122   *Cardinal legate*

by many historians since (Wilkie called it 'a tactless, almost child-ish effort to upstage') as an ostentatious display of his authority to his Italian colleague.[10] Showmanship and a concern for appear-ances were certainly characteristic of him – witness the reception of his cardinal's hat less than three years earlier. Yet, as on that occa-sion, Wolsey's actions do make a kind of sense if we accept that he wanted the Italian prelate to look as splendid as possible as the pope's legate, precisely in order that the two of them looked equally impressive alongside each other, as if both had come from Rome. Campeggio entered London on 29 July, received by the whole clergy, the guilds, the Mayor and aldermen of the city and conveyed to Bath House on the Thames where he was accommodated by Wolsey himself – the recently appointed Bishop of Bath and Wells. The high point of the reception came at Greenwich on 3 August where, with only Wolsey's legatine cross borne before the two cardi-nals, the king 'royally apparelled and accompanied, met them even as though both had come from Rome' – just as Wolsey intended. The joint-legatine commission to conclude a truce was read out, and they dined in state with the king before returning together through London. In all of this, the representatives of the English political, commercial and ecclesiastical elite at the court and in the city of London not only witnessed the arrival of an Italian cardinal legate but were effectively co-opted into the public acknowledg-ment of Wolsey as his fellow legate in England.[11]

Wolsey was ever conscious of international parallels. Sometime in September, amidst all the complex diplomatic negotiations he was then conducting, he found time to draft a long description for Henry of how the papal legate to France, Cardinal Bibbiena, had been received. According to the French ambassadors in England, Wolsey told Henry, the legate had been honoured with a canopy held over him, even in the king's presence. King Francis had met him on horseback and, placing the legate on his right side, escorted him into Paris. Wolsey pointed out that no oration was made at Bibbiena's formal reception, 'as was done here', but that hundreds of nobles continued to escort him everywhere until the legate had himself asked that they might be dispensed with. This description shows how important ceremonies that emphasised status were to Wolsey, as a man who had risen from humble origins, but more importantly, it suggests that he wanted Henry both to appreciate the full significance of his legateship, as at least the equal of any other, and also to be reassured of Wolsey's loyalty and commitment to him as expressed through the recent, and comparatively low-key, ceremonies in England inaugurating his own legateship.[12]

The legate reformer?

From the outset of his legateship, Wolsey presented himself to the papacy as entirely devoted to its interests and emphasised that continued legatine status was key to his service. One of the reasons for which he was ostensibly granted these powers was reform of the Church in England. What exactly the papacy meant by that is debatable, but at the very least Leo wanted his legate to have strict oversight of a Church conscious of its duties to the papacy. He wanted to ensure that canon law operated effectively, that the clergy were of good moral standing and also that the revenues owed to the papacy, through appointments to benefices and a plethora of other imposts, made their way to Rome regularly and unimpeded. Wolsey wanted that, too, but he also appreciated from the outset of his time as cardinal that the Church in England was also subject to royal authority and royal justice and that there were ambiguities in the demarcation line between the jurisdictions of the Church and crown in a range of matters concerning the clergy and its privileges; ambiguities he might well be required to deal with as legate.

Motivated in part at least by this awareness, Wolsey sought an extension of his legatine powers immediately after they were first granted, ostensibly to carry out Leo's instructions for reform of the clergy upon which he had begun to act and to raise a tax for the (now-superseded) papal truce between princes. Wolsey genuinely did want reform along the lines advocated by Christian humanist scholars like Erasmus. Although orthodox to his core and seeing no need for major doctrinal reform, nor for significant changes in the practice of religion in England, he was, nevertheless, sympathetic to calls for reform among the clergy. It was their duty to care for those in their charge, from the level of the village parish upwards, and Wolsey was determined that under his authority they would do this well. As legate, he therefore focused principally on the proper organisation and running of the episcopate, on reform of religious houses where needed to ensure high standards of observance, and on the promotion of an orthodox, well-educated and well-motivated clergy. These three, he reasoned, were the best ways to uphold the reputation of the clergy and protect the Church in already troubled theological times against the danger of heresy. As we shall see in the next chapter, he made serious efforts as an educational patron towards these aims with the foundation of university lectureships and his two colleges at Oxford and Ipswich, which promoted Christian humanist learning. These efforts were praised by Erasmus, by Bishop Fox of Winchester and Sir Thomas More and ultimately approved by both the king and pope.

Leo tolerated Wolsey's request for further legatine powers politely because he needed Wolsey to keep Henry on side against France. On 27 August 1518, Wolsey was given authority to 'visit', that is inspect, monasteries, including those of the Regular orders who were generally exempt from episcopal supervision. Wolsey and Campeggio made a largely ceremonial visit of this kind to the Benedictine community at Westminster Abbey in December that year. The same month he issued a summons to English bishops to attend a meeting with him the following March. In the spring of 1519, with Campeggio's departure in prospect, Wolsey demanded a further extension of legatine status. He instructed Worcester in Rome to remind the pope how assiduously and effectively he had hitherto served as legate and that a similar extension of authority had just been accorded to the 'bishop of Bussi' who had been made a papal legate *a latere* for one year for the realm of France after the return to Rome of Cardinal Bibbiena – Campeggio's counterpart. This was Adrien de Gouffier, Bishop of Coutances, Cardinal de Boisy. Wolsey insisted that he had thus far served the Curia far more assiduously than Boisy ever had.[13] Once more Leo initially resisted, conscious of potential trouble in giving a resident legate such power, but by June 1519, his wish to keep Henry allied after the election of Charles of Spain as Holy Roman Emperor meant that the pope extended Wolsey's authority to visit monasteries for a year from Campeggio's departure; the same arrangement as granted in France. This, despite the fact that Wolsey had completely failed to set about raising clerical taxation. There is no evidence that he ever did so in any of the meetings with the religious orders, the bishops or the secular clergy in the months that followed.

Cardinal legate 125

In March 1519, Wolsey duly met with the bishops for consultations and to formulate a set of legatine 'constitutions' or agreed laws that, among other things, determined the best way forward in carrying out supervisory 'visitations' of religious houses. This provoked the first real clash with Archbishop Warham, who thought the legate's demands would infringe directly on his own legatine (*natus*) jurisdiction and who attempted to block them. In the end he was forced to accept the supervening authority of Wolsey's *a latere* jurisdiction. Very little evidence survives of the legatine constitutions that were agreed in March, and not even a single copy of them is extant, although it is known that some concerned dress and the behaviour of those in clerical orders. It has, however, been suggested that given the lack of evidence of any serious or sustained opposition to them, and that none seem to have had any adverse financial implications for the clergy, they were probably not that radical in intent and were more in the way of Wolsey's putting himself personally in charge of the clerical housekeeping of the English Church. In May, Wolsey met with bishops and set out his priorities for the reformation of clergy and monasteries. At the top of his list was theologically sound preaching. The proper administration of the sacraments and due observance of the Church's liturgical calendar also figured. Clergy were to ensure marriages were conducted in the correct form and that their own personal lives were morally sound. He also wished to tackle absenteeism and much else besides. Many of the items on his draft list accord with contemporary criticisms of the clergy and suggest Wolsey was alive to the need for reform and perhaps the danger to the Church's standing if these criticisms went unheeded. Wolsey had planned to hold another consultation with the bishops that autumn, but due to plague in London, it was effectively cancelled.[14]

Campeggio left England on 24 August 1519 and arrived back in Rome in late November. He undertook much of the maintenance of papal relations with England in the following years, and he was rather successful in obtaining virtually all that Wolsey wanted. He also gave what may have been a somewhat misleading impression that England did indeed have sufficient and effective representation in the papal Curia. This was an impression Giulio de' Medici also did his best to affirm as cardinal protector.

Meanwhile, having consulted the bishops in March, and as Campeggio arrived back in Rome, Wolsey summoned the leaders of the religious orders to Westminster in November 1519 for consultations on his legatine authority, to oversee the many orders of monks, friars and nuns in England. The major monastic orders owned vast amounts of land and were deeply involved in the local communities of which they were a part, as landowners, farmers and employers. They offered basic health care to those around them, provided extensive alms and were, to a significant extent, responsible, directly and indirectly, for such education as was offered in the late-medieval period. Between them, they had the right to appoint priests to hundreds of parish livings all over the country. Of prime importance for late-medieval people was the fact that the religious orders, especially the monks, prayed for society in general, for individuals, whether exalted or humble, and crucially and for payment, they prayed for the salvation of the souls of the dead. Like the bishops, the abbots of the major orders sat in the House of Lords, an indicator of their social, economic, political and spiritual importance in the world.

The main problem was that in early sixteenth-century England, as elsewhere in Europe, there were simply too many monasteries, many of them decayed with only a few inhabitants and manifestly underfunded, whatever the terms of their original endowments. Consequently, they could do little good socially and spiritually for their own members, much less the communities around them which they were supposed to serve, and some at least were burdens on those communities. The good governance of such institutions, even the largest of them, was a perennial issue throughout late-medieval Christendom, and the conduct of men and women who belonged to them often concerned bishops and humanist commentators, not least the likes of Erasmus and, in England, Sir Thomas More and Bishop Fisher of Rochester. Their criticisms were not so much of the monastic lifestyle itself but of the number of houses, allegedly lax standards, or at least ineffectiveness, in some of them and the high-handedness at times of some in their dealings with episcopal authorities. 'Something must be done', was the usual cry, and something Wolsey determined to do, sympathetic as he was to these reformist trends. He saw ample scope for the rationalisation of monasticism and supported a drive towards improved education for the secular clergy and effective preaching in parishes, in town and country alike.[15]

Like Morton before him, Wolsey found a number of orders of monks and friars resistant to his supervisory authority. These included the Dominican and Franciscan friars and the Cistercians, three of the largest orders in England. The outcome of the Westminster meeting seems to have been some form of committee which brought forward a set of reformed statutes for the Augustinian Canons and the Benedictines. These were subsequently presented to the chapters of the orders and accepted in February 1520. The ones for the Benedictines do not survive, but those for the Augustinians suggest that, like those for the bishops, they were fairly uncontroversial, had no financial implications and were concerned with maintaining effective operations and good moral standards among members. Again, as with the episcopal constitutions of March 1519, they are probably best seen as Wolsey putting his stamp on the issue of monastic supervision and reform, gaining the apparent support of his brother clerics and allowing him to present himself to king and pope alike as fully seized of the matter, intent upon the good conduct of the religious orders, and as the right man for this job – as for all others.

Yet it was not just for appearances' sake. Wolsey meant business. In March, the cardinal wrote to the Augustinians at Leicester, enjoining upon them the need to conform to 18 articles which specified among other things that the canons were not to leave their establishment without leave. Nor were they to hunt or wear furs, and in general, they were to conform to the highest standards of their order's Rule in their personal conduct. Richard Fox wrote enthusiastically about Wolsey having engaged upon 'a more entire and whole reformation of the ecclesiastical hierarchy of the English people than I could have expected', and declared that Wolsey's skill in business, 'whether divine or human', would gain him 'true immortal honour from God and posterity'.[16]

Wolsey, the Church and royal authority

By January 1521, a series of bulls prolonging (but not enlarging in scope) Wolsey's legatine powers until August 1522 had been issued. This, despite Leo's expressed reservation about the impact of these powers on the jurisdictions of the English bishops. This did not satisfy Wolsey, who continued to badger Campeggio to obtain a further extension and, more importantly, a widening of his legatine authority. The much sought after extension of Wolsey's authority was finally obtained by bulls issued in April and June 1521. His delegated jurisdiction was amplified as never before to cover the reform of the Church as a whole, rather than just the religious orders, and to give Wolsey new powers to grant exemptions from episcopal supervision, to absolve excommunication, to grant licences in canon law matters and to establish his own legatine court. The death of Silvestro Gigli, Bishop of Worcester, in April 1521, allowed Wolsey to press his claims still further through strengthening ties with the pope's cousin Cardinal Giulio de' Medici, who was offered the vacant see of Worcester. Unsurprisingly, this nomination was confirmed by Leo in June. All of this happened in the context of England's place in the changing balance of power in Europe and Henry's decision to write a book against Luther in defence of the papacy, the *Assertio Septem Sacramentorum* or *The Defence of the Seven Sacraments*.[17]

On 12 May 1521, Wolsey presided as legate over the public pronouncement of the papal excommunication of Martin Luther and the banning of his works, copies of which were burnt in St Paul's Churchyard in London. A proclamation was made against printing or supplying these banned books. The highpoint of the event was Wolsey's announcement, by way of dramatic contrast, of the king's new book.

Henry had consulted some advisors on the project, but Wolsey was evidently not among them. Sir Thomas More later confirmed that he had been approached and that Henry had maintained his trenchant defence of papal authority, even against More's expressed reservations on certain points. Before representatives of domestic and international audiences, the cardinal made clear his own intentions to follow the king's lead and defend orthodoxy at home and abroad. Efforts were certainly made in Flanders and elsewhere to intercept condemned writings destined for England. Behind the scenes Wolsey sought to identify and quietly censure, and indeed censor, known educated heretics. Their books were confiscated, and their quiet abjurations secured by a mix of threats and offers. This enabled him to project Henry's England as being in no way seriously infected by Luther and ever a staunch defender of the papacy.[18]

Cardinal legate 129

In July 1521, Leo pressed Henry to send his treatise to Rome where it would be assured of a warm welcome. John Clerk, a Wolsey protégé, conveyed the text there. Meanwhile, Wolsey was at Calais negotiating with French and Imperial ambassadors, apparently to bring an end to the war that had begun the previous spring. By August, an Anglo–Imperial, anti-French alliance of the kind that the pope had been seeking for a year since the Field of Cloth of Gold, was in place, negotiated secretly by Wolsey in Bruges. The pope's response to the pleasing news of the treaty was, among other things, the extension of Wolsey's legateship for a further five years, and he was given additional rights to 'prevent' meaning, somewhat confusingly, to appoint members of his own clientele to benefices. Leo also offered demonstrative public and personal approval of the *Assertio*, presented to him by Clerk on 2 October. On 25 October, he issued the bull conferring upon Henry the title of 'Fidei Defensor', Defender of the Faith (a title Henry had already started using informally), held by English and British sovereigns ever since. Yet barely had Wolsey returned from Calais that autumn and re-established his routine at Westminster than he received news that Leo had died on 1 December.[19]

In the conclave that followed, Wolsey seems genuinely, if somewhat hesitantly and on the prompting of his king, to have sought the papal throne. Charles V's ambassador reported Wolsey as saying 'for no other purpose could he desire the Papacy, except to exalt your majesties'. In the event, Henry's agent Richard Pace arrived too late to have any influence. While Cardinal de' Medici had hopes of a smooth succession to his cousin, others objected to one Medici succeeding another and looked for alternatives in name and in spirit. No French candidates took part in the conclave, and attention soon fell on 'non-curial' cardinals such as Matthäus Lang in Germany and Wolsey in England. In that conclave, 26 votes were required for victory. According to John Clerk, still in Rome, Wolsey obtained 9 votes at the first ballot, 12 in the second and 19 in the third, but then support deserted him. Some objected to him on the grounds of his comparative youth; he was then between 48 and 50 years old. Even these modest figures may have been intended to flatter, and the reality was that Wolsey's chances were always slim, lacking the means to build a solid support base among Italian, curial cardinals against any Imperial candidate. As Clerk

130   *Cardinal legate*

reminded the cardinal, he had not worked that hard, 'because your grace at my departing showed me precisely that ye would never meddle therewith'. In the end it was indeed the emperor's candidate and former tutor, Cardinal Adrian of Utrecht, who was elected as Adrian VI on 9 January 1522.[20]

After initially refusing to recognise that election as valid, Wolsey renewed his effort to secure enhanced legatine status during Adrian's pontificate, but without success. Adrian had been acting as Charles's regent in Spain until his election. Perhaps Wolsey expected the new pope's gratitude for his work concluding an Anglo–Imperial alliance against France the previous year. Instead, Adrian refused Wolsey's request outright, clearly regarding the English cardinal as already having had ample power delegated to him by his predecessor. This was a view perhaps shared by Wolsey's fellow English clergy, some of whom had begun to express concern about how that power was being used, and in whose interests. The memory of clashes in the past and a wish to avoid them was an evident consideration in the way Wolsey, as legate, exercised his widened authority from the summer of 1521.

The problems of jurisdiction between Church and Crown had as long a history in England as anywhere else in Christendom. Henry VII had worked with Cardinal Morton to restrict sanctuary in churches, whereby those who had done acts punishable by death sought refuge. His successor followed in similar vein. There was also the question of benefit of clergy and the demarcation between secular and ecclesiastical jurisdiction in criminal cases involving the clergy. This was brought into focus in 1515, in the first few months after Wolsey became Archbishop of York, in a legal controversy, the key issue in which was the king's role in a matter which the Church would rather have dealt with on its own. Richard Hunne, a London merchant, was accused of heresy in the course of a long and bitter legal case he had begun over mortuary fees charged by a clergyman. On 4 December 1514, he was found dead, apparently a suicide, while in the custody of Richard Fitzjames, the Bishop of London. As part of the dispute, Hunne had raised a charge of *praemunire* against members of the clergy. That is, at its broadest, exercising ecclesiastical (including papal) jurisdiction in matters that properly belonged to royal justice. The 1393 Statue of Praemunire had laid down strict penalties of forfeiture and more for any individual or institution found guilty

Cardinal legate 131

of such a charge. It may be that the heresy charge on which Hunne was detained was an aggressive response to the *praemunire* allegation. The bishop's chancellor William Horsey and two accomplices were found guilty of his murder by an inquest jury. Given the controversy and the issues at the heart of the various legal proceedings, the king's council held an enquiry into the case in February 1515. When Horsey and accomplices were eventually arraigned before the King's Bench as they were required to be, they pleaded not guilty. The king ordered that their pleas be accepted. It has been suggested that Henry only did that because he believed, or chose to believe, that Hunne committed suicide and that his intervention sought to protect the Church from anti-clerical accusations to the contrary. The point is that the king understood himself as having the right and will to do so. The Church, in accepting his intervention and its damping down any imputation of *praemunire* alleged by Hunne in the wider circumstances of the case, gladly and tacitly acknowledged the same. Of course, the protection the king chose to give to the hierarchy in this instance, he could also take away.

That this was so was immediately demonstrated in a controversy over the issue of *praemunire* directly. Among the many traditional privileges (called liberties) of the priesthood was 'benefit of clergy'. This controversial practice allowed clergy to escape punishment by the crown in cases within certain circumstances. It was open to abuse and had been progressively restricted over the course of at least the previous century. In 1512, a law was passed that removed the practice of 'benefit of clergy' in cases involving murder in a church, highway or dwelling house. The legislation had proved controversial as between bishops in the Lords and the House of Commons, and in February 1515, Richard Kidderminster, Abbot of Winchcombe, preached that the statute contravened the clergy's immunity from secular legal jurisdiction in removing benefit of clergy from clerics not in major orders. More generally, he complained of mistreatment of clerics under the secular law. Henry VIII reacted immediately. The respected theologian Dr Henry Standish was commissioned by the king publicly to defend the law against Kidderminster's claims. Having done so very effectively, Standish was promptly accused of heresy by Bishop Fitzjames, and in November, he was summoned before convocation to account for himself. The London Franciscan Friars, of whom Standish was warden, appealed to the king and

Wolsey to protect him. In response the king's judges warned the bishops that whoever accused Standish of heresy would themselves be subject to the charge of *praemunire*. With growing interest in the controversy, especially among civil lawyers, the ecclesiastical authorities submitted the whole issue to Henry to arbitrate. William Warham, the Archbishop of Canterbury, rallied to the support of the Church's jurisdiction over its own, and it ultimately fell to Wolsey, by now a cardinal, to try to resolve the conflict by seeking Henry's pardon. In admitting the charge and submitting on behalf of the clergy, he still tried, as far as he reasonably could, to maintain (for clerical consumption at least) the integrity of the Church courts' jurisdiction, while capitulating entirely on the particular issues of the case, namely that the crown had the right to punish anyone convicted of murder or felonies – layman or cleric. The details of the resolution of the dispute were finessed but not before Henry had very clearly laid down his view, in response to Wolsey's submission, that the kings of England had no superior but God and:

> Wherefore know you well that we will maintain the right of our Crown and of our temporal jurisdiction as well in this point as in all others, in as ample a wise as any of our progenitors have done before us.[21]

This was a clear statement of Henry's belief that his rights could not be impinged by any ecclesiastical authority whatsoever. By the time the controversy died down at the end of the year, Wolsey was indeed in a tricky position because, as cardinal he was, notwithstanding Warham, the de-facto leader of the hierarchy of a Church that has been aptly described as a 'vital and vulnerable' part of the kingdom. As Chancellor, from December 1515, he was also now the highest administrative and legal official in England, responsible for ensuring that the writ of the king's authority ran as far as possible, over matters both secular and ecclesiastical, throughout Henry's realm. He was in a very real legal sense, the king's cardinal.[22]

Legate *a latere* for life

Perhaps in the light of these earlier controversies, Wolsey's first instinct, when his legatine powers were amplified in mid-1521, was to take any and all matters where questions of even a potential clash of jurisdictions could arise into his own hands. Pollard argued that Wolsey went well beyond that and sought to subsume all other jurisdictions to his own and to monopolise virtually all senior ecclesiastical patronage in England to the point of a 'despotism' over the Church. Subsequent research suggests this view has to be moderated significantly. Wolsey certainly did often pronounce on the fullness of his authority, implying at times that he could take control of any jurisdiction, diocese or religious house that he chose. He did this in much the same highly rhetorical way that he laid down the secular law as Chancellor. Warham was troubled by the jurisdictional implications of the presence of a resident legate *a latere* as a threat to his own *natus* legateship. As early as 1519, he had complained about Wolsey's legatine officials interfering in matters within his jurisdiction as archbishop of Canterbury, in derogation of his dignity and authority. By October 1522, Wolsey had established a legatine Court of Audience, a form of ecclesiastical supreme court which heard cases referred from diocesan canon law courts. Although its surviving records are little more than fragmentary, it seems that Wolsey, initially at least, did intend that it should supersede (or at least supervene over) the existing Court of Arches. The profitable business of probate, of proving wills concerned with property and bequests of more than £10 and in more than one diocese, was the preserve of the Court of Arches. After some opposition and further debate, in 1523, Wolsey and Warham agreed to share the proving of wills, with probate fees shared between them. Once again, however, little useful evidence survives of the workings of the joint-prerogative court. Wolsey's new court seems merely to have added another complicated layer to the existing ecclesiastical legal machinery under Canterbury's jurisdiction.

Under those powers first granted in April 1521, Wolsey apparently also summoned a Church Council at Westminster in 1523, principally to allow him to advertise his authority. It coincided with the king's calling of Parliament and issuing writs authorising the summoning of the northern Convocation of the Church, already under Wolsey as Archbishop of York, and the southern under Warham, who ordered a meeting at St Pauls. Hall says that Wolsey 'dissolved' the St Paul's meeting and summoned the clergy to Westminster instead. Polydore Vergil says this was an occasion of further

134   *Cardinal legate*

conflict between the cardinal and Warham, together with bishops Fox and Fisher who objected to the way Wolsey was carrying out his legatine responsibilities. The poet Skelton later mocked the episode and Wolsey in the lines: 'Gentle Paul laie doon thy sweard; For Peter of Westminster hath shaved thy beard'. It is not certain that any formal legatine 'council', as distinct from the usual convocations, actually met. Some gathering was evidently presided over by Wolsey at Westminster, but its outcomes are unknown.[23]

Another area where Wolsey's amplified legatine authority from 1521 did have an impact on bishops was the power to grant 'dispensations'. These were permissions that exempted individuals in particular cases from the rules of canon law that ordinarily governed a range of important personal and ecclesiastical issues, including marriage, ordination and the holding of benefices. For example, marriage dispensations were sought by the laity to enable couples within the prohibited degrees of consanguinity (that is being too closely related by blood) to marry. Most other dispensations were sought by the clergy over such issues as bars to ordination by reason of illegitimate birth, being underage for ordination to the priesthood, holding more than one benefice at a time (pluralism) and non-residence for various reasons, including study-leave at university. In addition, for some centuries beforehand, popes had devolved to legates, both *natus* and *a latere*, and also to some bishops, powers or 'faculties' to do a number of things, such as granting special 'graces' forgiving particularly grave sins in the places of their authority – but they usually had only limited powers of dispensation.

By the bulls of 1521, Wolsey was enabled to absolve from spiritual sanctions, award degree and papal titles and dispense upon a very wide range of issues concerning ordination and benefices. For example, he could forgive monks for the very serious, or 'reserved', sin of apostasy and transfer repented apostates to different orders. He had the faculty to reduce the age at which men could be admitted as sub-deacons, deacons and priests and could dispense to allow clergymen to hold up to four benefices in plurality. He had extensive powers to dispense in marriage cases, but he could not dispense in the so-called 'Levirate' cases, that is a marriage between a man and his childless brother's widow – exactly the situation faced by Henry VIII when he had wanted to marry Katherine of Aragon in 1509 and upon which much would, as we know, eventually turn.

So, while Wolsey was not unique in having power to dispense, his 'faculties' were more extensive than any other prelate in England precisely because he was a permanent, resident papal legate. His delegated jurisdiction allowed Wolsey to act almost as fully – though not quite – in response to petitioners of many kinds as could the papacy itself. Wolsey still pressed for further extensions of these powers, but Pope Adrian refused all demands, save extending his legatine status till August 1524.[24]

Clearly the pope had his reservations about the extent of Wolsey's authority, but the cardinal of England still had a friend in Rome in the person of Giulio de' Medici. In the spring of 1523, the papal chancellor warmly received John Clerk as the new English ambassador to the Holy See.[25] Both Giulio and Cardinal Campeggio supported Clerk's request for a lifetime legateship for Wolsey, but to no avail. Then, to Wolsey's private delight no doubt, Adrian died suddenly in September 1523. Once again Henry pressed Wolsey to become a candidate in the forthcoming conclave, although Wolsey told the king that his absence from Rome would count against him. He would, for himself, rather not put his hat in the ring as he did not have high hopes, but however things turned out, he would feel 'no less bound to the King than if he had attained the honour, to which he would never have aspired, except to please and serve the King'.[26] John Clerk went in to bat for Wolsey but from the outset warned that Cardinal de' Medici would be hard to beat, and so it proved. In November, he was duly elected as Pope Clement VII. That was still, in theory at least, an excellent result for Henry and Wolsey. For the second time in exactly 20 years, the Cardinal Protector of England had become the pope. He would understand the king of England's view of matters better than anyone else and be ready to work with such a loyal son of the Church as Henry – surely? Giulio's obvious successor as Protector was Campeggio, and this nomination was immediately sought by the man himself with the tacit approval of the new pope. Henry and Wolsey, however, made the king's agreement to such a nomination dependent upon a significant extension of Wolsey's legatine power. This time the new pope obliged handsomely. On 21 January 1524, Clement made Wolsey legate *a latere* for life, a position he had earnestly sought for six years. He did not, however, extend Wolsey's faculties any further, partly out of concern that the legate's omnicompetence was now

136   *Cardinal legate*

such that it might start to deprive the Curia of business and income from English and Welsh petitioners. Wolsey's predictable protests were quelled somewhat when, in April, he also gained Clement's formal authority for the foundation of what became Cardinal College, Oxford. Cardinal Campeggio was duly confirmed as absentee bishop of Salisbury later that year and held the post for a decade.[27]

Wolsey and the bishops

Armed now with lifetime delegated papal jurisdiction, Wolsey turned once more to the governance of the Church in England. As we have seen, his relations with the prominent members of the ecclesiastical hierarchy, and specifically the episcopate, were on the whole cordial, but his initial efforts to take their activity under his supervision, and some of their rights directly into his control, were resented by many, and very vocally by a few. Wolsey really had little to complain about when it came to his bishops. For a start, the English episcopate was, by any standards, first rate at the time Wolsey became legate in 1518. Archbishop Warham, Fox of Winchester, Fisher of Rochester, Ruthall of Durham and Tunstall of London led a group of men who were for the most part highly educated, orthodox, yet in varying degrees open to, and even patrons of, the 'new learning' Wolsey apparently championed. In contrast, for example, to so many of their French, German and Italian contemporaries, none were noblemen with any of the distracting dynastic ambitions and consequent political game-playing such status often entailed. Some had a gentry background, but most were of yeoman stock – just like Wolsey. Warham and Fox had held, before Wolsey's advent, two of the highest offices of state as Chancellor and Keeper of the Privy Seal, respectively. Cuthbert Tunstall, who became bishop of London in 1522, succeeded Bishop Ruthall of Durham as Keeper of the Privy Seal in May 1523. Many other bishops were also involved in aspects of royal administration, and a number, such as Nicholas West of Ely and the aforementioned John Clerk who became bishop of Bath and Wells, were royal secretaries and senior diplomats, as were Fox, Ruthall and Tunstall. These duties could take them away from the dioceses for long periods even if in most cases their duties were ably undertaken by vicars-general (or chancellors) and suffragan bishops, often drawn from the chapters of the cathedrals.

Cardinal legate 137

The majority of bishops still wanted to be active diocesan administrators and pastors. Most were committed to high standards of personal discipline and practice, which they were keen to impose alike on the parish clergy and monastic houses under their authority. Inevitably there were occasional rivalries and frictions between some bishops and the dean and chapters of their cathedrals over rights and privileges. Bishops sometimes clashed with each other along jurisdictional lines, and some frequently with Wolsey himself, but on the whole the legate seems to have acquired a remarkably competent and conscientious group of prelates. They were also quite long-lived, and there were comparatively few opportunities for him to appoint new men.[28]

These considerations, and the relatively little evidence that survives of Wolsey's actions as legate at diocesan level, might suggest that he had little real need to be concerned with the English episcopate. Yet, there were problems beyond absenteeism. Bishops were often thought too ostentatious, and a number of them, not least Warham and Wolsey himself of course, were enthusiastic builders of colleges or grand, luxuriously furnished, episcopal palaces. There were also simply too few bishoprics; 17 in England and 4 in Wales. By contrast, in Scotland, smaller in size and population than England, there were 12 dioceses. There were over 30 in Ireland. Nor were the English and Welsh dioceses equal in size or wealth. Wolsey was concerned about the sheer area of some and the capacity of their bishops properly to administer them. For example, the bishopric of Lincoln took in not only a considerable proportion of the west of East Anglia, but Oxfordshire as well and had an astonishing 1,736 parishes and 111 religious houses within it. That of York extended into much of the southern midlands. Winchester was also large, the bishop's lands extending to the southern border of London itself. The argument was that by creating new bishops and reducing the size of some of the existing dioceses, better pastoral care, visitations of parishes, religious houses and so on would be provided and that bishops would have a better impact on smaller areas.[29]

In November 1528, Wolsey was empowered, evidently in response to his own request, to dissolve a number of monasteries in order to create new cathedrals and dioceses. The bull also recognised the English crown's rights by giving Wolsey the capacity to appoint in Henry's name any first appointee to the proposed new

138   *Cardinal legate*

dioceses, only requiring their successors to be formally 'provided' to their benefices by the papacy – thus attracting annates to the papal treasury. Whatever their intention, these plans would have serious implications for those existing bishops whose dioceses would be reduced in area. Although the lands of the new dioceses would be paid for through the monastic dissolutions, the incumbents would still lose income from fees of different kinds. The monasteries proposed to be closed (or converted into cathedrals with chapters comprised of monks) might also reasonably be expected to object.

Clement VII was aware of these issues and asked whether the diocesan re-organisation Wolsey was proposing was really necessary. None of the detailed provisions of the bull allowing this to go ahead survive, but from his correspondence with Rome, it is evident that Wolsey sought authority to act without having to consult those concerned, precisely to avoid complicated legal and political opposition. Once again, however, no evidence of the cardinal's correspondence with the bishops about the proposed reorganisation has been found. The re-structuring of the episcopate and the appointment of more bishops of his choosing might seem to have been an ideal way for Wolsey to further his apparent concern for high standards. It would also allow him to determine new appointments, to act as patron and thereby increase his personal control of, or at least influence over, the episcopal hierarchy. In fact there were comparatively few appointments made to the episcopal bench during Wolsey's time, and of those, three were conferred on himself: Bath and Wells, after the deprivation of Castellesi in 1518, the bishopric of Durham in 1523, at the death of Thomas Ruthall and Winchester in 1529 in succession to his former patron Richard Fox. As we have seen, two others were occupied by Italians in the service of maintaining England's good relations with Rome. Worcester, held by Silvestro de' Gigli, went to Giulio de' Medici in 1521 and then to Girolamo Ghinucci in 1522. Salisbury went to Campeggio in 1524. All these appointments were as much the king's as Wolsey's, for his approval was needed for any of them, as the whole Consistory acknowledged on Campeggio's obtaining Salisbury.

Of the remaining seven new appointments between 1514 and 1529, there is little real evidence of Wolsey's patronage save in two instances. Archbishop Warham expressly thanked the cardinal for

Cardinal legate 139

making Cuthbert Tunstall Bishop of London in 1522, based in part at least on Tunstall's extensive diplomatic and administrative experience, both initially as Warham's chancellor and then as Master of the Rolls from 1516. The other was John Clerk, a canon lawyer and the man who, as we have noted, presented Henry's book to Pope Leo in 1521. He succeeded Wolsey in 1523 as bishop of Bath and Wells. He returned to Rome at the end of the year from where he specifically acknowledged that Wolsey had made him a bishop. Obviously talented, Clerk had come within Wolsey's ambit as early as 1514 with the death of his former patron Cardinal Bainbridge and, as we have seen, actively assisted Wolsey's first candidacy for the papacy. Theirs was evidently a close relationship.[30] He continued to serve occasionally as an ambassador. In August 1526, Clerk wrote to Wolsey from the French court about an encounter with the king's youngest son, Charles, then aged about four. As Clerk was speaking with Louise of Savoy, and to the amusement of his grandmother, Charles tugged at Clerk's hand and asked whether, as the ambassador of his father's friend King Henry, he would take him to see his older brothers then hostages in Spain. The episode shows Clerk to have had something of the diplomat's charm, and its relation in a letter like this suggests a reasonable personal familiarity with Wolsey.[31]

It has been suggested that John Longland's appointment as bishop of Lincoln in 1521 might also have been due to Wolsey's influence. He was an academic theologian and talented preacher, whom Warham commended for a set of reforming sermons he published. A correspondent of Erasmus, Longland became the bishop in 1521 and was shortly afterwards made royal almoner and confessor. He was present at Paul's Churchyard to hear Bishop Fisher's sermon and afterward initiated a search for heretical material in Oxford and Buckinghamshire. He worked with Thomas Cromwell on the dissolution of the monastic houses to provide funds for Cardinal College, and he preached at the laying of its foundation stone in 1525. As bishop, he seems to have shared and perhaps encouraged Wolsey's drive for reformed standards of behaviour among secular and monastic clergy in his diocese. He even intervened in the Augustinian priory at Dorchester in Oxfordshire, appointing a new prior there whom he thought more suitable.

The year 1524 appears to have been when the general pattern of relations between the bishops and the cardinal legate were

140   *Cardinal legate*

settled. In the spring, the bishops of Hereford, Ely and Longland of Lincoln became the first of a majority of English bishops who made 'compositions' or agreements with the cardinal whereby they secured their episcopal rights, including those to visit parishes and monastic houses and to prove wills where bequests were wholly within their diocese. In return Wolsey took a share, probably about a third, of the 'spiritualities', that is, the fees to which the bishops were entitled in carrying out these duties. Spiritualities generally comprised a relatively small but not insignificant proportion of a bishop's income. These arrangements in place, Wolsey appears broadly content to have shared their income, so the more 'business' they generated, the better for him. The plans for creating new dioceses never came to fruition under Wolsey but were in the spirit of reform of his time and were probably the basis of Henry VIII's later plans for restructuring. These would have increased the number of dioceses to 36, more or less along county lines, and would have allowed for incomes of about £1,000 per diocese. These, too, never came to fruition but, in the 1540s, the king did create six new English bishoprics; the short-lived Westminster, together with Bristol, Chester, Gloucester, Peterborough and Oxford.[32]

Wolsey and the monasteries

From 1524, Wolsey turned once more to the supervision of religious houses. He was met with a reasonable degree of cooperation, but some quarrels arose as well. Understandably perhaps, he saw the leadership of these communities as crucial to his reform initiatives and took a close interest in the elections of abbots and priors, often in controversial circumstances. Perhaps the most famous of these elections was the one for the prioress at Wilton in 1528 in which Wolsey interviewed all the prospective candidates and had chosen the woman he thought best for the position before Henry intervened directly, in the circumstances we have already considered (see Chapter 3). Less well known, but just as illustrative, is a dispute that had arisen earlier in the decade between Abbot John Birchenshawe of Chester and Bishop Blythe of Coventry and Lichfield within whose diocese Birchenshawe's abbey of St Werburgh was located. The abbot had asserted he was exempted from all episcopal supervision and entitled to wear bishop's vestments or 'pontificals'. Bishop Blythe demanded that the abbot be disciplined by Rome, and Leo had asked Wolsey to resolve the dispute. It was not, however, until 1524 that Wolsey finally acted. Now as lifetime legate, he sided with the bishop and deprived the abbot of his position. Nevertheless, as the county palatinate of Chester was a separate jurisdiction from England, he was careful while removing the abbot still to confirm the privileges of the abbey itself. These included exemption from supervision not just by the local bishop but of Canterbury as well. Birchenshawe's high and mighty behaviour was exactly the sort of thing Wolsey clamped down on in the Church as legate as he also did in wider society as Lord Chancellor. The new abbot was John Highfield, the sub-prior of the abbey, nominated to the post by Wolsey, doubtless to foster order and continuity in the community there and because he was a more amenable figure than his predecessor, more willing to finesse questions of privileges and exemptions and unwilling to provoke the local bishop. Abbot Birchenshawe had also been involved in a land lease dispute between two men, one of whom, George Legh, was the husband of Joan Larke, Wolsey's former partner. The resolution of the dispute took a long time, and contemporaries accused Wolsey of bias when it was finally resolved in Legh's favour, but the implications of the case for Chester's relations with the crown of its being heard in Chancery involved the cardinal's role as Chancellor rather than legate. Birchenshawe had the last laugh however. He was back as abbot at Chester soon after Wolsey's fall in 1529.[33]

In January 1525, acting under Wolsey's orders, Dr John Allen and the same Dr Henry Standish, who had been involved in the 'benefit of clergy' and *praemunire* controversy a decade earlier, attempted to conduct a visitation of the Observant Franciscan convent at Greenwich. Standish was now the Bishop of St Asaph (at the king's insistence over Wolsey's preferred candidate incidentally). So greatly did the community object that a substantial number of friars absconded, as a way of expressing their unwillingness to participate in the supervisory visit. The Greenwich convent belonged to a strict, reformist branch of the Franciscans, committed to the founding statues of the order – hence the name. The convent was also close to the royal family, having been founded by Edward IV and supported by Henry VII and his son in turn. The Greenwich Observants were, perhaps for these reasons, quite an independently

142   *Cardinal legate*

minded house. In common with the Order in general, they were formally exempt from episcopal supervision and guarded their autonomy from all ecclesiastical authorities apart from Rome itself. They asserted that their own internal supervisory processes were sufficient to maintain good standards of conduct among members. In August 1525, however, Wolsey as legate (in the person of his two agents or 'commissaries') was Rome suddenly come to them. He had by then secured a special bull to override the Observants' known objection to his intended visitation and had in return promised to use his legatine powers carefully and discreetly. Having got wind of this bull, the Observants had objected in Rome and got a two-year suspension of it, so their view was that in the summer of 1525, Wolsey's agents should not have attempted a visitation at all. In the end the leaders of the community had to accept it, but the absconding of some members expressed their profound reservations about what Wolsey was doing and his apparent lack of respect for the tradition of self-governance among the English Observants.[34]

It was not so much in the supervision or reform of monastic orders as in the dissolution of a significant number of religious houses that Wolsey's impact on the English Church was perhaps most direct. Wolsey suppressed over 25 religious communities in the south of England, the Midlands and East Anglia in order to fund his two educational institutions, Cardinal College at Oxford University and the College of St Mary – also known as Cardinal College – at Ipswich, a feeder school for his Oxford foundation. The establishment, and the curricula, of the two institutions will be discussed later, but for the present it is necessary to note how focused, efficient and speedy was the operation to dissolve them. The decision to establish these new centres of learning was legally and personally a joint project of the cardinal and king. For example, the papal bulls allowing Wolsey to dissolve St Frideswide's Augustinian priory in Oxford, which would become the site of Cardinal College, were issued on 3 April 1524, subject to the king's approval. This followed on 19 April, so speed was evidently paramount. That Henry was enthusiastic is clear from a letter written by John Longland in January 1525, who had been commissioned to dissolve St Frideswide's. He reported Henry as praising the cardinal's work and saying, 'that more good shall come of this your honourable foundation than any man can esteem'. Founding educational

Cardinal legate 143

establishments seemed to appeal to Henry in the mid-1520s. His later ambition to be a patron of education himself produced two places of learning. These were Trinity College, Cambridge, formed by the merger of two previously existing colleges, and King Henry VIII's College (subsequently Christ Church), Oxford, which was essentially the refoundation of Wolsey's establishment.[35]

The dissolving of each monastic house involved significant legal complexities with Wolsey having to be invested with ownership of the lands and property of each from the founder or his or her descendants or successors, in order that he could then legally convey the income to the two establishments at Oxford and at Ipswich. He had a team of lawyers, initially led by John Allen, a canon of Lincoln cathedral. He also had other specialists working on this, including the man who would eventually very closely supervise the whole operation, Thomas Cromwell. He first entered Wolsey's service in July 1524 and very quickly assumed a pivotal role establishing both Cardinal College and St Mary's at Ipswich. Initial permission was given for the suppression of 22 houses in the dioceses of Coventry and Lichfield, Lincoln, Salisbury, Rochester, Chichester, London and Norwich.[36] The members of these communities were re-homed, and some priors and abbots were appointed to leadership roles in other houses as compensation for losing their original places. The number of houses involved and the complexity of the operation provoked unease in some establishments, and several approached Cromwell, expressing concern as to whether their houses were on his not-so-little list. Wolsey was aware of this, and in February 1525, he assured Henry that everything was being done correctly according to the king's commission. With 'your gracious aid and assistance converting the same', he told Henry, he would ensure that the income from the dissolved houses would be given 'unto *your* intended College of Oxford for the increase of good letters and virtue'. His emphasis on Henry as, in effect, the patron of the whole project is significant. Even this enterprise, so wholly identified by others as his alone, Wolsey envisaged as a joint undertaking with the king.[37] Wolsey was occupied with a host of concerns in 1525 and spent very little personal time on his college projects, but by then had placed Cromwell in charge of virtually the entire process, and he kept the cardinal well informed of what was going on. Whether Wolsey did the same for the king is less likely.

144   *Cardinal legate*

In the controversy over the appointment of the abbess of Wilton in 1528, Henry would warn Wolsey to be careful as to how he went about raising funds for his colleges as rumours had reached the king that it was being done for Wolsey's own aggrandisement and without due care and attention and proper justification for the dissolutions in each instance. Similar allegations would surface at the time of Wolsey's fall in 1529.

The complicated process of winding up over 20 houses took the best part of four years to complete. Some of the revenues of the houses in East Anglia originally intended for the Oxford college had to be used in setting up the feeder school in Ipswich, leaving a deficit which Cromwell addressed in the last years of Wolsey's power. He concentrated his attentions during 1528 on the East Anglian school, which, in April, he reported to Wolsey was progressing well and that 'the like was never seen for largeness, beauty, sumptuous, curious and substantial building'. He also told the cardinal that the chapel was already up and running in good order.[38] The school itself was operating by September that year. A further three houses were dissolved at Felixstowe, Rumburgh and Bromehill that month, their possessions being transferred to Ipswich by January 1529. The following month, the lands of the houses of Stanesgate and Blackmore in East Anglia, by then belonging to Cardinal College, were also transferred to St Mary's. Cromwell was chiefly responsible for ensuring the orderly transfer of the monastic possessions to both Wolsey's foundations, leasing their lands once acquired, and more generally expediting all other administrative and legal business for them. This extensive experience and his knowledge of the cardinal's many different financial interests made him the ideal man to wind up his former master's affairs after Wolsey's death in 1530. That work in turn helped him to make his way, as quite a few others in Wolsey's household had before him, into the king's service by the early 1530s.[39]

Education and heresy

Wolsey saw education, and the founding of new schools and university colleges, as the best way to defend orthodoxy and guard against heretical ideas among the clergy. He has often been accused of being soft on, or indifferent to, heresy. It has equally often been

Cardinal legate 145

forgotten that during the early 1520s in England, as elsewhere, the boundaries between legitimate, critical, scriptural exegesis and heretical opinion were often unclear. Wolsey certainly drew a fine line between the new humanist exploration of the scripture in its original languages, as favoured by Erasmus, and the unforeseen consequences of such study in the formation of heretical opinion. He was content to allow scholars to continue their intellectual explorations, provided this was kept to academic circles and that they did not possess or distribute proscribed books. From 1514 he supported several evangelically minded scholars at Cambridge and more generally the 'new' learning, especially the study of Greek, strongly promoted there by Lady Margaret Beaufort and John Fisher, the university's Chancellor. Wolsey was splendidly received by the university in 1517 while on pilgrimage to Walsingham in Norfolk. More splendidly, in fact, than had been either Henry's sister Mary who visited in 1516, or Queen Katherine who came later in 1520, or even the king himself, when he visited the university two years later. Cambridge, the university where the humanist learning of which Wolsey apparently approved had first taken root, was clearly angling for greater patronage from him. Erasmus himself had been a visiting scholar at Queen's College. By contrast, Oxford remained more traditional and orthodox in its educational outlook and curriculum, and this was something Wolsey was trying to change.[40]

It was news of the publication of William Tyndale's English translation of the New Testament in Cologne in 1525 that prompted Wolsey to take up the fight against heresy anew. Probably tipped off by agents in Germany about the role of merchants in importing Lutheran-influenced materials into England, Wolsey ordered a 'secret search' for them, including Tyndale's translation, in London and surrounds. In January 1526, there was a raid on the German merchants of the Steelyard by a posse of king's councillors, knights and noblemen in which Sir Thomas More took a prominent part. The raid was not exactly forensic, but did result in the detention of a number of merchants on suspicion of heresy. The same month, the prior of the Cambridge Austin Friars, Robert Barnes, was also arrested after giving a very anti-clerical sermon on Christmas Eve 1525. He was interviewed personally by Wolsey on 8 February 1526. Barnes later described how mild and good-humoured

146   *Cardinal legate*

Wolsey had been during this meeting. Behind closed doors, Wolsey seems to have allowed Barnes to make his case to some extent at least, even accepting that he was one of its targets, before sending him before a group of specially appointed legatine commissioners, including John Clerk, Bishop of Bath and Wells, to whom Barnes (temporarily as it turned out) abjured his heretical or at least virulently anti-clerical opinions. Wolsey's commission was objected to by Cuthbert Tunstall, the Bishop of London, on the basis that it contravened his episcopal jurisdiction.[41]

On 11 February 1526, Robert Barnes and some four or five Hanse merchants arrested in January were paraded at St Paul's Churchyard, there publicly to recant their Lutheran heresy, and to witness their books being burnt – the first public abjuration of this kind in England. A proclamation was made that all copies of Luther's works and other banned writings in England should be surrendered by a certain date, under threat of excommunication and trial for heresy. Printers and booksellers compelled under financial penalties not to import heretical texts. Bishop Fisher of Rochester once again preached a sermon in the cathedral before an excited and noisy congregation. Partly for that reason, it was shortly afterwards published. Fisher preached before Wolsey who was seated on a scaffold or platform, accompanied by 36 lesser prelates and chaplains. Robed in purple, the colour of penitence, Wolsey listened as Fisher condemned Luther's heresy, warned of the consequences of heeding it and called on all who had been influenced in its direction to return to the tenets of the true faith.[42]

The difference between this event and the similar one in May 1521 was that it expressed a far more active concern and approach to investigating the extent and whereabouts of heresy in the capital and the two university towns at least. No longer was there a pretence that the legate was pre-emptively disinfecting the realm of heresy, as it were, by mere refutation of Luther's doctrine. Now the rhetoric was of repentance for its acknowledged presence and of combating it forcefully under the full rigour of the law. Yet as Craig D'Alton has pointed out, a carrot and stick approach continued to be adopted in individual cases, and Wolsey's emphasis remained on securing quiet, private abjurations from educated men like Barnes, wherever possible. They were given every opportunity to embrace orthodoxy again. This was thought to be a more effective way of

Cardinal legate 147

dealing with individuals. It was preferable to advertising the extent of Lutheran influence in society, limited though that always was in general terms, in public heresy trials. There were remarkably few such cases between 1526 and Wolsey's fall three years later.

Perhaps the most famous of these trials were those of Thomas Bilney (who had been influential on Barnes) and Thomas Arthur in November–December 1527. Both had spoken out against the 'insolency of the clergy', as John Foxe later put it in his account of their trial. Wolsey interviewed them personally, and again his use of his legatine status to do so became an issue. While the hearing had begun at Westminster, it concluded in London with Bishop Tunstall included among the commissioners. The defendants finally abjured before him, and he absolved them as Wolsey's commissioner, but also as the local diocesan bishop in whose jurisdiction they appeared.[43] Another Cambridge man examined by Wolsey was Hugh Latimer, then the university's Chaplain, who was critical of the clergy and advocated the publication of the Bible in English, despite the ban on Tyndale's translation. He defended himself so adroitly and eloquently that Wolsey gave him licence to preach anywhere in England. Five years after Wolsey's death, in a very changed political and ecclesiastical context, Hugh Latimer was made Bishop of Worcester in succession to Ghinucci.[44]

The case of Thomas Garrett raised some uncomfortable contradictions for Wolsey, not least the indirect role played in it by the man who was, by this time, the cardinal's most important servant and supporter in his educational programme. Garrett was an MA scholar at Cardinal College recruited not from Cambridge but from Oxford itself. Evangelical in outlook, he also operated as a distributor of books and other materials in Oxford and was arrested in February 1528 for supplying banned writings. Detained briefly, Garrett escaped the custody of the university authorities led by Dr John London, the Warden of New College who was also Wolsey's principal contact and investigator at the university. He revealed that it was one John Clerk, originally a Cambridge man and now a canon of Cardinal College (not to be confused with the bishop of the same name), who had been lent or sold suspect books by Garrett, together with some 22 or more students from Wolsey's and other Oxford colleges. Clerk was revealed to be the leader of an evangelical circle in Oxford. This provoked something of a scandal as men of Wolsey's

148   *Cardinal legate*

foundation were seen to be subverting the reformist but orthodox educational aims for which it had been established. How had Garrett and Clerk even become members of the college in the first place? The answer may well be through Thomas Cromwell. He was sympathetic to calls for reform within the Church generally and with Wolsey's desire that his two foundations become agents of educational development. Yet the kind of reform Cromwell wanted and what Wolsey sought to promote may have been two rather different things. By 1528, when the Garrett scandal broke, Cromwell was acting as both Surveyor and Receiver-General at Cardinal College. He was recognised as an influential man, not only in the college's establishment, but in its daily management as well, by those eager to obtain places for themselves or others on the staff or as students. His formal roles at Cardinal College focused on attracting scholars from Cambridge to Oxford, arranging their transfers and the like, but he evidently had some say in who was recruited. Cromwell had by then acquired significant insights into the state of monasticism in England. He maintained friendships with a number of reformist abbots, monks and friars, even as his misgivings about aspects of monasticism itself grew stronger. He was also known to evangelically minded men in Cambridge and other places in East Anglia where the bulk of his work on the dissolution of monastic houses was concentrated. Garrett was known to him through associates in Boston, Lincolnshire, where Garrett had at one time been the head of the local grammar school, and it is quite likely that Cromwell played some part at least in attracting him to Cardinal College.

Wolsey was desperate to secure Garrett's re-arrest and conveyance to Westminster, to expel this cuckoo from the nest. Yet Dr London and others urged that the whole matter be handled with the utmost discretion in order to minimise the reputational damage to the university. Accordingly, most of the erring young men were reprimanded privately. John Clerk was held within the cellars at Cardinal College, where he became ill and died in August 1528. Garrett was finally examined in London by a panel once again headed by Bishop Tunstall. He, too, abjured his heresy relatively quickly and quietly – but only temporarily. Garrett maintained his Lutheran beliefs and an association with Thomas Cromwell for a further decade. On 30 July 1540, he, together with Barnes, was burnt for heresy – two days after Cromwell's execution on Tower Hill.[45]

The legate's Church, or the king's?

Wolsey was a strong and powerful papal legate, but to what ends he directed that power remains debatable, as does the strength of the Church in England under him. Like Morton, Wolsey used his authority to enhance what might be called the 'monarchical church'. That is one where the demarcation lines between papal and royal authority over the Church were drawn as distinctly as possible and never in derogation of crown-established rights and Henry's authority as emperor within his realm – long before the break with Rome. As legate, Wolsey affirmed what Henry stated. Whatever the technicalities of their status under canon law, the English clergy were subject to royal jurisdiction. All of this, even as Wolsey supported the younger Henry's personal devotion to the Holy See and placed himself at the centre of the relationship, interpreting king to pope and vice versa. So far as he could, he finessed their contacts in ways that ensured the rights of each appeared to be respected and allowed relations between them to be conducted as far as possible amicably and to mutual satisfaction. Wolsey's legatine powers had first been renewed and finally made for life principally in order that he could raise revenue for the papacy and bring about reform of the clergy in England. He busily assured three popes in succession of his good intent on both these fronts.

Wolsey was genuinely interested in ecclesiastical reform, conscious, as was Henry, of the criticisms of Erasmus and other humanist scholars. He made large rhetorical claims for himself about his determination to bring it about. Typically, his approach was to arrogate to himself as much authority as possible as legate in order to carry this programme out, to the frequent consternation of senior clergy like Warham (himself a reformist) and supporters of leading monastic houses. As with his legal responsibilities, this centralising tendency was also often less effective than he pretended. It did not impress his fellow bishops, and both Popes Leo and Clement received complaints that Wolsey was throwing his weight around. This was particularly true of his much-vaunted legatine council. It published reforms which were largely traditional, and it was still very much up to the bishops to ensure these were implemented at local level. Wolsey was right that many of the 17 English dioceses were too large, making oversight difficult for incumbent bishops, even if the majority of those bishops were hard-working and capable administrators. Under their protection, the secular clergy within these dioceses were largely untouched directly by Wolsey's reforms.

Wolsey's attitude to monastic reform was characterised by the same authoritarian approach as towards the dioceses. The visitations his officers made to monastic houses were generally, although not universally, accepted, and they gave instructions for improved lifestyles among Benedictine and Augustinian houses. When it came to 'exempted' orders, particularly the Observant Franciscans, his interventions were perceived (probably correctly) to be more about asserting his authority as legate and being seen to do something than from any genuine need of serious reform. The real focus of Wolsey's reforming interest was education, which he saw as the surest way to instil in future clergy the knowledge, skill and moral standing needed to build and maintain high standards of behaviour in the Church as a whole, and as the best defence against the threat of heresy. This was the motive behind his foundation of public lectureships, his two colleges at Oxford and Ipswich and his plans for diocesan feeder schools. It also drove the considerable number of dissolutions he ordered, that Cromwell organised and that disconcerted very many within the monastic ranks.

There is little real substance to the charge that Wolsey was 'soft' on heresy, although his approach to it may have been 'softly softly'. It was a charge from which even the poet John Skelton, who was often a critic, was prepared effectively to defend him. He suggested obliquely in a poem, admittedly commissioned by and dedicated to Wolsey, that the trial of Bilney showed the Church's authorities were on top of the problem of heresy especially among university men to whose ranks it was almost (but never exclusively) confined. In fact, Luther's ideas reached into England beyond academics to the ranks of merchants and artisans in London and other towns and cities but never in sufficient strength seriously to challenge the authorities' capacity to respond.

Under Wolsey, they were reasonably effective in keeping a lid on the problem in the short-term. Nevertheless, it must also be admitted that some of the abjurations this policy secured proved worthless, and by them several prominent evangelicals slipped through Wolsey's hands. Men like Latimer and Barnes went on to have significant direct and indirect roles in influencing Henry's attitudes to the papacy and in the formulation of his religious policy in the years immediately after Wolsey's fall and the break with Rome. Wolsey's approach to heresy, as to episcopal and monastic reform (rather as to legal reform), was short-term and reactive, not fully articulated and not followed through as effectively as it might have been. His ambitions in this, as in virtually every sphere, ever outran his capacity to achieve them. Unlike his wider aims in the use of his legatine authority, however, his approach to heresy was supported by a majority of his clergy and by key members of the English episcopate. It was also evidently supported by the king. Whatever its longer-term consequences for the Church in England, to modern sensibilities at least, it redounds to Wolsey's credit that during his whole time as bishop and legate, the cardinal never personally sent a single individual to burn at the stake for heresy.[46]

Notes

1 Cavendish, pp. 16–17.
2 Pollard, pp. 165–216; P. Partner, *The Pope's Men: The Papal Civil Service in the Renaissance* (Oxford, 1990), pp. 20–46.
3 *LP* IV, 4881 Cameggio to papal secretary Sanga, 28 October 1528.
4 G. L. Harris, 'Cardinal Beaufort: Patriot or Usurer', *TRHS* 20 (1970): 129–48; see also G. L. Harris, *Cardinal Beaufort: A Study of Lancastrian Ascendancy and Decline* (Oxford, 1989).
5 C. S. L. Davies, 'Bishop John Morton, the Holy See and the Accession of Henry VII', *EHR* 102 (402) (1987): 2–30; S. Bradley, *John Morton: Adversary of Richard III, Power Behind the Tudors* (Stroud, 2019).
6 C. Richardson, *Reclaiming Rome: Cardinals in the Fifteenth Century* (Leiden, 2009), pp. 4–7, 21–4.
7 J. Dumont and L. Fagnart (eds.), *Georges Ier d'Amboise 1460–1510: Une figure plurielle de la Renaissance* (Rennes, 2013).
8 S. May, 'Establishing the Tudor Dynasty: The Role of Francesco Piccolomini in Rome as First Cardinal Protector of England', *Royal Studies Journal* 4 (2) (2017): 103–40.
9 W. Wilkie, *The Cardinal Protectors of England: Rome and the Tudors before the Reformation* (Cambridge, 1974), pp. 104–9.
10 Ibid., p. 110.
11 Hall, p. 593; *LP* II ii, 4333 An anonymous description of the reception of Cardinal Campeggio.

152   *Cardinal legate*

12 *LP* II, Appendix, 52 Draft of a letter to Henry in Brian Tuke's hand, dated from context September 1518; Bernardo Dovixi (1470–1520) was made Cardinal of Santa Maria in Portico by Leo X.

13 *LP* III i, 137 Wolsey to Gigli, Lambeth, 25 March 1519.

14 Gwyn, pp. 267–70.

15 Wilkie, pp. 112–14.

16 *LP* III i, 693; Fox, *Letters*, pp. 115–16.

17 Ibid., 1371 Charles V to his Audiencer Haneton, Brussels, 27 June 1521; 1297, 1298 Henry and Wolsey to Leo X, Greenwich, 21 May 1521 for Henry's offer of the book and of the bishopric of Worcester to Giulio de' Medici.

18 C. W. D'Alton, 'The Suppression of Lutheran Heretics in England, 1526–1529', *Journal of Ecclesiastical History* 54 (2) (April 2005): 228–53.

19 *LP* III i, 1802 Treaty dated Calais, 24 November 1521; *LP* III i, 1796 Memorandum of negotiating points with imperial representatives, November 1522; Gwyn, p. 157.

20 *LP* III i, 1884 Bernado de Mesa to Charles V, London, 19 December 1521 on Henry's enthusiasm; 1960 Clerk to Wolsey, Rome, 13 January 1522.

21 Gwyn, p. 50.

22 G. Bernard, *The Late Medieval English Church: Vitality and Vulnerability before the Break with Rome* (New Haven & London, 2012), pp. 1–16 for the most recent detailed consideration of the Hunne affair. See also R. Dale, 'The Death of an Alleged Heretic, Richard Hunne (d.1514) Explained', *Reformation and Renaissance Review* 15 (2) (April 2013): 133–53.

23 Hall, p. 657.

24 P. D. Clarke, 'Rivalling Rome: Cardinal Wolsey and Dispensations', in P. D. Clarke and M. Questier (eds.), *Papal Authority and the Limits of the Law in Tudor England*, Camden Miscellany 36, Camden Fifth Series 48 (Cambridge,2015), pp. 1–100, esp. pp. 1–9.

25 Wilkie, pp. 131–6.

26 *LP* III, 3372 Wolsey to Henry VIII, The More, 30 September 1523; 3464, 3514, 3592 for Clerk's reports from Rome on the conclave.

27 S. Fletcher, *The Popes and Britain* (London, 2017), p. 81; J. Curthoys, *The Cardinal's College: Christ Church, Chapter and Verse* (London, 2012), p. 5.

28 Bernard, *Late Medieval English Church*, pp. 49–76; C. Michon, *La crosse et le sceptre: Les prélats d'Etat sous François Ier et Henri VIII* (Rennes, 2008) for a comparative study of these two very different groups of prelates.

29 Pollard, pp. 194–208 cf. Gwyn, pp. 464–9.

30 *LP* III, 1972, 3594 for letters from Warham and Clerk respectively; Gwyn, p. 295 for the bishops and appointees under Wolsey; *LP* IV i, 986/7 Consistory letters to Henry and Wolsey regarding Salisbury, Rome, 2 January 1525.

31 BL, Cotton MS Caligula D IX, fos. 246–51 [*LP* IV i, 2416] Clerk to Wolsey; Amboise, 21 August.

Cardinal legate　153

32　S. E. Lehmberg, *The Reformation of Cathedrals: Cathedrals in English Society, 1485–1603* (Princeton, New Jersey, 1988), pp. 84–6.

33　Thornton, pp. 193–5.

34　K. Brown, 'Wolsey and the Ecclesiastical Order: The Case of the Franciscan Observants', in Gunn and Lindley, pp. 219–38.

35　*LP* IV i, 995 Longland to Wolsey, Eltham, 5 January 1525; R. Rex and C. Armstrong, 'Henry VIII's Ecclesiastical and Collegiate Foundations', *Historical Research* 75 (190) (November 2002): 390–407.

36　P. J. Ward, 'The Origins of Thomas Cromwell's Public Career: Service under Cardinal Wolsey and Henry VIII 1524–30' (Unpublished London University PhD dissertation, 1999), pp. 53–8 for the dating of Cromwell's entry into Wolsey's service and a list of the dissolved houses.

37　*St. P.* I, 153–6 Wolsey to Henry, 5 February 1525. My italics.

38　*LP* IV ii, 4135 Cromwell to Wolsey, 2 April 1528.

39　Ward, p. 20; D. MacCulloch, *Thomas Cromwell: A Life* (London, 2018), pp. 133–71 for the period of Cromwell's transition to direct royal service.

40　S. Wabuda, 'Wolsey and Cambridge', *British Catholic History* 32 (3) (2015): 280–92.

41　R. Barnes, *A Supplicacion unto the Most Gracyous Prince Henry the VIII* (London, 1534) [*STC* 1471].

42　Foxe, V, pp. 418–19.

43　Ibid., IV, pp. 620–32. C. W. D'Alton, 'The Suppression of Lutheran Heretics in England, 1526–1529', *Journal of Ecclesiastical History* 54 (2) (April 2003): 228–53.

44　Wabuda, pp. 290–2.

45　*LP* IV ii, 3968; III, 1193 Warham to Wolsey [re-dated by D'Alton to] 8 March 1528; On Cromwell's role see MacCulloch, *Cromwell*, pp. 64–74.

46　Hall, p. 708; M. J. Dowling, *Fisher of Men: A Life of John Fisher 1469–1535* (Basingstoke, 1999), p. 101; D'Alton, pp. 236–40; Gwyn, p. 480. At least four were burnt in Lincoln diocese during his chancellorship, but not for Lutheran heresy.

5 Cardinal benefactor

Wolsey's cultural and educational patronage

The study of humanities, hitherto somewhat fallen, is rebuilt; the liberal arts, still struggling with the champions of ignorance, are supported by your encouragement, protected by your power, gilded in your reflected glory, and nourished by your munificence as you offer princely salaries to attract outstanding scholars to come and teach.[1]

Thus, Erasmus of Rotterdam, sixteenth-century Europe's foremost man of letters, praised Thomas Wolsey as a patron of learning in the spring of 1519. As ever, Erasmus gilded the lily in flattering an important royal servant. Yet his words offer a comparatively rare, positive contemporary view of Wolsey as a significant cultural benefactor in early Tudor England. It is a view of him largely forgotten in the popular imagination and, until relatively recently, among historians as well. During his ascendancy, Wolsey's educational and architectural patronage exceeded that even of Henry himself and gave the lead, in scale and ambition at least, to much that followed him. His capacity to promote the arts and letters in the way that Erasmus endorsed depended upon the cardinal's power and wealth as an ecclesiastical and political patron. The maintenance of his exceptional status demanded constant affirmation and expression through the munificence expected of him. Although Wolsey's first examples in such munificence were set by his predecessors, particularly Cardinal Archbishop Morton, he also looked immediately to Continental exemplars such as Georges, Cardinal d'Amboise and his contemporary cardinals in France and Italy, more so, perhaps, than to any of his fellow English prelates.

Wolsey as patron

By the time Erasmus praised him, Wolsey was Archbishop of York, the cardinal legate of England and the Chancellor. Contrary perhaps to the popular misconception of the medieval English Church, Wolsey was exceptional among ecclesiastical peers because he held more than one principal benefice at the same time. As well as being Archbishop of York, he was bishop of Bath and Wells from 1518 to 1523, and for the following six years to 1529, he held Durham. From then until his death the following year, he held Winchester, the richest see in England (although Wolsey did not enjoy that wealth). He also effectively controlled the sees of Worcester and Salisbury, both held by absentee Italians. He was also commendatory abbot of St Albans from 1521. These positions, together with his role as Chancellor, his pensions from the king of France and the emperor and presents given him on particular occasions, provided him with an annual income estimated at·the height of his power to be the astronomical sum of £30,000, comfortably exceeding that of the dukes of the realm and rivalled only by that of the king himself. Something of the scale of Wolsey's wealth is conveyed in Giustinian's description of what is probably York Place given to the Venetian Senate at the end of his embassy in 1519. The cardinal, he noted:

> has a very fine palace, where one traverses eight rooms before reaching his audience chamber, and they are all hung with tapestry, which is changed once a week. He always has a sideboard of plate worth 25,000 ducats, wherever he may be; and his silver is estimated at 150,000 ducats. In his own chamber there is always a cupboard [display shelves] of vessels to the amount of 30,000 ducats.[2]

Wolsey's various bishoprics brought with them rights of appointment to hundreds of church benefices and dignities, quite apart from his supervising authority over benefices as legate *a latere*. His wealth enabled him to recruit considerable numbers of clergy and gentry servants, assistants and advisors to his household and immediate entourage and then to appoint them to places in his gift. Wolsey focused the recruitment to his household on the sons of noblemen, gentlemen and yeomanry who showed the necessary aptitudes. They formed the core of a wider circle of clients that fed directly into the royal affinity. For this pattern of patronage to continue and increase, education was essential. Valuing his own education as he did, and the opportunities for advancement it had afforded him, Wolsey intended to found many schools and at least one university college to promote learning certainly, as Erasmus said he should, but chiefly perhaps in order to train young men for service in the Church and for the crown.

It is important to remember in this context that as a 'self-made man', in our terms at least, Wolsey was not an ecclesiastical dynast. In this respect, he was very similar to his English episcopal colleagues but very different from many of his Continental ones. He had no large family of brothers, uncles, nephews and other kin in the upper ranks of the Church as did the cardinals of the Medici, Este or Farnese families. He could not therefore build a personal affinity centred on wide and complex family connections as they did. On the other hand, he was spared the need to promote relatives' dynastic ambitions and having to deal with family rivalries and disputes. True, he protected and promoted as far as he could Joan Larke's two brothers and his natural son, Thomas Wynter. Thomas Lupset, one of the foremost English scholars of his day, was the boy's tutor when both went to Padua in 1522 when Wynter was about 12. By October 1526, Wynter was in Paris, there to continue his studies in Latin, Greek and French. He was met and looked after by Dr John Taylor, then the English ambassador at Francis I's court, who oversaw his settling into the house of his first Parisian tutor, the Scots humanist Florens Volunzenus. Wynter lived in a small residence called the Commanderie de Saint Jean-de-Lateran in the university quarter. Despite this support and apparently ideal setting for his studies, Wynter seems to have lacked application and had made no significant progress by 1529.[3] Perhaps this did not matter so much, as his father looked after his clerical career very well. From 1523 onwards, Wynter collected a series of livings including the archdeaconries of York, Richmond and Suffolk. He was also made Dean of Wells. Towards the end of his time in power, Wolsey tried unsuccessfully to obtain further benefices for his son. Yet one son, even one so generously provided for, does not an ecclesiastical dynasty make.

Cardinal benefactor   157

As ever, the key to Wolsey's power remained the king, not his genetic family, and since his earliest days in Henry's service, that power had made him the realm's foremost patronage broker. This brokerage was centred first and foremost on his own household which, as George Cavendish was at pains to emphasise, was large, multi-faceted and, in the contemporary general sense of the term, constituted his 'family'.

Cavendish's description of the household estimates it to have had between 400 and 500 inhabitants. No complete list of household officers survives against which to check this. The main evidence for its size comes from three lists for parliamentary subsidy assessments made between 1523 and 1527 that are principally concerned with laypeople. The first list has a total of 429 persons. The subsidy lists are not definitive, and there are men who can be identified as part of Wolsey's household at various times who do not appear on them. Nor do they include members of the household whose wages or moveable goods were less than the minimum threshold for taxation so that a good proportion of the lower household do not appear, suggesting that Cavendish may not have been far from the mark.

Unlike that of a secular nobleman, Wolsey's household was predominantly a clerical establishment and virtually an all-male environment. There were a large number of young noblemen, some still in their teens, including Edward Stanley, Earl of Derby and perhaps most famously Henry Percy, heir to the earldom of Northumberland and sometime suitor of Anne Boleyn. These provided him with the 'honourable' company any great lord expected to have around him. Wolsey is said to have been escorted at the meeting of the two kings at the Field of Cloth of Gold in 1520 by 50 such gentlemen. Approximately one quarter of the servants in Wolsey's household whose origins can be identified were from gentry families. Virtually every county in England was represented at some level in the household, although the bulk of the men from land-owning ranks came from Essex, Bedfordshire and Yorkshire, the latter perhaps no surprise as it was the largest county in the kingdom and Wolsey was Archbishop of York. The majority of those non-clerical members of Wolsey's household, of yeoman and common status, came from Wolsey's native part of the world in Lincolnshire and East Anglia.[4]

Wolsey's court was divided into the departments of the Chapel, the Chamber and the Household proper, the latter two loosely

158 *Cardinal benefactor*

corresponding to the 'upstairs/downstairs' arrangements of wealthy Victorians and Edwardians. Cavendish emphasised the considerable clerical component of the household in the department of the Chapel, headed by a Dean who was, by the late 1520s, Robert Shorton, former Master of St John's College and concurrently Master of Pembroke College, Cambridge. The sub-dean of the Chapel did much of the day-to-day management of a team of priests, sacristans and ancillary staff. The choristers and musicians of the Chapel will be discussed later. His first almoner was Lawrence Stubbs, one of Wolsey's chaplains and his Receiver-General, or bursar-accountant. He supervised many of Wolsey's building projects, including at York Place and Hampton Court. He was succeeded as almoner in 1527 by Dr William Capon, who also became the Dean of Wolsey's foundation of St Mary's College, Ipswich. The cardinal's confessor through the middle 1520s was the aforementioned Thomas Larke, the brother of his partner, Joan.

Wolsey's Chamber was staffed by noblemen and gentlemen, rather than clerics, under the direction of the Chamberlain, Sir Thomas Denys, from Devon. He was also a royal servant in that county and by 1526 had become Comptroller of the household of Princess Mary in the Marches of Wales. He seems to have been succeeded by one Sir William Fitzwilliam, who also acted as treasurer of the household and who was also prominent in the Merchant Taylors' Company. He should not be confused with the more famous royal courtier Sir William Fitzwilliam who later became first Earl of Southampton and who was, to some extent, also a protégé of Wolsey. With his deputy, the Chamberlain supervised Wolsey's 12 gentlemen ushers, among whom were George Cavendish and Richard Warren (who had organised Wolsey's accommodation for the Field of Cloth of Gold). Wolsey also had 6 gentlemen ushers for his private suite of rooms, or 'privy chamber', together with table servants of various kinds numbering some 40 men in all, assisted by 46 yeoman ushers who did most of the fetching and carrying within the cardinal's personal quarters. In common with royal and noble practice, many of these men would have served in three-month-long stints, known as quarters, so that not all of them would be in service at any one time. Like that of the king, the staff of the Chamber looked after the cardinal's personal accommodation, dress, nutrition, health care and personal security. They

Cardinal benefactor 159

were also responsible for ensuring that his personal adornment and presentation was at its most splendid, at all times. Wolsey's physician was the Italian doctor Agostino Agostini, who would play an important part in the cardinal's final demise, although not for medical considerations. He was assisted by the cardinal's personal apothecary. Wolsey retained a team of men to assist him with his vast administrative burden, including two secretaries, clerks and four legal counsellors.

Beyond the Chamber was the usual and extensive range of domestic officers and servants in the department of the Household proper, responsible for the accommodation and provisioning of the cardinal's entourage. Wolsey's household Treasurer was (from 1523 at least) Sir William Gascoigne, a lawyer from Cardington in Bedfordshire, of which county he had been sometime sheriff. By 1527, the Comptroller, responsible for daily financial administration, was John Gostwick, also from Bedfordshire, who had by then been in his household for a decade and whom Wolsey described in the last year of his life as his 'old and trusty servant'. The Steward of the household, responsible for all the 'below stairs' service departments, was Robert Carter. He presided over a large complement of kitchen staff, both communal (responsible for feeding the entire household) and of the privy kitchen which prepared the meals of Wolsey himself and his personal guests. These were supported by an extensive ancillary staff in the various sub-departments such as the buttery and cellar, larder and scullery, laundry and so on.

The household also had a number of marshals and porters charged with gate-keeping and security. It had a large department of the stables, responsible for the transport of the cardinal, his hunting expeditions and for the care of his horses and other animals. Wolsey's personal saddler was one Forde or Ferror. A surviving account for one year shows he was paid 60s a year and that materials for the saddles themselves cost £10. The account shows Wolsey as having 5 mules for his own use; 6 horses for riders who bore the cardinal's crosses and his maces, or pillars, before him in procession; 6 spare horses and 11 pack horses and mules. Nine keepers were each paid 26s 8d a year. In addition to this was the cost of the hay and other food for the horses. These expenses are only indicative, and surviving accounts are sparse and scarcely more detailed. An undated declaration was made of its expenses over three years between 1516 and 1519. This includes costs for horses, wages, livery, boats on the Thames, Wolsey's pilgrimage to Walsingham in September 1517, journeys to and from the royal court, wherever it was, and even for his tonsure as a man in holy orders (31s 2d in 1516–17). Total estimated outgoings rose from just over £2,485 in 1516–17 to just over £2,897 in 1518–19 (a particularly busy year for the cardinal).[5]

Like his master, Wolsey seems to have been a good judge of talent and attracted to his service a number of figures who would later play key roles in Henry's regime. The most famous of them was of course the lawyer Thomas Cromwell, who worked for Wolsey from 1524. His knowledge of the complicated process of dissolving religious houses, and of Wolsey's property, helped him to make the transition to royal service in the years after Wolsey's fall.[6] Within a few years, Cromwell employed his former colleague, Wolsey's comptroller, John Gostwick, as his own treasurer. Gostwick eventually became treasurer of the court of First Fruits and Tenths and was knighted in 1540. Another member of Wolsey's household who became a royal servant in turn, and who worked with Cromwell, was Thomas Heneage from Hainton in Lincolnshire. Born in or before 1482, he had become one of Wolsey's gentleman ushers by 1521 and had by then already served on peace commissions for Lincolnshire, something he continued to do into the mid-1520s. Wolsey arranged for his transfer to service in the king's privy chamber in 1528, possibly as a way of keeping himself informed of events there, in the way Sir William Fitzwilliam had been doing for some time, although how helpful Heneage was may be doubted. At Wolsey's fall the following year, Heneage rapidly disowned his former master and was soon in the circle of his one-time colleague in Wolsey's household, Thomas Cromwell. He went on to become the royal Cofferer by 1532. By 1536 he was Keeper of the King's Privy Purse, and after the execution of Henry Norris in May that year, he was made joint Chief Gentleman of the king's Privy Chamber with Sir Francis Bryan – probably on Cromwell's advice. He was also Groom of the Stool and thus Henry's most personal body servant.[7]

In 1523 the University of Cambridge authorities sent letters to Wolsey borne by one Stephen Gardiner who soon afterwards entered Wolsey's service as a chaplain and secretary. Like other high-profile members of Wolsey's household and wider affinity, Gardiner was also in effect on royal business in his work for the cardinal because the whole of Wolsey's work in which they assisted was the king's government. Gardiner handled a good deal of the cardinal's correspondence with the king. By the time of his first master's fall from power, Gardiner had joined the royal household as the king's secretary. He succeeded Wolsey as Bishop of Winchester, acted often thereafter as an ambassador in France and elsewhere and became one of the king's leading advisors until the early 1540s.[8]

It has been estimated that about 60 members of Wolsey's entourage also held an identifiable position in the royal household at some point; often while still in the cardinal's service. This demonstrated Wolsey's high status in the kingdom to those within it and beyond. It certainly declared to any ambitious young gentleman or promising scholar that the household of the leading royal administrator, as opposed to that of a middling ranked noble, was now a more reliable and direct pathway to royal service and ideally favour. It made Wolsey a very attractive patron. To house this considerable entourage and wider quasi-royal affinity, Wolsey had necessarily and quickly to become a patron of building on a grand scale.

Domestic architecture

Wolsey's first property was at St Bride's, Fleet Street, which later became Bridewell Palace. The parcel of property consisting of a house and garden was granted to him by Henry in 1509. The house was soon embellished with guest chambers in which its new owner began to entertain in a manner to which he was evidently determined to become accustomed. In 1515, Henry acquired the property after Wolsey had taken on the more substantial residence, York Place, on his appointment as Archbishop in August 1514. Yet Wolsey continued to have an interest in the further development of Bridewell, including the construction in 1516 of a long gallery ending in a water gate on the Thames.[9] Bridewell was a timber-framed structure standing on a brick base. In or about 1516, a total estimated cost of around £21,000 was given for its renovation, including £2,033 for the cost of foundations, £450 for timber and £1,083 for bricks. Glazing came to £686 13s 4d. Bridewell had no hall but was set around two brick-built courtyards.[10]

York Place, where Wolsey resided by November 1514, was located on what is now the area occupied by Inigo Jones' Banqueting House

162   *Cardinal benefactor*

and the Ministry of Defence at Whitehall. Wolsey used it as his principal London residence until 1529, together with the manor of Bridge Court in Battersea, which effectively became the administrative office for his architectural patronage. There he set up a brick kiln, storage yards and offices for the works. Materials were shipped across the Thames from Vauxhall to a nearby wharf, rented for the purpose. At York Place, Wolsey significantly increased the number, size and splendour of its reception rooms and accommodation for himself and his entourage. The first major undertaking was the great chamber, or principal reception room, which was ornately decorated and lit by a large bay window. This structure rested on an under croft, still in existence, now relocated under the Ministry of Defence buildings. This work cost in the vicinity of £500 and was carried out under the supervision of Henry Redman, Westminster Abbey's master mason, who headed a team of craftsmen and builders drawn from royal service and from various colleges at Cambridge.

The work at York Place continued intermittently for over a decade. By the spring of 1520 Wolsey had bought a section of riverside land to the south of York Place. Over this he built what became the distinguishing feature of his residence. This was a long gallery at first floor level running out from the cardinal's private lodgings, more or less parallel to the Thames on its eastern side, overlooking the house's garden and an area of grassland and trees known as an 'orchard' to the west. At its southern end, away from the house, it ended in an extension at right angles to it, affording views out over the river. Towards its northern end were projections apparently containing two rooms. Cavendish described 'two chambers adjoining the gallery, the one called the gilt chamber and the other, most commonly called the council chamber' at York Place, and they seem to have been part of what was in effect an extension of the cardinal's private apartments. In 1523 Wolsey purchased 12 pieces of tapestry 'of the story of Jacob and Joseph provided for the gallery at York Place at Westminster, having 24 windows'. In 1531, the Venetian ambassador Mario Savorgnano saw the gallery at York Place and reported that it had

> windows on each side, looking on gardens and rivers, the ceiling being marvellously wrought in stone with gold, and the

wainscot of carved wood representing a thousand beautiful figures; and round about there are chambers, and very large halls, all hung with tapestries.[11]

A second major phase of works opened in late 1527 or early 1528 when Wolsey moved to Durham Place temporarily in order that a complete refurbishment of the hall and chapel could be undertaken, the cardinal 'intending most sumptuously and gorgeously to repair and furnish the same'.[12] This refurbishment was not completed in Wolsey's lifetime but had progressed sufficiently by November 1529 for the king to take up temporary residence at York Place after he made Wolsey vacate it. The gallery, its features and its novelty, together with the ornate public and private rooms at York Place, were deliberately intended by Wolsey to advertise his splendour, his architectural and artistic taste and his authority, secular and sacred. Yet under Wolsey it remained at heart a practical, albeit magnificent building, a *pied-à-terre*, close to Westminster Hall to which he rode each day in the legal term to carry out his many and various responsibilities as Chancellor. After Henry took over York Place, it became the heart of his own redesign of what was eventually the Palace of Whitehall, his principal residence, the centre of his government from the 1530s and, at his death, the largest metropolitan palace in Europe.

Much more extensive as a palace for Wolsey was Hampton Court, upon which he took out a 99-year lease at £50 per year from the Knights of the Order of St John (Hospitallers) in 1515. Since 1505, the manor house had been leased to Giles, Lord Daubeney, Henry VII's Lord Chamberlain. This moated manor house on the north bank of the Thames quickly became his principal residence outside Westminster and London and the cardinal's main entertainment venue – a showcase for his architectural and artistic patronage. Wolsey owned the house as his private residence and, unlike York Place, did not acquire it in right of his ecclesiastical titles. From the outset, therefore, it reflected his personal tastes and needs more fully than some of his other properties. Moreover, within four years of its acquisition, as cardinal legate of England, Wolsey was the highest ranked ecclesiastic of the realm and entitled to status and honour accorded to the pope himself. Hampton Court therefore became the principal venue for the display of that status, and of

164   *Cardinal benefactor*

Wolsey's awareness of his equal standing with his fellow Continental cardinals and legates. The extension and renovation of Hampton Court provoked John Skelton's most famous satirical poem 'Why come ye not to Court' with its oft-quoted opening stanza:

> Why come ye not to court? To which court?
> To the King's court, Or to Hampton Court?
> Nay, to the king's court! The King's court
> Should have excellence, but Hampton Court
> Hath the pre-eminence. And York's Place,
> With my Lord's Grace! To whose magnificence
> Is all the confluence, suits and supplications,
> Embassades of all nations.[13]

Lord Daubeney had already created a substantial residence centred around what is now Clock Court. The lease from the Knights of St John was transferred to Wolsey by Daubeney's son, Henry. Wolsey immediately began building, using a team of technicians and artisans overseen by Lawrence Stubbs. The first major project was extending the house westwards, with a new outer, or lower, 'Base', court. This was 104 feet north to south and 155 feet east to west. This addition virtually doubled the area of the original house and required the re-digging of the dry moat to encompass the increased area the whole building occupied, a task completed by the end of the summer of 1515. The four ranges of the outer court were terminated in a four-turreted gatehouse, five storeys high (reduced by two storeys in the early 1770s). The models for these sort of base courts with lodgings around them include Knole, which dates from the 1460s, and Dartington from the 1390s. Cardinal-Archbishop Morton of Canterbury created a similar arrangement at Lambeth, but whereas that court was built to house members of the archiepiscopal household, Wolsey's new court provided accommodation for his household and a large number of guests. Some 36 rooms of single and double size were created; each reached from a sheltered corridor that ran all around the courtyard. These lodgings, which included a three-room suite in the gatehouse, were furnished luxuriously when occupied, allowing the cardinal to display the sort of magnificent generosity expected of someone of his high conciliar and ecclesiastical status.

Cardinal benefactor 165

In planning Hampton Court, Wolsey may have been conscious of Italian models like the palace of the Montefeltro dukes of Urbino, adapting neo-classical notions of quiet and elegant spaciousness seen there to the English context. He may also have been aware of Paolo Cortesi's book *De Cardinalatu* published in 1510, in which the author set out the pattern for the Renaissance cardinal's ideal palace based on a series of graded spaces from the fully public to the most private living quarters – much in the manner of royal and noble households. It should provide a fitting environment for him as a powerful figure in the Church and as a patron, fostering an orderly and virtuous life and impressing on all the political importance of the owner.[14] The new courtyard made the original Daubeney courtyard, now known as Clock Court, the effective centre of the palace. The programme of renovation work in these ranges included a new Great Chamber, the principal reception room of the cardinal, outer lodgings and ancillary buildings, including the kitchens. It was completed in time for the visit to the palace of the emperor Charles V in the summer of 1522.

Hampton was chosen in part for its health benefits for a man whose constitution seems at once to have been generally robust, but prone to sudden onsets of illness. Contemporaries mention that Wolsey suffered from kidney stones and colic and had frequent bouts of dysentery, including his last illness. These complaints and the regular outbreaks of contagious diseases to which all were subject, notably the virulent 'sweating sickness', affected Wolsey's health frequently – the latter first and almost fatally in 1512. He suffered another bout in the summer of 1517, and his recovery from it prompted his pilgrimage to Walsingham in September. He was reported to have retreated from London in November the same year to avoid the plague. The cardinal was sensitive about hygiene and his health and is described by Cavendish (and depicted subsequently) as leaving his privy chamber

> holding in his hand a very fair orange, whereof the meat within was taken out, and filled up again with the part of a sponge, wherein vinegar and other confections against pestilent airs; to the which he most commonly smelt unto, passing among the press.[15]

166   *Cardinal benefactor*

With good reason did Wolsey regard the environment of the capital and its immediate surrounds as unhealthy. The environs of Hampton and its distance upriver and upwind from Westminster and London afforded him a country retreat in more senses than one. Others thought so, too. Once, while recovering from a serious illness, Archbishop Warham wrote to Wolsey to thank him for the cardinal's invitation to come to recuperate at his 'most wholesome manor of Hampton Court'.[16] The palace's water supply, essential to its health and proper functioning, came from springs at Coombe Hill near Kingston, from where it ran to the palace through three miles of newly laid lead pipes.[17]

The initial programme of extensions and renovations to 1522 do not seem to have included the hall of the existing manor house, although this is a matter of debate among architectural historians. One view is that Wolsey *did* build a new first floor hall, enlarging the one built by Daubeney, and that this was completed by about 1521. Its significant surviving feature is the oriel window in its south-east corner, which has strong affinities with the near-contemporary oriel window in the Hall of Wolsey's college at Oxford. In this view, the new hall was an important aspect of how Wolsey used Hampton Court to display himself as a cardinal of European standing who modelled his household, its principal rooms and ceremonial arrangements, on the manner of his curial contemporaries but in an English vernacular context. The majority view remains, however, that Wolsey only augmented Daubeney's hall with the oriel, that he was otherwise content with it for the time being at least, and that the present Great Hall was the work of Henry VIII.[18]

Some of the archaeological evidence relied on by the majority view also indicates, in the absence of any surviving building accounts, that a new programme of renovation at the palace was put in hand from 1523. The most important elements of this were the creation of new stacked lodgings on three storeys along the east wing of what is now Clock Court. Here Wolsey created suites of rooms ostensibly for the royal family. On the ground floor were rooms for Princess Mary; on the first floor, those for the king, and on the second floor was a similar suite for the queen. These were used from time to time by those for whom they were intended, although never all at the one time. They remained the core of the

Cardinal benefactor 167

royal lodgings after Henry took effective possession of the palace in 1529.[19]

In 1526, Wolsey decided to build new lodgings for himself centred on a tower on the south side of the inner court, near where Clock Court now meets Base Court. These lodgings had two principal rooms on each of their three levels, and some of the rooms survive to this day, notable for their intricate ceiling decoration and the period linenfold panelling on their walls (although this may originally have been elsewhere in the palace, or from another building altogether). The new lodgings incorporated a long gallery which projected into the gardens along the river side of the palace. It was 16 feet wide and 55 feet long, terminating in a tower. The gallery had windows on either side with views out to the river and over the palace's fashionable knot garden. A short passageway also connected the gallery to the king's rooms on the first floor of the east wing of the principal court. Given the tower lodgings built for Wolsey were probably intended for his use while the king was in residence, this arrangement would have afforded the two men an ease of private communication and time together that the cardinal ever sought but did not always easily find. How often Henry actually made use of these rooms, however, remains uncertain. He paid at least 16 visits to the palace between 1515 and 1528, and on such occasions, Cavendish assures us, 'such pleasures were then devised for the King's comfort and consolation as might be invented or by man's wit imagined . . . in so gorgeous a sort and costly manner that it was an heaven to behold'.[20] Yet the king was not there very often in the middle years of that period, at the height of Wolsey's power.

Hampton Court's ceremonial spaces, and particularly its chapel, had also to express Wolsey's high ecclesiastical status. The chapel was rebuilt as part of the second phase of renovation in the mid-1520s but was not completed by the time Henry assumed responsibility for the works in September 1529. In keeping with Oxford traditions out of which he had grown, Wolsey's chapel was T-shaped rather than strictly cruciform. Unlike those college chapels, however, Hampton Court's included holyday closets on the first-floor level at its west end to enable the king and queen to attend services when they were in residence. The east end was lit by long, stained-glass windows depicting the Crucifixion, below which were figures of the palace's principal residents, Wolsey, the king and queen and

168   *Cardinal benefactor*

Princess Mary in the guise of various supplicant saints, together with a figure of St George, the patron saint of English chivalry. In common with royal palaces, ecclesiastical ones needed processional ways and links between the hall and the chapel, both public spaces, and within the private lodgings of the owner, only the merest remnant of which survive today.

Hampton Court also provides the home for two legendary creatures associated with Wolsey. The first was the 'Cardinal Spider' that by 1890 was being referred to in guides to the palace. This large reddish-brown spider, *Tegenaria domestica*, was apparently more common in the Thames Valley area in the nineteenth century than it is today. It was popularly linked with Wolsey at Hampton Court either because it was a spinner of webs, like him, or somehow an augury of his downfall. Rather more appealing is the legend of Wolsey's cat, or cats, that supposedly accompanied him at all times, even when in Chancery. One variant of the legend has it that the cat was kept because Wolsey was fearful of the spiders, and it chased them away. Alternatively, it protected them because Wolsey regarded the spiders as lucky. It is a nice idea, but no documentary evidence has been found for Wolsey keeping or feeding a cat at Hampton Court or anywhere else – yet!

In common with senior nobles, Wolsey quickly adopted the practice of flattering Henry, and highlighting the grandeur of Hampton Court, by commonly referring to it and formally including it in the 1526 Eltham Ordinances as one of the king's houses. Despite an enduring tradition, deriving from Hall, that Wolsey surrendered Hampton to Henry in some sort of exchange for the use at least of Richmond Palace in 1525, he retained ownership of it until at least September 1528. That month, the king demanded that Wolsey vacate Hampton Court so he could entertain the papal legate Campeggio who had arrived in England apparently to resolve the issue of the king's annulment. Wolsey readily obliged. A popular tradition has it that he made it over as a gift either to Henry or Anne Boleyn in an attempt to curry favour with her. There is no evidence for that claim, but what is clear is that Henry never returned full possession to the cardinal. Wolsey evidently continued to live there until the autumn of 1529 after the failure of the legatine court, 'hiding' in those months of disgrace, according to the French ambassador Du Bellay, before he returned

Cardinal benefactor 169

to York Place for what proved to be his final, short stay there in October.[21]

Second only to Hampton Court Palace as Wolsey's site of royal and ambassadorial entertainment was the manor of 'The More' near Rickmansworth, Hertfordshire. Wolsey acquired its use when confirmed as commendatory Abbot of St Albans in 1521. The name derives from the Anglo-Norman word for marshland. Unfortunately, no building records survive for this residence, but it was surveyed in the Elizabethan period, and its form has been reconstructed from modern archaeological excavations undertaken by Martin Biddle in the 1950s and by Channel 4's *Time Team* programme in 2012. Like Hampton Court, as Wolsey inherited it, The More was a moated residence, with the original house occupying perhaps less of the platform surrounded by the moat than at Hampton. This space Wolsey used in his programme of enlargement, creating U-shaped lodgings around three sides of the original house. In its final form, the ranges extended to the edge of the moat and terminated in a two-towered inner gatehouse. The whole structure seems somewhat to have resembled Oxburgh Hall in Norfolk. The inner house contained a chapel, and in 2012, traces were found of expensive Flemish-stained glass, probably for the east window of the chapel. Multi-coloured, tin glazed floor tiles were also recovered, and the remains of classical columns decorated with stone-carved foliage were identified – faint traces of the opulence of Wolsey's surroundings. The columns may have been set on plinths on either side of the gateway into the main lodgings of the manor. Here, too, Wolsey built a long gallery that led north from the principal lodgings across the moat and out into the privy garden. At some 253 feet, it was over twice as long as the one at Hampton Court and terminated with two towers, giving views out over extensive parklands to the north. These could, at times, pasture as many as 400–500 deer, and hunting was an important aspect of the entertainment Wolsey offered his guests at The More.

To the south side of the moated main house, Wolsey built a base court with lodgings for guests on three sides, with corner towers and terminating in a four-towered gatehouse, much as at Hampton. It differed however in that the base court lay beyond the moat and was connected to the central court by a bridge. Its cobbled central area was not that much smaller than at Hampton. The Anglo-French

170 *Cardinal benefactor*

peace agreement signed in the aftermath of Francis I's defeat at Pavia took the name of the house, where it was negotiated in part and then signed in August 1525.[22] The French ambassador Jean du Bellay, thought The More to be superior in splendour and comfort to Hampton Court. He was Bishop of Bayonne and would himself later become a cardinal. Du Bellay was a considerable patron of architecture in France and an early adopter of the Italian Renaissance style. Wolsey may well have exchanged ideas about architecture and decoration with the ambassador, who became something of a friend and who was not alone in being entertained well by Wolsey at his various properties.[23]

On being made Bishop of Winchester in 1529, Wolsey had also acquired another manor house, at Esher in Surrey. He was not here very long and undertook no major works there. In October 1529, he was ordered to go to Esher after being dismissed as Chancellor. From here he moved briefly to Richmond in early 1530 before beginning his first and last journey to York.[24]

Sculpture, tapestry, plate and glass

Because so little of what he commissioned survives, Wolsey is not often numbered among the first ranks of English patrons of Renaissance arts such as sculpture. In fact, his contribution was significant and innovative. His best-known commission today is undoubtedly a set of eight painted and gilded terra cotta roundels recorded as 'octo rotundas imagines, ex terra depictas et deauratas' of classical figures, since commonly referred to as Roman emperors, now at Hampton Court Palace. These were made by the Florentine sculptor Giovanni da Maiano who was second only to Pietro Torrigiano among Italian sculptors working in England in the early years of Henry's reign. De Maiano had arrived in England certainly by 1521, and probably the year before, and is likely to have worked on the temporary palace at the Field of Cloth of Gold. The roundels cost £2 6s 8d each, and Da Maiano also produced roundels or panels depicting three stories from the life of Hercules (which have long since disappeared), each costing £4. In June 1521, he was still owed £21 14s 4d for the work, about which debt he wrote to Wolsey. The terracotta roundels were probably intended to imitate very similar marble roundels commissioned by Cardinal Georges

Cardinal benefactor 171

d'Amboise for his château at Gaillon, although there is no consensus as to their original distribution or positioning at the palace.[25] They were, however, the first such medallions in England and thus amongst the earliest examples of using Renaissance forms to decorate and modernise traditional Gothic architecture. Such work, and the example set by Wolsey, were taken up by the king in the following decades. From 1528, da Maiano received an annual salary from the crown of £20, and similar terra cotta roundels and panels made by him or others appeared at royal palaces, including Greenwich and the Holbein Gate at Whitehall.

Of equal importance as evidence of Wolsey's innovative sculptural patronage is a terracotta panel of the cardinal's arms above the gateway of Clock Court at Hampton, which is most likely to have been the work of Torrigiano but in which Giovanni da Maiano may also have been involved. When it was rediscovered around 1845, Wolsey's arms had been cut away and replaced by the royal arms, and his cardinal's hat had been covered over with a wrought-iron crown. The panel was originally dated 1525 and included Wolsey's monogram above it, which no longer survives, and his motto below it, which does. The central panel, now in situ, features Wolsey's arms, with his archiepiscopal cross behind (nineteenth-century replacements of the lost or destroyed originals) surmounted by his cardinal's hat, supported by two winged putti, themselves flanked by Corinthian columns, all of which are original (see Figure 2.1). The panel sits above egg-and-dart moulding supported by brackets decorated with acanthus leaves. In addition to this panel, numerous items of terracotta in the Renaissance style, including capitals and window mouldings, have been recovered at Hampton Court in the course of archaeological excavations since the nineteenth century.[26]

Impressive though the terracotta panel, roundels and remains are, the single greatest sculptural project upon which Wolsey engaged was an immense tomb for himself. As he left no will, there is no definite evidence as to where he first intended it to be located, but in 1530 he indicated it should be in York Minster. It might originally have been intended for St George's Chapel Windsor or the immense chapel Wolsey planned for Cardinal College, Oxford, where it would form the centre of a monument to his own achievements. The design owed much, as did the life it was intended to commemorate, to European models of the ideal Renaissance cardinal

172   *Cardinal benefactor*

set within an English context. It was to be built in the same mix of marble and gilded bronze as Torrigiano's tomb of Henry VII and Elizabeth of York in Westminster Abbey, but on a far grander scale. Wolsey commissioned yet another Florentine sculptor, Benedetto da Rovezzano, whom Vasari described as 'among our most excellent craftsmen', to design and build the tomb. He had begun work by the summer of 1524, assembling a team of Italian and Flemish carvers and guilders. Much of the mundane organisation and funding of the project was handled by Thomas Cromwell, whom Benedetto described as 'a man of great talent and exceptional skill'. It was to Cromwell as Wolsey's 'counsellor' that the sculptor later wrote seeking a final payment for his work prior to his return to Italy.[27] Benedetto also produced two inventories (possibly for Cromwell and certainly used by him) of completed pieces for the tomb, with their measurements. They included a recumbent figure of Wolsey – or as the man himself called it, 'of myne image with such part of the tombe as it shall please the King that I shall have' – when instructing Cromwell to have it sent to York in 1530. By then, as Wolsey evidently realised, many of the pieces were being re-directed for use on a projected tomb for Henry himself, whose design the king had long before committed to Wolsey and upon which the cardinal had first worked with Torrigiano.[28] For a decade from 1530, Benedetto and Giovanni da Maiano worked jointly on the king's monument, but in the end neither tomb was ever completed. In 1808 the black marble base and the sarcophagus taken from Wolsey's monument, which had been moved to St George's Chapel at Windsor in 1565, were used for the tomb of Admiral Lord Nelson in the crypt of St Paul's Cathedral in London.

Several other pieces for Wolsey's tomb have since been identified. These include four bronze candlesticks now in St Bavo's Cathedral in Ghent and the four classically garbed bronze angels bearing candelabra now in the Victoria and Albert Museum. The inventories and remnants have formed the basis of several conjectural reconstructions of the tomb, which show how the design reflected Wolsey's ideas. It was to have been on a massive scale and quite unlike any previous English ecclesiastical funerary monument. In its use of costly marble and gilt bronze, it has far more in common with English royal tombs, and its overall design was influenced by French ones. In its size, expense and Renaissance style,

Cardinal benefactor   173

the tomb emphasised Wolsey's unprecedented ecclesiastical and political importance in England, and in Europe beyond. It was perhaps these very considerations that, ironically, made it a model for an even grander tomb for Henry. By the same token, it is hardly surprising that it was never completed in the aftermath of Wolsey's fall from favour. Yet this fact itself suggests how powerful an expression the tomb would have been (just as Wolsey intended it should be) of the cardinal's status within the kingdom, and Christendom beyond, as statesman and patron.[29]

The acquisition of expensive furnishings, primarily tapestries and hangings of rich cloth of various kinds, was central to Wolsey's display of his high status. On a practical note, the extensive additions of accommodation at York Place, Hampton Court, and The More required the purchase of significant amounts of tapestry and other ornate materials used to insulate and decorate the walls of halls, galleries and rooms, as panel covers, altar frontals and as parts of bed furnishings. Wolsey's first acquisitions of high-quality tapestry were by gift or perquisites from the royal collection and by purchase during his time in Tournai in 1513. According to Cavendish, Wolsey shortly afterwards had acquired hangings and other possessions of William Smith, his predecessor as Bishop of Lincoln, and those of Cardinal Bainbridge, his predecessor as Archbishop of York, both of whom died in 1514. These acquisitions formed the real basis of his own collection as cardinal from 1515, and a number of items from such collections and Tournai have plausibly been identified in an inventory of Wolsey's possessions taken around 1522. By then Wolsey was collecting, in a more focused and ambitious way, Flemish work of the late fifteenth century and catching up perhaps with the kind of prestigious works of both sacred and secular subjects from Tournai and Antwerp that Henry and many of his nobles would have inherited, or begun to purchase, but which Wolsey had not initially been able to afford. Several of these sets were woven with, or given additional, borders showing the cardinal's arms and motto.

In the months before the Field of Cloth of Gold, Wolsey purchased several sets of continental tapestry through the London merchant Richard Gresham. Their religious themes emphasised his high ecclesiastical status as cardinal and papal legate in England and may have been used in his accommodation at the

174   *Cardinal benefactor*

Anglo-French meeting. The king also purchased very expensive sets of tapestries to be used at the event, chiefly in the temporary entertainment palace the English built where, as we have seen, Wolsey had a set of richly decorated rooms next to the king's which impressed all who saw them (see Chapter 2). No detailed description of these apartments survives, but according to one observer, the first two chambers were hung with 'silken tapestry without gold, of astounding beauty'. Campbell has suggested that these hangings may have been at least part of a set of the *Triumphs of Petrarch* that appear to have been made for the cardinal in 1520, on a design first presented to Louis XII by Cardinal George d'Amboise in about 1503.[30] This set was one of two Wolsey had acquired by about 1522–3 when the inventory was drawn up. One of the sets, which may have been the one at the Field and now in the Victoria and Albert Museum, includes a panel titled the *Triumph of Fame over Death*, which features what is apparently a portrait of Wolsey. The figure of the cardinal, his dress, colours and the features of his face are certainly reminiscent of those in the de Boucq collection (see Chapter 1) and to a lesser extent the one in the National Portrait Gallery.[31]

In December 1521 Gresham provided bespoke purchases for furnishing the extended accommodation around the inner and base courtyards at Hampton Court Palace, only a few of which survive today. A second set Gresham provided in April 1522 were probably commissioned in anticipation of the visit of Charles V in the summer of that year. The bulk of these tapestry sets were of Old Testament subjects, but also included sets of the *Seven Deadly Sins* (for Wolsey's bedchamber at Hampton Court) and *The Nine Worthies*. The 1522 inventory, with various interpolations from later years, includes one 'rich cloth of estate embroidered with my lord's arms', a large number of other less expensive hangings, together with table carpets and items of domestic furniture and bedding and so on. It indicates that Wolsey continued to acquire hangings and other furnishings from third parties, such as Sir John Yonge, Master of the Rolls; Thomas Docwra, the Prior of the Knights of St John; and Thomas Ruthall, whom Wolsey succeeded as Bishop of Durham in 1523. With these acquisitions, Wolsey is estimated to have had more than 600 pieces of tapestries of varying quality by the mid-1520s.[32]

Cardinal benefactor 175

Wolsey also had a collection of table, window and floor carpets, many of which he obtained through Venetian sources. Over the course of about two years from December 1519, the Venetian ambassador Antonio Surian communicated his requests to the republic's authorities for 60 Damascene and Cairene carpets that Giustinian had promised Wolsey. The Senate eventually authorised the purchase of about that number of medium-sized and small carpets at a total cost of 600 ducats. Wolsey received them in October 1521. As late as August 1529, Wolsey was again pressing the Venetians for more gifts, this time 45 yards of 'tawny damask' which the Senate agreed to acquire. Along with everything else, the carpets and perhaps this cloth passed into royal hands at his fall.[33] Cavendish reports that textiles were a substantial part of the Chancellor's possessions inventoried at York Place in November 1529. He noted, among many other things brought out to be inventoried, rich sets of vestments which the cardinal had intended for his own use or that of the Deans of his Ipswich and Oxford colleges. There were many lengths of silk of various colours, together with velvet, damask and a thousand yards of 'Holland cloth', a very rich linen. The walls themselves were covered with 'cloths of gold and tissue of divers makings, and cloth of silver likewise on both sides, and rich cloths of baudkin of divers colours'. Even after his fall from power, Wolsey, with the king's help, maintained a certain splendour at Esher and then at Cawood House near York. The plate there was inventoried on the orders of the earl of Northumberland at the cardinal's arrest.[34]

As his gentlemen usher well knew, as with tapestries, textiles and vestments, Wolsey's patronage of goldsmiths' work was on a grand scale and was yet another means of displaying his wealth and his status as England's pre-eminent churchman. Giustinian and Hall left descriptions of the cardinal's spectacular displays of his silverware on tables and shelved sideboards in his principal palaces of Hampton Court and York Place. Cavendish noted that the sideboard in the cardinal's Presence Chamber, specially built for the reception of the 1527 French embassy (see Chapter 6), was as wide as the end wall of the room and six shelves high. The silver-gilt plate displayed on these shelves was 'very sumptuous and of the most newest fashions'. The lower shelves displayed items of pure gold and two great candlesticks of silver and gilt, which together

176   *Cardinal benefactor*

cost about £200. As was customary on great occasions, the plate on display was not used during the banquet offered to the ambassadors, there being sufficient other for actual use. The five leaders of the embassy were also presented with gifts of silver pots, a basin and ewer and drinking bowls. This was also customary and a display of Wolsey's munificence.[35]

In his account of the inventorying of Wolsey's possessions at York Place, Cavendish observes that he 'had two chambers adjoining a gallery, one of which was commonly called the council chamber in which had been set two broad and long trestles, whereupon was set such a number of plate of all sorts as almost incredible'. These are likely to have been the gallery chambers seen by Savorgnano, noted earlier. Cavendish specifies that in the 'gilt' or decorated chamber off the gallery were tables set with 'nothing but gilt plate', and there was also a dresser under a window set completely with 'clean' or pure gold vessels, some of which were garnished with pearl and other precious stones. As Giustinian had reported, plate was on semi-permanent display whenever Wolsey was in residence. In 1529, all of this was already inventoried in books which were available to those taking possession of his goods in the king's name. There were also, under the tables in both rooms, baskets 'with old plate which was not esteemed but for broken plate and old, not worthy to be occupied [used]'. This was the kind of plate which Wolsey sometimes used to pay back part of his debts to Robert Amadas and other goldsmiths.[36]

A good proportion of Wolsey's plate was purchased through agents in European cities. Some of his earliest purchases were made in Paris in 1515 by Sir Richard Wingfield, who was a member of the embassy sent to congratulate Francis I on his accession. Much more was supplied by London goldsmiths, principally Amadas, who also did a huge amount of work for the king. There exists an incomplete series of accounts of Amadas's work for Wolsey between 1517 and 1527, containing the weights in ounces of gold and silver of items made or refurbished for the cardinal. It shows that Wolsey spent £5,002 9d on work from Amadas's workshop, and he still owed him just over £1,690 at his death. Most of the items listed are tableware of various kinds, including cups and plates, candlesticks and salt-cellars. There are also several items of altar plate and other items for ecclesiastical use,

Cardinal benefactor 177

such as processional crosses, crucifixes and the like. There are also several items given by Wolsey to Henry as New Year's gifts, usually gold 'standing' cups with covers, generally costing between £120 and £135. Many entries in the account are for new items such as these gifts, but there are also numerous entries for repair of broken pieces, refurbishment or polishing of others and reworking elements of others still. Some of this work was parcelled out to other London goldsmiths, including Cornelis Hayes, who did more for the cardinal in the later part of the mid-1520s. Work was carried out for items at York Place, but Wolsey also commissioned numerous items of altar and table plate for St Alban's Abbey; Cardinal College, Oxford; and St Mary's at Ipswich.[37]

As with his fabrics and furnishings, little of Wolsey's vast collection of gold and silver plate, tableware and church silver can now be identified, apart from pieces which were inventoried towards the end of his life around the time of his giving up the Great Seal in 1529 and afterwards at Cawood a year later, and which then turn up in inventories of the royal Jewel House in the 1530s. Their existence can be verified in these lists by reference to the distinctive heraldry of the cardinal's hat, his coat of arms or the choughs from them (inaccurately described in the lists as martlets), and his motto, *Dominus mihi adjutor*, which marked most of his important pieces.[38]

Virtually all those items were, however, redistributed or melted down for their metal in the course of the century afterwards. Some of this plate was obtained by perquisite or gift in royal service, as gifts from English noblemen and as diplomatic gifts from monarchs. For example, at the conclusion of the Field of Cloth of Gold in 1520, Francis I gave Wolsey a number of gold basins and ewers decorated with the king's initial 'F' and with one of his personal badges, the Franciscan friars' knots, appropriate perhaps on a gift to an ecclesiastic and a punning reference to his own name. They were estimated by the Mantuan ambassador there to be worth some 20,000 crowns. From Louise of Savoy, Wolsey received a jewelled crucifix said by observers to be worth about 6,000 crowns.

In 1527 at the signing of the Treaty of Amiens, the king of France was even more generous to Wolsey. He gave him a chalice or cup known as 'the emperor's cup', specially refashioned 'with crowned roses and other devices'. He also presented the cardinal with a large

178   *Cardinal benefactor*

silver-gilt 'tableau', a sculpture in low-relief, garnished with porcelain cameos and pearls, incorporating a reliquary and depicting the Crucifixion. Wolsey also received a figure of St Francis of Assisi, the king's patron saint.[39]

An inventory of the Jewel House of 1533 includes a number of items 'late the lord cardinal's' that includes 'two basins and ewers with friars girdles by the French king'. These sound very likely to be those given to Wolsey in 1520. It also records 'a table of camewiss set in silver' weighing 446 oz, also 'by the French' king. The object's weight, description and origin strongly suggest the gift given by Francis in 1527. Other items identified in an inventory of 1533 of 'Plate to be broken by the king's command', as being 'late the lord cardinals', include, 'a pair of cruets chased in the feet, the spouts like dragons and the lids with leopards heads', and two 'parcel-gilt pots, embossed with the cardinal's arms and hats'.[40]

There is one area of artistic patronage in which Wolsey is conspicuous by his absence and that is portraiture. Despite his evident interest in all aspects of the fine arts, it seems curious that, so far as we know, Wolsey did not have a significant collection of pictures, although tapestries certainly performed an analogous function. Wolsey is not known to have commissioned a portrait of himself.[41] This, despite the presence in England during the mid-1520s of Hans Holbein the Younger, one of the greatest portraitists in the history of art. With the support of Erasmus, whom he had by then painted three times, Holbein arrived in England in the autumn of 1526 when Wolsey was at the height of his power. Over the next two years he carried out a series of works for the king and others in circles quite close to Wolsey. At Greenwich Palace he painted a battle scene and a 'cosmic' or astronomical ceiling for a temporary banqueting house in which the two Anglo-French treaties of 1527, Wolsey's greatest diplomatic triumphs, were both celebrated. At this time Holbein was preparing one of his most important projects, a separate portrait of Sir Thomas More, and a large painting of More with his extended family. More was a man whom Wolsey admired and with whom he worked closely. Holbein also painted William Warham, Archbishop of Canterbury, and made portraits of prominent courtiers, including Sir Henry Guildford and his wife, Mary, and the famous *Lady with a Squirrel and a Starling* (possibly Anne Lovell). Wolsey could not have been

Cardinal benefactor 179

unaware of the young German painter's presence in England or his growing reputation. Perhaps Wolsey did not care for likenesses of himself, for political or personal reasons – although the grand plans for his tomb argue against any such reticence. Giustinian thought him 'very handsome', and another Venetian envoy described him as 'hale and of a good presence'. Skelton referred to some sort of facial disfigurement, 'a flap before his eye' and, if true, this may have dissuaded Wolsey from sitting to Holbein. It is, however, more likely to have been one of Skelton's slurs, and the French sketch of 1567 depicts no such disfigurement.[42] Sampson Strong's Christ Church image depicts him, Oliver Cromwell-like, with warts, an artistic invention which rather nods to Skelton (see Figure 5.1). Perhaps

Figure 5.1 Cardinal Wolsey by Sampson Strong, c. 1610, Christ Church, Oxford

180   *Cardinal benefactor*

Wolsey was painted by Holbein and the portrait was subsequently lost? The fame of both the sitter and the artist make this unlikely. How different, and how much better-informed, might our view of Wolsey be had such a portrait been made? What vivid sense of him would Holbein's charcoals and paints have left us, to set alongside the pen-portraits of Cavendish, Vergil and Skelton? What kind of Wolsey might the genius of Holbein have shown us?

Educational patronage

The words of Erasmus quoted at the outset of this chapter accurately summarise Wolsey's ambition, if not finally his achievement, as an educational patron. Yet the cardinal's ecclesiastical and educational patronage might arguably be, indirectly, the longest-lasting part of his legacy. As with every other aspect of Wolsey's patronage, that of learning and theological training was intended to equal, or indeed exceed, the efforts of his European contemporaries and his English predecessors.

In the fourteenth century, William of Wykeham, Bishop of Winchester, had established Winchester College as a school for boys who then went on to New College, which he founded at Oxford. Henry VI established Eton College and King's College, Cambridge, in the 1440s. Perhaps the nearest exemplar for Wolsey's education patronage was William Waynflete's foundation of Magdalen College in 1458. Waynflete established several schools from where students could progress to his college at Oxford. Wolsey's patron Richard Fox, Bishop of Winchester, established Corpus Christi College by 1517, and its statutes were closely mirrored by those written for Wolsey's college. His establishment was to be dynamic and outward looking, with a mission to combine sound orthodox theology with the more contemporary approach to scriptural exegesis developed by the biblical humanists, like Erasmus and John Colet, and in which Cambridge had thus far taken the lead.

The first step in the foundation of Cardinal College was taken in April 1524 when Wolsey, newly made papal legate *a latere* for life, received authority from Pope Clement VII to supress St Frideswide's Priory in Oxford. The papal bull was brought to England by Thomas Hannibal, newly appointed as Master of the Rolls. The royal licence for the Oxford college was formally granted in July 1525, by which time building had already begun, and it continued for five years until Wolsey's fall in 1529. It has been estimated that the construction to that point cost an astronomical £22,000. The various elements of the establishment were essentially the same as for any other collegiate foundation, but Cardinal College was always intended to be on a much larger scale than Oxford had seen before.[43]

The buildings of the former priory of St Frideswide formed the core of the plan, but in order to accommodate the large number of staff and students Wolsey envisaged, a new Great Quadrangle (now Tom Quad) was laid out, requiring the demolition of two or three bays of the priory church which lay at its south-east corner. The quadrangle was intended to be cloistered, and the footings for the colonnade can still be seen around it today. Accommodation for students and staff occupied the remainder of the south wing, and the east and west wings of the quadrangle. The shortened priory church then became the chapel of the college, although Wolsey had plans to build an entirely new one to rival that at King's College, Cambridge, along the north side of the quadrangle, on the wing opposite the dining hall. This hall was, like the whole college of which it was part, the largest in Oxford. It still is. Behind it were the kitchens set within a separate, tall, cubed building – for fire safety – together with many offices, larders and storage spaces and housing for servants. Work progressed quite fast in the first few years, but by the time Wolsey fell from power, the building was still far from complete, and much of the old priory still remained. Two sides of the quadrangle were finished and most of the west front of the building on St Aldate's was completed, but it took a further two centuries before, by 1681, it was adorned by Tom Tower, built on a design by Sir Christopher Wren.

The college constitution provided that it should be headed by a Dean who oversaw a large and complex administration. The first was John Higden, who had been President of Magdalen since 1516 and who took up his new office in 1525. There were a number of public professors, together with lecturers who, between them, taught all the subjects available in the university at undergraduate and postgraduate level. The students, 100 in all, were called canons, together with chaplains, lay clerks and choristers, music and choir masters, and an organist. There were 60 canons of the

182   *Cardinal benefactor*

'first order' who were ordained graduates, elected from dioceses all over the country. Most were in effect postgraduates, studying higher degrees. The remaining 40 'petty' or 'minor order' canons, the equivalent of modern undergraduates, were to be elected from the many grammar schools Wolsey proposed.[44]

Typically, Wolsey had intended to establish a large number of such feeder schools, ideally one in each diocese, right across England. In fact by the time of his fall, only one such had been established, in his home town of Ipswich. The provisions and licence for the 'Cardinal College of St Mary', dating from June 1528, indicate that it was intended to dovetail with the Oxford college in relative size and educational objectives. The construction of new buildings for the college began in the summer of 1528 with extensions from the church of the suppressed priory of St Peter and Paul. In September 1528, Cromwell and others delivered to the new college parcels of vestments, plate and hangings and assisted with their installation. While its statutes do not survive, evidence from January 1529 indicates that the college was already proving popular, providing education for a larger number than the eight 'singing boys' proposed for the initial intake. With Wolsey's fall from power later that year, however, work ceased on the college, and it passed to the crown together with all the founder's other properties. Unlike at Oxford, no attempt was made to maintain or re-found it under royal patronage.[45]

There is comparatively little information about what sort of education Wolsey intended to provide for the scholars he hoped to attract to his foundations at Oxford and Ipswich. What does survive is enough, however, to get a sense that he favoured to a considerable extent what was known at the time as the 'new learning' or the 'studia humanitatis' based on the teaching of classical languages, rhetoric and history, together with the contextual biblical studies epitomised by the scholarship of Erasmus, whose praise of Wolsey was quoted at the outset of this chapter. This followed the announcement the previous year of the establishment of six public lectureships in the humanities at Oxford. The first of these was John Clements, who lectured in Greek and Latin literature, although who Wolsey's other appointees were, and whether, indeed, all the lectureships were finally established, remains uncertain. With some success, Wolsey pressed the university to alter its timetable

Cardinal benefactor 183

to enable and encourage students to attend Clements' lectures in addition to those in the more traditional areas of logic, dialectics and moral philosophy. By 1523 Wolsey had also appointed Juan Vives, the Spanish humanist and former tutor to Princess Mary, but despite Erasmus's further praise in his letter that Wolsey offered 'princely salaries' to attract the very best, there seem to have been no further international appointments. Nevertheless, Wolsey was influential in promoting the study of classical literature at Oxford, even if the conservative scholastic traditions at that university going back to Duns Scotus were fully maintained. The 'schoolmen' of Oxford and elsewhere had been satirised by Erasmus, Sir Thomas More and others in the first decade of the sixteenth century – a satire with which Wolsey would perhaps have concurred. After all, he was no insular academic himself. Yet, as Peter Gwyn suggested, with the rise of Lutheranism in the early 1520s and growing uncertainty about the boundaries between legitimate criticism, satire and heresy, the essentially conservative Wolsey emphasised the inculcation of rigour in argument in those who would be responsible for defending doctrinal orthodoxy.

Books and music

Books were inevitably a major part of Thomas Wolsey's life. In his many and varied ecclesiastical roles and as a practising judge as the Chancellor, he used liturgical, theological, legal and linguistic texts virtually daily. Like everything else, books were an important part of the display of his high status and dignity with their cost, appearance and number. In the letter of May 1519, Erasmus went on to flatter Wolsey as a great book collector: 'In the getting together of libraries richly furnished with good authors of every kind you rival Ptolemy Philadelphus [king of Ptolemaic Egypt 283–246 BCE] himself, who owes his fame to this even more than to his crown'.[46] Perhaps in this aspect of his patronage, more than any other, it remains difficult to gauge accurately the extent of Wolsey's efforts or success. His principal library is thought to have been at York Place, where he spent most of his time during the legal terms each year, but he may have had a significant part of his collection at Hampton Court and other residences. Although it was not fully established during his lifetime, Wolsey had evidently intended to found in Oxford what

184   *Cardinal benefactor*

would have been a truly exceptional collection for England and one to rival many on the Continent. The revised 1527 statutes for Cardinal College make clear how the library was to function and be supervised, who would have access to its collection and on what terms. Readers were instructed as to how to treat the books to avoid damaging them. Policy for protecting and enhancing the value of the collection was outlined, and two catalogues of the library were to be kept. Wolsey sought to build the library's collection, especially of texts in Greek, by purchase and donation. He approached several English scholars as well as European sources, principally the Vatican and Venice. He sought copies of manuscripts donated to the Republic by Cardinal Bessarion (1403–72) after the fall of Constantinople. Unfortunately, it is not known whether any of the texts Wolsey sought ever arrived in Oxford before his fall. One inventory survives of liturgical books sent from Hampton Court to Oxford in 1525 'to the use of my lord's new college there', but these were for use in the chapel rather than the library.[47]

Recent scholarship has established that at least 31 books gathered from various monasteries were in Wolsey's possession at his death, all identified by the distinctive 'TC' monogram, and all of which deal with theology and English history. There are traces of some others which made their way to European collections by gift or subsequent purchase. Cardinal Campeggio gave Wolsey an exquisite fifteenth-century Book of Hours, now in the collection of Stonyhurst College. A number of works dedicated to him have also been identified among Henry VIII's collection, including a cosmographical treatise written in Germany in 1523, an encomium for the year 1529, two translations of Galen's medical text by Thomas Linacre and a treatise of civil law by Sylvester Dario, the papal collector in England. Wolsey is also known to have had two orthodox preaching texts. The first was a copy of Aelfric of Eynsham's *First book of homilies in Anglo Saxon*. The second was John Capgrave's collection of the lives of English saints, the *Nova legenda Anglie*, printed by Richard Pynson, the royal printer, in 1516. Perhaps the two best known books associated with Wolsey are an epistle lectionary now at Christ Church and a gospel lectionary now at Magdalen College, Oxford. Richly illuminated, the two books were designed as a pair, and their decorative schemes are dominated by Wolsey's badges, arms and motto and reflect his

Cardinal benefactor   185

various roles and achievements. They were most likely intended for the cardinal's own use, probably at York Place, rather than for either of his collegiate foundations, and it was probably from this location that they, along with the majority of his books, were removed to the royal collection after his fall.[48]

The patronage of music was, almost inevitably, an important aspect of Wolsey's cultural patronage in his own household, in those abbeys and cathedrals of which he was at least titular head and in his educational establishments. His primary concern was for the many religious services which marked his household's weekly, monthly and yearly cycles at Hampton Court and elsewhere. He provided music for its leisure time as well, together with frequent entertainments he hosted for guests, including foreign ambassadors and the king. His household players could sometimes be supplemented by other musicians, including those of the royal entourage. Cavendish relates one occasion when Wolsey entertained Henry, and although he gives neither place nor date, his description suggests Hampton Court. The king arrived with a dozen other maskers disguised as shepherds with false beards of gold, silver and silk. They were greeted with salvoes of small cannons before being brought into Wolsey's presence chamber to participate in an elaborate game in the course of which Wolsey 'discovered' the king and ceded the place of honour to him. A sumptuous banquet and dancing followed, and the whole occasion was, Cavendish notes, accompanied 'with such a number of drums and fifes as I have seldom seen together at one time in any masque'. Shakespeare incorporated this event into *Henry VIII*, and it was reputedly the misfiring of cannons during this scene that set fire to the roof and destroyed the Globe Theatre in Southwark in June 1613.[49]

Wolsey also used ceremonial and celebratory music very consciously as part of what might now be called his 'soft power' in diplomacy. Choral and instrumental music was an important element in the signing and solemnisation of the Treaty of Universal Peace in 1518 and that of The More in 1525. At the Field of Cloth of Gold, Wolsey's choir, or elements of it, attended him and may have joined with members of the Chapel Royal for the various masses celebrated during the course of the event, most famously the Mass of the Holy Spirit on 23 June when both French and English choirs sang parts of the Mass. The cardinal's musicians and choir also accompanied him on his other two visits to France. In August 1527, he offered musical entertainments to the French king's mother Louise of Savoy and the ladies of her entourage, also heard by the king, when he was at Amiens. Cavendish relates how the cardinal's musicians played 'so cunningly and dulce [gently] all night' that Francis asked to borrow them for the following day when they again played so much that, he assures us, one of the shawm players died. Wolsey's musicians also featured in the entertainments given to the French ambassadors a few months later at Hampton Court when, according to Cavendish, as Wolsey's guests were served, they were offered 'such a pleasant noise of divers instruments of music that the Frenchmen (as it seemed) were rapt into an heavenly paradise'.[50]

It was principally, however, with the full choirs that Wolsey assembled to perform the elaborate choral polyphony then fashionable that he made his mark as a patron of music. They were reputedly among the best in the kingdom. According to Cavendish, the singing staff of Wolsey's own chapel totalled 32 priest-chaplains and clerks or 'singing men' and 12 boys, which eclipsed the choir of the chapel royal and was as large as that of St Paul's Cathedral in London. Wolsey's choir served him in his three principal residences.[51] Regrettably, virtually none of the music or music books used by Wolsey's choir is known to have survived. Evidence does, however, survive indicating that he patronised Richard Pygott (1485–1549) and John Taverner (c.1490–1545). Pygott was master of the choristers of Wolsey's chapel and worked alongside fellow composers Avery Burnett and John Mason. He wrote several sacred works together with secular songs whose forms anticipate the emerging domestic madrigal. John Taverner, England's greatest composer of the early sixteenth century, was the first organist and master of the choristers at Cardinal College. His most celebrated work is the *Missa Gloria tibi, Trinitas*, but there are also settings of the *Ave Maria*, all likely to have been composed during his four years at Oxford till 1530. Some of the music books used at Cardinal College have survived, including settings of the Mass by Tavener among others, including another important early Renaissance composer Robert Fayrfax (1464–1521), who rose from the chapel royal of Henry VII and enjoyed royal patronage until the end of his life.

A few of the names of the clerks and boys who served in Wolsey's chapel choir have survived, partly because of the stiff competition between choirs at the time for the best singers, who became the subject of correspondence. Wolsey, it seems, enjoyed the right of impressment of singers for his own choir and of protecting it from the predations of others. There are several examples of him pinching talented singers from churches in London, and from Canterbury Cathedral, but in March 1518, he was unable to prevent Henry demanding the transfer to the chapel royal of a boy in his choir named Robyn who was evidently highly gifted. In addition to his own chapel, Wolsey established choirs for both his collegiate foundations. At Cardinal College there were 42 individuals employed in the choir, including 12 chaplains, 12 lay clerks and 16 choristers. As we have seen, the college at Ipswich had proportionately less, with eight choristers. As was the case with his household choir, Wolsey sought to retain the best singers and musicians available for each of these foundations, and there are similar trails of correspondence seeking impressment of singers for them. He also insisted upon the highest skills in the choir masters of these establishments and received reports that they and their choirs were well regarded in their respective colleges and beyond.[52]

Wolsey's personal taste in music, both secular and sacred, and his promotion of it in his court and educational establishments, has been described as conservative rather than particularly experimental. They show virtually no sign of Continental innovations, such as the accompaniment of instruments, in the way Wolsey would have seen and heard done in France in 1520 and in 1527. Instead, he favoured the kinds of liturgical settings that allowed his choirs to make the best of the ancient plainsong tradition as well as the luxuriant and expansive polyphonic sound of the late-medieval style. These forms, and the forces deployed in his choirs to produce them, proclaimed both his dependable orthodoxy in already-troubled times and the grandeur of his status in the kingdom and beyond, as the foremost churchman and cardinal legate of England.

Wolsey's cultural influence

As with so much of Wolsey's committed and determined activity, his musical patronage served his immediate needs very effectively, but its influence was limited largely to his own life span. Wolsey's choirs of the mid-1520s were all broken up within a short time after his fall

188   *Cardinal benefactor*

as other patrons made use of their talented singers. Nevertheless, this dispersal into royal and other services was a kind of legacy through which he contributed to the generation of English music that followed. In virtually every area of cultural endeavour, it was Henry who was the prime beneficiary of Wolsey's patronage. This is because he appropriated virtually all Wolsey's possessions for himself, as well as a great deal of the expertise that the cardinal had acquired for his own service. The king's own architectural patronage and sheer quantity of possessions eventually eclipsed the cardinal's, in part because Wolsey's collection made such a substantial contribution to the royal one. During his lifetime, it was Wolsey who was the foremost patron across a widest range of artistic and intellectual activity. Claims have been made that it was Wolsey who taught Henry how to be a patron and set the example for all that followed. These are hard to substantiate on closer inspection, but there is no doubt that the king and his chief servant did both enjoy architecture and discussed, even collaborated on, plans for Henry's palace of Beaulieu in Essex, on the temporary palace at the Field of Cloth of Gold and perhaps elsewhere, such as at Bridewell. In one sense, Hampton Court and York Place became collaborative insofar as Henry extended and embellished significantly what Wolsey had begun. Henry's planned tomb, it will be recalled, borrowed both materials and design ideas from Wolsey's. Cavendish and Vergil give sufficient evidence of a mutual appreciation between the king and the cardinal of music, of rare objects and new technology, and the way that Wolsey often showed the king these kinds of things. Gifts exchanged between them at New Year and other occasions were perhaps conventional, cups and the like, but decoratively would typically have been of the 'newest fashions', as devised by Amadas, Hayes, Twistleton and others. So, discourse on artistic patronage of all kinds there was between Wolsey and the king, and it is reasonable to assume that they influenced each other at times. The king's own instincts were encouraged and perhaps shaped to an extent by interactions with Wolsey, principally in the way both looked to the 'antique' or Italian Renaissance style. Yet we should not forget that it was Henry, not Wolsey, who was the first major English patron of Torrigiano. Henry eventually owned more of everything than Wolsey ever did, but the one area where he clearly eclipsed Wolsey as a patron was portraiture. Henry is most famous precisely because of the series of portraits done of, and for, him, principally by Hans Holbein the Younger in the 1530s. Because of Holbein's genius, Henry dominates the story of artistic patronage during his reign, as he does Holbein's canvases, and makes it almost wholly his own. Henry's patronage was indeed considerable and a conscious product of his own reputation-building and royal munificence. Yet, we should not allow that compelling image entirely to obscure the figure of his sometime companion in arts and the other, single-most significant, cultural patron of Henry's reign – Cardinal Thomas Wolsey.

Notes

1 *Collected Works of Erasmus: Correspondence of Erasmus*, ed. D. F. S. Thompson (Toronto, 1980), vol. 6, pp. 366–7; Erasmus to Wolsey, 18 May 1519.

2 Rawdon Brown, II, p. 314.

3 Richardson, 'Anglo-French Relations', p. 166 for further details on Wynter's accommodation.

4 Lewycky, 'Serving God and King', pp. 23–54; see also Appendices 1–5.

5 *LP* IV, 3 for stable costs; *LP* II ii, 4623 December 1518.

6 M. Everett, *The Rise of Thomas Cromwell: Power and Politics in the Reign of Henry VIII* (New Haven & London, 2016), pp. 26–36; see also Ward and MacCulloch, *Cromwell*.

7 'Heneage, Sir Thomas', by Michael Riordan, *ODNB*.

8 G. Redworth, *In Defence of the Church: Life of Stephen Gardiner* (Oxford, 1990).

9 S. Thurley, 'The Domestic Building Works of Cardinal Wolsey', in Gunn and Lindley, pp. 76–102, at p. 83.

10 H. M. Colvin, *The History of the King's Works* (London, 1963–82), vol. IV, pp. 53–8.

11 Cavendish, p. 102; *CSPV* IV, 682 Savorgnano to unknown recipient 25 August; S. Thurley, *Whitehall Palace: An Architectural History of the Royal Apartments, 1240–1698* (New Haven & London, 1999), pp. 13–22.

12 *LP* IV ii, 4251 Edward Foxe to Stephen Gardiner, 11 May 1528; Thurley, 'Domestic Building Works', p. 85.

13 Skelton, *Why Come Ye Nat to Corte?* Lines 398–412, www.exclassics.com/skelton/skel065.htm.

14 K. Weil-Garris and J. D'Amico, 'The Renaissance Cardinal's Ideal Palace: A Chapter from Cortesi's "De Cardinalatu"', *Memoirs of the American Academy in Rome* 35 (Ann Arbor, 1980), pp. 45–119.

15 Cavendish, pp. 24–5.

16 TNA, SP1/26, fo. 273. I am grateful to Dr Alden Gregory for this reference.

190 *Cardinal benefactor*

17 Matusiak, pp. 156–8; *CSPV* II, 987.
18 J. Foyle, 'A Reconstruction of Thomas Wolsey's Great Hall at Hampton Court Palace', *Architectural History* 45 (2002): 128–58; D. Ford and M. Turner, 'The Kynges New Haull: A Response to Jonathan Foyle's "Reconstruction of Thomas Wolsey's Great Hall at Hampton Court Palace"', *Architectural History* 47 (2004): 53–76.
19 S. Thurley, *Hampton Court: A Social and Architectural History* (New Haven & London, 2003), pp. 30–5.
20 Cavendish, pp. 26–7.
21 Thurley, 'Domestic Building Works', pp. 90–1.
22 Report of the Time Team dig at The More, 2012, www.wessexarch.co.uk/our-work/time-team-series-20-wolseys-lost-palace-manor-more-northwood.
23 F. Barditi, 'Jean du Bellay, bâtisseur passioné de la France à Italie', in C. Michon and L. Petris (eds.), *Le Cardinal Jean du Bellay: Diplomatie et culture dans l'Europe de la Renaissance* (Rennes, 2014), pp. 193–220.
24 Thurley, 'Domestic Building Works', pp. 91–3.
25 K. Rawlinson, 'Giovanni da Maiano: On the English Career of a Florentine Sculptor (c.1520–42)', *Sculpture Journal* 26 (1) (2017): 37–52.
26 P. G. Lindley, 'Playing Check-Mate with Royal Majesty? Wolsey's Patronage of Italian Renaissance Sculpture', in Gunn and Lindley, pp. 261–85 at pp. 280–5.
27 MacCulloch, *Cromwell*, pp. 54–7.
28 *LP* III i, 2 Henry's instructions to Rovezzano, 5 January 1519.
29 Lindley, pp. 278 and 272–3 for a suggested design of the tomb.
30 L. Fagnart, 'Les biens meubles du château de Gaillon', in J. Dumont and L. Fagnart (eds.), *Georges Ier d'Amboise 14601–1510: Une figure plurielle de la Renaissance* (Rennes, 2013), pp. 169–87.
31 Campbell, *Henry VIII and the Art of Majesty*, pp. 130–1.
32 Ibid.
33 *CSPV* III, 130; IV, 493; M. Hayward and P. Ward (eds.), *The Inventory of King Henry VIII*, vol. 2: *Textiles and Dress* (London, 2012), pp. 135–8.
34 TNA, E 36/171, fos. 1–5v.
35 Cavendish, pp. 71–3.
36 Ibid., pp. 102–3.
37 Christ Church Oxford Archive: Deanery Papers iv.b.2; Printed in J. Gutch, *Collectanea Curiosa* (2 vols; Oxford, 1781), vol. II; P. Glanville, 'Wolsey and the Goldsmith', in Gunn and Lindley, pp. 131–48; *LP* II I, 129,159, for purchases of plate for Wolsey in Paris.
38 BL, Harley MS 599, fos. 1–116 [*LP* IV iii, 6184] inventory of Wolsey's household.
39 BNF, MS français 10,390, fos. 49–51.
40 TNA SP1/75, fos. 102–49 at fo. 117 [*LP* VI, 339, 13 April 1533].
41 See Chapter 1 for discussion of two best known posthumous portraits.

42 Rawdon Brown, II, p. 314; *CSPV* III, 232.

43 Curthoys, *The Cardinal's College*, pp. 3–15.

44 E. A. Bond, *Statutes of the Colleges of the University of Oxford* (3 vols; Oxford, 1853), vol. II, part 11, pp. 11–20.

45 J. C. Cox, 'The Cardinal's College, Ipswich', in *A History of the County of Suffolk: Volume 2*, ed. W. Page (London, 1975), pp. 142–4.

46 *Collected Works of Erasmus*, as cited in note 1.

47 *Statutes of the Colleges of the University of Oxford*, II, 11, pp. 112–13; J. Willoughby, 'Thomas Wolsey and the Books of Cardinal College Oxford', *Bodleian Library Record* (December 2016), pp. 114–34 at p. 118.

48 www.wolseymanuscripts.ac.uk; J. Carley, 'Thomas Wolsey's Epistle and Gospel Lectionaries: Unanswered Questions and New Hypotheses', *Bodleian Library Record* (August 2016): 43–59; see also J. Carley, *The Books of King Henry VIII and His Wives* (London, 2004), pp. 80–4.

49 Cavendish, pp. 26–30.

50 Ibid., pp. 61–3 for the episode at Amiens, and p. 73.

51 R. Bower, 'The Cultivation and Promotion of Music in the Household and Orbit of Thomas Wolsey', in Gunn and Lindley, pp. 178–218, at p. 180.

52 Ibid., pp. 202–3.

6 'Cardinalis pacificus'

Wolsey's 'Eternal Peace'

> *Now was there made divers pageants for joy of his coming, who was called there and in all other places within the realm of France as he travelled, Le Cardinal Pacifique; and in Latin, Cardinalis Pacificus, who was accompanied all that night with divers worthy gentlemen of the country thereabout.*[1]

Wolsey's gentleman-usher described Cardinal Wolsey's entry in July 1527 to the town of Montreuil-sur-Mer in France as a personal triumph. The cardinal's reception was made on the orders of Francis I who came to Amiens to meet Wolsey. There the two men concluded a treaty of 'Eternal' or 'Perpetual' peace and alliance between England and France. Doubtless Wolsey enjoyed the praise heaped upon him by the good people of Montreuil and throughout his journey to Amiens as the 'cardinal of peace', but his visit was really part of his efforts to make good his claims for Henry as the 'prince of peace' in Europe, which he had first essayed almost ten years earlier in 1518.

In the months after the Field of Cloth of Gold in 1520, there had been some scepticism in England at least about its real significance and whether peace in Europe would be achieved. This was expressed in a sermon given at the time by Bishop Fisher of Rochester, who thought that although Henry and Francis had promised much,

> these princes (of whom we spoke before) were not so, but they had divers wills, diverse council and no endurable amity, as

'Cardinalis pacificus' 193

after that did well appear. These princes were mortal and mutable and so their will did change and not abide.[2]

Fisher had a point. The Universal Peace upon which Wolsey had set so many hopes and ambitions for himself and his sovereign proved impossible to implement, let alone maintain for any length of time. The rivalry between Francis and Charles V was simply too great for that to happen. Immediately after the Field of Cloth of Gold, Francis had returned to the royal château of Saint-Germain-en-Laye where, in August, his fifth child, Princess Madeleine, was born. By then he had received news of Henry's meeting with Charles at Calais in July and also assurances that nothing had been done there to his prejudice. He expressed his gratitude to Henry and Wolsey through the resident English ambassador, still Sir Richard Wingfield.[3] Wolsey was clearly anxious to provide further reassurance of Henry's goodwill, and soon after Wingfield was succeeded as ambassador by his fellow Knight of the Body in the Privy Chamber, Sir Richard Jerningham. The new ambassador's instructions were drafted by Wolsey. They made clear that the change reflected the wish to emphasise the steadily growing importance of the personal links between the two sovereigns through men who, since the expulsion of the minions, held court offices close to the king, but who were also men whom Wolsey trusted. Jerningham's instructions incorporated a full report of what had transpired at Calais, particularly that Henry had not agreed to any offensive alliance with Charles against Francis. This was the truth, but not the whole truth. They had concluded a mutually defensive alliance, each promising to aid the other if he were attacked. It was this alliance, more than the provisions of the Universal Peace itself, upon which Charles later relied in dealings with England. Nevertheless, there was nothing in the treaty that contradicted the pre-existing Anglo-French alliance agreement for Mary's marriage to the dauphin, agreed in 1518. Charles and Henry also agreed to send special representatives to Calais within two years to work towards increased co-operation between them, but no plans for an attack on France were laid, much to Charles's frustration. Henry had kept his promise to Francis, and, Wolsey urged, Francis should ensure that he did likewise and do nothing to Henry's disadvantage.[4]

In the weeks around the Field of Cloth of Gold, Pope Leo, who had never really been supportive of the Universal Peace as organised by Wolsey, made considerable efforts to induce him to persuade Henry to break the alliance with Francis. He promised to extend the cardinal's legatine status (always of great importance to Wolsey) apparently for life if he secured a Franco–Imperial alliance. This Wolsey resolutely refused to do as he did not want Henry dragged into an expensive war for the aims of the emperor or the pope. His legatine status technically ended shortly after his return to London after the Field. Given that he had neither secured the anti-French alliance Leo wanted, nor raised the clerical taxation for which, among other things, the authority was originally granted, Wolsey might have been worried. Somewhat surprisingly, however, in January 1521, Leo agreed to a further extension of Wolsey's legatine powers, not for life as he hoped but for a further two years. Yet more followed. In April and in June 1521, Leo further extended Wolsey's legatine status for ten years and extended his powers over the English Church considerably. He had, in the end, more or less honoured the promise of which he had spoken the previous summer. He did so because, despite having ample reasons to be frustrated with Wolsey, the cardinal remained the only way for Leo to get to Henry, and he still hoped for English cooperation against Francis.[5]

Francis was well aware of Leo's hostility towards him, and this added further to his anxieties. Whatever assurances he received from Henry and Wolsey, he was still unsettled by the implications of Charles's election as Holy Roman Emperor and the 1518 Universal Peace. Francis did not so much fear a direct attack on France as that the emperor's power would encircle France and threaten his own hold on the duchy of Milan. Charles had a claim to Milan as well through his grandfather Maximilian, and he was nervous of French power in northern Italy, a fear he shared with Leo. Francis also feared that Charles might perhaps prevent him making good his claim to the kingdom of Naples, inherited from his predecessors Charles VIII and Louis XII. He was right to be concerned. By 1520, the Treaty of Noyon, which Charles and Francis had agreed four years earlier to sort out competing claims between them, had effectively expired. Francis felt compelled to return to Milan to reinforce his hold over it, and he fretted that the longer he waited to do so, the more time he gave Charles to consolidate such financial and military power as he had there. Francis in turn expected Henry to support his claim to Naples, but this was of course precisely what the Universal Peace had been designed to prevent him pursuing.

At Aachen on 23 October 1520, Charles was crowned as the elected ruler of the German lands and acclaimed as 'King of the Romans', the first of a two-part formalisation of his full Imperial status. This event, together with his continuing fears about Milan, seems to have provoked Francis into what proved a disastrously short-sighted attempt to force Henry and Wolsey to side with him as the apparent victim of Imperial aggression. In the spring of 1521, Robert II de La Marck, duke of Bouillon and lord of Sedan, an Imperial subject, attacked his overlord's territory in Luxembourg, covertly supported by the French. At about the same time, two French noblemen, André de Foix, lord of Lesparre, and Henri d'Albret attacked Navarre in support of Henri's claim to that kingdom. Naturally the emperor counter-attacked, as the French surely expected he would. They immediately called for Henry's assistance according to the terms of the Universal Peace. It was as well for them that they did because, by the end of May, Charles V's commander, Henry of Nassau, had thrown La Marck out of Luxembourg. He did not stop there but overran the lordship of Sedan and threatened France itself. Meanwhile, after initially taking Navarre, Lesparre over-reached himself and attacked Castile, but was eventually forced back out of Navarre. Charles immediately called on Henry and Wolsey to implement the terms of the Universal Peace and to stand with him against French aggression, under the terms of the mutual alliance agreed at Calais in July the previous year. In June, Pope Leo X publicly repudiated Francis, having signed a treaty with Charles in which he promised to invest him with the kingdom of Naples and formally invited him to enter Italy to receive from his hands the Imperial crown.[6]

Wolsey quickly appreciated the consequences of the fighting on the French borders, the calls for assistance from both Charles and Francis and Leo's intervention. He advised Henry that the king's status would be enhanced, not by backing one side against the other as they wished, but by arbitrating the dispute, strictly within the terms of the Universal Peace. As he told Henry:

> In this controversy between these two princes it shall be a marvellous great praise and honour to your grace so by your high wisdom and authority to pass between and stay them both, that ye be not by their contention and variance brought unto the war.[7]

Accordingly, Sir Richard Jerningham was sent to ask Francis to agree to arbitration. At the same time, two French ambassadors sounded Henry and Wolsey out once more on possible support against Charles. Their resolutely negative response eventually elicited Francis's agreement to arbitration on 9 June 1521.[8]

Accordingly, the cardinal arranged a peace conference between the parties, chaired by himself, at Calais. He arrived, amidst his usual pomp, on 2 August 1521 armed with authority to resolve the dispute from Henry, the pope, Charles and Francis. The grand claims and promises of the Universal Peace reached their acid test, and Wolsey apparently worked hard to make good on them. Peter Gwyn argued persuasively that Wolsey's real commitment at the Calais conference was, however, to ensure Henry did not lose the advantageous position he had achieved by the Universal Peace, rather than to defend peace itself in the way envisaged in 1518. Whatever he told the king, Wolsey knew, almost certainly before he even arrived in Calais, that Henry must eventually be drawn into the conflict on one side or the other if it continued. It was best, then, to bring it to an end if at all possible, and Wolsey never lacked self-confidence. But if not, then Henry must at all costs be kept on the winning side. That is why, on 16 August, after two weeks of conducting intense and apparently indifferent negotiations between the French and the Imperialists, Wolsey went to Bruges, there to negotiate with the emperor's representatives for an alliance against France which had first been offered a year earlier in the days immediately after the Field of Cloth of Gold. Ostensibly he went still as the arbiter and honest broker of the dispute, but barely ten days later an alliance was concluded.[9]

The strongest evidence that Wolsey did want peace, but only for as long as there was no better alternative, is a letter he wrote to

'Cardinalis pacificus' 197

Henry on 14 November explaining this alliance, pointing out that the king's reputation would be enhanced by taking the opportunity to attack Francis, whose power and resources were rapidly being diminished by the war with Charles. On 24 November 1521 a final treaty of alliance was signed. This agreement also included the papacy, something Leo had been wanting for a year or more.[10] By then Francis was on the back foot in the fighting. Milan had fallen to Imperial forces, and he was unable to raise the siege of the city of Tournai (for which he had paid Henry handsomely in 1519). It capitulated to the emperor's army in December 1521, by which time the duchy of Milan had also fallen to Imperial forces.

The weakness inherent in the Treaty of Universal Peace and its design for collective security was revealed at Calais. It could not deal with agendas too big for Henry or Wolsey effectively to control. Wolsey was perhaps fortunate that this first collapse of his ambitious foreign policy did not worry Henry too much. He had, after all, failed to provide the king with the kind of dominant position and reputation through peace-making and peace-keeping that he had promised would be his. But by then, Henry had convinced himself that Francis was indeed to blame for the breach of the peace and had been unreasonable in the negotiations at Calais, and this allowed, indeed demanded, a resumption of the conquest of France begun almost a decade earlier.

Wolsey swung quickly and completely behind plans for war with France. In early March 1522, notwithstanding an outbreak of the sweating sickness that Lent, an embassy of Flemish courtiers arrived in England for discussions and planning. On Shrove Tuesday, Wolsey entertained them and the royal court with an elaborate masque and banquet at York Place, or at Hampton Court. The king took part in the masque as one of a group of eight knights who successfully attacked, with dates and oranges, a castle of love or virtue defended with rose water and sweets by no fewer than 16 ladies. The knights captured their 'prisoners' and danced with them in a light-hearted and romantic allusion to success in warfare, and of the kind often enjoyed by the Tudor court.[11]

The new Anglo-Habsburg alliance was shortly afterwards inaugurated on a much grander scale. The 1521 Bruges treaty had provided that Charles would visit his uncle and ally and confer

198   'Cardinalis pacificus'

upon the details of Henry's actual entry to the conflict. He duly arrived in England, with an entourage of almost 1,000 people, on 26 May 1522. He was in high spirits, as the war against Francis seemed by then to be going his way. Wolsey left York Place to meet him at Dover accompanied by an augmented retinue which, Hall specifies, included 8 bishops, 10 abbots, 30 chaplains; 2 earls, 36 knights, 100 gentlemen and 700 yeomen. He welcomed the emperor to England at Dover at about 4.00PM and escorted him to its castle. He then helped Henry with one of those carefully contrived moments of apparent spontaneity which often marked sixteenth-century diplomacy. The king was supposed to meet Charles as Wolsey escorted him from Dover to Canterbury a day later, but there were delays in getting all the baggage across to Dover. Accordingly, Wolsey advised Henry to come to meet the emperor at the port. Henry agreed but told Wolsey that only he was to know so that Charles would think Henry's 'coming [to Dover] to be of his own mind and affection towards the emperor'.[12] Henry took Charles to inspect his flagship the *Henri Grâce à Dieu* together with other ships, moored outside Dover harbour. Charles was entertained by the king with jousts and banquets at Greenwich, before, on 6 June, he was received into London with a series of flattering pageants given by the city. Wolsey hosted the emperor at Hampton Court for two days, the first occasion he had entertained there on a grand scale. Charles stayed in England for the rest of the month on progress with Henry through Berkshire and Hampshire, hunting as they went, before the emperor embarked for Spain from Southampton on 6 July. A portrait of the two of them as allies and friends (now in a private collection) was painted either at the time, or retrospectively, to commemorate this visit. Meanwhile in France, on 29 May, Clarencieux Herald formally declared war on Francis I.[13]

Had Francis enjoyed better fortune on the battlefield in the early part of the year, it is doubtful that Wolsey would have allowed Henry to get anywhere near declaring war. Even now, he wanted to postpone further any actual English invasion of France for at least a year, and longer if possible, apparently on the basis that God might yet dispose Christian princes to a peace. This postponement was agreed in a treaty signed at Windsor during the emperor's visit.

'*Cardinalis pacificus*' 199

In fact, Wolsey wanted more time to build up the required funds, and he even suggested 1525 as the entry year at one point. He was never squeamish about effective warfare with France, and few men better appreciated the charm it held for Henry, but neither did he underestimate the cost or difficulty of an invasion and had little confidence in Charles as a military tactician.

Things being thus, it is quite possible that England might never have actually entered the war but for the fact that in 1522 the duke of Bourbon, the greatest magnate in France after the king, sought support from Charles and Henry for a revolt against Francis. The two had been in dispute over Bourbon's landholdings in central France and their future following the death in 1521 of Bourbon's wife, Suzanne, the daughter of Pierre de Beaujeu.[14] The prospect was now raised of a three-pronged attack on Francis. Charles would invade Guienne in the south, the English would attack Picardy in the north, and Bourbon would attack the royal army that Francis was then leading from Lyons towards Milan in an effort to wrest it back from Charles. After complex, year-long negotiations, an agreement was finally reached, and in August–September 1523, an English army led by the duke of Suffolk invaded French territory from Calais with initial orders only to besiege the neighbouring coastal city of Boulogne with a view to establishing a base for further operations.

Wolsey had initially agreed with this strategy but then began urging the king to send the army south towards Paris, to link up with Charles's army and that of Bourbon who was presumed at this stage to have risen against Francis. He wanted a quick war to force Francis into a bargaining position, not the protracted and expensive siege of one city. Henry disagreed but was eventually persuaded, and in late September Suffolk's army was ordered to march towards Paris. It did so rapidly and was 50 miles from the royal capital a month later. By that time, however, Henry had effectively been abandoned by his allies. Charles's army had been stopped in its tracks by the French commander Lautrec and was nowhere near where it should have been to rendezvous with Suffolk. Bourbon's revolt, always half-hearted, had collapsed ignominiously, and he fled France to enter the emperor's service. Reluctantly, Henry accepted that the attack, urged on by Wolsey, had failed, and the army was recalled.[15]

The return to peace, 1524–6

In January 1524, Bourbon wrote from Genoa to one of his associates asking him to urge the king of England to renew the fighting in France. That seems to have been Henry's clear intention, yet a month later, Wolsey was writing to the new pope Clement VII praising him for his efforts towards peace between princes and assuring him that he was 'ready to devote his goods, or even his life if necessary, to his service. He may depend on the King as a firm ally, whom Wolsey will continually strengthen in his good purpose'.[16] By the summer he had also begun secret exploratory talks with Louise of Savoy, who was regent while her son was on campaign. These secret negotiations were initially undertaken by Jean Joachim de Passano, an experienced Genoese diplomat with whom Wolsey had dealt before. Talks progressed over the autumn and some initial progress was made, but with the French re-conquest of Milan looking at that point quite likely, Louise wanted to concede as little as possible.[17] All that changed, however, with the news of the defeat and capture of Francis at the Battle of Pavia on 24 February 1525. He was taken to Spain shortly afterwards as the prisoner of Charles. Henry was informed of the news in March by a messenger sent from the Imperial commander at the battle, the receipt of whose report sent the king wild with delight. To cap his unearned triumph, Henry learnt that the last Yorkist claimant to the throne, Richard de la Pole, 'the White Rose', had been killed at Pavia.

Wolsey probably did not entirely share his master's happiness at Francis's defeat but was immediately busy in mustering troops and attempting to raise the extra-parliamentary Amicable Grant (see Chapter 3) so that Henry could invade France in person as the king was now determined to do. As we have seen, however, the widespread resistance to the grant and the opprobrium heaped on Wolsey in consequence expressed the nation's reluctance to pay for more war against France. Henry's coffers were empty. Charles, too, was penniless, and he had thus far avoided any immediate or detailed response to Henry's call for a joint invasion of the apparently defenceless French kingdom. He was sure in his own mind that he had been handed literally a God-given opportunity to impose an advantageous settlement on his most dangerous foe, and he was not about to let Henry's chivalric ambitions in France get in the way of that.

Louise of Savoy anticipated exactly Henry's response to her son's defeat and turned urgently to Wolsey in search of a settlement with England.[18] Wolsey seized on negotiations in order to capitalise diplomatically and financially on Francis's defeat. At the same time, a French plan was coming together with Venice for an anti-Habsburg league, into which it was hoped Henry would be drawn. Accordingly, when Jean Joachim de Passano, now seigneur de Vaux, and his colleague Jean Brinon came to England in the summer of 1525, they were far more accommodating of Wolsey's demands for massive sums of money in exchange for a truce, and eventually a peace agreement. Wolsey persuaded the king to respond favourably, reminding him how little Charles was now offering him in comparison. He also pointed out the rapidly growing demand for action against the emperor's now preponderant power in Italy.[19] Wolsey negotiated hard with the French, and five separate agreements, together constituting the Treaty of The More, were signed on 30 August. The most important of these bound Francis to pay Henry two million crowns in yearly instalments of 100,000 crowns. In return, Henry would demand that Charles release Francis from captivity in Spain.[20] Wolsey did not lose out either. The French ensured that he benefitted financially from his work in their interests. As part of the Treaty of The More, they agreed to pay Wolsey a total of 121,898 crowns, which sum represented a pension he had previously been granted together with an amount to compensate him for the revenues of the bishopric of Tournai which he had never finally secured.[21] As we have seen, a number of leading English political figures were given pensions by the French. Charles Giry-Deloision showed that in 1525 their number increased. It was Wolsey who actually drew up the list of recipients, and he tended to favour his own adherents. This angered some of the English nobility. In 1521, Francis had awarded Thomas Grey, second marquis of Dorset, an annual pension of 1,000 crowns. In March 1525, Grey wrote to Wolsey expecting to have this pension restored. It was, but at a reduced rate of 475 crowns per year – much to Dorset's annoyance.[22] An Anglo-French truce was proclaimed at Lyon on 25 September 1525. Perhaps in anticipation of its future use in international treaties, that year Henry ordered Wolsey to have a

202   *'Cardinalis pacificus'*

new Great Seal of England cast and engraved, incorporating the king's title including 'Fidei Defensor' and showing the king 'sitting in majesty in a chair, crowned with the crown imperial'.[23]

Wolsey's 'Eternal Peace' of 1527

As 1526 began, Louise of Savoy and others were urging Wolsey to ensure that England was at the forefront of on-going efforts to oppose the power of Charles and to assist in securing her son's release from captivity. In fact, having taken Henry out of the war against France with financial advantage, Wolsey was determined once more to limit England's commitments to expensive wars elsewhere. Yet he was genuinely concerned that the emperor's potential hegemony might limit his own master's international prominence and to that extent favoured Francis's restoration to his kingdom and the re-establishment of the Anglo-French alliance. In a way it was not dissimilar to the situation back in 1514 when Henry had first been deserted by an Iberian-based ally (his father-in-law, Ferdinand) and so allied himself with his French counterpart to turn the tables on him. That was one thing, but Wolsey refused to commit Henry formally to another international league, or at least not one which was not of the cardinal's own making.

Although they lent weight to a negotiated settlement between Francis and Charles, Wolsey and Henry had no direct influence on the terms of the Franco–Imperial peace eventually agreed under the Treaty of Madrid, signed in January 1526. Its terms were onerous indeed. Essentially, Francis had to give up all his claims to Milan and the kingdom of Naples and to return the duchy of Burgundy and most of its appurtenant territories to the emperor as the successor to the Valois dukes. His two eldest sons were to be sent to Spain to be held as hostages for their father's performance of his obligations. He had also to marry the emperor's sister Eleanor.[24] Doubtless somewhat assured by England's support as well as that of Venice and having little real choice anyway, Francis reluctantly signed the agreement. He eventually returned to France on 17 March after being exchanged, on a pontoon moored in the middle of the Bidassoa river (the border between France and Spain) near Fuenterrabía, for his sons, François and Henri. Accompanied by a small group of intimates and servants, the king then rode to Bayonne where he was reunited with his mother.

'Cardinalis pacificus' 203

Meanwhile, Wolsey had spent January 1526 principally occupied with the Eltham Ordinances. These had important implications for his negotiations with France thereafter. As we have seen, Wolsey's court reforms effectively recognised, for the first time, that the Gentlemen of the Privy Chamber had a legitimate role in the king's dealings with Francis, and indeed with Charles V, as personal representatives and special ambassadors (see Chapter 3). This left Wolsey with a dilemma. On the one hand, the embassies of Wingfield and Jerningham, both Knights of the Body in the Privy Chamber, had shown how royal intimates could indeed foster good communications between Henry and Francis. Such direct links were now highly desirable for Wolsey's revived ambitions for peace and a restoration of Henry's international prominence – no longer in harness to the Habsburgs. On the other hand, for the implementation of this pro-French policy, he relied in part on men whose view of what was in the king's interests might differ from his. Most monarchs, including Francis, sent clerics to handle business alongside ambassadors of gentry or noble rank. Yet this was quite different to the situation before the 1522–5 war where gentlemen ambassadors such as Wingfield and Jerningham were formally intimates of the king, but also royal councillors and thus directly accountable to their peers on the council and to Wolsey. The cardinal was forced to discard the advantages of this system in order, as far as possible, to restrict the overtly political role of the gentleman ambassadors in dealings with Francis, so as to keep matters as far as he could in his own hands. This tendency, and perhaps tension, is evident from a letter that Dr John Taylor sent to Wolsey in January 1526 when his colleague Sir William Fitzwilliam was returning to England. Taylor had first become resident ambassador in France in September 1525 after the Treaty of The More. He asked to be sent frequent news so that he would have plenty of reason to go to court. This would confirm, he said, 'the opinions of them here . . . that think and say openly that I am in some favour with your Grace and say that Mr Treasurer (Fitzwilliam) was sent by the king's highness, and I from your Grace'.[25]

It is unclear whether Taylor considered that giving such an impression was appropriate, but his remarks reveal an awareness of how royal intimates like Fitzwilliam were viewed in France and how their complementary roles could be manipulated to Wolsey's advantage. Fitzwilliam had indeed been as much a protégé of the cardinal as he had been of the king. He was recalled to become Treasurer of the royal household pursuant to the Eltham Ordinances. Lawyers and churchmen like Taylor and his successor, John Clerk, the Bishop of Bath and Wells, knew that they owed their first allegiance to Henry. However, to a far greater extent than for Henry's gentry companions, their loyalty to the king was more naturally expressed in closer cooperation with Wolsey. Clerk and Taylor shared the role of resident English ambassador in France between them, occasionally supplemented by other clerics or Gentlemen of the Privy Chamber, until Wolsey began to lose power in mid-1529.

John Taylor was amongst the first foreign ambassadors to greet Francis on his return from Spain. Seeking to press home the English advantage, Henry and Wolsey ensured that a much grander embassy led by Sir Thomas Cheyne, a Gentleman of the Privy Chamber, who had been the last ambassador in France before the war, was now sent to congratulate Francis on his release. Although Dr Taylor had been 'hastily ordered' to greet Francis, the instructions drafted by Wolsey said, nevertheless, Henry could not forbear 'or be satisfied until such time as His Grace immediately and with diligence upon the said deliverance, had visited, seen and saluted the said French king by some one of his most secret familiars of his Privy Chamber'.[26] The sense of intimate friendship they evoke could not be clearer. In what are in effect Wolsey's words, Henry does not simply greet Francis, but metaphorically 'visits' him in the person of Cheyne who, because of his rank as a Gentleman of the King's Privy Chamber, embodies, or impersonates, his master in the truest sense of the word.

Wolsey was once more in his element. A revived momentum in personal relations between the two kings, of the kind that he had carefully cultivated in the years between 1518 and 1520, would once more spearhead an international peace or league on a much bigger scale than the proposed international alliance then being negotiated on the Continent. Perhaps a re-created Universal Peace of 1518 could yet be made to work to the advantage of Christendom in general, and Henry in particular? So Wolsey's thoughts seem to have run in the spring of the year. Francis was certainly keen to pick up the threads. Cheyne met him in Bordeaux on 9 April.[27] Wolsey was keen to assess Francis's attitude to the Treaty of Madrid. Dr Taylor was instructed, 'by such learning he has in the law', to assure Francis that he was not bound by an agreement signed under duress. This was music to Francis's ears, and he told the ambassadors as early as 13 April that, as Wolsey had anticipated, he had no intention of abiding by it. Wolsey threw his diplomatic effort behind the plans for an anti-Habsburg alliance, but still stopped short of committing Henry to it. It was eventually concluded in May 1526 as the so-called Holy League of Cognac, comprising France, the Papacy, Venice, Florence and the Sforza family, still claimants to Milan. Henry was declared its 'protector' but not included formally. Wolsey assured all that if the emperor would not come to more reasonable terms, England might yet enter, but that this mighty threat was best kept as a last resort. In July, Wolsey told his master that by remaining connected to, but not part of, the League, he would constrain the emperor to come to new terms with Francis and thus preside over 'a universal peace' in Christendom.[28]

Once Francis knew the League of Cognac was viable, he repudiated the Treaty of Madrid and refused to give up Burgundy. He claimed, with the support of the duchy's provincial Estates, that to do so would breach the 'fundamental laws' of France and was beyond his legal power as king to perform.[29] Almost immediately war broke out in northern Italy. At first things went well for the forces of the League, but Francis remained curiously aloof, not committing troops, despite the fact that the alliance had indirectly been formed for his support and protection. The emperor threw his forces into his stronghold of Milan in response, and Francis in turn looked to Henry to enter the conflict with him. In mid-August, John Clerk was sent to France as ambassador in place of John Taylor but brought no glad tidings with him.

Then, in October 1526, Wolsey received a full report from Sir John Wallop, in Cologne, of the battle at Mohác the previous August and the death of Louis II of Hungary. The threat from the Ottomans appeared greater now than it had ever been in the days of Leo X and what became the Universal Peace of 1518. Wolsey saw this as an opportune moment for Henry, judging from his letter to the king from Hampton Court on 9 October. In it he urged Henry to provide 30,000 or 35,000 ducats to pay for Swiss mercenaries to support the League, thereby, he said, securing peace, obtaining the gratitude of the pope, keeping the friendship of Charles and providing a basis for peace and action against the Ottomans – all while saving himself the greater expense of committing his own forces to the struggle and not having to help Francis.

The same month, the body of Queen Claude of France, who had died at Blois in 1524, was brought to Paris and interred at the royal abbey of Saint-Denis. Clerk warned Wolsey that, in accordance with the Treaty of Madrid, the next queen of France was due to be Eleanor, the sister of Charles V, and that notwithstanding Francis's repudiation of the demand for Burgundy, his second marriage might give him an excuse to seek to limit his obligations to Henry under the Treaty of The More, especially financially. Wolsey's response was to propose, somewhat embarrassingly for Francis, that the French king should marry Princess Mary instead. If he did, England would join the League, and Henry would demand the release of Francis's sons as hostages. In December, Sir William Fitzwilliam returned to France with proposals for a new peace and marriage alliance.[30]

Francis's equivocal but encouraging response was conveyed to Wolsey and the king by a high-powered team of ambassadors led by Gabriel de Grammont, the Bishop of Tarbes, that arrived in England in February 1527. It was the bishop who, Henry later alleged, had first alerted him to the uncertain state of his marriage in canon law to Katherine of Aragon. Later, as a cardinal, Grammont acted to support the annulment case in Rome. Wolsey welcomed the embassy warmly, making it clear that a new and yet more comprehensive Anglo-French peace settlement and alliance was his foremost aim. Meanwhile Charles's ambassador in England, Inigo de Mendoza, resisted demands that his master should accept a revised settlement with Francis. His voluminous correspondence with the emperor in the opening months of 1526 offers an insight into how Wolsey and Henry could work hand in glove. Each offered assurances of Henry's regard for Charles, while informing him on the progress of talks for an Anglo-French alliance and, alternatively, expressing impatience at the emperor's apparent unwillingness to come to new terms. Each pressed the ambassador to secure Charles's consent to a new mediated settlement between himself, Francis and Henry – which pressure Mendoza resisted stoutly. Sometimes Wolsey would take the initiative, sometimes Henry. Wolsey would usually be the more adversarial of the two, although at times Henry could be aggressive while Wolsey might earnestly assure the ambassador of his good faith, as a priest, towards the emperor and peace. They were evidently good at playing 'hard cop, soft cop'.[31]

The French ambassadors in England at the same time made similar observations about Wolsey's negotiating techniques, and if Mendoza was having a hard time of it, they were collectively astonished that, having pressed Francis to accept Mary as an alternative bride to Eleanor, Wolsey now told them that before he would discuss any marriage proposal, the French must confirm, once and for all, Henry's huge annual pension and a share of the profitable French salt trade which had been agreed under the Treaty of The More. He was, in effect, suggesting that the French should buy out Henry's ancient claim on the French throne. Only by offering a permanent or 'Eternal' Anglo-French (no longer 'Universal') peace, as it would thereafter be called, could Henry demand such a high price. The marriage negotiations must now await a totally re-negotiated peace agreement. Neither the 1518 Treaty of London, nor the Treaty of The More, were, Wolsey assured them blandly, ever intended to be anything other than short- to medium-term measures![32]

As the spring came on, the situation for the League of Cognac in Italy deteriorated rapidly. The emperor's forces were steadily taking hold of strategic points in the north – hence Charles's continued delays in committing the resolution of the quarrel with Francis to Wolsey and Henry. Francis could provide no financial support to his allies, though continued to promise it, and Pope Clement vacillated between remaining part of the league and coming to terms with the emperor. In these circumstances, Francis had little choice but to accept the deal on offer from England. The Treaty of Westminster was finally signed on 30 April. It provided for a marriage either between Mary and Francis or between her and his second son, Henry, who was then still a hostage in Spain. A joint embassy was to be sent to Charles to demand the release of the young French prince and his older brother. The rhetoric of international peace was echoed in the April treaty, but its real ancestor was not that of 1518, but the first Treaty of London, of 1514. As in that agreement, the king of France bound himself to acknowledge Henry's rights in France and the value of his friendship by paying him, in effect, a huge indemnity in return for his support. That done, Anglo-French joint power could be brought to bear to assist both kings in their complex relations with the rest of Europe and with Charles V in particular.

Henry ratified the treaty at Greenwich on 5 May, and the entertainments offered to the French embassy to mark the occasion were on a lavish scale, reminiscent of those of 1518 or the Field of Cloth of Gold.[33] They were renowned at the time, principally for the richness and innovation of the temporary building, the banqueting and 'disguising' house or theatre, built at Greenwich Palace, to accommodate them. This was a showcase for the technical and artistic talent marshalled by Henry's patronage of Hans Holbein, and the astronomer royal Nicholas Kratzer, among others.[34] Yet, even as celebrations for the third Anglo-French rapprochement of Henry's reign got underway, Imperial troops commanded by the duke of Bourbon had marched on Rome, as the headquarters of the League of Cognac, and thus enemy territory. On 6 May they broke through the walls and sacked the city, forcing the pope and those cardinals with him to flee to safety in the Castel Sant'Angelo and leaving him virtually a prisoner of Charles, with what would prove to be dire consequences for Wolsey.

In late May 1527, Arthur Plantagenet, Viscount Lisle, Thomas Boleyn, now Viscount Rochford, Anthony Browne and John Clerk were commissioned to accept Francis's ratification of the April treaty. They were officially received by the king on 8 June and entertained with a series of splendid banquets designed, as ever, to outmatch the hospitality given to the French ambassadors in England the previous month. The king of France met them and spoke 'very gently and discussed with us of hunting and building and divers other things'. The pageant of the 'Ruin of Rome' which was presented at one of these festivities was not described in Lord Lisle's written account of his embassy, but its subject matter is easy to imagine from its title.[35] As Wolsey grasped the implications of the Sack of Rome, he rapidly came to see that the Anglo-French peace had to be amplified, and quickly, into a platform for direct action in Italy. He was busy, full as ever of self-importance and confidence – all good things in international negotiations. Yet, as ever with Wolsey, appearances could be deceptive. By then he had another matter to deal with for which he had no similar enthusiasm but whose urgency could not be denied. This was the king's wish for an annulment of his marriage, to which we will return.

On 11 July 1527, Wolsey crossed the Channel hoping to turn 'the ruin of Rome' to Henry's advantage by amplifying the April peace treaty into a fuller and longer-term Anglo-French alliance. He wanted thereby to build a coalition of European powers greater than the League of Cognac that would enforce the pope's release and his agreement both to another international peace and, crucially, for a favourable resolution of Henry's marriage question. The cardinal was accompanied by a large entourage comprised of his own household, including his secretary Dr Stephen Gardiner, augmented by royal councillors and courtiers, chief among whom were Cuthbert Tunstall, the Bishop of London, Lord Sandys and Sir Thomas More. Wolsey was acutely aware of the responsibility of his vice-regal status, just as he had been in 1520 when last given such power to negotiate with the French king. Cavendish reported that Wolsey was still very concerned with appearances and told his entourage that he expected to have from them, 'all such service and reverence as to his highness's presence is meet and due'. In other words, they were to treat him as if he were the king himself which, as plenipotentiary for the negotiations, in truth he was. They were always to distinguish themselves as 'men that knoweth your duty to your sovereign lord and to your master'.[36]

Although then principally occupied with reasserting his authority over his realm, Francis personally oversaw plans for Wolsey's reception in France. At Boulogne, Montreuil-sur-Mer, Abbeville and finally at Amiens, Wolsey was presented with a succession of street pageants and orations in which he was praised as the peacemaking cardinal and saviour of the Church. When on 4 August Francis came out of the town of Amiens to meet the cardinal personally, just as he had done at Ardres before the Field of Cloth of Gold, Wolsey ensured that he had changed 'into more richer apparel' for the occasion. Once again, he greeted the king on horseback, as an equal. Wolsey told Henry that at Amiens, he had found his lodgings 'richly and pompously apparelled with the French King's own stuff'. Francis had a large collection of furnishings and plate brought to Amiens from his châteaux at Blois and Amboise for the occasion, and some of this was evidently used in Wolsey's rooms. These were set out, as they might have been for Henry himself, more in the English than the French manner with a sequence of Presence, Privy and Bed chambers, all richly decorated.[37]

210   'Cardinalis pacificus'

In these rather splendid surroundings, Wolsey got down to nego-tiations with the French representatives, keeping Henry informed in minute detail of their progress. They were concluded compara-tively quickly. The Treaty of Amiens was signed and sworn to by Francis on Sunday, 18 August. The treaty documents themselves were brilliantly illuminated, depicting among other things the two royal coats of arms, heraldic flowers and Francis's salamander emblems. Celebrations and orations praising the Anglo-French 'Eternal Peace' followed. Francis had commanded the preparation of a number of expensive gifts which were probably presented to the cardinal by the king himself either at Amiens at the conclusion of the negotiations, or perhaps when they met again at Compiègne a few weeks later.

The ostensible business of his mission having been concluded by mid-August, it might be expected that Wolsey would have returned to England, but he stayed on in France for a further month. This was because, having secured the alliance, he was now entirely focused (as he assured Henry) on the king's 'great matter', and it was easier to work on that from France than England – or so he thought. Wolsey was by now pursuing two related strategies. On the one hand, he tried to use the new alliance to put pressure on Charles to grant a truce enabling the pope to be released. On the other, he sought, with the help of the French king and his cardinals, to have himself appointed, during Clement's continuing indispo-sition, a papal vicegerent or 'acting pope'. He knew better than anyone that his power as a cardinal legate depended on having a pope with whom he could communicate and who could do things for him – even if that meant temporarily, extraordinarily, becom-ing that pope himself. Henry was already losing patience with this complex concatenation and, as we shall see, decided to take a very different and very direct course for himself.

Wolsey's plan for a papal vicegerency never had any real support among his fellow cardinals. As soon as he realised this, he hurried home, anxious to lay his latest triumph in France (if it was still thought of as one) at his master's feet and to catch the mice who had been at play while the cat was away. As far as relations with France were concerned, Wolsey stressed to the king the advantages of the new alliance in garnering support for his annulment case in Rome. He also lost no time advertising other alleged advantages to

'Cardinalis pacificus' 211

the political nation more widely. As Hall informs us, at the start of the new legal term in October, Wolsey summoned the king's council, the Mayor and Aldermen of London, the king's judges and the justices of the peace from the shires to the Star Chamber at Westminster. There he praised the Anglo-French alliance, urging his audience to 'be merry my lords' for the king would never again need to demand taxes or forced loans for wars in France. With the failure of the Amicable Grant in his mind, he went on to assure his audience that Henry would, by this new alliance, become 'the richest prince of the world', for he would 'have more treasure out of France yearly than all his revenues and customs amount to'. Wolsey had worked a pious miracle, he inferred, bringing the king and the nation both peace and profit in *secula seculorum*. He showed the great and the good before him the immense 'bulla' or seal of the king of France in fine gold attached to the document; physical proof, as it were, of the durability of the alliance concluded. The implied promise was that the annoying subsidies that Wolsey had done so much to introduce and refine would be, at the very least, less frequent. This would heal the wounds caused by the demand for the Amicable Grant. It is significant that in his effort to impress his audience, Wolsey made no mention of international peace or the honour to Henry from apparently managing the affairs of Christendom as he had done in proclaiming the universal peace nearly a decade earlier and in his more recent correspondence with the king. Wolsey told his audience only that he had turned a military war into a financial one, and that Henry was its acknowledged victor.[38]

Even as Wolsey spoke, the final French embassy to England in 1527 was on its way. It was commissioned to receive Henry's ratification of the Treaty of Amiens and to invest him with the Order of Saint Michael, the French order of chivalry, to which Henry had been elected, as an expression of the 'eternal' friendship and alliance between France and England that Wolsey had negotiated. From this distance, this seems a fitting gesture as between sworn allies and something Wolsey would have suggested. In fact, the idea was Francis I's. He had first suggested an exchange of membership of chivalric orders in the months before the Field of Cloth of Gold. Henry had turned him down flat. Francis appreciated why, given the Order's heritage, Henry had hesitated to bestow the Garter upon him. He would, after all, be the first French monarch ever elected to the English order, founded by that great enemy of France and Henry's ancestor, Edward III. Yet, if Henry could be forced to respond, Francis's election would defuse some of the Garter's anti-French ethos. Moreover, given the tradition of strict reciprocity between them, Henry would effectively recognise the Saint Michael as equal in status to the Garter. Accordingly, at Amiens, Francis had taken the opportunity to press Wolsey, reckoning, rightly, that if anybody could persuade Henry to agree, it was Wolsey. Wolsey must have undertaken to do so. That is why Henry was unilaterally elected a member of the French Order in September 1527. It was still a close run thing. Henry did not finally decide to reciprocate until 21 October when the French delegation, bearing the insignia of their Order, was already in England.[39]

The French embassy was led by Anne de Montmorency, Great Master of the French king's household, one of his oldest friends and his most trusted advisors. He and Wolsey had known each other since Montmorency had first come to England on diplomatic visits at the time of the Field of Cloth of Gold, and his support had been essential in securing Francis's agreement to both the peace treaties signed in 1527. He was accompanied by the new resident ambassador to England, Jean du Bellay, with whom Wolsey would soon build a good working relationship, together with a very large entourage of noblemen. Henry received the French at Greenwich on 22 October. On All Saints Day, Wolsey celebrated High Mass at St Paul's attended by a group of 24 bishops and abbots with full ceremonial as cardinal legate. Henry and Montmorency swore to uphold the new alliance at the Mass after Wolsey read out the main articles of agreement. On 10 November at Greenwich, Henry was presented with the collar and mantle of the Order of Saint Michael. After a tournament that afternoon, the Frenchmen were entertained in the same banqueting and disguising houses built for the April embassy. These had been entirely renovated, and the pageants presented after the banquet recalled those which had greeted Wolsey in France. They played up his role in supposedly delivering the pope from captivity and his work to try to free two French princes from the emperor's clutches.

Yet however flattering the vision of the omnicompetent churchman was intended to be, the cardinal tried to project a rather

'Cardinalis pacificus' 213

different and perhaps more engaging image of himself to his French guests. A few days after the Greenwich banquet, Wolsey entertained the French ambassadors at Hampton Court, just as he and his entourage had similarly been entertained at Compiègne in the summer. As he explained to his household, according to Cavendish, he intended to entertain his guests with 'such triumphant cheer as they may not only wonder at it here, but also make a glorious report in their country to the King's honour and of this realm'. For some time beforehand, preparations went on preparing suites of accommodation for the French guests. On this occasion, Wolsey displayed his own wealth deliberately and ostentatiously. Each of the ambassadors had his own well-furnished room, most accommodated around the Base Court, and attendants throughout his stay. The three reception rooms where the banquet was served were all laden with gold and silver plate 'very sumptuous and of the newest fashions'. Wolsey's guests ate as they would have done at a royal banquet, prepared by a team of cooks drawn from London and elsewhere, using the finest ingredients available. The ambassadors spent the day hunting in a deer park at Hanworth, not far from Hampton, and arrived towards evening. After resting in their rooms, they were all individually escorted to the banquet. Wolsey was strategically absent at the start of the meal. At the end of the first course he arrived dressed, not in his clerical robes as a cardinal, but in riding gear, 'booted and spurred all suddenly', as if coming in from a journey or a hunt. He greeted the company profusely, bidding them remain seated and enjoy the food. Then, without changing his clothes into anything finer (something he usually tended to do before meeting ambassadors), he called for a chair and sat down amidst the company 'laughing and being as merry as ever' Cavendish had ever seen him. This was yet another instance of that carefully calculated, but apparently spontaneous, behaviour that punctuated Anglo-French dealings during Wolsey's time, intended to communicate an apparent openness and suggest genuine friendship.

The meal continued, the highlight of which were the 'subtleties' or edible constructions, depicting among other things, St Paul's Cathedral (where the treaty had been sworn), jousting knights, figures of men and women and an entire chess set that Wolsey gave as a gift to one of the members of the embassy. At some point, Wolsey took a huge gold bowl filled with hypocras (spiced wine) and drank a toast to Henry and to Francis. He bid Montmorency do the same and then gave him the cup, estimated by Cavendish to be worth 500 marks. Only then did Wolsey retire to change and eat a little privately, before then 'circulating' as we might say, greeting individual ambassadors and being the perfect party host 'so that they could not commend him too much'. In short, at the banquet Wolsey presented himself less as the 'cardinal peacemaker' or Chancellor, than as a powerful, wealthy nobleman, a man of influence and action – hence the staged business of arriving in riding gear. He probably did this in order to impress upon his guests the fact that he was, effectively, Montmorency's political equal in England as the king's right-hand man. The leader of the French delegation was genuinely committed to peace with England as part of his wider hope of enabling Francis also to come to peace with the emperor – a peace Montmorency believed was genuinely in the realm's best interest. Wolsey was similarly invested in the 'Eternal Peace' with France as being in Henry's financial and strategic interests, and his best way of securing an ally that gave him some freedom of movement with the otherwise all-powerful Charles. The stakes were high for both men personally, and Wolsey seems to have been showing himself to be a man with whom Montmorency could do business.[40]

Eternal peace, immediate war

As 1527 ended, Wolsey's favour with Henry seemed to have been restored, and he was building on the French alliance as promised. Once more there were grand promises but also hard cash for Henry in pursuing the path of peace with France. There were also good grounds for thinking that Henry's prominence in Europe would be restored after the hiatus of 1525, and he could escape the isolation in which his Habsburg ally had, once again, been prepared to leave him. Once more, he was in a position to teach that unreliable ally the importance of keeping him on side as Wolsey sought to draw Clement VII into a revived League of Cognac against Charles V.

On 28 January 1528, Francis I was, as Henry's 'good brother and perpetual ally', installed by proxy in St George's Chapel, Windsor, as a Knight of the Order of the Garter. A week beforehand, he and Henry had declared war on Charles for, among other things, endangering the security of the pope. In February, a French army under Marshal Lautrec invaded the kingdom of Naples and by the spring was besieging that stronghold of Imperial power in Italy, assisted by the naval mercenary commanders Andrea and Filippino Doria, whose galley fleet blockaded the city. This suited Henry and Wolsey well insofar as it put pressure on Charles and offered apparent hope to Pope Clement that, with English support, the French would enable him to escape the power of the emperor. On the other hand, it antagonised Charles, and Henry and Wolsey could never be sure how much Francis would really do for them if he once got his hands on the prize of Naples.

Doing its part in the alliance meant that England had already begun an economic war with the emperor's dominions in the Low Countries. This was, understandably, hugely unpopular with London's merchants who, quite rightly, pointed out that it disrupted valuable trade with Bruges, Ghent and especially Antwerp. Trade with those cities completely eclipsed anything done through French cities which were geographically further away and less well organised for international trade than those in Flanders. The supposed direct economic advantage for Henry of Wolsey's pro-French policy was outweighed by its indirect consequences in lost trade and with it lost customs revenue. It also caused popular unrest in towns and villages in East Anglia and elsewhere dependent on the cloth trade. Wolsey's pro-French policy was being countered effectively by Charles and his aunt, Margaret of Savoy (his regent in the Netherlands), who shut even more ports to the English and imposed tariffs on imports. In short, the economic war did more harm to England than it did to the Netherlands, and, with bad harvests in 1527 requiring the import of grain, it had to be abandoned, leaving England in a weak position diplomatically. For all this, Wolsey was blamed.[41]

In February 1528, Imperial troops finally withdrew from Rome, allowing Clement to contemplate the possibility of a return to Rome himself. Even as he set out, however, Admiral Doria withdrew a fleet he had provided in strategic support for the French siege of Naples. In the summer, the French commander, Lautrec, died of the plague along with many of his troops, and, unable any longer to sustain the siege, the French withdrawal from Naples and southern Italy followed soon after. Helped by Doria's desertion of the French, Charles had faced down the League of Cognac, which,

216 'Cardinalis pacificus'

without support from England, soon collapsed. Seeing all of this, the pope's main priority by the end of 1528 became to secure the emperor's assistance in restoring his own power and his family's authority in Florence. Everything else, including Henry's matrimonial difficulty that first became public and the subject of formal action in 1527, was subservient. This had dire consequences for Wolsey that would unfold in 1529.

Notes

1 Cavendish, p. 53.

2 *Here after Ensueth Two Fruitful Sermons Made and Compiled by the Right Reverend Father in God John Fisher Doctor of Divinity and Bishop of Rochester*, printed by William Rastell in 1532 (reprinted 2010); also quoted in Russell, pp. 216–19 [Appendix D] at pp. 218–19.

3 BL, Cotton MS Caligula D VII, fos. 242–3 [*LP* III i, 923] Wingfield to Henry VIII, Poissy, 19 July 1520.

4 TNA, SP1/21, fos. 20–7 [*LP* III i, 936] Undated draft of instructions; *CSP Sp.* II 287 Treaty between Charles V and Henry VIII dated 14 July 1520; see also *LP* III i, 908, 914; BL, *Le triu[m]phe festifz bien venue [et] honorable receiul faict par le roy da[n]gleterre en la ville de Calais a la tressacree Cesare catholiq[ue] maieste* . . . (Arras, 1520), www.bl.uk/treasures/festivalbooks/pageview.aspx?strFest=0009&strPage=001

5 *LP* III i, 1216, Leo X to Wolsey, Rome, 1 April 1520. Full text of Leo's letter of 27 June 1521 detailing amplified powers is printed in Clarke, 'Rivalling Rome: Cardinal Wolsey and Dispensations', 1–100, at 31–9.

6 Knecht, pp. 175–7.

7 BL, Cotton MS Vitellius B XX, fo. 239 [*LP* III i, 1213] Wolsey to Henry VIII.

8 TNA, SP1/22, fos. 193–96 [*LP* III i, 1338] Francis's response to Henry's request; see also *LP* III ii, 1339, 1341–2, 1344 for further correspondence about the appointment of negotiators.

9 *St. P.* I, p. 90; P. Gwyn, 'Wolsey's Foreign Policy: The Conferences at Calais and Bruges Reconsidered', *HJ* 23 (4) (1980): 755–72.

10 *LP* III, 1802 Treaty with Charles V, signed 24 November 1521; Gwyn, pp. 144–58. esp. p. 153; Scarisbrick, pp. 88–96; see also Knecht, pp. 185–99 on Francis's financial crisis during these years.

11 Hall, p. 631.

12 *LP* III ii, 2289 Wingfield, with the king, to Wolsey, Canterbury, 26 May 1522.

13 Hall, pp. 634–42; BL, Cotton Caligula D VIII, fos. 223–4 [*LP* III i, 2292].

14 Knecht, pp. 201–6 on Charles de Bourbon and the reasons behind his rebellion against Francis.

15 S. J. Gunn, 'The Duke of Suffolk's March on Paris in 1523', *English Historical Review* 101 (1986): 596–634.

16 BL, Nero B VI, fo. 52 [*LP* IV, 38] Bourbon to the Comte de Ponthievre, Genoa, 13 January 1524; *LP* IV, 119 Wolsey to Clement VII, London, 25 February 1524.

17 BL, Cotton MS Caligula D VIII, fos. 128–9 [*LP*, 789, 790]; PRO 31 8/137, fos. 284–5 [*LP*, IV i, 1093] Louise of Savoy's instructions dated 16 February; *St. P.* I, pp. 153–6. Wolsey to Henry, February 1525, reporting on progress of negotiations.

18 G. Jacqueton, *La Politique exterieure de Louise de Savoie. Relations diplomatiques de la France et de l'Angleterre pendant le captivité de François Ier. 1525–1526* (Paris, 1892), pp. 74ff.

19 TNA, PRO 31 8/137, fos. 193–6, 199 [*LP* IV, 1525, 1573] Instructions to ambassadors for the treaty; BL, Cotton MS Caligula D IX, fos. 138–9. A letter of intelligence points out Louise of Savoy's difficulties and her need to settle with Henry in order to strengthen her own hand with Charles V; *St. P.* I, pp. 159–61.

20 TNA, PRO 31/8/137, fos. 193–6, 197, 198, 199–200, 201–4 [*LP* II i, 1525, 1531, 1537 1573, 1578] for correspondence with Louise of Savoy detailing the progress of negotiations; Rymer, XIV, pp. 48–74 [*LP* IV i, 1600–6].

21 *LP* IV i, 1774 Obligation signed by Louise of Savoy for the total sum, 8 November 1525.

22 Giry-Deloison, pp. 28ff.

23 *LP* IV i, 1859 Draft of letters patent to Wolsey dated 17 Henry VIII [1525]. No place or date given.

24 Knecht, pp. 246–53 on the negotiation of the Treaty of Madrid.

25 BL, Cotton MS Caligula D IX, fo. 147 [*LP* IV ii, 1901]; Fitzwilliam had been appointed Treasurer of the royal household by October 1525.

26 BL, Cotton MS Caligula D IX, fo. 172v [*LP* IV i, 2039] Instructions dated 20 March 1526.

27 Ibid., fo. 187 [*LP* IV i, 2087].

28 *LP* IV ii, 2325 Wolsey to Henry, Westminster, 19 July 1526.

29 Knecht, pp. 255–9.

30 TNA, SP1/40, fos. 88–93, for Morette's recommendation from Wolsey and Fitzwilliam's credence and draft proposals for a marriage alliance; *LP* IV ii, 2554 for Wallop's letter to Wolsey from Cologne; 2556 for Wolsey's letter to Henry, 9 October 1526.

31 *CSP Sp.* III ii, 32, 37, 66 for Mendoza's key correspondence with Charles V in the spring of 1526.

32 BL, Cotton Caligula E II, fos. 80–2 [*LP* IV ii, 2791–4]; BL, Additional MS 12192, fos. 43–79 esp. fos. 44–5; a copy of a French report on the embassy. The original is BNF, MS NA 7004.

33 G. Lehmann, 'Henry VIII's Great Feast at Greenwich, May 1527', *The Court Historian* 23 (1) (June 2018): 1–12.

218 'Cardinalis pacificus'

34 See essays in D. Starkey, *A European Court in England* (London, 1991), pp. 54–93.

35 TNA, SP1/42, fos. 70–5 [*LP* IV ii, 3171] Lord Lisle's narrative of the embassy to Paris.

36 Cavendish, pp. 50–1; Rymer, XIV, pp. 199–200 [*LP* IV ii, 3186] for Wolsey's commission, dated London, 18 June 1527.

37 Ibid., pp. 55–6; *St. P.* I, p. 239 Wolsey to Henry VIII, 11 August 1527.

38 Hall, p. 732.

39 *LP* IV ii, 3516; *St. P.* VII, p. 11 Henry VIII to Francis I, Greenwich, 25 October 1527.

40 Cavendish, pp. 71–7.

41 S. J. Gunn, 'Wolsey's Foreign Policy and the Domestic Crisis of 1527–8', in Gunn and Lindley, pp. 149–77.

7 The Cardinal's greatest matter

Wolsey and the annulment

With that quod my Lord Cardinal, 'Sir, I most humbly beseech your highness to declare me before all this audience whether I have been the chief inventor or first mover of this matter unto your majesty, for I am greatly suspected of all men herein'. 'My Lord Cardinal' quod the king, 'I can well excuse you herein. Marry indeed, ye have been rather against me in attempting or setting forth thereof.[1]

So, Cavendish narrated the encounter between Wolsey and Henry VIII in the moments after Katherine of Aragon had dramatically left the court convened at Blackfriars in June 1529 to judge the validity of her marriage to Henry. The king's 'Great Matter', his demand for an annulment of that marriage, had, by that time, become the greatest matter, crisis, and perhaps opportunity, that Thomas Wolsey had ever faced. Cavendish's account of the interaction between the two men – master and servant, trusted confidants and friends – is replete with tragic irony. Henry apparently spoke in defence and support of his cardinal and went on to own responsibility in conscience for the case. Yet, for Cavendish at least, his words had a double meaning. Wolsey had never indeed been 'the chief inventor' of the annulment case. Yet when it was committed to his charge by Henry, he had worked as hard as he knew how to bring the annulment about. He wanted to succeed in this as much as anything else, for his king, and for himself. If it could be secured by his means, it would prove decisively his indispensability to the king who had made him. It would also vindicate his power as England's cardinal legate and his relations with the papacy, conducted for 15 years very largely on his own terms. Unfortunately for Wolsey, at Blackfriars he reached the limitations of his powers with king and pope, and of the personal charisma upon which he so often relied. He was confronted at that moment with Henry's already firm, if errant, conviction that in working for the annulment in the way he had chosen to do, according to the necessary curial proceedings, Wolsey had in some sense betrayed him. In that moment it was the king's friendship with Wolsey that was on trial.

Standing there at Blackfriars that day, it may have seemed to Wolsey a long time since the spring of 1527 when he had taken the first steps in the matter of the king's marriage. He had understood Henry's dilemma immediately upon being informed of it, probably in the early months of the year, by his protégé, Bishop Longland of Lincoln, who was the king's confessor. He comprehended perfectly well the royal anxieties about the lack of a male heir and Henry's wish to remarry in order to secure the succession, in terms consonant with his own heightened sense of masculine kingship. That Wolsey also knew Henry loved, or was at least in love with, Anne Boleyn by the spring of 1527 is also reasonably clear. Whether Wolsey realised the extent of their mutual and firm commitment to marriage at that point is rather less certain. By the end of that year, understand he certainly did.

The initial case for an annulment

During the spring months there must have been reasonable grounds for optimism. As legate *a latere*, Wolsey had wide dispensing powers in matrimonial causes (see Chapter 4), and Henry's first thought and hope might have been that, armed with these, Wolsey might resolve his dilemma for him as soon as the facts could be established. Even if Wolsey's authority did not extend as far as Henry hoped (and that was almost certainly the case), popes had often annulled royal marriages for political and dynastic considerations. The most recent similar case was that of Jeanne de France, the daughter of Louis XI, whose marriage to Louis XII was ended by papal dispensation so that the king could marry Anne of Brittany. The difference there was that Jeanne had agreed to dissolve the marriage and enter a convent – something, as Wolsey would soon enough discover, Katherine resolutely refused to do.

The Cardinal's greatest matter 221

The parallel with French dynastic politics reminds us of the international context of Henry's marriage dilemma. Katherine was the aunt of the most powerful ruler in Western Europe, Charles V, and, as we have seen, his rivalry with Francis I had given Henry his most recent opportunity to pursue his own dynastic ambitions against France. As we have also seen, however, Anglo–Imperial military co-operation came to nothing in the war between Charles and Francis of 1521–5. In the spring of 1527 Wolsey was principally engaged in allying Henry once more with Francis, who was now again at war with the emperor in Italy. At Greenwich, on 5 May, Henry ratified a comprehensive Anglo–French peace under the Treaty of Westminster. Even as he did so, news came of the Sack of Rome. Charles's unpaid and rebellious troops had looted and ransacked the city, killing thousands and forcing the pope himself to flee to the safety of the Castel Sant' Angelo, a short distance from the Vatican. There he relied on the protection of the emperor and was, in effect, his prisoner. The circumstances of Henry's case were thereby radically altered.

Nevertheless, on 17 May, the French ambassadors having departed and even as he was drafting instructions for a return English ratification embassy to France, Wolsey opened the first secret trial of the validity of the king's marriage at York Place. Katherine was not informed of it, much less represented. Assisted by Warham as Archbishop of Canterbury, the papal legate called the king as defendant and put the proposition to him that his marriage was unlawful under canon law. Henry appeared in response and presented the dispensation bull of 1504, formally protesting that his marriage was valid, as proved by the dispensation. He appointed Dr John Bell as his defending counsel. Bell's task was, of course, to argue the exact opposite of what the king really wanted, and to assert the legality of the royal marriage in the full expectation of losing the case. The court sat for barely two weeks before rising, without giving a verdict, on 31 May.

Although it is commonly and conveniently referred to as Henry's 'divorce' case, it is important to note that he sought an annulment of his marriage, not a divorce. That is, a finding that he had never been validly married, not that his marriage had somehow failed and should be ended, as in modern divorce law. Amateur biblical scholar from his teens and a published author after all, Henry had

222   *The Cardinal's greatest matter*

established, to his own satisfaction at least, that his marriage to Katherine was invalid by divine, not just canon, law. It fell directly within the terms of Leviticus 18:16 *Thou shalt not uncover the nakedness of your brother's wife; it is your brother's nakedness*, and Leviticus 20:21 *If a man shall take his brother's wife, it is an impurity; he hath uncovered his brother's nakedness; they shall be childless*. Henry said that he had done exactly that, and his lack of a son, which, for him, was the same thing as being childless, was proof of God's anger. He had been living in sin for almost 20 years, and the only way to repent and rectify the wrong was to end his marriage to Katherine.

To this 'scruple' in the king's conscience there was an obvious and comforting resolution. Pope Julius II had given a dispensation for the marriage, and it had taken place fully and legally in the eyes of the Church before the king and queen were jointly crowned in June 1509. Not so, said Henry. The pope might dispense upon canon law, in effect, human law matters. He could not dispense upon divine law as set forth in scripture. Yet even if this were the case (and Catholic orthodoxy denied it), Henry's circumstances, it was countered, were covered by Deuteronomy 25:5, which stated that *when brethren dwell together, the wife of the deceased shall not marry to another; but his brother shall take her, and raise up seed for his brother* – exactly Henry's situation and the evidence to date suggested that all was well. After all, he was not in fact childless. He had a daughter, Mary, evidence in herself that even in divine law his marriage was sound. He had not suffered God's reproof in the Levitical penalty. Henry's necessary objection to this was that the text in Deuteronomy referenced a specific Jewish custom that, since the advent of Christ, had been superseded. Deuteronomy was ambiguous anyway and irrelevant to his case. His situation sat squarely within the injunction of Leviticus 20:21, and the only question was whether the pope had the competence to dispense in the special circumstances – which Henry maintained he did not. This assertion was grounded primarily on the alleged insufficiency of papal authority in scriptural law but also that the kings of England were 'emperors' in their own kingdom and acknowledged no authority higher than their own in the realm. At first, this was asserted almost incidentally, implicitly. It was for the present pope to recognise the errors of Julius II, to void the 1504 dispensation and to annul the marriage, in conformity with divine law.[2]

The Cardinal's greatest matter   223

Wolsey's training in theology and his experience in the law as the Chancellor accustomed him to legal and doctrinal technicalities, and it was on these rather than theology that he first sought to ground the king's matrimonial case. This was that the original dispensation granted by Julius II for Henry to marry Katherine had been defective. Among other things, it was maintained that the bull had been issued at Henry's behest, and that this had been wrong as he had been a party to the case. The marriage had been contracted to keep Anglo–Spanish peace, but in fact the kingdoms had not been at war and were not likely to be at the time the dispensation was granted. Another point was that Henry was only 12 when the dispensation was obtained and so was underage to marry, and he had in any case subsequently repudiated the intended marriage to Katherine under his father's instructions, rendering the bull null and void. A 'new' marriage to Katherine without a new dispensation was invalid. The most significant of these faults was, however, the impediment of 'public honesty'. Katherine's marriage to Arthur, even if unconsummated, had been celebrated publicly and thus could be considered a genuine one that created a bond between her and the close blood relatives of her husband, including his brother. The impediment existed only in canon law, and the Pope could easily dispense with it. However, Julius II's 1504 bull had failed specifically to do so. Therefore, Katherine's marriage to Henry could be said to be invalid on that basis. Katherine argued that the dispensation had implicitly removed the impediment of public honesty. These were indeed rather technical arguments (and there were many more on both sides), but if the pope were willing to act for Henry, they gave him ample scope to do so. That, at least, is how Wolsey wanted to deal with the matter.

Wolsey had the assistance of what today might be called counsel to the enquiry, one Dr Richard Wolman, who investigated the circumstances of Henry's marriage and his wife's previous marriage to Prince Arthur. This he did with great skill, calling as his chief witness Bishop Fox of Winchester, who had been part of Henry VII's royal council that had first sought the papal dispensation allowing Henry to marry Katherine. He built a reasonably tight case against the validity of the dispensation, in accordance with the king's real intentions. Yet, there was evidently some debate as to whether Wolsey might have declared the king's marriage null and

224   *The Cardinal's greatest matter*

void on a technical basis, especially on the issue of public honesty, by virtue of his 'dispensing' powers as legate – a claim sometimes still advanced by historians. This was certainly not the view taken by Bishop John Fisher, whom Wolsey consulted in late June. He strongly backed the idea that, given the delicacy of the case, it was best referred directly to the pope. Aware of this, Wolsey hesitated. It was axiomatic in his exercise of Henry's delegated authority that he always double-checked that he had sufficient power to do something. It seems that, in this instance at least, he showed the same caution in dealing with the papacy. Everything had to be done by the book to avoid any possibility of appeals based on Wolsey's alleged or actual misuse of his legatine authority. The problem for Henry was that the adjournment of the secret court meant delays and raised the possibility that if Wolsey did not in fact have sufficient power as legate to rule in a case of the first degree of consanguinity, then it might have to be heard in Rome – something both of them very much wished to avoid. Obtaining authority directly from the pope to give a verdict, however, ought not to be that difficult. Or so Wolsey reasoned.[3]

Henry probably understood his cardinal's caution. He too wanted a failproof solution to his dilemma. But it did not sit well with him. From the start, Henry saw the issue not as one of technicalities but in national and fundamentally theological terms. Once convinced of his position, Henry held to it throughout the case. The pope was duty bound in scripture to find the 1504 dispensation invalid and thus annul Henry's marriage. Wolsey understood Henry's theological perspective as well, whatever doubts or misgivings about it he may have had. His view was still that the case best went forward on the more technical matters, outlined previously, less hostile to the issue of the sufficiency of papal spiritual authority as such.

Measures were, however, evidently in hand in case those technicalities should prove insufficient. There exists in the British Library a draft of a papal letter, or *breve*, which, from its contextual references, must date from May 1527 or shortly thereafter. It may have been drawn up immediately after the adjourned secret trial, or perhaps for Wolsey to take with him when he went to France in July that year. A papal *breve* was a legal document issued by the papal secretariat for the pope's signature. It was an expression of papal authority and something of an alternative to the more ample bull

The Cardinal's greatest matter 225

ordering or sanctioning something, issued by the papal Chancery under the pope's seal or 'bulla' – hence the name. As was customary with both, the supplicant first drew up a draft version, which was then scrutinised, perhaps amended, and hopefully approved, before being signed by the pope. There is no named addressee on the 1527 draft *breve*, but it was evidently to be provided for a legate who sought an extension of his authority when the pope was indisposed. It delegates to its intended recipient 'power to concede all dispensations and other graces both within and beyond papal authority, even relaxing divine law, as if the pope could grant divine power outside his Petrine commission'. It has long been presumed, surely rightly, to have been drawn up by Wolsey, or at his behest, to secure unequivocal approval for action of the kind that popes alone, even in the fullness of their power, *might* take, in Henry's circumstances. It has aptly been described as 'a dispensatory blank cheque'. There is no evidence, however, that Clement VII ever actually received the draft, and he certainly never issued a final *breve*. Yet the draft shows us that Wolsey was aware of the lengths he might need to go. As early as the summer of 1527, and in the wake of the Sack of Rome, he wanted the king's annulment every bit as much as the king did, precisely because the king did. Moreover, he wanted it achieved under his own auspices, as cardinal legate of England. Rome must concede the fullest amplitude of power it had already granted to him as legate for life.[4]

In one sense, the circumstances for this draft *breve*'s receipt could hardly have been less propitious. The pope was safe enough in his fortress in Rome, but his court and administration, which alone could give effect to the draft, was rapidly fragmenting around him. On the other hand, given his vulnerability and need for help, what might a pope not do for a king who extended the hand of friendship and arm of protection in his hour of need? Clement might at least have been happy to clarify and amplify Wolsey's legatine powers to ensure he had competence in the matter of the king's marriage. That was the idea behind the drafting of the papal *breve*, and although it was never sent, it impelled Wolsey's conduct of Henry's case thereafter until its final collapse at Blackfriar's in July 1529.

In June 1527, Henry confronted his wife with his view that their marriage had always contravened divine law and must end. She was overwhelmed by this announcement and protested her loyalty and love for him. Not unnaturally, Henry was moved to comfort the wife whom he had in truth loved before they were married, promising that all would yet be well and requiring her, on the obedience she had always shown, to keep secret what he had said to her. That may be so, but it is also clear that Katherine understood from the start that the key to the defence of her marriage to Henry was that the previous one to Arthur had never been consummated. She had married Henry as a virgin and therefore could never have been within the first and prohibited degree of consanguinity. In effect, Julius II had dispensed upon nothing in 1504, and her marriage was valid in canon *and* divine law. To that resolution she would hold as determinedly as Henry held to his. She was soon afterwards able to contact her nephew Charles, who immediately objected to Henry's plans and promised support for her in Rome. Among other things Katherine requested Charles to make every effort to have Wolsey deprived of his legatine powers, lest they should prove sufficient for him to act unilaterally, something she evidently feared.[5]

Wolsey, meanwhile, had seen the potential consequences of the military attack on Rome, for good and ill, for Henry's matrimonial case. Drawing the king and Francis even closer together in an alliance of mutual advantage against the emperor became his main aim in the summer of 1527. As we have seen, he travelled to France in July, and an amplified Anglo–French alliance, known as the 'Eternal Peace', was agreed on 18 August under the Treaty of Amiens. The coincidence of these events has led to the suggestion, first made by Polydore Vergil and Tyndale, that Wolsey even initiated the annulment proceedings himself in order to free Henry to marry again, pursuant to his pro-French policy. This may have been something that Katherine herself believed. But that really was to put the cart before the horse. Wolsey's influence with Henry had certainly caused tensions at times between Katherine and the cardinal and had been something that the queen had been required, over time, to come to terms with. Instinctively, Wolsey always treated her with the respect to which she was entitled as queen but took his orders from the king. He may even have had some sympathy with her circumstances and the series of miscarriages and still-births she had suffered – he was a father himself after all. Nevertheless, his abiding rule was that Henry got what he wanted. Henry later used comments apparently casting doubt on the legitimacy of his marriage,

The Cardinal's greatest matter 227

made by a French diplomat, the Bishop of Tarbes, as part of his explanation for his scruple of conscience. Yet, at no stage in the discussions that led to the peace and alliance of 1527 was the validity of the king's marriage or Princess Mary's legitimacy as Henry's daughter, as the prospective bride for Francis's son, Henry duke of Orléans, ever questioned publicly by Wolsey, let alone the French ambassadors negotiating that alliance. Had it been considered a real issue, the French would not have agreed to the treaties of that year.

Throughout his time in France, Wolsey wrote frequent and long letters to Henry assuring him that, while negotiating, he was also 'daily and hourly musing and thinking on your Grace's great and secret affair and how the same may come to good effect and desired end'. This, in order that Henry might be delivered from the 'dolorous life' that he was in. As he explained, he planned to travel on to Avignon (the seat of the popes during the so-called Babylonish Captivity in the fourteenth century) and there assemble as many cardinals as he could. With their support, he hoped to obtain permission from Clement to undertake nothing less than the leadership of the entire Church, as a papal vicegerent, for as long as the pope remained a hostage of Imperial troops. Having that power, Wolsey told Henry, he would resolve the king's dilemma and approve an annulment without needing even to consult Clement, 'which shall be a good ground and fundament for the effectual execution of your Grace's secret affair'. In other words, the sort of action Henry now needed and favoured to resolve his dilemma.[6]

The earnest and reassuring tone of Wolsey's letters testify not only to his fear of being too long separated from the king, but a growing awareness that the case was no longer entirely in his own hands. He was warned by Sir William Fitzwilliam on 31 July that the king was surrounded by a large entourage, including the dukes of Norfolk and Suffolk and Sir Thomas Boleyn, who were dining with Henry. By then Anne herself was more often in Henry's company than not. The king was keeping a 'very great house'.[7] Wolsey knew, too, that Katherine was not going meekly to accept the ending of her marriage and was being advised on her next steps. He therefore pressed on with his own plans, sending a group of officials, including Ghinucci, the Bishop of Worcester and Gregorio Casali, the English ambassador in Rome appointed in October 1525, to obtain a commission from the pope to confer a vicegerency over

228   *The Cardinal's greatest matter*

Christendom upon him. The pope, having already been alerted to the case by Imperial ambassadors, received Wolsey's representatives well enough and promised aid, but did nothing immediately, pleading the circumstances of his refuge in the Castel Sant' Angelo and his fear of alienating the emperor.[8]

Wolsey redoubled his efforts to reassure the king, telling him in a further series of letters after the treaty of Amiens had been signed that he would bring Francis on board with his plans for a papal vicegerency and Henry's annulment but, 'in so cloudy a sort that he shall not know your utter (final) determination'.[9] Henry read Wolsey's letters and replied to them, giving the impression that he supported the papal vicegerency–annulment conjunction. Yet, as both men knew, as desirable as that outcome might be, it would take time, money and complicated diplomacy to bring about. This was meat and drink to Wolsey of course, but increasingly frustrating for Henry, who wanted not more delegated papal authority for the cardinal but a shorter, more direct approach to the pope for himself.

For a decade, as cardinal legate, Wolsey had conducted relations with the papacy by his own means and according to his own instincts. He had often exaggerated the degree of influence he had as a way of flattering Henry. He also knew better than anyone how that agency had now to prove effective as never before. But just when Wolsey wanted decisively to demonstrate his influence with the papacy, Henry's faith in him faltered. At the end of August, Dr William Knight, the king's secretary, was sent as ambassador to Rome on a mission intended to establish personal communications between Henry and Clement. Knight himself informed Wolsey of the new situation. He wrote on 29 August advising the cardinal that he was to consult with him at Compiègne, while en route to Rome, but to proceed there in the matter of the marriage on the king's final instructions alone.[10] Never, since Wolsey's becoming a cardinal in 1515 had Henry approached the papacy for any cause, let alone one that touched his kingship so near, without his advice and agency. Overnight, it seemed, all that had changed.

Wolsey was appalled when he received Knight's letter on 3 September. He understood that he had been, really for the first time, brushed aside by Henry, who, as Fitzwilliam had told him, had been constantly in the company of members of the nobility who had little love for him and were determined to support any plan, however hare-brained, that would reduce his influence with Henry in order to secure the annulment to which Anne was also now committed. Wolsey's response to this letter, written on 5 September, was probably the occasion during his time in France that Cavendish recalled how once Wolsey had risen at 4.00AM and, without changing into his daytime apparel, sat at his desk for 12 hours. 'All which season', Cavendish writes, 'my lord never rose once to piss, ne yet to eat any meat but continually wrote his letters with his own hands, having all that time his nightcap and keverchief on his head'. In his letter he urged the king to recall Knight and allow Wolsey to manage matters still. After seeing his letters despatched by a messenger, one Christopher 'Gunner' Morris, who was instructed to ride fast and directly to the king and to bring word back as soon as possible, Wolsey walked for a while in the garden, said his evening office of readings and prayers, had some supper and went to bed – surely anxious and exhausted.[11]

Knight and Wolsey had worked together before. The cardinal knew he had some experience of negotiation but nothing like enough for the task with which he was now charged. In Rome, Knight would be an outsider who threatened his own elaborate plans for managing the king's case, to the detriment of Henry's honour – and Wolsey's, too. How could the king possibly think that a mere secretary could have more influence with the pope than he had as Clement's papal legate to England, and as Henry's cardinal before the pope? It was not to be believed. Wolsey urged the advantages of using Ghinucci, Casali and the papal nuncio Uberto Gambara instead. They were all experienced Italian diplomats, far better able than Knight to handle this extremely sensitive issue according to the etiquette and culture of the Curia. Unlike Knight, all three had the insider's awareness of who in Rome might best assist the king. Wolsey himself could not be there, but these men were his eyes and ears in Rome and were the king's as well if he would but use them. The trouble for Wolsey was that he was then in France, and usually resident in England, and had never been in Rome. How could it be otherwise given his many responsibilities? At this vital moment, however, there was no one like Cardinal Bainbridge to represent the English king directly in the Curia. For more than a decade since Bainbridge's death, Wolsey's nomination of Italians

230　*The Cardinal's greatest matter*

to English bishoprics in return for their support in Rome had made sense in itself. Suddenly it looked clumsy, even amateurish, and left English business dangerously at the mercy of a range of competing pressures and only ever indirectly represented, by foreigners.

The Defender of the Faith steps in

All of this may have played its part in Henry's thinking in the summer of 1527 when he decided it was time to deal with the pope himself. Had he entirely lost confidence in Wolsey's approach? Subsequent events suggest not. But was Henry at that moment wanting to see for himself whether the relationship which he had built with the papacy through Wolsey really was as strong as the cardinal maintained? If it was, the king seems to have reasoned, ought not the pope to respond as well (or better) to a direct approach from him, as to one from Wolsey? Anne and her circle may well have encouraged the king in this direction, not necessarily at this point from any wish to do Wolsey down, but from the hope of a quick solution of the kind they knew the king was looking for and which Wolsey could not promise him. They also wanted to test the strength of the cardinal's competence in the matter. If the king could get what he needed from Clement through Knight, rather than Wolsey, so much the better.

Realising from Fitzwilliam's warning that something like this might be afoot and using his powers of persuasion on paper to the uttermost, Wolsey wrote painstakingly to restore himself to his accustomed place as trusted advisor. He offered assurances of loyalty and pleaded his competence to his sovereign. All of this, Henry politely ignored. He knew Wolsey would never have agreed to the course of action upon which he had now embarked, for the request Knight carried with him was indeed an extraordinary one. He was, in the first instance at least, to present the pope with a draft bull that, if approved, gave Henry a dispensation to allow him to marry another woman, even while he was still married to Katherine – that is, a licence for bigamy.[12]

The conventional sequence of events on Knight's mission is based on a set of instructions to him which he apparently acknowledged on 13 September, three days after he arrived at Compiègne ostensibly to confer with Wolsey. The cardinal asked him to remain

The Cardinal's greatest matter 231

until the messenger Christopher Morris had returned with further instructions in response to his letter of 5 September urging Knight's recall. This is usually thought to be because, by then, Wolsey had somehow got wind of what Knight's mission was really about and tried to stop it. Christopher Morris did indeed return to Compiègne but with no instructions countermanding Knight. Knight went on to Rome, and as there was nothing further to be done in France, Wolsey returned to England, assuring Henry that he travelled with such diligence as 'my old and cracked body may endure'.[13]

In the conventional view, even as these events unfolded, the king had decided to abandon the bull for which Knight had been sent (for Henry to marry again even while still married to Katherine) as being 'too much to be required and unreasonable to be granted'. Knight was to admit this to Wolsey and tell him that the king and the cardinal would together draft another bull, more moderate in scope, perhaps for a legatine commission in England or something similar, but having put Wolsey off the scent, he was to press on to Rome.[14] He would be sent another, different, draft bull (that does not survive), but in no circumstances should this be disclosed to Wolsey. This second bull was to be the king's request, 'which I above all things do desire', for a dispensation allowing him to remarry only *after* his marriage to Katherine had been found unlawful but, crucially, to any woman, even one connected to him in the first degree of affinity. It is an important point that Henry stood within the same degree of prohibited consanguinity to Anne Boleyn as he said he did with Katherine because of his prior relationship with Anne's sister, Mary, who had been his mistress.[15] Henry was asking Clement to sanction, in respect of Anne, the very thing he denied Julius II had the power to do in respect of his marriage to Katherine. Such was the inelegant position that Henry's love for Anne and his theological convictions had now placed him.

Tellingly, Henry instructed Knight to ask the pope to grant it 'in consideration of such service as I have done or hereafter may do to his holiness and the church'.[16] This revised demand was in one way put on the same basis as the English crown had always dealt with the papacy, but in the immediate context of Henry's marriage to Katherine and his argued grounds for annulment, still a rather big thing to ask Clement to approve. Clearly, as early as the summer of 1527, Henry saw the papacy, and Clement personally, as being in his debt, rather than the other way around. His belief in the authority of the papacy itself ultimately to determine such matters evidently still stood – at this point. Knight was also specifically ordered to get access to the pope, if it all possible, *without* the assistance of Wolsey's men in Rome. These instructions and the demand of the pope flatly contradicted Wolsey's advice on the annulment to disclose as little as possible about Henry's future hopes in matrimony. Hence the need for Knight's secrecy and Henry's deception of Wolsey.

David Starkey has offered a somewhat different chronology. He suggests that Wolsey did not know about even the first draft bull, allowing Henry a bigamous marriage, until *after* he got back to England. He first met the king, in Anne's presence, and virtually by her leave, at Richmond on 30 September. He was able to confirm for himself that Anne was now inseparable from the king. Some-time shortly afterwards, he found out about the bull, to Henry's displeasure and 'by whose means I know well enough', Henry told Knight.[17] Wolsey then understood just what sort of scheme had been devised by Henry and Anne's supporters in his absence. He remonstrated with the king and apparently succeeded in getting Henry to drop the whole thing and to return the management of the case to him. In fact, Henry then issued the new and secret orders to Knight, discussed previously. He had kept them so secret that, as Henry told Knight, they would never be revealed 'for any craft of the cardinal or any other can find'.[18] In other words, the undated instructions, conventionally associated with the first stage of Knight's journey in early September, when he met Wolsey at Compiegne, in fact date from later in the autumn – after Wolsey had consulted with the king. Wolsey's objections to Knight's mission in September were not specifically about the proposed bull, about which he then did not know, but were more general complaints about Knight's insufficiency as an envoy to Rome. It is agreed on all sides that Henry's instruction letter to Knight was delivered by one John Barlow, 'by whom', Henry told Knight, 'you may assur-edly send me whatsoever you will'. Barlow was a chaplain to Anne Boleyn's father, Thomas. John Barlow first caught up with Knight, not at or near Compiègne in September as is implied in the con-ventional chronology, but at Foligno in Umbria in early November 1527. The messenger who brought letters to Knight at Compiègne which he acknowledged on 13 September was, as Knight himself affirmed at the time, not Barlow, but the same Christopher Morris who had taken Wolsey's letter of 5 September to the king.[19]

Whether Wolsey knew the real intent of Knight's mission as early as 10 September, or not until his return to England, perhaps matters less than the fact that Henry had decided to deceive Wolsey as early as August 1527 and continued to do so even after he returned to England at the end of September. That special, instinctive and mutual trust between them, evoked in Gilbert's later depiction of the two men, had evidently broken down at this time (Figure 7.1).

Figure 7.1 'Me and My King' by Sir John Gilbert RA c. 1886
© Chronicle/Alamy Stock Photo

234   *The Cardinal's greatest matter*

The conventional chronology, even in its most recent iteration, has always struggled to account for how, precisely, Wolsey knew the details of Knight's mission immediately upon its being set on foot and why the king, just as immediately, and apparently unprompted, changed his mind about the purpose of that mission. Starkey's suggested chronology more plausibly accounts for the contradictory sequence of events over a slightly longer timescale, while allowing that Wolsey knew in France that September that he had somehow lost the king's confidence. It was now for him to regain it.

Wolsey regains the initiative

By the time Barlow met Knight, news had spread that the pope expected to be released from the Castel Sant' Angelo. Despite instructions from Henry to the contrary, Knight could barely get anywhere without some help from Wolsey's agents in Rome, and Henry himself seems to have been persuaded that they could be trusted to act for him. Wolsey's elaborate plan to be vicegerent was reduced to nothing the moment Clement was free, so as Barlow travelled to Italy, he mobilised these agents apparently to assist, and certainly to monitor, Knight's mission. The nuncio Gambara was at Foligno to meet him and arrange a safe conduct to Rome. Using that or otherwise, Knight did get into the city and managed, through the good offices of Cardinal Pisani, to get into Clement's hands the second (but now principal) draft bull. Having read this astonishing document, the pope nevertheless signified that, as soon as he was at liberty, he would do what Henry required of him. Clement did duly escape, with the emperor's connivance, on 6 December and went to Orvieto where Knight met him again, expecting to receive the dispensation for which he had come. Instead, the matter was taken up by the Papal Datary, Cardinal Pucci, for review and consideration.[20]

Wolsey's first direct instructions to Gregorio Casali to act as Henry VIII's ambassador in Rome told him to join Knight with the pope at Orvieto and give him every assistance. Wolsey gave a precis of the king's case based on conscience to be presented to the pope and making no mention of any second marriage – although that cat was already well out of the bag. The instructions are particularly noteworthy as the first occasion when Wolsey threatened

The Cardinal's greatest matter 235

the pope with the international consequences of failing to accede to Henry's demands. He told Clement that he foresaw the breakdown of English solidarity with Rome unless the issue of the succession was settled. Without it, Henry's capacity to aid the papacy against its enemies, temporal and spiritual, in the way he had always sought to do, was hamstrung. He went further still. In a letter sent early the following year, Wolsey threatened England's 'declining from obedience to the Holy See' if the pope did not allow him to settle the annulment question in England. This was tactical manoeuvring certainly, and still within the bounds of the approach Wolsey had favoured since May 1527, but it shows that he now understood just how far Henry was prepared to go to get what he wanted. In Henry's mind the issue was rapidly becoming principally about his authority within his kingdom, its security and his international reputation as a monarch.[21]

Casali was instructed by Wolsey to use that insider's expertise he claimed to have, to distribute favours on Henry's behalf, apparently to the extent of offering Cardinal Pucci a 'gift' of 2,000 crowns to ensure a favourable reading of the draft bull of dispensation. This was politely declined. Pucci made numerous amendments but finally approved the draft. Nevertheless, its import, intended to clear and simplify the matter, tipped the whole divorce and remarriage plan into the lap of the Roman Curia where there were ample supporters for Katherine and Charles, and it effectively ended Henry's chances of exactly the kind of swift, if unconventional, settlement it had been intended to bring about in the first place.[22] By the start of 1528 then, when Knight left Rome, all that Clement had conceded was a general commission to Wolsey to enquire into Henry's marriage by virtue of his powers as legate, with any verdict still subject to appeal to Rome. It got Henry only a little further than he had been in May 1527. Worse still for him, the papacy was now well aware of his real matrimonial intentions. Clement assured Knight that when, as he hoped, the French forced a withdrawal of Imperial forces from Rome, he would be better able to do as Henry asked. Knight began his journey back towards England. He was never reconciled thereafter to Wolsey, who despised him for what he regarded as a personal betrayal.[23]

The news of Clement's limited dispensation and commission for Wolsey reached England in late January 1528, and the documents

236 *The Cardinal's greatest matter*

themselves arrived with the nuncio Gambara not long afterwards. Wolsey at once saw their deficiency and the limits of what had been achieved. Henry had done his best, but it had proved less than good enough. Bereft of any new ideas, the king gradually allowed Wolsey to take charge again, causing Anne and her supporters to reconsider, and only for a time, the benefits of Wolsey's technical expertise in dealing with the papacy. The cardinal oversaw the detailed redrafting of the dispensation bull. He also prepared a demand, not for a general commission to investigate the marriage as had been the case till now, but a decretal commission to hear the case, and to give a definitive, hence 'decretal', verdict in England that would prevent any appeal to Rome from Katherine. Wolsey's command of the case is evidenced in the despatch back to Rome on 12 February of Gambara, together with Edward Foxe and Stephen Gardiner, both Wolsey protégés, the former already sworn of the king's council and the latter soon to become his principal secretary. Reassured perhaps by the renewed energy and initiative Wolsey now showed, Anne thanked him for his assistance in a sequence of warm letters. Complimenting him as patron, she politely requested fish from his ponds at Hampton Court that Lenten season. She was evidently still prepared to trust Wolsey, provided he could get the job done. Wolsey readily responded, at least with equally friendly letters.

The return of Cardinal Campeggio

Meanwhile, riding at pace, Foxe and Gardiner arrived at Orvieto on 21 March 1528, exhausted in body and even lacking suitable clothing for presentation to the pope due to the rapidity and conditions of their winter journey. They were greeted by Casali who accommodated them in his own lodgings in the town and smoothed their way into the papal court. Wolsey's man, and now the king's too, was at work again.[24] The international situation was more favourable for their mission as the French siege of Naples looked likely to succeed by early summer. Clement's hands now appeared to be freer to act for Henry in the way he had promised Knight he would do. Nevertheless, after a month of relentless negotiation by Foxe and Gardiner, the most he would grant was a 'new' dispensation for Henry to marry whomever he wanted after his first marriage had been annulled; the one that had been painstakingly redrafted

The Cardinal's greatest matter 237

under Wolsey's direction. He did that with remarkable ease in fact, doubtless hoping this show of goodwill towards Henry would be appreciated. A decretal commission, however, proved a bridge too far. The most he would grant was another general commission for a trial, but to give the whole thing apparent personal approval, he would also send Cardinal Campeggio to England. Wolsey and he would together convene a legatine court to hear the case. In such matters, Clement soothed, two cardinals were better than one. All verdicts were still subject to appeal to Rome, but he offered meaningful but informal promises, called 'policitations', that these would not be heard, or at least heard without prejudice to Henry's case. The documents were sealed on 13 April, and Foxe departed immediately for England, leaving Gardiner behind to await further developments. Yet, for all their diplomatic and forensic skills and their commitment to carry out their instructions to the uttermost, the two talented English diplomats had actually obtained nothing very much more than had Knight the previous December.

This, Wolsey realised as soon as Foxe returned (with astonishing speed) to England by 2 May. He first reported the following day to Anne and Henry at Greenwich, having missed the cardinal there by some few hours. He had been delayed somewhat by the mayor of Canterbury who had insisted on entertaining this royal envoy fittingly. Leaving the two of them much encouraged, even delighted, with the situation, he came on the same night to Wolsey at Durham Place where his news was greeted rather less excitedly. The documents Foxe brought appeared to demonstrate Wolsey's influence in Rome, based as they were on his redrafting, but without a clear decretal commission, they were still insufficient. After deliberating for some days and taking advice from lawyers already concerned in the case, such as Wolman and Benet, Wolsey issued new orders to Casali and Gardiner to obtain from Clement a secret decretal commission giving Wolsey (and Campeggio) the authority to act decisively in the case, for the interests of the English realm and in the best interests of its relations with the papacy, insofar as Wolsey, being able to give the king what he most needed, would better be able to bind him further to the Holy See. As Foxe informed Gardiner, Wolsey, 'as of himself, for the discharge of his own conscience, with the consent of the other prelates here . . . desires you to press the Pope with all possible persuasions to grant the commission decretal'. Foxe continued that it would assist the Holy See if, armed with the decretal, Wolsey 'were of such authority and estimation with the King that whatever he should advise, Henry would readily assent to'. If granted, the decretal would be shown to nobody

> but only to the King as a means of augmenting his [Wolsey's] own influence with Henry, 'of which thing his Grace willeth also you make faith and promise *in animam suam*, under most sacred oath and obtestation,' that you still urge his Holiness to pass the said decretal.

This insistent emphasis that the diplomats should swear to explain to the pope the importance of Wolsey's influence reinforces the view that he was wholly committed to the annulment case, not because he liked it, but as a demonstration of his own power and authority as legate. Wolsey needed to reassert himself as the king's principal advisor and, crucially, as the sole channel of communication between the king and the pope, and he needed to do what Henry wanted.[25] He wrote to Campeggio and asked him to urge the Pope 'to grant what will be sufficient for the cause, and what can never be subject to revocation or appeal'.[26]

With the danger from Imperial troops lessened during the spring, for the time being at least, Clement moved his court from Orvieto to the statelier town of Viterbo, the traditional summer residence of the popes. Hoping perhaps that these new surroundings better disposed Clement to decision-making, Gardiner at once renewed the assault, assisted by Casali. He demanded the decretal commission Wolsey wanted and was finally successful, as he told Henry on 11 June. Campeggio was commissioned to go to England, armed with the secret document. Casali, who was still smarting after a castigating letter from Wolsey about his alleged incompetence, kept the momentum up and pressed Campeggio to start for England as soon as possible. The Italian cardinal had been his patron some years beforehand. He now did as he was told by his English masters, even to the extent of deceiving Campeggio into thinking that Clement had only granted the decretal commission on the understanding that Campeggio would take it to England personally. Refusal to do so would put him in direct conflict with Henry, something

Campeggio wished to avoid at all costs. Casali arranged galleys for the journey, and Campeggio sailed for France on 25 July, arriving in Paris on 14 September. He eventually landed at Dover on 29 September and, wracked with gout, reached Canterbury by 1 October 1528, a decade after his first visit to England.[27]

Wolsey and Henry were eager for a quick resolution of the matrimonial question, not least because news had by then reached them of French reverses in Italy with Admiral Doria's defection to the emperor and the failure of the siege of Naples. This was also probably the high point of Anne Boleyn's hopes in the cardinal. As we have noted, the two had exchanged a series of friendly greetings in the spring, and again in summer, of 1528 as Campeggio made his way to England. Carefully, each sought to position themselves advantageously with the other. If Wolsey really was committed to securing the annulment which she needed as much as Henry, it made sense for Anne to encourage and support him. It may have seemed to Anne that, notwithstanding his sometimes fantastical schemes and the setbacks to date, the cardinal was now serious about the annulment, if only because he knew how intent upon it Henry was. For Wolsey, Anne's present position alongside the king being unassailable, her support would be helpful in several ways. Not the least of these would be in maintaining good relations with France. Anne readily endorsed Anglo–French peace and had personal connections at the French court, particularly through Francis's sister Marguerite de Navarre. She might prove a powerful ally to Wolsey in that cause if they could work together. What Wolsey really needed her to do immediately, however, was to settle Henry's nerves and enable him to keep the conduct of the matter in his own hands while he squared Campeggio as to what was required.

Alas for Wolsey, Campeggio already knew well enough what he was expected to do. Even as he bore the legatine commission to England in one of those diplomatic bags, Campeggio had in his back pocket, so to speak, instructions from Clement to delay, delay and then delay. His first effort to do so on arrival was personally to persuade Katherine to enter a convent. Henry and Wolsey must have told him that this was pointless, but they had nothing to lose (and Campeggio had time to gain) from one more try. Unsurprisingly, after meetings with the two cardinals and other clergy on 24 and 26 October 1528, Katherine affirmed that her marriage to

240   *The Cardinal's greatest matter*

Arthur had not been consummated. She had no intention of taking the veil, and she wanted to remain in a marriage that she regarded as thoroughly lawful. Meanwhile Wolsey ordered Casali to plead with Clement to issue another full, clear and unequivocal, decretal commission. Despite his best efforts, and as he advised, in sending Campeggio with the 'secret' commission, the pope had done all he was ever going to do for Henry in the matrimonial cause.[28]

Campeggio's limited commission, which he showed the king on 24 October, empowered the two cardinals to enquire into the 1504 bull of dispensation. Its political basis had been that the marriage between Henry and Katherine was essential to maintain peace with England and Spain. This, Henry now said, was wrong at the time and thus invalidated the dispensation. In the autumn of 1528, however, Katherine obtained not only a copy of the bull, but also a copy of one of those papal *breves* we encountered earlier, through the offices of the Spanish ambassador in England, Diego di Mendoza. This *breve* had been addressed, not to an English recipient, but to Katherine's devout mother, Isabella of Castile, at the time of her death in 1504. There was a crucial difference between the text of the bull and the *breve*. The latter said that a dispensation had indeed been granted to maintain Anglo–Spanish peace but also 'for certain other reasons'. These other reasons were not specified, but given its effective co-equal status with the bull, the language of the *breve* was crucial. It covered any flaws there might be in the bull itself, and if it stood, then the decretal commission had nothing to decide upon and the whole weary process would have to start again.[29]

The panicked reaction of Wolsey and Henry at the appearance of what became known as the 'Spanish brief' shows its powerful potential. They immediately questioned its validity and demanded to see the original, held by Charles V. Katherine was prevailed upon to write to her nephew to ask for it to be sent. Naturally, Charles refused her request, saying all that he would provide was an attested copy. Meanwhile, the start of the king's case had to be postponed yet again, to Wolsey's immense frustration and doubtless to Campeggio's relief. Wolsey had now to busy himself on instructions for new ambassadors to Rome. Once more assisted by Casali, Peter Vannes, Sir Francis Bryan and Gardiner were to investigate the validity of the *breve* and seek a new decretal commission to enquire into it.

The Cardinal's greatest matter   241

Henry's hopes of a quick resolution, and Anne's too, were dealt a punishing blow from which they never again recovered. For the first time, but with a determination that characterised him once he had decided upon something, Henry earnestly began to search for another way as a matter of dynastic and national urgency. Then, as if in divine approbation of this new resolution, came news that the pope was dead.

The ambassadors in Rome were immediately instructed to press Wolsey's candidacy in the expected conclave to their uttermost. They were to offer anything that might be promised to anyone who would take it in order to secure his election. It was the only time in Wolsey's entire career that he genuinely wanted to become the Supreme Pontiff. As Clement's successor, he could resolve at a stroke the entire mangled conundrum of the annulment that had so bedevilled the second Medici pope. But no sooner had these instructions been despatched, and Wolsey began calculating how and where to gain support for his election, than news came that Clement was certainly ill but, alas, not dead. There would be no conclave. Eventually Gardiner was able to meet the ailing pope and demand that he denounce the Spanish *breve* as a forgery – no original copy of it could be found despite searching through the curial archives.

In the face of all of this, Henry's patience with the two legates ran out, and as the Imperial ambassador Mendoza reported in February, Henry no longer held Wolsey in his customary esteem. For almost two years since his return from France, Wolsey had been assuring the king that all would yet be well, while urging, sometimes berating, envoys to make greater efforts in securing papal cooperation. Yet his exclusive control of communications between Henry and the pope had never been fully recovered. The ambassadors sent to Rome, Gardiner, Vannes and Bryan, reported to Wolsey of course, but they worked ultimately for Henry and freely gave him their own assessments of the situation in Rome, as they were bound to do. In April 1529, Bryan ended a series of worried reports with his most telling statement since arrival that, as far as he could see, 'the pope will do nothing for your Grace' and that whoever made Henry believe otherwise had not done him the best service. In May, he stated flatly that Campeggio gave the king but 'fair words' and that he was the pope's cardinal, not Henry's.[30]

242 *The Cardinal's greatest matter*

The French ambassador Jean du Bellay, who took up his post anew that spring, reported that Wolsey was in trouble and that Suffolk, Norfolk and those around them had it in for him.[31] Historians have detected in this and similar reports from the new Imperial ambassador Eustace Chapuys, who arrived in August, the origins of an effort by a faction of courtiers close to Anne, including the two dukes, her brother and her cousin Sir Francis Bryan, deliberately to bring the cardinal down. The group he identified certainly had been to the fore in the king's affairs since the summer of 1527, and whether by coordinated action or not, they had undoubtedly done their best to discredit Wolsey whenever it appeared that his suggestions were not working, or even when the king showed impatience with them. The question has been asked, however, in so doing were they setting the agenda, or simply taking their lead from the king? Everyone after all agreed with him that the annulment was necessary. The only question was whether Wolsey could deliver it.[32]

Wolsey knew Henry was angry with him and that he needed friends. He asked Du Bellay to go to the king and declare Francis I's support for him. That, the ambassador did not do, but he did ask his master to support Wolsey and reported his further request that Francis send one of the gentlemen of his chamber to the pope to impress upon him how much he supported Henry's cause.[33] In May, Suffolk and Sir William Fitzwilliam were sent to Francis to try to forestall any reconciliation between the king of France and the emperor, of which talk was in the air after the failure of the French siege of Naples. Du Bellay urged Francis to assure them of his support for Henry's cause, and for Wolsey. In fact, Francis took the opportunity to damn Wolsey with faint praise. In response to Suffolk's question, asked on the king's instructions, as to Francis's opinion of Wolsey (and as Suffolk gleefully reported), the French king said ambiguously that as far as he could tell, Wolsey wanted the annulment to go ahead because he did not love the queen. Nevertheless, Francis apparently went on, for all the cardinal's much vaunted influence with his peers in Rome, they seemed unwilling to help Henry, and the best remedy would be for the king 'to look substantially upon his matters himself', as he understood Henry now to be doing. Or words to that effect – we have only Suffolk's letter to go by. A subsequent argument between Suffolk, Wolsey and Du Bellay about the veracity of this statement strongly suggests that the duke had at the very least taken Francis's words out of context.[34]

Yet the real harm that Francis did to Wolsey was far more serious than giving Suffolk ammunition against him. Suffolk and his circle may or may not have wanted to get rid of Wolsey, but Francis I certainly did. The French army in Italy was finally defeated at Landriano on 21 June 1529. With that, Clement announced, with uncharacteristic decisiveness, that he was now firmly committed to the emperor. He had little real choice anyway. On 29 June, scarcely a week after Landriano, he agreed the Treaty of Barcelona with Charles. He allied with the emperor and promised to crown him, finally enabling Charles to assert his full status as Holy Roman Emperor, a decade after his election. In return, his Medici relatives were to be restored to power in Florence, by force of Imperial arms if necessary. This had been Clement's prime concern for the previous two years and was certainly a higher priority for him than Henry's annulment case. Seeing his defeat in Italy and the pope and emperor now reconciled, Francis was constrained to open peace negotiations, raising the unthinkable possibility for Wolsey of an agreement between Charles and Francis to which Henry was not central. Such a thing had not happened for a decade. Wolsey was desperate to get himself involved in negotiations to prevent it. Aware of this, Francis deceived him, and Henry (and perhaps even du Bellay), about the extent to which he was determined to reach a negotiated settlement with the emperor.

The legatine court at Blackfriars

Armed with Bryan's opinion and apparently encouraged indirectly by Francis, Henry once again took back some measure of control over the annulment case. He formally authorised, in effect told, the two legates to proceed under the terms of the pope's secret commission, while still awaiting the hoped-for fuller decretal commission. Henry probably just wanted to have done what had to be done, but for one last time he affirmed, if not exactly his faith then at least his hope, that Wolsey the magician might once more pull the rabbit out of the *galero*. The two legates duly met and set a date for the trial. Campeggio also met Katherine on 14 June in response to her request for news of Charles's demand that the case be revoked

244 *The Cardinal's greatest matter*

to Rome, made in April. He took the opportunity again to plead with her to enter a convent. Once more she refused. Accordingly, the trial proceedings began at the Dominican Friary in London, Blackfriars, on 18 June 1529, after a preliminary private hearing in which Katherine formally notified the court of her appeal to Rome. Henry appeared by proxy. The queen repeated in public her appeal against the legates, and they formally recognised it. On 21 June, the court met to hear evidence. This time the king and queen were both present. As Edward Hall and George Cavendish report, when summoned, Henry, standing under a cloth of estate, addressed the court, briefly laying out the nature of his case and his belief that his marriage to Katherine was invalid and asking for the legates' judgement. Wolsey formally replied, assuring the court that they would judge impartially, according to the facts. After exchanging a few hurt words with Henry, Katherine suddenly arose from her place and, coming around the benches of the lawyers, threw herself on her knees in front of her husband. 'Alas, sir, wherein have I offended you, or what occasion of displeasure have I deserved against your will and pleasure?' she asked. She pleaded with him to accept the validity of their marriage, the legitimacy of their daughter and to respect her honour as a true wife and loyal queen of England. She specifically reasserted that she had been a maid when Henry had married her, the core of her case after all, and challenged the king 'whether that be true or no, I put it to your conscience'. She reminded him that at the time both English and Spanish counsellors had considered the marriage 'good and lawful'. She asked to be excused 'the extremity' of the trial and demanded independent counsel, before standing and leaving the court.[35] Three times she was called back, but accompanied by her close household servants, she pressed on and never returned. In consequence, she was declared 'contumacious', that is, in contempt of court, which made her subject to a summary verdict. Yet, as Jean du Bellay noted, she had departed to shouts and cheers of encouragement from women outside the courtroom. As he put it: 'If the matter was to be decided by women, he [Henry] would lose the battle'.[36]

An awkward silence followed, broken by the king uneasily admitting that Katherine had indeed been to him as 'true, obedient and as comfortable a wife as I could in my fancy wish or desire' and praising her many virtues. At which point Wolsey, seated alongside

The Cardinal's greatest matter   245

Campeggio, arose and there followed the exchange with Henry quoted at the outset of this chapter. Henry went on to explain in further detail before the court, the 'certain scrupulosity' he had felt in conscience about his marriage.

Ever since William Knight's mission to Rome in 1527, there had been deep unease between Henry and Wolsey as to the best way forward. Despite, or because of, Anne's supporters' best efforts, Henry's confidence in Wolsey was by then much reduced but not yet extinguished. The desired outcome of the trial might still put things right between the two friends. That must surely have been Wolsey's hope. According to Cavendish at least, he went out of his way to test Katherine's defence team at every turn, deliberately to demonstrate his commitment to the cause as far as he could. Henry was also evidently keeping the pressure on from behind the scenes. A few days after Katherine's dramatic withdrawal from the court, he summoned Wolsey to Bridewell for an update on the case. They spent an hour or more together. Afterwards Wolsey returned to York Place by barge, accompanied by the Bishop of Carlisle, who remarked that it was a hot day. Wolsey retorted, 'Sir if you had been as well chafed as I have been within this last hour, ye would say it were very hot'. Arriving at home, Wolsey was evidently so distressed by that royal heat that he went straight to his bed, only to be roused two hours later by the arrival of Thomas Boleyn with an urgent command from the king that Wolsey return to Bridewell with Campeggio the same day. There, they were to persuade the queen to turn the whole matter over to the king's hands and to avoid the shame and dishonour of the trial. In fact, despite her 'contumacy', Katherine had done a pretty good job for herself of ruining the trial in England. Charles V's revocation request was already lodged in Rome, the documentation of her own appeal was on its way there via Brussels and her dramatic public confrontation with the king, couched as it had been in humble but devastatingly telling words, had publicly exposed the weakness of the king's case. It panicked Henry. What he was preparing to offer Katherine, or threaten her with, at this stage in the proceedings may well have been the subject of the heated conversation between himself and Wolsey earlier that day. We shall never know, but if Wolsey had been told of it, his going to bed immediately afterwards perhaps tells us what he thought of it. He angrily blamed Thomas Boleyn and the other members of the royal council for this summons, assuming they had supported what he probably regarded as Henry's pointless course of action – just as they had done back in the summer of 1527. When the cardinals met her, Katherine was all humility but changed her position not one iota. As Cavendish reported, 'We in the other chamber [next to the queen's privy chamber] might sometime hear the Queen speak very loud, but what it was we could not understand'. The cardinals left to report the outcome to the king. Doubtless that meeting, too, was heated.[37]

While these royal histrionics played out, the trial went on. Meanwhile at Cambrai, the peace negotiations between the emperor's aunt Margaret of Savoy and Louise of Savoy, Francis's mother, made progress, and Francis continued to deceive Wolsey as to their true import. As late as 17 June, Francis told Jean Du Bellay that matters were going slowly, only for Wolsey and Henry to discover scarcely five days later that they were in fact so far advanced that a final settlement was expected imminently. Henry was again furious with Wolsey for, as the ambassador reported, 'to this hour he has always been assuring his master, both in public and in private, that you [Francis] would do nothing without them'. Through Du Bellay, Wolsey begged Francis to write to Henry declaring himself willing, even at this stage, to accommodate Henry fully in the settlement because of the legate's intercession. Francis never did. The last thing he wanted was for Wolsey to be able to turn the whole thing to Henry's advantage – as he had always done before.[38] By the end of the month Du Bellay was urging Francis to allow the English representatives, Cuthbert Tunstal and Sir Thomas More, who had belatedly been appointed to go to Cambrai, to take a meaningful part in the negotiations. He also communicated Wolsey's request that Francis write to Campeggio and ask him to treat the king of England's matter as a personal favour to himself. Again, there is no evidence that Francis ever did so.[39]

Katherine's appeal reached Rome by 5 July and there found powerful supporters. After the usual prevarication from Clement, it was upheld and the 'advocation', that is the revocation, of the case to Rome was decreed by the cardinals in Consistory on 16 July. As Casali told Wolsey, 'His Holiness fears and trusts only the Emperor', neatly summing up the whole sorry tale of the king's matrimonial cause.[40] No one in Rome knew then that the

The Cardinal's greatest matter 247

Blackfriars' trial was coming to an end of its own accord. Wishing to anticipate events in Rome, the king's lawyer demanded judgement in the case. On 23 July 1529, it was delivered – or rather, it wasn't. Campeggio, ill and under enormous pressure from the papacy on the one side, and Wolsey, Henry and anyone else who mattered in England on the other, stood and announced that the trial would be 'prorogued and continued', in fact adjourned, from the end of that month until October. He declared himself unable to pass judgement in a case 'too high and notably known through all the world' without further consultation with the Holy See. He protested his impartiality, wishing to avoid any 'hasty judgement' and assuring all that he adjourned the matter out of respect for the king's honour and dignity. The fact was that he could not pass judgement in Henry's favour not knowing whether or not Clement had already revoked the case (which of course he had). Yet, if he pronounced himself unable to pass sentence, the commission empowered Wolsey to give a verdict alone or perhaps with Warham, and he knew what that would be, even if this was still subject to advocation. In the end, Campeggio took the only reasonable course available to him.

There was shock, even uproar in the court room. The duke of Suffolk, according to Hall and Cavendish, speaking as 'from the king and by his commandment' (suggesting that Henry probably knew what Campeggio was going to say), stepped forward and declared thunderously, 'It was never merry in England whilst we had Cardinals among us'. Wolsey certainly knew beforehand what Campeggio intended. Ashen-faced, he saw Suffolk's 'vehement countenance' and understood for whom the duke spoke. Standing beside his fellow legate, Wolsey was unable to do or say a thing. Now the ecclesiastical slipper really was on the other foot. In 1518, Wolsey had patronisingly bundled Campeggio (and Pope Leo X) into his grand scheme for Henry's international prominence, the Treaty of Universal Peace. Now he stood helpless as Campeggio carried out Clement's instructions and, by so doing, humiliated Wolsey's king before all the world. A revocation now seemed almost inevitable. Henry could be summoned to Rome to appear, not as the embodiment of English national sovereignty and the fount of justice himself, but as respondent to an appeal to an authority higher than his own, and at his wife's behest. It was unthinkable.

248　*The Cardinal's greatest matter*

Wolsey's limitations

In early August, news of the papal advocation of the case arrived in England. Wolsey had now to work as fast and as cleverly as he had ever done before to extricate the king, and himself, from this awful dilemma if at all possible and only if Henry would still give him the chance to try. Wolsey used his habitual mix of blandishments and threats to obtain the agreement of Katherine's lawyers that to avoid Henry having to accept the advocation summons personally, he and Campeggio would accept it on the king's behalf. Henry grumbled at even this and suggested that Clement's *breve* of 9 July, indicating the advocation had been granted and 'inhibiting' any further action in the case, should suffice. Katherine's lawyers finally agreed to take no immediate further action against the king on the understanding that nothing prejudicial would be done to her legal interests, and the trial in England was abandoned.[41]

Campeggio remained Wolsey's only reasonable means of advice and support. He persuaded his Italian colleague to promise that he would do his best to intervene with the pope to prevent Katherine's case actually being heard. Why this undertaking should have given him or Henry any particular comfort, given Campeggio's recent action, may be wondered at, but if his words in the legatine court were taken at face value, the Italian legate appeared still to be well-disposed to the king. His dependence on Campeggio illustrates Wolsey's dilemma. He had worked as hard as he could and used every means at his disposal to bring about the result that Henry wanted. He deployed the considerable diplomatic, legal and theological expertise of Foxe, Gardiner and Casali in furtherance of this objective and flattered and threatened his fellow cardinals, foreign ambassadors and the pope himself in an effort to secure the annulment. He was imaginative but also conventional in his thinking, as was the king at this point and most of those others whose advice he also sought. In the end it was not the theological and canon law intricacies of the case that finally defeated Wolsey's attempt, but the complexity of the international situation which, for once, Wolsey was powerless even to influence, much less control, in the way he once apparently could.

The Treaty of Cambrai, also known as the 'Peace of the Ladies', was signed on 3 August 1529. Two days later it was sworn to in

Cambrai cathedral in the presence of the king of France. The English king had formally been comprehended in the Valois–Habsburg peace but practically excluded from any real influence on its terms. In order to keep Francis on side, Henry agreed to forgive some of the French king's debts to him on the understanding that the money be spent instead on ransoming Francis's eldest sons, still held captive by Charles after the Treaty of Madrid.[42]

This was a disaster for Wolsey, worse even than the Blackfriars trial. For a decade past, he had ensured that his king was at the fore-front of any significant European peace, using English support for one side or the other to maintain an imbalance of power advanta-geous to Henry. Trapped in the trial proceedings at Blackfriars and held responsible for their fruitless outcome, Wolsey could not work his accustomed magic abroad. He now faced his sometime appren-tice in international relations, friend and sovereign who seemed to be at his weakest point since the start of his reign.

This situation was the very antithesis of everything Wolsey had striven to provide for Henry as king of England. Henry knew that, too. He was bitterly disappointed with Wolsey, who had proved unable to give him the one thing he needed more than anything else he had ever asked of him. He was fearful for the future of his dynasty and his personal reputation, for his 'honour', as the king of England. Henry felt betrayed by the one man who, he was con-vinced, had from the outset denied him the treatment that befit-ted his high sovereign status and his devoted service, ever since his accession, to the Church Universal. That man was Pope Clement VII. Coldly furious at this betrayal, the Defender of the Faith now struck out vengefully against the Church in England – and first at its head, Cardinal Wolsey.

Notes

1 Cavendish, pp. 85–6.
2 Scarisbrick, pp. 163–97 for what remains the fullest, concise, exposition of the canon law of the annulment, although it has its critics.
3 Ibid., pp. 153–6.
4 Clarke, 'Rivalling Rome', pp. 12–14. Text at Appendix IB, pp. 41–3.
5 *CSP Sp.* III ii, 113, Mendoza to Charles V, 13 July 1527; 131 Charles's response, 29 July 1527.

6 *St. P.* I, pp. 230–3 Wolsey to Henry, 29 July 1527.

7 *LP* IV ii, 3318 Fitzwilliam to Wolsey, 31 July 1527.

8 C. Fletcher, *Our Man in Rome: Henry VIII and His Italian Ambassador* (London, 2012), pp. 3–15.

9 *St. P.* I, p. 256 Wolsey to Henry, Amiens, 16 August 1527.

10 J. Sharkey, 'Between King and Pope: Thomas Wolsey and the Knight Mission', *Historical Research* 84 (224) (May 2011): 236–48.

11 Cavendish, p. 62; *St. P.* I, 267 [*LP* IV 3400] Wolsey to Henry, 5 September 1527; Sharkey, 246–7; D. Starkey, *Six Wives: The Queens of Henry VIII* (London, 2003), pp. 302–3 on the identity of the messenger 'Gunner'.

12 J. Gairdner, 'New Lights on the Divorce of Henry VIII', *EHR* 11 (44) (1896): 673–702 at 684; Starkey, *Six Wives*, pp. 301–6; cf. Sharkey, pp. 242–3.

13 *St. P.* VII, p. 3 [*LP* IV ii, 3422] Knight to Henry VIII, 13 September 1527.

14 Sharkey, p. 242.

15 Gairdner, p. 685 Henry VIII to Knight undated; Scarisbrick, pp. 159–60; Sharkey, p. 242.

16 Ibid., pp. 685–6.

17 Ibid., p. 685; Starkey, *Six Wives*, pp. 305–6.

18 Gairdner, p. 685.

19 *St. P.* VII, p. 3 [*LP* IV ii, 3422] Knight to Henry VIII, 13 September 1527 'I have received your letter by Chr. Morris'.

20 Gairdner, p. 687.

21 *LP* IV ii, 3641 Wolsey to Casali, 5 December 1527; 3913 Wolsey's instructions to Gardiner and Fox, January 1528; see also W. Rockett, 'Wolsey, More and Unity of Christendom', *SCJ* 35 (2004): 133–53.

22 Fletcher, pp. 16–21 on Knight and Casali's efforts to bribe Pucci.

23 Gairdner, pp. 690–2; Starkey, *Six Wives*, pp. 306–13.

24 Fletcher, pp. 26–30.

25 *LP* IV ii, 4251, Foxe to Gardiner, 11 May 1528.

26 Ibid., 4249, Wolsey to Campeggio, 11 May 1528.

27 *St. P.* VII, pp. 68–9 [*LP* IV 4289] Wolsey to Casali, London, 23 May 1528.

28 Ibid., pp. 102 ff [*LP* 4897] Wolsey to Casali, London, 1 November 1528; *CSPV* IV 383; Fletcher, p. 54.

29 J. Gairdner, 'New Lights on the Divorce of Henry VIII (Continued)', *EHR* 12 (46) (April 1897): 237–53 on the significance of the 'Spanish Brief'.

30 *LP* IV iii, 5255 Mendoza to Charles V, London, 4 February 1529; *St. P.* VII, pp. 166–9 [*LP* IV iii, 5481] Bryan to Henry VIII, Rome, 21 April 1529.

31 *Correspondance du Cardinal Jean du Bellay*, ed. R. Scheurer (2 vols; Paris, 1969), p. 22 [*LP* IV iii, 5581]; see also *LP* IV iii, 5601.

32 E. Ives, 'The Fall of Wolsey', in Gunn and Lindley, pp. 286–315; G. Bernard, 'The Fall of Wolsey Reconsidered', *Journal of British Studies* 35 (3) (July 1996): 277–310, at 292.

33 *Correspondance*, pp. 15–16 [*LP* IV iii, 5547] Du Bellay to Anne de Montmorency, London, 15 May 1529.

34 *St. P.* VII, p. 182; *Correspondance*, pp. 64–9; see *LP* IV iii, 5862 for Du Bellay to Montmorency, 23 August 1529, for an account of the argument about what Francis had said to Suffolk.

35 M. Dowling, 'Humanist Support for Katherine of Aragon', *Bulletin of the Institute of Historical Research* 57 (135) (May 1984): 46–55 for Katherine's defence counsel and their advice.

36 Cavendish, pp. 83–5; *LP* IV iii, 5701/2 Du Bellay to Montmorency and to Francis I, 22 June 1529.

37 Cavendish, pp. 89–92.

38 *LP* IV iii, 5701/02.

39 Ibid., 5741, 5742; for the English ambassadors' commission, see 5744.

40 Ibid., 5780 Casali to Wolsey, Rome, 16 July 1529.

41 Starkey, *Six Wives*, pp. 253–5.

42 *LP* IV iii, 5829 for the terms of the Treaty of Cambrai; Knecht, pp. 283–6.

8   The turn of Fortune's wheel

Wolsey's fall

'Well, well, Master Kingston' quod he, 'I see the matter against me, how it is framed. But if I had served God as diligently as I have done the King, he would not have given me over in my grey hairs. Howbeit this is the just reward that I must receive for my worldly diligence and pains that I have had to do him service, only to satisfy his vain pleasures, not regarding my godly duty. Wherefore I pray you with all my heart to have me most humbly commended unto his royal majesty, beseeching him in my behalf to call to his most gracious remembrance all matters proceeding between him and me from the beginning of the world unto this day, and the progress of the same'.[1]

The words 'But if I had served God as diligently as I have done the King, he would not have given me over in my grey hairs' were apparently uttered by Cardinal Wolsey in the last hour of his life. They are often read as the words of a talented but arrogant man, ruined, and perhaps deservedly so, by the tyrant he served. Read thus, the words have a shameful pathos that has shaped and coloured perceptions of Wolsey since his death. In an ironic twist, they seem to anticipate the final brave words of his successor as Chancellor, Sir Thomas More: 'I die the king's good servant, but God's first'. The ascetic More, the martyr for the ancient Church in England, stands in saintly contrast to Wolsey, its leader for over a decade. For his critics, Wolsey was, at his last, the bloated, sick embodiment of that Church's greed and pride – soon to be swept away by the same king who ordered the death of More. The fateful words recorded by Cavendish have virtually become his epitaph.

Wolsey loses power

What is less well appreciated, but more revealing of Wolsey, is the rest of what Cavendish attributes to him in the passage quoted at the start of this chapter. It begins a long and assertive, even defensive, death-bed speech. It has a certain, presumably intentional, affinity with Cavendish's account of Katherine of Aragon's speech to Henry at the Blackfriars trial the previous year. Both appear humble and deferential before their sovereign, but both stand on their record of dutiful service. They recall it to the king's mind and reproach him (by implication at least) for treating them unfairly and remind him that they know what has really passed between them, whatever he maintains to the contrary. In Wolsey's case, his sense of grievance played some part at least in bringing him to his final disgrace and regret.

After the effective conclusion of the Legatine Court, Wolsey spent the next six weeks until mid-September 1529 mainly at St Albans and at his manor houses of The More and Tittenhanger. He and the king agreed a process of winding up the legal proceedings and strategies to delay or prevent Henry's being summoned to Rome. That done, Henry left Wolsey and spent the remainder of the summer in the company of Anne Boleyn, hunting across the southern Midlands and Oxfordshire throughout 'the grease season', when the deer were in their prime and before the autumn rut. On the surface, all appeared to be alright. In the king's absence Wolsey kept watch, as he had done for more than a dozen summers past, on royal business, corresponding and generally ordering minor administrative matters in the way second nature to him. Perhaps he clung to these daily responsibilities as never before, knowing that there was little he could now do directly about the two things that really mattered: the king's marriage and the consequences of the treaty of Cambrai. For, as was being daily borne in upon him, true authority was shifting. Wolsey's advice on policy was no longer routinely sought. His former protégé and secretary, Stephen Gardiner, was appointed royal secretary on 28 July. He took up his duties immediately and with them a distinctly altered attitude towards his former master. On the king's instructions, Gardiner liaised with Wolsey on the transfer of the temporalities of the vacant see of Durham, that Wolsey had exchanged for Winchester,

254   *The turn of Fortune's wheel*

to Thomas Boleyn, now Lord Rochford. During August, Wolsey was alternatively summoned to, or banned from, the court as the king pleased. Writing to Wolsey on 24 August, and while observing every courtesy, Gardiner more instructed than advised the cardinal, willing him in the king's name to come to arrangements with the queen's counsel, to dissolve the legatine court along the lines they had agreed when the king had recently been at Tittenhanger, and to do so promptly. Wolsey doubtless fumed but complied without significant demur in these matters. He tried to see the king at the end of August but was rebuffed and told to offer his opinions on a range of matters put to him by the king, in writing.[2]

The new Imperial ambassador, Eustace Chapuys, arrived at the end of August. He was the first envoy in almost two decades who did not meet Wolsey before an audience with the king. Nor, when he had his first meeting with Henry on 14 September, did the king refer Chapuys to Wolsey to discuss the details of his instructions and mission, as he had almost invariably hitherto done with ambassadors. Chapuys knew better in the circumstances than to even mention Wolsey. The times had indeed changed. He and Henry then conducted a polite but difficult discussion over the import of his mission, the annulment case and the implications of the treaty of Cambrai.

From the outset, Chapuys was naturally well-disposed towards Katherine and ill-disposed towards Anne. In his first despatch to the emperor, he echoed the language of his predecessor Mendoza, describing Anne as effectively the head of a group of courtiers who had 'sworn to the cardinal's ruin' and said that she had 'spoken and acted the most openly against him'. Much has been made of these remarks, together with those of Du Bellay earlier in the year, by those who see Wolsey as the victim of a Boleyn faction. Yet Chapuys also said that the cardinal's fate, and doubtless the reasons for it, were being quite openly gossiped about. He said he was unsure what to believe, and for that reason, he told Charles, 'when at Court I will make inquiries and ascertain what truth there is in the general report, in order to shape my conduct accordingly'.[3]

On September 11, the two legates gave up their powers in the matter of the king's marriage. There was nothing now for Campeggio to do but return to Rome. By then, he had long since wanted to see the back of England anyway, and its king

The turn of Fortune's wheel 255

the back of him. All sides kept to the polite and perhaps reassuring fiction that he was still England's trusted cardinal protector at the heart of the Curia, there to do all he could for Henry. Under that colour, it was agreed that, with Wolsey, Campeggio should come to Henry at Grafton in Northamptonshire on 19 September, there to take his leave. The evidence is patchy, but it seems that Wolsey had not seen the king for at least a month. Chapuys reported that the visit was to be without their usual legatine crosses and other paraphernalia and that each was to have no more than 10–12 servants.[4]

On arriving at Grafton, Wolsey found that while Campeggio was offered rooms in which to change out of his riding clothes and to prepare to meet the king, there was literally no room for him at the small manor house. Henry Norris, the Groom of the Stool, Henry's closest body servant and head of the Privy Chamber, that department of the household Wolsey had helped to create but could never master, offered the cardinal his own rooms. The two ecclesiastical princes met the king in front of an expectant court. Everyone showed their accustomed deference, but as one observer of the scene commented, 'what they bear in the hearts I know not'. Henry greeted Wolsey with open arms and 'with as amiable a cheer as he ever did', which was followed by an animated conversation by a window (as was their usual custom). They dined separately, Wolsey with the other lords of the council, and Henry with Anne. She evidently tried to dissuade him, with some pretty strong language, from seeing the cardinal further. Henry responded that he knew she was not the cardinal's friend. Nevertheless, he and Wolsey met again and once more conversed 'in a great window' and then in complete privacy in the privy chamber for the rest of the day. Yet still there was no accommodation for the cardinals that evening. They had to travel some three miles by torchlight to Easton Neston, where they stayed in the residence of Sir Thomas Empson. The following day, Wolsey and Campeggio returned. After sitting with the council and being treated with as much respect as ever, Wolsey met Henry again privately for some time. Then the king, already dressed for hunting, gave leave to both cardinals. At Anne's insistent suggestion, he rode off to inspect a new and appropriately named hunting park, called Hartwell. Neither Henry nor Wolsey could have known that day that, after 20 years of work together, of

256   *The turn of Fortune's wheel*

friendship and interdependence as master and servant, they would never see each other again.[5]

On 3 October 1529, Wolsey returned to York Place amidst another outbreak of the pestilence in London and in anticipation of the start of the legal term at Westminster. That day Jean du Bellay met the king's council at York Place. He confirmed to Francis what Chapuys had by then also told Charles, that Lord Rochford was the new manager of the king's affairs generally and in the future of Anglo–French dealings particularly. This was confirmed by the appointment that month of his son George as the new ambassador to France. Du Bellay believed, as did Chapuys, that Wolsey would be brought down by the Parliament shortly to convene. Both had got wind of a list of some 44 accusations against the cardinal that had been framed by Lord Darcy and agreed by a group of noblemen, all of whom had grudges against Wolsey. These were apparently first shown to the king during the summer, and Chapuys at least thought they would become the basis for depriving him of his offices. Some trivial, some serious, the allegations were intended to demonstrate that 'by his great orgueil and pride, and insatiate covetousness to maintain the same', as Chancellor and especially as papal legate, Wolsey had enriched himself, impoverished others and exceeded his authority, to the king's discredit at every turn. The king had done nothing when first presented with these accusations, but had evidently pondered them over some months because they eventually became part of concerted action against Wolsey in the king's name as the autumn began.[6]

Wolsey took part in several meetings of the council at which the dukes of Norfolk and Suffolk were prominent, and which formulated the business for the coming parliament. These meetings were dominated by Henry's increasingly anti-clerical agenda on which he sought the advice of the lay nobility. Common law lawyers made perennial accusations of malpractice among secular priests and various religious houses in matters such as fees for probate. Alerted to these accusations anew, it now suited Henry to have Parliament debate and perhaps legislate to remedy such abuses. On 9 October, the legal term began, and Wolsey again took up his functions as Chancellor, with all his accustomed pomp and ceremony, doubtless glad to be back at work and in public once more. The same day, however, a writ of *praemunire* was brought against him by the Attorney-General, Christopher Hales, in the court of King's Bench.[7] Wolsey was specifically accused of using an illegally obtained legatine authority to appoint two clerics to benefices without specific royal approval and profiting personally in doing so. This was complete nonsense. As both the king and Wolsey knew, his being made a papal legate in 1518 had been done perfectly legally and at Henry's insistence (see Chapter 2). It could not have been in any common meaning of the term without the king's approval, and Wolsey had documentary proof of the same. Since when, Wolsey had exercised that authority primarily in the king's interests, and most prominently at the legatine trial at Blackfriars. Importantly, *praemunire* also constituted a form of technical treason insofar as anyone convicted was held to have acknowledged an authority other than the king's within his realm. That was the point of course. Moreover, to charge the highest-ranked churchman in the land with the offence implied that the whole hierarchy, which had obeyed his legatine authority since 1518, was complicit, an implication that in due course Henry would follow up aggressively. The *praemunire* charge gave the king the legal means to act against the cardinal, but it was really about the English monarch using English law to reassert his rights and authority over the Church. It was a way of emphasising the crown's independence from the papacy, to the protection of which Henry was as committed as any of his predecessors. It was the first step down the road of using English law in the circumstances of his marriage that would lead ultimately to Henry's supreme headship of the Church in England.

Nunc Dimittis: Wolsey's dismissal

The *praemunire* charge against Wolsey has often been thought of as the first move in Henry's planned destruction of him, at Anne Boleyn's insistence. Wolsey himself believed that Anne was behind the moves against him. Her loss of confidence in Wolsey (and indeed Campeggio) and her wish for Henry no longer to rely on him is clear from the early summer of 1529, affirmed by Du Bellay and, as we have seen, reported as virtually common knowledge by the newly arrived Imperial ambassador Chapuys. Eric Ives believed that Henry dismissed Wolsey under pressure from a group of Anne's supporters while maintaining a private sympathy with him and that

258   *The turn of Fortune's wheel*

relations remained good until they differed over the ramifications of the treaty of Cambrai. On the last occasion they met, at Grafton on 19 September, Henry had treated Wolsey with every sign of courtesy, respect and even affection. George Bernard has argued that, despite this, Henry had lost virtually all confidence in Wolsey by the late spring of 1529. The twin disasters of Blackfriars and Cambrai had merely confirmed this.[8]

Anne's father, her uncle Norfolk, her cousin Francis Bryan, her brother and other supporters had pushed her forward in her close relationship with the king in the hopes of advantaging themselves. There is little evidence that, as a group, they set out in a coordinated fashion to 'ruin the cardinal' in the way that Du Bellay and Chapuys characterised them as doing. What they did, however, with Anne in the lead, was to challenge the king's long-held confidence in Wolsey when it wavered. They may have questioned the cardinal's motives and sincerity at first, but it was increasingly his methods that they found fault with, anywhere and as often as they could. They did so because the king already had his doubts about them and with good reason, as Bryan confirmed from Rome in May 1529. Anne's determination to secure an annulment matched Henry's. If Wolsey could deliver it, then Anne and her supporters would work with him. They had no more need to ruin him than had the gentry and the nobility of England more generally during the two decades of his ascendancy. If he could not, however, then Anne had no fascination with the cardinal's supposed omnicompetence. The collapse of the trial exposed his limitations which had left Henry weak and isolated internationally. Wolsey had nothing new to offer strategically. Anne believed that she and her supporters had, and Henry was increasingly willing to listen to them. The evidence of Wolsey's apparent wrong-doings had been presented in July, tending to prove as it did his over-reaching himself in all spheres of his authority as Chancellor and as legate. The form of necessary redress began to take shape in the king's mind. Henry needed no prompting from Anne Boleyn to ponder the dismissal of Wolsey during the summer of 1529, but he surely had her fervent blessing in doing so.

Yet it is also evident that Henry still needed Wolsey at times in August and September for his technical expertise on aspects of the treaty of Cambrai and limiting the damage of the advocation of the

The turn of Fortune's wheel   259

matrimonial case to Rome. This was done at the direction of the royal council and communicated usually through Gardiner. Anne's annoyance at Grafton was perhaps less because she thought any meeting with Henry after a month would result in Wolsey's immediate recall, as is sometimes imagined, but because in her view the king was treating Wolsey with too much honour and privilege for one who had failed him so completely. Perhaps it was that Henry's anger against Wolsey personally had abated somewhat. They were old friends, and Henry understood as well as anyone just what a bind Wolsey had been in. Perhaps, stickler for form that he could be for all his spontaneity, Henry also accorded Wolsey that day the honour of the office he still held and what it represented. And that was the rub of it; what Wolsey represented was the clear and present problem. By the end of September, the technical details of the case and the Cambrai treaty had for the time being at least been sufficiently dealt with. Doubtless more details would arise in due course, but other smart advisors like Gardiner, Sir Thomas More and Richard Sampson, were rapidly mastering their briefs on both these situations. New initiatives were in hand, such as consulting universities at home and abroad on the validity of the king's case, and with which Wolsey could be of no service. The new legal term now begun, Henry could not have the personal representative of the papacy, and a man charged in *praemunire*, exercising legal and royal authority in the realm and presiding over Parliament. Cardinal Wolsey was therefore dismissed as Lord Chancellor of England on or about 16 October 1529.[9]

Wolsey was also dismissed from all his English ecclesiastical offices. He could not, of course, be deprived of his cardinal legateship as that lay outside Henry's gift. On 17 October, the dukes of Norfolk and Suffolk arrived at York Place to inform Wolsey of his dismissal and to demand from him the Great Seal of England. For himself, Wolsey acknowledged, all that he possessed had come from Henry, and it was the king's right to appoint whomever he wanted as Chancellor. Yet, aware of his rights, convinced of his innocence at law and still in his own mind the kingdom's chief legal officer, he sent the two dukes packing. That seal, he told them, had been entrusted to him by the king himself for life under Letters Patent, and their mere verbal demand for it, even as peers, was insufficient. It was perhaps a last, small victory, as technical in its way as the charge of *praemunire* was, but equally symbolic of Wolsey's robust response and his insistence on proper dealings. Only when the two dukes returned the following day with letters from Henry, the reading of which, Cavendish tells us, 'was done with much reverence', did Wolsey yield up the Great Seal and prepare to obey the king's further order to vacate York Place and move to Esher, a manor house belonging to the bishopric of Winchester. The contents of York Place were then inventoried (some record of which survives), trussed up in wicker baskets and cases and taken to Greenwich where they were viewed by Henry and Anne some days later.[10]

All sources indicate that Wolsey left York Place for the last time within a few days of his dismissal, probably on 19 or 20 October. Rumours had spread that he was to go to the Tower of London, and again according to Cavendish, a crowd had gathered on the river to enjoy the spectacle of his disgrace. Wolsey chided his treasurer William Gascoigne for believing the tittle-tattle, assuring him that he had not been arrested and had no fear of the Tower. Doubtless he disappointed onlookers when his barge left York Place and turned upstream towards Putney. On arrival there, to continue the journey to Esher by land, Wolsey's hopes of being recalled seemed suddenly to revive. Sir Henry Norris, the man who had offered him his rooms at Grafton in September, appeared on horseback bringing Wolsey a gift of a ring from the king. As Cavendish explains, 'which ring he knew very well, for it was always a privy token between the King and him when so ever the King would have any special matter dispatched at his hands'.[11] The cool public composure Wolsey had thus far affected utterly deserted him. His anguish and relief burst forth at once. He leapt from his mule like a man half his age and threw himself on his knees before Norris. In frustration he tore at the strings of his clerical hat, to bare his head in the presence of the man who, Archangel-like, had brought him the good news of his apparent salvation. For a time, Norris, too, knelt with Wolsey in the muddy road. In thanks, Wolsey gave him a gold crucifix containing a piece of the true cross.

Henry was evidently deeply disappointed in the man who, from his youngest days as king, had been his most trusted advisor and friend. Wolsey had suffered the consequences of that disappointment in his dismissal from office. As they rode together, Norris and Wolsey talked for some time, and we may be sure their subject was more than the weather. What was the 'special matter dispatched at his hands' that Henry wanted, the ring betokened, and of which Norris now spoke? Wolsey was already at the king's mercy and protection; they both knew that. It is most likely that the oft-noted assurances Norris had brought came as part of a deal. If Wolsey publicly accepted the fault of *praemunire* and its implications about Henry's authority, then Henry would ensure that he did not suffer unduly, despite the urgings of those around him to do away with Wolsey altogether. This would, however, have to be something just between Wolsey and the king. No one could better convey that message than 'gentle Norris', as he was known. Although angered by Wolsey's inability to do what was needed, Norris may have said, the king was yet mindful of the cardinal's friendship, his many years of work for him and wanted to protect him from those who wished him ill – if Wolsey helped him. If he did not, Norris need hardly have reminded him, the means of the cardinal's utter destruction were already in the king's hands, with or without Anne Boleyn's say so.

We do not know of course, but a conversation along these lines accords closely with several statements Wolsey later made as to why he did not contest the charge of *praeumunire*. These were given to Thomas Cromwell, to the judges sent to examine him in October, to some legal officials of the council the following year, and to Cavendish. Wolsey understood his own situation, and its implications for the Church, from his dealings with Hunne's case and with the 'benefit of clergy' dispute involving Abbot Kidderminster years earlier (see Chapter 4). Charging him with the offence of *praemunire* was a legal ploy, but a very serious one and politically motivated. He responded in an equally political manner. As he later made clear, he refused to fight the case on legal grounds and wanted as far as possible to keep the matter between himself and Henry and threw himself upon the king's mercy.

He had, after all, very good grounds to defend himself. Not the least of these, as he told his interrogators on the *praemunire* charge, was that he had the king's licence 'under his hand and broad seal' to exercise legatine authority 'in the largest wise within his dominions', although this had now been taken from him with his other papers. We are also told that as he and Norris parted, Wolsey gave him his fool, a man named Patch, as a gift for the king. He was

262   *The turn of Fortune's wheel*

'for a nobleman's pleasure, worth a thousand pounds'. Fools were licensed to speak to their masters as nobody else could. Was he the means, then, to 'patch' things up with the king along the lines Norris discussed with Wolsey? All of this took place, we should remember, in the few days before 22 October when, by an indenture between himself and the king, Wolsey formally admitted his guilt in *praemunire*. Moreover, Wolsey, who had stood on his dignity for proper proceedings since the start of the month, capitulated completely scarcely a week later on 30 October and formally submitted to the king's mercy.

That a deal was done is confirmed by the secret visit made to Esher by Sir John Russell, late one very rainy night on or about 1 November. Russell bore another ring from Henry, and he and Wolsey were soon in 'very secret communication'. He had brought news of a pardon. We know this because Wolsey thanked Henry profusely for it in a letter, praying him that as soon as 'it will stand with your honour, it may be openly known to my poor friends and servants that you have forgiven me mine offences, and delivered me from all danger of the laws'. Despite the inclement weather, Russell refused Wolsey's invitation to stay the night as his mission was to be kept utterly confidential.[12]

On 23 October, the day after Wolsey's formal admission of *praemunire*, Henry had nominated Sir Thomas More his successor as Chancellor of England. He received the Great Seal from Henry on 25 October and formally took his oath at Westminster the following day. The new Parliament, whose proceedings More superintended from the Lords, opened at Blackfriars on 3 November 1529. Henry came up from Greenwich to Bridewell Palace for the opening. Standing by the king, More made a speech praising Henry as the good shepherd of his flock who defended it from all danger. With that wit upon which he prided himself, the new Chancellor satirised Wolsey the arch-cleric, telling the assembled Lords and Commons that Henry as the 'good shepherd' (one of the images of Christ himself of course) had cast out of the flock the 'great wether which is of late fallen as you all know', for foolishly attempting to deceive the all-seeing sovereign. He had suffered deserved but 'gentle' correction. Know, henceforth, More went on, no other clergyman should presume to do the same. The Chancellor's speech appears designed to encourage the febrile anti-clerical mood in the Parliament. In fact, it seems to have been intended to direct or diffuse it. Wolsey, More was saying, was being punished by the king himself, there was no need for Parliament to become involved in this matter. This was less about protecting the cardinal himself (although More felt a certain loyalty towards him), than about the staunchly conservative Chancellor pre-empting any efforts to punish Wolsey that might threaten the clerical estate as a whole.[13]

The first session of the so-called 'Reformation Parliament' was an orchestrated effort by the king and his advisors to put new and direct pressure on the papacy to resolve the annulment issue in his favour. To do this, Henry, ever the dutiful son of the papacy after all, presented himself to Clement and the Curia in Rome as the protector of an English Church that had, under the cardinal, overreached itself into areas of national life and governance where it had no place to be. Like Wolsey himself, many of its members had shown themselves to be arrogant, incompetent, or both, and popular indignation and resentment had grown steadily. This had now found voice in parliament, the kingdom's proper forum for the 'redress of grievance' with demands in both the Lords and Commons for urgent reform. To this, Henry could not remain indifferent, he would tell Clement, but with that keen sense of justice and equity that he naturally possessed, he would see to it that the wrongs were righted and that by his authority alone, the pope's men would be protected. All of this, it was strongly implied, yet again demonstrated Henry's dutiful loyalty to the papacy which ought to be matched with an understanding and cooperative dealing with his case in Rome.

The terms of the petitions against probate and mortuary fees, non-residence and pluralism, and commercial activity by priests among other things, were drawn into three bills. Hall's *Chronicle* notes how novel such complaints were and that 'at this Parliament men began to show their grudges'. Prior to this, he asserted, such complaints would be termed heresy because the 'bishops were chancellors, and all had the rule about the king' (another dig at Wolsey among others of course). Clerical malfeasance had indeed generally been dealt with under canon law and in the ecclesiastical courts. The bishops, especially John Fisher, objected to the legislation amending probate fees, and to the populism at the root of these moves against the rights of the Church, hinting darkly at Bohemian or Hussite heresy. When confronted, Fisher equivocated, denying this was any accusation against the Commons itself. With an eye to the papacy no doubt, Henry responded as the apparently indifferent arbiter between Church and Commons, insisting that the bills be toned down and redrafted, but they were finally passed as acts curbing a range of clerical malpractices. A cap was put on the sliding scale of fees for probate, and abbots were also prevented from conducting or profiting from a range of trades in the local areas. Fisher's intervention may have been significant in dissuading the Commons from pressing on with further anticlerical legislation, but Henry made a proclamation forbidding the publication in England of any authorisation or decision of the papal court in any matter that touched his sovereignty.[14]

Given the parliament's attitude to the Church, it is easy to see why Wolsey worried about its view of him. He was very eager for Henry to make public the pardon he had granted privately before the session opened in respect of *praemunire* and other matters, and he was formally brought back under the king's protection as early as 18 November. Even so, one of the petitions tabled in that first session was a document based on Lord Darcy's accusations first shown to the king in the summer. Wolsey had himself been forced to sign this in October, which turned it into a public confession of his apparent wrong doings. Some articles concerned individual clerics or noblemen (not least Lord Darcy) who had apparently suffered miscarriages of justice at his hands. Most were generalities, including that he illegally took control of people's lands, properties, and even children in the case of wards. He appointed unsuitable people to posts in the king's service, dissolved some religious houses on spurious grounds and protected others that he favoured. He had abused his papal dispensing powers and had, it was strongly implied, even plotted with foreign princes. The worst colour was put on those phrases that he had habitually used to assure ambassadors of the close understanding between himself and Henry in order to accuse him of claiming equality with the king.[15] Perhaps his accusers overreached themselves, for in trying to show Wolsey's wrongdoing in virtually every aspect of government, Darcy's articles make Henry seem, by implication, a rather weak monarch who had been easily gulled by his wily servant. Perhaps they played a part in More's fulsome oration about Henry's vigilance as the good

The turn of Fortune's wheel   265

shepherd. They certainly enumerate, like some of John Skelton's poems, the sort of grievances that Wolsey's authority and manner had caused among the political elite over the course of his time in Henry's service.

On 1 December, More also signed a parliamentary petition against Wolsey, which drew heavily on Darcy's articles. It was debated in the House of Commons, and some wanted it to be the basis of a bill of attainder. Perhaps the strongest voice defending Wolsey in Parliament, but not the only one, was that of Thomas Cromwell. He had feared that Wolsey's fall would mean the end of his own career, and being the cardinal's friend did not exactly make him popular at the time. Cromwell obtained the seat for Taunton for that Parliament, due in large measure to the assistance of court friends and the duke of Norfolk. He and Cromwell had met and worked together to some extent on the establishment of Wolsey's college at Ipswich. Norfolk would have had ample opportunity to see for himself the same talents in Cromwell that Wolsey prized, and Cromwell had acted for the duke in a small legal matter the previous month. Cromwell probably saw getting into Parliament as much about regaining credibility and asserting his independence from the cardinal as it was about securing a position from where he might assist him. He seems to have lent his support to the bills that curbed clerical abuses in general, but opposed anything that touched Wolsey directly.[16]

Parliament duly took note of Wolsey's offences but left the penalty to the king, just as Henry wanted. It was prorogued on 17 December 1529, and Cromwell immediately sent the cardinal news that no action had been taken against him. Wolsey was doubtless relieved, and glad of the king's protection, but he was also angered by the whole episode and made his view of the articles clear to Cromwell. They were, he said, for the most part untrue, and even those that seemed most serious were such that 'by the doing of them no malice nor untruth can be justly arrected unto me, neither to the prince's person, nor to this realm'.[17] In other words, that he had done nothing materially wrong. Cromwell's response over the coming months was to try to dampen down this sort of dangerous talk and to get Wolsey to accept his fate as he had promised to do, often pointing out how little he had personally suffered in the *praemunire* business and enjoining patience on his master.[18] Cavendish at times gives the slightly misleading impression that Wolsey was completely friendless. Apart from Cromwell, upon whom Wolsey relied first and foremost, Sir William Fitzwilliam, the Treasurer of the royal household, the king's Vice Chamberlain John Gage and Sir John Russell (who brought secret news of Wolsey's pardon in November 1529) all spoke for him in the teeth of opposition from Anne Boleyn and her supporters. Ralph Sadler, then in Cromwell' service, was doing business with the likes of Norfolk when required. On Cromwell's instruction, he was also doing his best for the cardinal. When Wolsey fell seriously ill after Christmas, Henry (at Cromwell's plea) appointed a team of no fewer than four doctors, including his personal physician Dr William Butts, to attend him till he recovered. He sent Wolsey a third ring in token of favour and insisted that Anne Boleyn also send him a gift, which she did. The king declared himself still very well disposed towards Wolsey at the start of 1530. As far as Henry was concerned, their deal was holding. Whether Wolsey felt quite the same is rather less clear.[19]

During the 1529 Parliament, Henry had used Wolsey's former residence of York Place, now renamed Whitehall. He spent Christmas at Greenwich but returned early in 1530. During the autumn, while the legal implications of Wolsey's admission of guilt in *praemunire* were still working themselves out, Henry had sent Sir William Shelley, Chief Justice of the Court of Common Pleas, to persuade Wolsey to concede the king's right to the property. This provoked a careful but spirited response. York Place, said Wolsey, belonged to the diocese of York as part of the patrimony of the Church. Hampton Court Palace was his own property. He had some time since freely made it over to the king's use and now accepted its surrender to him. York Place, by contrast, was not his to relinquish on a mere royal whim. By what right did the king presume to take it from the Church and what precedent would it set if he did? This riposte was really directed at the anti-clerical mood prevailing that autumn. The former Chancellor, whose court of Chancery looked at cases in 'conscience' or fairness, reminded the king of justice; a prime duty and quality of true kingship. More than most, Wolsey knew the king with whom he dealt; 'put no more into his head than the law may stand with good conscience', he told Shelley. Let the king act out of the fullness of justice, not legal technicality. 'For law without conscience is not good to be given unto a King in counsel to use for a lawful right, but always to have a respect to conscience, before the rigour of the common law'. Wolsey was clearly angry at what had happened to him and how he and the Church he led were being made to feel the brunt of Henry's frustration over the annulment case. Given the precariousness of his own position, however, he had very few ways to express that anger. York Place was, so to speak, solid ground on which he could stand if still in a very technical and circumscribed way. He had little choice but to obey the king's order. It was also, after all, a test of his continuing loyalty to Henry at whose mercy he remained. Perhaps there were those around Henry who hoped he might fail that test? Wolsey complied but discharged his own conscience by charging those of Shelley and the council. Remind the king, he told Shelley finally, 'that there is both heaven and hell'. Carefully but assertively, Wolsey had now started bargaining with Henry.[20]

As the first months of 1530 passed, his finances were rapidly diminishing. It was his friends to whom he turned once more in hope of reaching a fuller settlement with the king, particularly on the question of the see of Winchester and its ample revenues. It was also to Cromwell that Wolsey entrusted the unhappy business of his tomb when, in January 1530, its architect and sculptor Benedetto da Rovezzano announced his intention of quitting the project and returning to Florence. Cromwell, it seems assisted to some extent by Norfolk, persuaded the king, against the advice of the majority of his council, to reach at least an interim settlement with the disgraced cardinal. Wolsey was formally and publicly pardoned and restored to the Archbishopric of York with all its revenues on12 February. In a document dated 14 February, he was given £6,374 3s 7 1/2d in a combination of plate, furniture, hangings and clothing with various other gifts. He also obtained a pension of £1,000. Three days later, on 17 February, Wolsey regained the titles, but ceded to the king all the revenues, of bishop of Winchester and abbot of St Albans. The windfall of some of these revenues at least was parcelled out to interested parties, including Anne's father, made earl of Wiltshire the previous December. Yet Wolsey remained a formidable figure in the English ecclesiastical estate. This was More's 'gentle correction' indeed.[21]

Cavendish also credits Cromwell with obtaining, without knowledge of the royal council, Henry's permission to leave Esher, where

268   *The turn of Fortune's wheel*

he had been since the early autumn and which now, unsurprisingly, 'waxed unsavoury' after four months of continual occupation. He moved to a small lodge in Richmond Park where he spent February, before then moving to lodge with the monks of the Charterhouse at Richmond near the royal palace. Having reached the financial settlement Wolsey had been seeking since before Christmas, Norfolk and others put pressure on him to put distance between himself and the king. In response, Wolsey offered, a touch disingenuously perhaps, to go to Winchester. This was still unacceptably close to the king for Norfolk and his circle, and as they pointed out, Wolsey, restored to full possession of his title, properties and rights as Archbishop of York, ought now to go to minister to an archdiocese whose lands and people were still entirely foreign to him. And that he was soon commanded to do.

The Archbishop of York comes home

Setting off on 5 April, Wolsey made slow and stately progress northwards. He spent Easter at Peterborough Abbey, there taking a full part in its solemnities as Cardinal-Archbishop, washing 59 poor men's feet as was customary (and from which Cavendish suggested his age at the time). In full pontifical vestments, he gave a plenary indulgence to all at Mass on Easter Sunday. He spent four days after Easter at Milton Manor, the home of Sir William Fitzwilliam, sometime treasurer of the cardinal's household, before resuming his journey and arriving at Southwell near Newark on 28 April. There he remained for the rest of the summer. While there, Wolsey had a conversation with Cavendish apparently in response to enquiries from well-disposed men in London as to why he had not contested the charge of *praemunire*. Wolsey told him that he knew the charges against him were politically motivated and that he could not possibly have contravened the relevant statutes. He had calculated that it was better to admit the charge, rather than in effect accuse Henry of making a false accusation. Had he done so it would have been seized upon by 'the night crow' (Anne) to do him harm. Better, then, to do what he knew the king wanted, secure clemency and his freedom, however reduced his circumstances. Wolsey seems genuinely to have believed, at least initially, that Henry would feel remorseful, and admit to himself that he had treated him badly. He

The turn of Fortune's wheel   269

hoped that in due course, it might give rise to a new appreciation of his service and talents. In other words, he seems to have expected that he would eventually be restored to authority with Henry.

While apparently willing to bide his time and demonstrate his continuing loyalty to the king, in practice Wolsey found this very difficult. Surprisingly, he seems not to have anticipated the loss of the revenues of Winchester and St Albans, telling Cromwell in January that he had been assured 'at the making of my submission' that he 'should not have to part with any of my promotions' and that since then he had 'fair words, but little comfortable deeds'.[22] Despite the fact that the titles were restored to him, and that he had been given more than a duke's yearly worth to tide him over for the time being, Wolsey still chafed at the loss of his income. Like Cavendish, Cromwell again urged patience. Then in July, Wolsey received a real body blow when he heard from William Capon, the Dean of St Mary's College, Ipswich, that the school had been dissolved on Henry's orders. He also found out that Cardinal College at Oxford was under a similar threat. He wrote to Gardiner, entreating him to do what he could to ensure that even if the king took control of it, the college would not be dissolved, but he can scarcely have hoped for a favourable response from the royal secretary. In August, he was once again worried that his lands and revenues of York might yet be taken from him. He complained to Cromwell that the king ought to have regard to his 'poor estate and old service'.[23]

Wolsey finally left Southwell on the last stage of his journey to York in late September and by October was at Cawood Castle, his country residence as archbishop, about seven miles south of York on the banks of the river Ouse. In one way, he was acutely aware of being seen acting for his own personal interests or pleasure. He scrupulously declined the earl of Shrewsbury's invitation to hunt in his park at Worksop. On the other hand, the whole way north, Wolsey called attention to himself as archbishop, now coming home to his archdiocese. He seemed to be making more of an episcopal progress than a journey imposed upon him. He made very sure to meet local dignitaries, as well as common people who came to see him apparently in great numbers, with every courtesy and show of apparent humility without loss of dignity. According to Cavendish, he also prayed regularly with the members of the

270 *The turn of Fortune's wheel*

monastic communities with whom he stayed at various points on the journey. He also confirmed many, many children at churches and cathedrals en route. Cavendish portrays him, not unnaturally, as priest and bishop, finally recalled to his duty and ministering to his flock. Probably he was making the best of it, and surely he *was* entitled to be received honourably on his way as the archbishop? It would have been odd if he had not.

Yet, as Cromwell told him, while many in the south commended this new-found pastoral zeal, his enemies accused him of aggrandising himself in the north, keeping too great a household and once again building, at Cawood. This was only to make the place habitable Wolsey countered, but he also fretted. Cromwell reassured him that he still had the king's favour but advised an abatement of building works and urged Wolsey to forget 'all vain desires of this world'.[24] That, it seems, he could never quite do.

Not long after his arrival at Cawood, Wolsey summoned the northern Convocation and plans began for his installation as Archbishop, set for 7 November. Cavendish said Wolsey had wanted a minimum of fuss. Perhaps he had finally heeded Cromwell's advice? He would not even stay in the residence of the archbishop in the city for the event, he said, but go to York and return the same night to Cawood, to avoid any appearance of grandly taking possession of the city. Edward Hall, of course, relates a rather different Wolsey, one eager to summon the northern clergy to his side, to overawe the populace with his splendour as cardinal-archbishop, and says that he ordered a huge throne to be set up for him in York Minster. There may be something to this if Wolsey was trying to re-establish a power base for himself in the north. Yet Hall almost certainly misattributes to Wolsey's ambition the motives and arrangements of the city's ecclesiastical and civic authorities to whom Wolsey had been a reasonably effective patron. It was they who wanted the enthronement ceremony to be grand, to reflect the city's sense of its high status as the archbishop's seat.

Wolsey's installation never took place, and he never made it to York. Even as preparations went ahead, on 1 November 1530, a warrant was issued for the cardinal's arrest. Wolsey's former ward and protégé Henry Percy, Earl of Northumberland, was despatched north with a large armed escort to take him into custody. It included Sir Walter Walsh, one of the gentlemen of the king's privy chamber. They rode at some pace, arriving at Cawood on Friday, 4 November. Taking the keys of the castle and placing his own guard at its gates, Northumberland entered the hall. The earl encountered Wolsey as he came down the stairs from his presence chamber, where he had just finished dinner. Wolsey gently remonstrated that Northumberland had sent no warning of his coming so that proper arrangements could be made to entertain him. He escorted the earl into a private chamber. There, without further warning but with 'a faint and soft voice', Northumberland laid a hand on Wolsey's arm and said, 'I arrest you of high treason'.[25]

Stunned momentarily by this statement, Wolsey demanded to see the warrant for his arrest. As with his response to Norfolk and Suffolk a year earlier, he stood upon his dignity and ample experience of exercising royal authority. He insisted that he would do nothing until he had proof of instructions. Sir Walter Walsh then met Wolsey. He was no 'gentle Norris', yet, in striking contrast to his attitude to Northumberland, the cardinal said he was content to place himself in Walsh's custody without sight of any warrant because, as he told him, he was 'a sufficient commission in yourself in that behalf inasmuch as ye be one of the king's privy chamber'. In so doing, Wolsey effectively admitted defeat in a battle that had been going on for a decade between himself and these special royal servants. His submission also subtly demeaned Northumberland, who had been not only Wolsey's ward and a member of his household, but also Anne Boleyn's one-time suitor. According to Chapuys at least, Wolsey's arrest was a product of Anne's angry insistence, but the decision was Henry's. Meanwhile Wolsey's Venetian physician, Agostino Agostini, was detained and bundled hastily towards London where he would provide much of what passed for evidence of Wolsey's supposed treachery. Over the next two days, Wolsey's property and papers were seized. Only five of his servants, including Cavendish, were permitted to remain with him. On Sunday, 6 November, amidst tearful farewells to his household, Wolsey left Cawood. We should be sceptical of Cavendish's statement that some 3,000 people gathered to see him, but some large number evidently shouted their good wishes to him. From Cawood, he came to Pontefract Priory where he stayed overnight before continuing to Doncaster where, by torchlight, more well-wishers greeted him. He then moved on to Sheffield Park and was the guest of the same

272   *The turn of Fortune's wheel*

earl of Shrewsbury who had invited him to hunt in his park scarcely two months earlier. There he stayed for about 18 days, preparing himself to face the charges levelled at him.[26]

Traitor to England?

What, then, was the basis for Wolsey's arrest for treason? It was set out in letters Henry sent to Sir Francis Bryan, once more his ambassador in France, in mid-November 1530, explaining the indictment so that it could be communicated to king Francis. The allegation in these letters, particularly in one of 16 November, was that Wolsey had plotted outside the realm in various ways, and especially with the papacy, in the furtherance of his ambition to be returned to power. It was known about principally through the aforementioned Dr Agostini who knew that Wolsey was in regular contact with the Imperial ambassador Eustace Chapuys and with Jean Joachim de Passano, seigneur de Vaux, Jean du Bellay's successor as French ambassador in England.[27]

The evidence for this accusation is remarkably thin and circumstantial. It is true that in March and April 1530 Wolsey had been in personal contact with Vaux and Chapuys, apparently seeking their favour on his master's or his own behalf.[28] On the one hand, this looks bad for Wolsey. Being in communication with foreign ambassadors after being dismissed from office might be suspect. On the other hand, he had known Du Bellay for two years and Vaux since as far back as their negotiation of the Treaty of The More in 1525. He had been deprived of office but not dismissed from royal service, much less obedience. The ostensible reason for contact was to discuss Wolsey's French pension, but that may just have been a cover for discussion about Francis's pension debts to Henry in the light of the treaty of Cambrai, the details of which no one knew better than Wolsey. He would have seized eagerly on any opportunity to be useful to the king, and there is no sense that his meetings with either ambassador were secret. They could scarcely have been in the circumstances. Close to the time Wolsey left Richmond, he had been visited by Vaux once more. On these occasions he evidently asked the ambassadors to ask their masters in turn to put in a good word for him with Henry. This was of itself neither treasonous nor unexpected. Commendations of good service and affirmations of

The turn of Fortune's wheel   273

the high representatives of one sovereign sent to another were quite routine. Both Charles V and Francis had often praised Wolsey's adroitness in the past when it suited them to do so.[29]

In June 1530, however, Wolsey was again in contact with Chapuys, this time with admittedly 'rather obscure' advice on resolving Katherine's case in Rome. As Peter Gwyn insisted, asking the pope to expedite the king's matrimonial matter (if that is in fact what Wolsey did) was at the time no more treasonous than seeking commendations. Katherine was entitled to advice and the help of friends towards the correct conduct of her case in Rome – even Henry admitted that. Yet in his letters Wolsey seems to have taken things a small but crucial step further. He told Chapuys that the time was right for stronger action from the pope in bringing the case to an end and that Clement might 'call in the assistance of the secular arm, since so little nerve was shewn [on the other side]', that is on Henry's. Chapuys was not quite sure of Wolsey's meaning but said in his view, 'Your Majesty ought to have matters brought to a crisis at once'. Wolsey, Chapuys told the emperor, had agreed with him that Clement's ordering Henry to repudiate Anne under threat of excommunication would do the trick. That done, others could take over the management of the case, 'by which he means himself'. Sceptical perhaps as he was, Chapuys nevertheless encouraged further contact and, as late as August, reported that he was receiving letters daily from Wolsey, then in Southwell, although he did not reveal their contents in his own reports of them to Charles.[30]

In July, during a conversation about Henry's relations with Francis I, Norfolk told Chapuys that he believed that the French were working to restore Wolsey (though he almost certainly did not think that), but it would do neither him, nor them, any good, and that though 'the Cardinal might use all the artifices he could conjure up, he would never again either see or speak with the King'. Norfolk went on, in that context, to say that he knew Wolsey had recently 'been plotting in the most ingenious and subtle manner, only the means of execution had failed him'. Three men involved as messengers had revealed his plans to the duke, 'thus enabling him to countermine it, and take precautions for the future'. What he meant, he did not make clear to Chapuys. This was a reference to Wolsey's concurrent correspondence with Vaux, the French ambassador who had been open with Henry's regime about seeing Wolsey. Norfolk's

274   *The turn of Fortune's wheel*

words suggest that in July Wolsey posed no immediate threat that could not be dealt with. Had he been thought otherwise, he would presumably have been arrested at once, not in November. Perhaps, in the finest traditions of espionage, Wolsey was being given time to incriminate himself further.[31]

Wolsey does seem to have been trying to secure the support of Charles and Francis, deploying varied, obscure and even contradictory pieces of advice and suggestions with a hope of eventual assistance in his being restored to power. But was Wolsey's reference to 'the secular arm' really, as it might first appear, a call for war against his own king, whom he had served faithfully for almost 20 years? Did he instead mean greater diplomatic pressure, or at least energy, on Charles's part in bearing in upon Henry with the threat of ex-communication which, Wolsey still believed, was the only sanction that might yet bring Henry to his senses? He admitted to Chapuys that he was unclear what the king's intentions now were, and he certainly does not seem to have appreciated just how far and how fast Henry was then moving on the subject of the basis of his relations with Rome. In none of the surviving correspondence from Cromwell or anyone else at the time is that shift even alluded to, much less discussed. Whatever Wolsey meant in the letters to Chapuys (and he may well have overreached himself), he was primarily wanting to be seen supporting Katherine's cause. He offered such advice as he did to secure a credibility with Charles that he almost certainly had no idea, at that moment, quite what he would do with. After all, he could claim, he had only ever acted under papal and royal authority in the king's case, had nothing personally against Katherine, sought to act only in the king's best interests (in getting rid of Anne) and had several times in the past been the means of advantageous agreements, reconciliations even, between Charles and Henry. Given the chance, he could say, he would prove to be so again, to Henry's advantage no less than the emperor's.

When it came to Francis I, an even greater sense of his indispensability, and entitlement, is noticeable. Wolsey seems genuinely to have regarded Francis as being in his debt for the several Anglo–French treaties of 1525–7 that had, in his reckoning, enabled Francis to regain his kingdom after the disaster at Pavia. There was something to that perhaps, but Wolsey had always sold Henry's friendship at extortionate rates, and the king of England had not always delivered fully on its promised benefits. The French (and doubtless the Imperialists, too) were pleased that in July 1529 Wolsey had been caught at Blackfriars and could not be at Cambrai himself, there to use peace-making to Henry's advantage once more. Yet in 1530, Wolsey still seems to have expected that Francis would make genuine efforts in his defence and for his restoration. Jean du Bellay had sympathy and perhaps regard for Wolsey, presenting him to Francis as key to maintaining good Anglo–French relations. Wittingly or otherwise, he had fed Wolsey's expectations of his master. Francis was in fact delighted at the cardinal's dismissal from the Chancellorship because his rival was thereby deprived of his most able minister, and he, Francis, had no longer to pay Wolsey a pension to keep him on side, or deal with Wolsey's pompous and frustratingly clever conduct of England's relations with France.[32] Chapuys himself would soon afterwards assert that Francis had lost nothing by Wolsey's fall. The members of the Boleyn extended family, led by the earl of Wiltshire and the duke of Norfolk, were carrying on the cardinal's pro-French policies in hopes of their support at Rome for the annulment, and at considerably less cost and inconvenience to Francis.[33] Unfortunately for Wolsey, but perhaps understandably, du Bellay's successor, the seigneur de Vaux, shared his master's view. He earned favour from both kings by informing them of his communications with Wolsey, precisely to discredit him completely and prevent his having any further influence on Anglo–French dealings. It was to these communications that Norfolk referred in July.

Even if it is accepted that Wolsey's dealings with Chapuys and Vaux were about him trying to get himself restored to favour through the good opinion of foreign princes, and nothing more, he had certainly been sailing very close to a rapidly shifting wind. In Henry's letter to Bryan of 16 November, however, it was alleged that there was even more to it than that. In October, letters from Wolsey to Vaux were intercepted that contained lines in cipher. Vaux was then near Dover visiting a religious shrine that he patronised. It is important to note that it was later reported to the duke of Milan 'that the cipher merely contained a request for some favour and intercession on the part of his most Christian Majesty with King Henry'.[34] Wolsey seems to have been up to his old tricks again, still trying to ingratiate himself with Francis. Perhaps, by then, however, that was enough to damn him. Yet it was not these letters upon which Henry himself relied in his account of the reasons for Wolsey's arrest in his letters to Sir Francis Bryan in November. The most substantive evidence the king adduced, such as it was, was supposed to come from a letter that Agostini wrote on Wolsey's behalf to Vaux, setting out a plot to have Wolsey restored to power, but never actually sent. Agostini subsequently, and rather conveniently, lost or destroyed the letter but remembered its contents in detail. According to Henry, it was in that letter that Wolsey sought to encourage the French to bring England into a war with the pope and emperor. This would result in Henry being placed under a papal interdict, so that, the theory ran, Francis would then be free to ignore his onerous monetary and other treaty obligations to Henry. He might even attempt to recover Calais and could certainly assist the Scots to invade England. Faced with this situation, it was alleged, Wolsey hoped to see an insurrection and chaos such that he would be recalled to office to sort out the mess at home and abroad.[35] At the very least, it was further alleged, Wolsey wanted the king of France to put pressure on Henry to have him restored to his full rights and income as Bishop of Winchester and Abbot of St Albans. That much at least is consistent with what was reported to the duke of Milan. When, later in the month, Chapuys reported all this to Charles and identified Agostini as its source, he noted that the Italian had been well treated at the home of the duke of Norfolk and had been 'singing the tune' he was expected to. In other words, it was all rubbish.[36] When Bryan informed him of the allegations against Wolsey, king Francis was naturally quick to distance himself from any suggestion of complicity. He was glad Henry had foiled a treasonous plot, he said, and condemned Wolsey to the worst death possible. He could also say confidently that he knew nothing about any kind of plot involving himself – for the very good reason that it had never existed.

The central problem with accepting that Wolsey concocted this fantastical scheme is everything we know about Wolsey himself. Although not directly in contact with Henry at this time, his own intelligence and instinctive understanding of the complicated relations between England, France, the Empire and the Papacy, that he had helped to fashion over nearly two decades, would have told him how improbable of success was any such plot. Wolsey already

The turn of Fortune's wheel   277

knew that Charles had reached a rather advantageous settlement with Francis at Cambrai which he would be unlikely to upset. It was also better for Francis than the 1526 Treaty of Madrid had been, and the French king was unlikely to have wanted to upset the applecart with Henry or Charles at this point, for Wolsey's sake. He continued to need Henry's immediate help with the financial obligations to Charles pursuant to the Cambrai treaty. He wanted Henry's agreement to suspend the annual French pension payments, and partly in return for that assistance, he had given Henry permission to consult the French universities on the theology of the annulment case. Those consultations were in progress during the spring of 1530 (something Wolsey knew) when this plot is supposed to have been hatched, and there was no advantage to Francis in fermenting war at this stage. There is also no evidence from Henry's ambassadors in Rome in 1530, always on the lookout for any news relevant to Henry's case, of contact between Wolsey and Clement about any of these possibilities, or indeed any other subject. It was also hardly in Clement's interests to get himself involved in a plot to attack England, in concert with Charles V, just to restore Wolsey to a power which it was by no means clear he would use in the papacy's interests. After all, he had never done so before! Why would Clement countenance a plot to restore Wolsey when the cardinal's pro-French policies were well known to him? Why would Clement now need to trust Wolsey to act primarily in Katherine's interests when he already had the means to assist her in his own hands? A papal nuncio, Antonio de Puello, did arrive in England in September to discuss possible military action against the Turks. He probably had contact with Wolsey by letter but had been instructed to be guided in the conduct of his mission, not by Wolsey, but by the French ambassador Vaux. His letter to Clement of 16 September reporting his mission does not even mention Wolsey at all.[37]

Perhaps it was, then, Wolsey's overweening pride and fury at his loss of status, in the absence of friends to advise or warn him to the contrary, that made him forget all he knew about how European international relations worked and to embark upon a foolish and treasonous course? The suggestion was made at the time and often since, and was the inference drawn by Gardiner in his discussion of Henry's letters to Bryan.[38] Cavendish certainly describes him as anxious, fearful, even weeping and wailing sometimes – but this is usually in response to items of bad news rather than his being in a general state of emotional collapse and irrationality. Wolsey *did* have friends, who all urged patience and tried to reassure him, and by the time he got to Cawood, they may well have been succeeding. He evidently had the composure to participate in the religious life of the communities with whom he stayed on his journey north, to present himself apparently sanguinely to people of high and low status throughout.

What is far more likely than outlandish plotting abroad as a way back to power is that Wolsey was looking to establish himself finally and properly in his archdiocese, just as he had been instructed to do by the king and council. Perhaps to his own amazement, when he got north of Watford, he found himself proving popular. His entertaining well and showing every sign of attracting people to him reassured him and boded well for his future use to Henry's regime. Perhaps, he may have begun to think, his energy and talents, concentrated in the archdiocese, working in conjunction with Tunstall in the episcopal palatinate of Durham, might bring an administrative and pastoral coherence to the north that, as he knew better than anyone, it had ever lacked. This would surely please Henry and be his best means of demonstrating again those talents which the king prized in him above all his other councillors. Looked at thus, his warm reception in Yorkshire, and even (if we credit them) suggestions that he wanted a grand enthronement at York, might well be construed as evidence of his successfully carrying out royal orders. Though Chancellor no longer, he was still, after all, cardinal legate *a latere*, Archbishop of York and Primate of England, Bishop of Winchester and Abbot of St Albans. This was far from the nothing with which he had begun in his days as Sir Richard Nanfan's chaplain at Calais. His circumstances considered, what possible need had he for risky and ridiculous plotting abroad? What better power base could Wolsey have had, and upon what surer basis could he have hoped to have a continuing role in England's governance at the highest levels? This man was a seasoned politician and courtier who was used to exercising patience, even if it did not perhaps come easily to him. How else could he have so successfully handled so volatile a man as Henry, and for so long? Now, how better might he bring himself soonest back into full favour with

The turn of Fortune's wheel   279

Henry than by establishing himself securely as the king's Cardinal-Archbishop of York?

Yet, as Cromwell never shrank from admitting, Wolsey had enemies as well as friends, and for them, Wolsey's obedience was also his conceit. They took the darkest possible view of everything Wolsey did in the north such that, as Cromwell warned Wolsey, to them, 'it might well appear that ye desired as much authority as ever ye did' – and they were right. He did, but not at any cost. This was of course the paradox of his final days. Despite his fall and withdrawal from the political capital, Wolsey was still too powerful for his enemies. Anne Boleyn and her supporters would now not have him in charge of so much as an Ipswich butcher's shop, never mind the north of England. That would not have mattered apart from the fact that, by the autumn of 1530, Henry, who had protected him for a year, was rapidly coming to the same view.

As he does so often, Edward Hall presented what became the official view of Wolsey's final disgrace by the end of Henry's reign. The cardinal, he writes, 'grudging at his fall and not remembering the king's kindness showed to him, wrote to the court of Rome and to divers other princes'.[39] Hall rarely has a good word to say for Wolsey. Yet, his pointing to Wolsey's 'grudging' and the papacy is indicative – not so much of the cardinal's actions, but of the construction the king now chose to put upon his words in letters to Chapuys. When Agostini was arrested, he evidently spoke freely of the contacts he had with Chapuys and Vaux since April and had probably revealed Wolsey's suggestions in June about it being the right time for some kind of 'firm action' to be taken by the pope against Henry. Yet, as we have seen, these were so vague that Chapuys himself said he did not care if he was questioned about them as he had nothing to reproach himself for. By the time Henry wrote to Bryan in November, this had been elided by the king, by Norfolk, and the council with a supposed plot with France, apparently evidenced in Wolsey's letter to Vaux, never delivered (but remembered) by Agostini and now conveniently lost. This was made to sit with the ciphered parts of the letters that were delivered to Vaux when he was in Dover, that had formed the initial basis of the warrant for Wolsey's arrest, about him wanting Francis's help to be restored to power. Vaux was not thereby implicated as a conspirator himself. Indeed, his very openness with the council about his contacts with Wolsey demonstrated that he was not. In other words, the king and council got out of Agostini's head what they wanted to hear and doubtless expanded upon it and distorted it as they deemed necessary. Maximum use could be made of whatever it was that Wolsey had said, while no definite proof needed immediately to be adduced, and no damage whatsoever was done to Henry's relations with either Charles V or Francis I. This left Wolsey skewered, before the whole of Christendom, on the most serious charge imaginable: high treason at an international level with the connivance of Rome.[40]

In a way it was a terrible testimony as to how much Henry still needed Wolsey. The hostility of Anne and her circle towards him, Henry had first tried to settle or diffuse, sometimes suppress, then frequently avoid and even ignore. He is known to have expressed regret at the loss of Wolsey's service, but his protective attitude towards the cardinal began to shift in the summer of 1530 as Henry's view of the Church itself changed. Fortified by the favourable verdicts of the English and a number of Continental universities in the annulment case, he moved once more to curb the power of the Church in England, thereby to send a message to Rome that it had better, finally, respect his authority. On 12 June, Henry had obliged a group of leading laymen and ecclesiastics of the realm (including Wolsey) to sign a letter to the pope demanding that a rapid and favourable resolution be found to the matrimonial case. The language of the first draft had to be moderated somewhat before its signatories subscribed, and it did finally leave authority in the case with the pope, but it made clear that Henry expected his rights and authority in England to be respected, and hinted that should this not be forthcoming, he might resolve the matter for himself. If this was not exactly a conciliatory carrot, Henry followed up with the stick. He issued a proclamation that nothing prejudicial to his authority and 'prerogative royal' could be published in England, probably in order to prevent any further action being taken on behalf of the queen, or because an appeal had been made to Rome against the legislation passed against pluralities the previous year. Then in July, pursuant to that proclamation, 14 leading churchmen, including Fisher of Rochester, the leading defender of the Church against Henry's moves to date, were accused of *praemunire* on the basis that they had recognised

The turn of Fortune's wheel 281

the illegal authority of the cardinal who had himself been found guilty of the same offence.[41]

Henry's aim in his unusually busy summer of 1530 was to intimidate the whole English clerical establishment by implying that for so long as it supported papal authority in the matrimonial cause, it recognised a 'foreign' power in the realm, denying the king's true authority. It was, it could be implied, even an enemy within, because its leading members, like Fisher and Standish, had not supported what, to the king's mind, was necessary for securing the succession and thus the security of the realm. By October, Henry's attitude hardened still further in the face of Clement's apparent indifference to his recent letter-writing. He now denied that he could be summoned to Rome at all, as a foreign jurisdiction, and as being contrary to the privileges of the realm of England, indeed (and this for the first time) that his authority was 'imperial', subject to no other earthly power. If the pope expected his authority in England to be respected, he would soon tell Clement, let him not interfere with his. He should remit the annulment case to England where, it was now implied, it would be resolved through the Church.[42] Who, then, was still the notional head of that Church in England and, just as importantly, the representative of an authority to which Henry no longer considered himself finally subject? Who was still Clement's personal representative in England, who, Henry could now believe, had been aggrandising himself in the north and, it appeared, much worse? A report from Bologna in October, of a papal brief apparently prohibiting Henry's remarriage, triggered action.

Wolsey was arrested for treason as part of Henry's determined campaign in the second half of 1530 to put unprecedented pressure on the papacy to give him what he wanted. Perhaps Wolsey had not completely fulfilled his side of the deal struck with Norris at Putney a year earlier. He had sought to bargain with the king where he should have acquiesced, and Henry's patience with him finally tired just at the time the king felt once more, and with greater force yet, the conviction that his royal authority in amplest form must be respected in England and beyond. As we have seen, during those months Henry reached out against the papacy in various ways, and that reach encompassed Wolsey. Henry's intentions in charging Wolsey with treason are as impossible to prove as the grounds upon which the charge itself was laid. Perhaps Henry intended to put him on trial to show how untrustworthy the representatives of the papacy could be? It is not easy to see how that would have assisted any of the several lines of argument he was currently running with the papacy, much less induce Clement to cooperate with him. Perhaps he wanted to force Wolsey's capitulation and admission of the king's authority in as full a manner as he now conceived it, and his endorsement of the king's demand for a favourable outcome? Again, it is hard to see what that would have gained. Wolsey under arrest for treason would be a broken reed. What authority could such a man lend to Henry's case? Besides, he had already signed the letter in June that effectively supported Henry's demands. Perhaps Henry did not, in November 1530, yet know exactly what he wanted to do with Wolsey, but at least he wanted to stop him showing himself off to the people in York and to have the cardinal again directly under his control. He had no need to invent elaborate conspiracy theories to achieve that. He could simply have ordered Wolsey back to Esher, and his friend would have returned eagerly. Yet Anne and her circle would never tolerate a free Wolsey being again anywhere near the king. But a Wolsey under arrest and kept the king's close prisoner – that might be another matter entirely.

Wolsey's final journey

While Wolsey was at Sheffield Park, he expressed his fear of just such an outcome – that the accusation of treason was made so that his enemies could finally do away with him. He had seen Buckingham's fate, even as he tried to distance himself from it. He insistently asked Northumberland to ensure to the best of his powers that he would be able to see the king and talk with him personally, which he felt sure would enable him to clear his name. We already know what Norfolk thought about that idea, and he spoke for Anne. The king's apparent response was to send Sir William Kingston, the Constable of the Tower of London, with an escort made of some of Wolsey's former guardsmen to escort him on the rest of his journey south. Both Shrewsbury and Cavendish tried to put the best face on the appearance of this evidently unwelcome arrival. Despite their repeated assurances to the contrary, Wolsey was convinced, surely rightly, that Kingston's appearance meant that he was destined for the Tower. Kingston said Wolsey could take his time, that the king would see him and expected him to be

The turn of Fortune's wheel   283

able to acquit himself. Wolsey knew that, despite his warm words, such an outcome was not in Kingston's gift. He remained sceptical and anxious. Who could blame him?

Throughout his life, Wolsey had suffered from bouts of various stomach and intestinal illnesses, including dysentery, and while at Sheffield Park he became ill once more of the 'flux', or diarrhoea. The stress he was evidently under almost certainly contributed to his physical collapse. He had first felt ill before Kingston's arrival with symptoms of indigestion which appeared to have been relieved by a prescription from his apothecary, but he grew worse the evening after his first conversation with the Constable. On 24 November, still very ill, he moved to Hardwick Hall in Derbyshire. The following day he came to Nottingham and stayed there before travelling to Leicester. Arriving at the Abbey, he told Abbot Pexall that he knew he was dying and, with a typically theatrical touch, had 'come to leave my bones among you'. He was taken to bed immediately that evening. It was Saturday, 26 November. He became even more ill during the following day, and by Monday morning Cavendish was convinced that Wolsey was indeed dying. His master was by then somewhat delirious, confused about whether it was morning or evening, and told Cavendish that at eight o'clock he would lose him. Kingston came to see him, and in Cavendish's narrative there followed a long discussion between them which began about a sum of £1,500 recorded as ready money in an account at Cawood discovered by Northumberland but not one penny of which could be found by him. Where had it gone, Kingston asked. Wolsey said that the money in question had been lent to several people, whose names he gave him, assuring the Constable that it was in safe-keeping. Kingston left him for the night.

At about 4.00AM the following day, Wolsey awoke and asked Cavendish for some food. He took a few mouthfuls of the chicken broth served to him but stopped, observing that it was the eve of St Andrew's and a fasting day. His chaplain and confessor, Mr Palmes, excused him by reason of his illness, but Wolsey refused to eat any more. He and Palmes were then together for an hour as he made his confession, and afterwards Wolsey seemed a little better. According to a report sent home by the Milanese ambassador, Wolsey then did something very deliberate and significant for a conventional Catholic of the early sixteenth century. It was about 7.00AM. The

284   *The turn of Fortune's wheel*

cardinal asked Kingston to bring all the members of the guard into the room, something Cavendish confirms. He told the assembled company that the previous day he had taken the sacrament and knew that he would soon face judgement before his creator. He then said, 'I pray God that the sacrament may be damnation of my soul if ever I thought to do disservice to my king'. This was also confirmed in Chapuys report of Wolsey's death to the emperor.[43]

The company was then dismissed, and there followed the conversation, the essential part of which was quoted at the outset of this chapter, in which Wolsey offered Kingston advice for himself and for the king. We cannot be sure how much of this the cardinal spoke at the time. It may well be that Cavendish, writing over two decades later, puts into Wolsey's mouth a compendium of thoughts expressed on different occasions. This, for dramatic effect as fortune's wheel turns for his subject one last time and in order to give him a good Catholic death. Wolsey offers a retrospective of his main concerns, ranging from personal dealings with the king, to his apparent sympathy with Katherine of Aragon's plight (something that might have played well with Cavendish's readers during Mary I's reign when the book appeared), his impatience of popular protest and the spiritual and political dangers of Luther. In his experience, Wolsey told Kingston, the king was by nature noble and brave, and very determined to have his own way in all things. He recounted how he had sometimes spent an hour or more on his knees before the king in his privy chamber trying to persuade him to do something against his will. In an echo of the advice he gave to Chief Justice Shelley about York Place, he warned Kingston (and through him all royal councillors) to be very careful how they advised the king for once an idea was put into Henry's head, he said, 'you will never pull it out again'. After delivering himself of a final expression of hope for the health of the king and realm under God's blessing, Cavendish tells us, Wolsey's eyesight began to fail him. He received the last rites of the Church from the Abbot and, as he had foretold, Cardinal Wolsey died as the clock struck eight on the morning of Tuesday, 29 November 1530.

As soon as his death was confirmed, one of the guards who had stood in the cardinal's chamber and witnessed it was sent post haste to tell the king. When Wolsey's body was examined, it was found to be clad in a hairshirt under a fine linen one. This was

The turn of Fortune's wheel 285

evidently a custom Wolsey had adopted from the time he was briefly resident at the Charterhouse in Richmond. The body was placed in an open coffin made of rough wooden boards, dressed in full pontifical vestments of an archbishop with crozier, ring and mitre. The mayor and aldermen of Leicester were sent for to witness that Wolsey was indeed dead. The corpse remained on display it seems to all who wanted to see it for the remainder of the day. That evening the coffin was taken down into the Lady Chapel of the abbey Church and placed on a hearse. After First Vespers from the Office of the Dead, the traditional vigil was kept all that night by the monks and some poor men of local parishes, in keeping with the Sarum Ritual for the burial of bishops. Matins (the dirge) was followed by a sung requiem Mass at about 4.00AM, and Wolsey's body was interred below the floor of the church before the monks sang Lauds from the Office of the Dead. Despite a popular tradition that they were buried not far from those of Richard III, the precise location of Wolsey's remains is still unknown. The appropriate obsequies were completed just before dawn on St Andrew's Day.

Notes

1 Cavendish, p. 183.
2 *LP* IV iii, 5864, 5865, 5893 and 5936 Gardiner and Wolsey's letters 24 and 12 September; Bernard, 'The Fall of Wolsey Reconsidered', 277–310 at pp. 301–3.
3 *CSPSp* IV i, 132 and 135 Chapuys to Charles V, 1 and 4 September 1529 and see 160 for his conversation with Henry.
4 *LP* IV iii, 5953 Campeggio to Salviati, Canterbury, 7 October 1529.
5 Cavendish, p. 100; *LP* IV iii, 5953 Thomas Alvard to Cromwell, St Albans, 23 September 1529.
6 BNF, MS français 3077, fo.125 [*LP* IV iii, 5983] Du Bellay to Montmorency, London, 4 October 1529; *LP* IV iii, 5749/50 dated 1 July 1529 for the accusations against Wolsey under Darcy's name, and an anonymous response to them, purportedly by Wolsey.
7 Hall, pp. 759–60; *LP* IV iii, 6035 for the indictment; P. J. Holmes, 'The Last Tudor Great Councils', *HJ* 33 (1) (1990): 1–22.
8 E. Ives 'The Fall of Wolsey', in Gunn and Lindley, pp. 286–315; but see also Bernard, 'The Fall of Wolsey Reconsidered'.
9 *LP* IV iii, 5996/7 Credence for George Boleyn and John Stokesley sent to the French court; 6011 Jean de Bellay to Montmorency, 17 October 1529.

286   *The turn of Fortune's wheel*

10 Hall, p. 759; Cavendish, pp. 101–2; *LP* IV 6018, Du Bellay to Montmorency. He confirms that the cardinal's goods were inventoried on or by 19 October; *LP* IV iii, 6184 for the inventory.

11 Cavendish, p. 105.

12 *St. P.* I, p. 234; Cavendish, pp. 114–15.

13 *LP* IV iii, 6025 for More's appointment.

14 Hall, pp. 765–7, 772–4; *Tudor Proclamations*, p. 130.

15 *LP* IV iii, 5749 'Protestation articles against the Cardinal of York, shewed by me Thomas Darcy, only to discharge my oath and most bounden duty to God and the King, and of no malice', July 1529.

16 Ward, p. 223; see also MacCulloch, *Cromwell*, pp. 89–93.

17 *St. P.* I, p. 354 as discussed in Gwyn, p. 615.

18 *LP* IV iii, 6114 Wolsey to Cromwell, Esher, December 1529, expressing gratitude for Cromwell's efforts on his behalf; MacCulloch, *Cromwell*, pp. 98–101.

19 *St. P.* I, p. 367 [*LP* IV iii, 6571] Wolsey to Cromwell.

20 Cavendish, pp. 120–2.

21 *LP* IV iii, 6213, 6214, 6220 for Wolsey's pardon and settlement, 14–17 February 1530.

22 *St. P.* I, p. 355 [*LP* IV iii, 6181] Wolsey to Cromwell, January 1530. He wrote to Gardiner in similar, if more direct, terms.

23 *LP* IV iii, 6529 Wolsey to Gardiner, Southwell, 23 July 1530.

24 *CSP Sp.* iii, 657 Cromwell to Wolsey, London, 18 August 1530.

25 Cavendish, pp. 158–9.

26 Ibid., pp. 162–7.

27 BL, Add MS 48066, fo. 184 r/v; Henry VIII to Sir Francis Bryan, York Place, 11 November 1530, quoted in L. Gardiner, 'Further News of Cardinal Wolsey's End, November–December 1530', *Bulletin of the Institute of Historical Research* 57 (1984): 99–107.

28 *CSP Sp.* IV i, 257 at pp. 448–57 Chapuys to Charles V, 6 February 1530, reporting Wolsey's contact with Vaux; 270 at p. 486 Wolsey in contact through Agostini about income due from the see of Palencia, 16 March 1530; and 290, at pp. 600–1 Wolsey seeking the favour of the emperor through Chapuys, 23 April 1530.

29 Gwyn, pp. 600–4.

30 *CSP Sp.* IV i, 354 Chapuys to Charles V, 15 June 1530.

31 Ibid., 373 Chapuys to Charles V, 11 July 1530.

32 *St. P.* VII, p. 211 [*LP* IV iii, 6733] Bryan to Henry VIII, Blois, 21 November 1530.

33 *CSP Sp.* IV ii, 995 Chapuys to Charles V, 15 September 1532.

34 *Calendar of State Papers and Manuscripts Relating to English Affairs, Existing in the Archives of Milan*, ed. A. B. Hinds (London, 1912), p. 637. Augustino Scarpinello to Francesco Sforza, Duke of Milan, 2 December 1530.

35 BL, Add MS 48066, fos. 186–7; Henry to Bryan, 16 November, see Gardiner, 'Cardinal Wolsey's End', pp. 103–4.

36 *LP* IV iii, 6738 Chapuys to Charles V, London, 27 November 1530.

37 Ibid., 6618 Antonio de Puello to Clement VII, 16 September 1530.

38 Gardiner, pp. 104–5. Gardiner accepted the validity of Wolsey's unsent letter, or rather Agostini's report of its contents, and that Wolsey was planning a triumphant installation at York.

39 Hall, p. 773.

40 *LP* IV iii, 6720 Vaux to Montmorency, London, 10 November 1530. Vaux had been assured that Henry and the council had no suspicion of him.

41 Scarisbrick, pp. 255–92, for these charges in the context of Henry's rapidly developing views of his royal supremacy in 1530.

42 *St. P.* VII, p. 261 Henry to Benet, Ghinucci and Casale, 7 October 1530; *LP* IV iii, 6759 Henry to Clement, Hampton Court, 6 December 1530; Scarisbrick, pp. 255–92.

43 See note 35; *CSP Sp.* IV ii, 522 Chapuys to Charles V, London, 4 December 1530.

Conclusion

The Cardinal's legacy

Of all which things he hath had in this world the full felicity as long as Fortune smiled upon him; but when she began to frown, how soon was he deprived of all these dreaming joys and vain pleasures! The which in twenty years with great travail, study, and pains obtained, were in one year and less, with heaviness, care, and sorrow, lost and consumed.[1]

Characteristically, Cavendish blamed Fortune for Wolsey's sudden death and the loss of all he had. Of Henry's immediate reaction to the news of Wolsey's demise brought to him at Hampton Court by one of the cardinal's guards, we have no evidence. It is by no means certain, however, that had he arrived in London, Wolsey would immediately have been put on trial for treason, found guilty and executed, as is the common modern assumption. It was one thing for Henry to execute a man who had been his Lord Chancellor, the head of his realm's parliamentary and judicial system. He would indeed do just that five years later with Sir Thomas More. Wolsey was, however, a cardinal, a prince of the Church Universal and the personal representative of the pope in England. True, Henry would within those same five years also execute a cardinal, John Fisher. But we should remind ourselves that the Henry of the autumn of 1530 was not yet quite the Henry of the summer of 1535.

Clement himself barely marked Wolsey's fall from power and his death by natural causes. In one way, his sudden disappearance simplified matters to an extent for the pope and might even have made it easier for him to persuade Henry of his good faith towards him, as the pope still wished to do. The execution of Cardinal Wolsey, even with compelling evidence that proved his guilt beyond all doubt, would have been a very different matter altogether. It could not have been ignored. It would almost certainly have provoked Henry's excommunication and conceivably even given grounds for the very war Wolsey was said to have been plotting. Henry may have been angry with Clement and searching avidly now for another way forward in the annulment matter, but he also had no wish to alienate or antagonise the papacy to no effective purpose. It has been argued here that no hard or genuinely convincing evidence of Wolsey plotting existed and that the king knew it. Such 'evidence' as had been adduced by the regime was already considered unreliable internationally. Nevertheless, as Cavendish reminds us, the last year of his life saw Wolsey lose much of what he once valued so highly during more than 20 years of service to the man who now accused him of betrayal.

To try a cardinal?

Henry probably had no idea what he really wanted to do with Wolsey in November 1530, beyond having him in his custody. More likely, perhaps, than an immediate trial and inevitable execution would have been Wolsey's imprisonment pending further developments in the king's matrimonial case. He was far more useful to Henry in that context alive than dead. Hard though it now is to imagine, had all gone well for Henry and the pope granted an annulment, and Anne become queen, the charges against Wolsey might eventually have been quietly dropped, although he might well have remained in the Tower of London for a long time, perhaps even died there as all this played out. Any restoration to secular or ecclesiastical responsibility seems barely possible – although with Wolsey, one should be wary of saying that anything was ever impossible.

When Cavendish met the king barely a week after Wolsey's death, on 5 December, he was questioned on 'divers weighty matters concerning my lord', including presumably his last days and hours. Henry said that he wished that 'rather than twenty thousand pounds he had lived'; a conventional, if revealing, expression of regret at Wolsey's loss and, incidentally, an estimate of his monetary worth to him! He asked Cavendish what had happened to

the £1,500 'missing' at Cawood. Cavendish's answer evidently satisfied Henry who then swore the usher to secrecy about the matter,
saying he never wanted to hear about it again – from anyone. He
would throw away the cap he wore, he said, if it knew his private
thoughts. Why this was so Cavendish does not reveal, but the royal
council, chaired by Norfolk, was already busy about the sort of
enquiry that would have been instituted had Wolsey been alive and
awaiting trial in the Tower. A posthumous public trial of Wolsey
in absentia was still not out of the question. The council doubtless
acted on Henry's authority, but did it do so on his orders? Did he
really want it looking into the matter of the dead cardinal, or did
he want it just keeping up appearances of doing so? Something
about his demeanour in the conversation with Cavendish suggests
the latter. Henry knew that Wolsey could now do him no further
service. Nor could he do him any harm. Safe from the prospect of
Wolsey contesting the charges against him, was Henry now indulg-
ing himself in the luxury of regret over his recent handling of his
most able and devoted servant, and friend, even if he remained
aggrieved that Wolsey had failed him? Did Henry now also want
forgotten pressing concerns about Wolsey's behaviour in order to
disown the elaborate treason plot that he had alleged against him in
his letter to Bryan earlier that autumn? What further use could the
accusation have with Wolsey dead and gone, and Henry now wanting to shift the basis of his annulment case on to his incipient royal
supremacy in England anyway? In other words, was it not just the
Cawood money, but the whole sorry saga of Wolsey's fall and last
days that Henry now wanted to hear nothing more about? Obeying
the king's implicit instructions, when Cavendish was summoned
to the council shortly afterwards, he excused himself as unable to
help. Perhaps this played its part in his decision, two decades later,
to publish his account of Wolsey's life and to offer the defence of
the cardinal he could not in 1530.

Afterwards, his loyalty to the king thus proven, Henry offered
to make Cavendish a gentleman usher in his own household. Norfolk did likewise. These were generous offers, but also intended
to keep him close. Cavendish evidently wanted to remain his
own man henceforward. He made clear his intention to return
home. Unable to keep him, Henry then wanted him gone.
He paid his wages, £10 in arrears, gave him £20 as a reward and

allowed him to retrieve his baggage that had been put in the Tower along with Wolsey's possessions. He gave him horses and a cart to take it all home and five marks for his journey. All this Cavendish politely received. He collected his things, went back to his native Suffolk and never returned to Henry's court again.

Wolsey and the king

Thomas Wolsey's career in the service of Henry VIII sprang from a natural talent and an astonishing capacity for work, but it was grounded on his innate understanding of Henry's personality and respect for his authority as king. When Henry was still barely out of his teens, Wolsey established an unrivalled relationship of trust and dependability with the king. No one, certainly not Cromwell or Norfolk, but not William Carey, Francis Bryan or Nicholas Crew either, had the king's confidence and trust in the way Wolsey did, and for so long. The reason is that Henry recognised in Wolsey someone who genuinely understood him, who took his ambitions as king seriously in a way his other councillors at the time did not and whose intelligence and imagination he admired.

Henry also recognised in Wolsey someone who could never threaten him. From the start of their relationship, Wolsey 'belonged' to Henry, was his 'creature' as contemporaries would have put it, in a way that none of the king's noble or gentry friends, not even Suffolk, were. This, Henry found deeply reassuring and useful, and he lent Wolsey so much authority because he knew it would never be turned against him. Moreover, in Wolsey's hands, it could be used to curb the potential ambitions of the kingdom's most powerful men. Wolsey, of course, never forgot that he owed Henry everything, although he frequently gave other, powerful people the impression that he had. Men like Norfolk and Buckingham had to work with him, and they did reasonably co-operatively most of the time, but they always resented such power and wealth being conferred on a man who they regarded as undeserving by reason of his lowly birth. Above all, these men, their families and supporters, resented that unique trust and confidence the king reposed in Wolsey. For them, Wolsey was always the too-clever-by-half schoolboy whose talents and hard work had propelled him to high offices that he then had the temerity to occupy as fully as possible. Very quickly, Wolsey

292   *Conclusion*

displayed, as earnestly as any nobleman born to privilege could, not just the trappings and ceremonies of rank, but real conviction in the exercise of delegated royal and papal authority. This suited the milieu into which he had been drawn by royal service and was surely required of him. He had to exercise authority unapologetically at times and always with conviction. Without that he could not have been an effective royal agent.

Yet Wolsey was also a man who was conscious of his own humble origins in a society obsessed with rank, ancestry and breeding; a consciousness that often expressed itself, paradoxically, in a love of legal and ecclesiastical ritual and ceremonial display. This was the way with his processions through Westminster, to Greenwich, and to France with his cardinal's *galero*, crosses, pillars, the Great Seal and all the other paraphernalia of authority with which he projected, and protected, himself. His lordly public demeanour was intended to compel deference at the very least and, hopefully, respect. Yet it often secured the opposite. What he saw as behaving with a dignity that became his many high offices, others at the time, and since, saw only as insufferable personal arrogance and pomposity. His forceful treatment at times of nobles and gentlemen in the equity courts, in his own household, and of bishops and abbots, and even occasional bullying of ambassadors, all added powerfully to this perception. Henry never had to deal with that side of Wolsey. He only saw the deferential, politic and urbane right-hand man. But others chafed under Wolsey's delegated authority such that when, in the context of Henry's relationship with Anne Boleyn and the annulment case, an opportunity arose to cast doubt on Wolsey's capacities, they seized on it eagerly. Anne was not responsible for Wolsey's fall in quite the way the cardinal feared, and Cavendish imagined, but her influence with Henry, on the marriage issue at least, more than matched Wolsey's. For the first time, those who resented Wolsey's authority had someone behind whom they could rally. She did play a crucial role in shaping occasional, if persistent, resentment of Wolsey into hardened opposition to him. Anne may not in fact have sought to destroy Wolsey, but she did want him curbed and to have him working unequivocally for her interests. These, she saw as contiguous with those of the king. Anne and her supporters sought to expose the limits of Wolsey's imaginativeness and competence, to demonstrate the strength of their own in turn,

Conclusion 293

and thereby to break the cardinal's monopoly of influence with Henry. They eventually succeeded in their aim, but it took some time. But it was not, finally, Anne who wanted Wolsey brought down. It was Henry.

Wolsey's record

It is hard to portray Wolsey as transcending his time and putting in place major changes or developments that profoundly influenced English constitutional arrangements, its Church governance or its civic administration in ways that might have satisfied historians like Pollard and Elton – still his chief modern critics. He certainly presided over no 'Tudor revolution in government' – but then, as it turns out, neither did anybody else. Yet, there are important aspects of the governance of the Tudor state and its Church to which Wolsey contributed significantly. He may not have transcended his times, but he answered to them more fully than many statesmen have. Conscious of the work of Warham, mentored by Richard Fox and aware of the record of Cardinal Morton, Wolsey continued a line of able and imaginative administrators at the highest level of English government. In his own protégés in turn, particularly of course Thomas Cromwell and Stephen Gardiner, he provided, albeit inadvertently, a secure succession in that same line. Wolsey developed the Tudor monarchy's capacity to assert its authority over the kingdom and to maintain its dominant position over the rest of the nobility of England.

Of all the areas of responsibility that Henry gave him, it was the conduct of the king's international relations that most engaged and energised Wolsey. His organisation of Henry's first war against France not only taught him much about administration on a large scale, but also cemented his place as Henry's principal advisor. When the international situation changed in 1514, Wolsey guided him into accepting that 'magnificent peace' could be more glorious and profitable than unsuccessful war. Though conventional in outlook, Henry had the imagination to see what Wolsey was advocating. Keeping Henry at the forefront of international affairs, whether by warfare or peace-making, became their joint project for the next 15 years. Together, they made England and her king a European power again, and they did so by trying to maintain not a 'balance of power' in a nineteenth-century sense, but an imbalance in Henry's favour between Francis I and Charles V. After Wolsey's fall, this policy was maintained by the king and by those who succeeded Wolsey as advisors, but none were as adroit as Wolsey. Cromwell's disastrous effort to change direction proved fatal for him. Wolsey's approach gave England an influence out of all proportion to its population or resources, such as it had never had before and would not have again until part of Britain in the late seventeenth century, under William III and Queen Anne.

For almost two decades no significant international treaty signed in western Europe escaped Wolsey's influence in some way or other. The terrible irony for Wolsey is that his apparently limitless capacity to arrange international affairs to Henry's advantage led the king to imagine that there was nothing that Wolsey could not do for him. Wolsey seriously misjudged the extent to which his complex and always demanding diplomacy alienated the very people upon whose cooperation it most depended and whom he genuinely saw as being in his debt, namely Francis I and Charles V. It is a mark of his effectiveness in placing Henry at the centre stage of European affairs for so long (even if contrary to his own expectations) that these two powerful monarchs more rejoiced at Wolsey's fall than lamented it.

At home, Wolsey's formal responsibilities as Chancellor took him into virtually all spheres of government, but it was in the provision of effective and impartial justice that he most prided himself and upon which he made his most frequent public statements. The evidence, partial as it is, strongly suggests that he did indeed highlight the advantages to users of the various equity tribunals over which he presided. He also made very effective use of them to bring to heel commoners and nobles alike – and for him that was the point – reducing instances of bribery, jury-stacking and other kinds of judicial malfeasance at local level. He had an enormous workload that occupied most of his time, and he very directly assisted the Crown in obtaining greater numbers and greater direct control of administrative and judicial officers in the localities to enhance its authority throughout most of England and Wales, or as Wolsey would have put it, give due attention to the 'indifferent' administration of the king's justice.

Conclusion 295

Crown finance also came within Wolsey's purview, and he proved to be an effective manager of the kingdom's revenues. While he made no wholesale reforms of the financial accounting system as such, he continued the trend of his recent predecessors in trying to maximise revenues – always a difficult task when Henry was bent on expensive wars and extravagant spending on his court. He improved auditing procedures and encouraged the efficient collection and disbursement of taxation revenues. The subsidy assessment reforms and procedures he oversaw raised significant sums in direct taxation, but also proved unpopular. As we have seen, he carried the can for Henry and had finally to accept the near-total refusal of the Amicable Grant of 1525. These considerations directly informed Wolsey's conduct of diplomacy with France and help to explain why he sought peace so often (it was so much less expensive than war) and why he drove such a hard bargain to obtain the largest possible financial settlements from the French. These settlements, he hoped, would reduce the king's need as far as possible on the direct parliamentary taxation, let alone extra-parliamentary grants, that were always difficult to secure. Cromwell would do his best in the decades that followed to regularise taxation further than Wolsey could.

The other major area of Wolsey's responsibility was of course the Church. His legatine authority gave him delegated papal jurisdiction that he valued and always sought to increase and extend. He was a leading churchman much in the mould of his mentors and predecessors, Fox and Morton. He sought those powers to enable him to do things that he saw needed doing to make the Church in England run as he wanted it to, and broadly in keeping with reformist trends across Europe. His efforts at episcopal regulation and reorganisation were genuine enough, and there were real issues to be addressed. His manner of going about this with legatine constitutions and council got clerical backs up at times, and he faced accusations of abusing his authority in ecclesiastical matters as much as he did in the legal or international spheres. The real focus of Wolsey's reforming interest was education, which he saw as the surest way to instil in future clergy the knowledge, skill and moral standing needed to build and maintain high standards of behaviour in the Church as a whole, and as the best defence against the threat of heresy. This was the motive behind his foundation of public lectureships, his two colleges at Oxford and Ipswich and his plans for diocesan feeder schools. It also drove the considerable number of monastic dissolutions he ordered, that Cromwell organised and that disconcerted very many within the monastic ranks. His patronage of humanist learning was genuine, whatever its final shortcomings compared to his ambitions. The cardinal's active endorsement of the 'new learning' authenticated and supported its development in England and kept the kingdom an active agent in important trends in European philosophy and education more widely. Wolsey's legatine authority was the source of his highest status internationally and arguably at its most effective in that context. He exercised it at home in order to do such things as he saw needed to be done to make the Church operate effectively in its central and important place in the state and society of England, rather than in the furtherance of papal authority within the kingdom as such. In the governance of the Church, as in all other spheres, Wolsey was first and foremost, the king's cardinal.

Cardinal Wolsey's artistic and cultural patronage was on the same grand scale as every other part of his endeavours. Aware of the patronage of his Continental counterparts and well informed of developments in arts and architecture, Wolsey was determined to show himself as their equal. His determination to follow these examples, as well as those of his English predecessors, proceeded first and foremost from a sense of himself as a royal and papal representative of the highest rank. It was further enjoined by the practical considerations of housing, feeding and entertaining his considerable entourage and guests. His building projects proceeded at a remarkable pace, and all were intended to impress with their size and sophistication. The plans for the chapel at Cardinal College in particular were on a monumental scale. Unlike a number of his fellow European cardinals, however, Wolsey commissioned no churches, hospitals, alms houses or other buildings for public benefit. He had serious money from his many benefices from about 1517, and virtually all of it seems to have been used to set himself up as he thought best. Perhaps this cardinal-in-a-hurry envisaged public benevolence of this sort once his own needs had been met, but if he had plans, no evidence of them survives.

Wolsey has some genuine claim to connoisseurship in the fashionable Italian 'antique' style as his commissions to sculptors, not least for his own tomb, attest. He was not alone, and his originality has perhaps sometimes been exaggerated as has the extent to which he informed or influenced the king's own artistic and architectural tastes. Henry's building at Newhall in Essex predated Wolsey's projects even if the two shared ideas about it, and Henry was a patron of Italian sculptors before Wolsey. Nevertheless, because of his disposable wealth, Wolsey was the leading patron of new artistic work and of education, in a word of the Renaissance, in the kingdom during the 1520s, and Henry was arguably its greatest beneficiary. The king profited from his artistic exchanges with Wolsey and after the cardinal's fall, had virtually all of his possessions. He took, discarded or remade everything from entire buildings to tapestries, gold plate and books, according to his own preference and without regard to the man who once owned them. The buildings now seen at Hampton Court are more Henry's than Wolsey's, although the Base Court remains essentially his. Not a single piece of metalwork inventoried by Amadas or others for Wolsey now survives. Henry also took from the pool of talented people that Wolsey had assembled those whom he wanted for his service, whether they were solicitors, secretaries or choristers. Cavendish proved an exception in declining the offer of royal employment.

Return to Ipswich

Wolsey's sudden fall was the result of Henry's deep disappointment with him over the failure to obtain an annulment by conventional means. All the power and authority with which Henry had invested him was taken back into royal hands, really for the first time in the reign. They had ruled as a partnership, and Wolsey was the manager and implementer of policies once determined. But Henry set the agenda. Wolsey's arrest on charges of treason in the autumn of 1530 was also part of the king's agenda because Henry now needed and wanted Wolsey to be the pope's cardinal, rather than his, as never before as part of his way of striking back at the papacy and compelling it to recognise the reality of his power and personal authority over the Church within the realm of England; a power that Wolsey had helped to build and consolidate.

Wolsey was much more, however, than just a manager. He was a significant force in enabling English royal government to operate to its fullest extent and a patron who drew significant numbers of adherents into the royal affinity. His record of achievement in the service of the Crown, in the Church and the arts demand better appreciation than they have sometimes been given. Wolsey was a complex man, possessed of an extraordinary imagination, intelligence, perspicacity and outward confidence, even charm, that transformed his own world, and the world in which he lived, and without which he could not have done a quarter of what he did in his public career. His fall was sudden and terrible for him and, after an agonising 12 months, proved fatal. He did indeed return to an obscurity more profound than that of his origins about which so many concerned themselves. We do not even know for certain where the body of the greatest English cardinal, and the once so-called *alter rex* of England, now lies.

It has taken almost 500 years for anything like a serious commemorative monument to be raised to Wolsey. It is not to be found in the places of his power, Westminster or York or even Oxford, but in a street in Ipswich, below the main shopping precinct, and near to where the boy Thomas once lived. Unveiled in June 2011, the statue by the Scottish sculptor David Annand portrays Wolsey not as a towering Lord Chancellor of England or enthroned Papal Cardinal Legate, but seated, as a teacher and patron of learning (see Figure 9.1). Holding an open book before him in his left hand and looking ahead, he addresses the viewer at eye level. His right arm is extended, his hand open in a gesture of exposition and invitation. His cardinal's *galero* hangs casually from the back of his professorial chair. From one side, partly draped in ecclesiastical tassels, his legendary cat stares ahead rather fiercely, quite protectively, of his master. Perhaps he has spotted one of those 'cardinal' spiders – or Anne Boleyn! The cardinal's bulky form and jowly face, sporting warts about the chin, still owes something to tradition, but he is not obese, and this is undeniably a more human, indeed humane, Wolsey than has often been presented in writing. He looks relaxed, freed as he is here from tragedy and confessional attacks. It is perhaps how Wolsey might have wanted us to see him, at least sometimes – the schoolmaster or university don that he might have become, had talent and ambition not given him a very different life and career. His two educational foundations were part of what he would like to have been remembered for. Perhaps he might have

Conclusion 299

Figure 9.1 David Annand's statue of Wolsey at Ipswich

300   *Conclusion*

preferred the statue to be at Christ Church? But his grand tomb project also reminds us that he wanted to be remembered for much else besides. Nevertheless, it is a more positive representation and memorialisation than he has often been accorded. The Protestant Edward Hall bid God forgive him his Cardinal sins, and the Catholic Cavendish made him Fortune's victim. In a 'post-Christian' age, we should try to be fairer. As Dylan Thomas's Reverend Eli Jenkins puts it: 'We are not wholly bad or good, who live our lives under Milk Wood'.[2] Perhaps it is time, finally, to allow Thomas Wolsey to join the rest of us.

Notes

1 Cavendish, p. 192.
2 D. Thomas, *Under Milk Wood: A Play for Voices* (Everyman edition; London, 1977), p. 82.

Suggestions for further reading

Primary sources

As with any aspect of the reign of Henry VIII, the key source for Wolsey's administration and correspondence as cardinal and Chancellor during that reign is J. S. Brewer, J. Gairdner and R. H. Brodie (eds), *Letters and Papers, Foreign and Domestic of the Reign of Henry VIII* (21 vols; London, 1862–1932); now available in digital form through *British History Online*. The full texts of many documents related to Wolsey were published in *State Papers Published under the Authority of his Majesty's Commission, King Henry VIII* (11 vols; London, 1830–52), now also online (but less easily available). See also the *Letters of Richard Fox, 1486–1527*, ed. P. S. Allen and H. M. Allen (Oxford, 1929) and J. Strype, *Ecclesiastical Memorials Relating to Religion and the Reformation of It etc.* (3 vols; London, 1822).

As indicated in the Introduction, the nearest contemporary chronicles in which Wolsey features prominently are Edward Hall's [*The*] *Union of the Two Noble and Illustre Famelies of York and Lancastre*, ed. H. Ellis (London, 1809), known as Hall's *Chronicle*, also available online; and Polydore Vergil's *Anglica Historia*, ed. D. Hay (Camden Series, 3rd series 74, 1950) also online.

Foreign ambassadors reported frequently on Wolsey and their negotiations with him, see *Calendar of State Papers, Spanish*, ed. G. A. Bergenroth and others (13 vols; London, 1862–1964); *Calendar of State Papers and Manuscripts Relating to English Affairs, Existing in the Archives and Collections of Venice etc.*, eds R. Brown, C. Bentinck and H. Brown (9 vols; London, 1864–98); see also *Four Years at the*

302   *Suggestions for further reading*

court of Henry VIII. Selection of despatches written by the Venetian ambassador Sebastian Giustinian . . . 1515 to 1519, tr. by R. Brown (2 vols; London, 1854). An important source for Wolsey's last years is *Correspondance du Cardinal Jean du Bellay*, ed. R. Scheurer (2 vols; Paris, 1969); many items are in English in *Letters and Papers*.

The full texts of the treaties, some diplomatic correspondence and some papal documents relevant to Wolsey are contained in *Foedera, conventiones, literae et cuiuscunque generic acta publica*, ed. T. Rymer (20 vols; London, 1727–35). The Eltham Ordinances promulgated by Wolsey in January 1526 are included in *A collection of ordinances and regulations for the government of the royal household made in diverse reigns* published by the Society of Antiquaries of London (London, 1790).

Traces of Wolsey's possessions may be found in *The Inventory of Henry VIII*, ed. D. Starkey, vol. 1, published by the Society of Antiquaries of London (London, 1998) and vol. 2 *Textiles and Dress*, ed. M. Hayward and P. Ward (London, 2012).

Secondary sources

Biographies

As indicated in the Introduction, the first recognisable biography of Wolsey was Cavendish's *Life and Death of Cardinal Wolsey*; the standard publication of the original text is by the Early English Text Society (Oxford, 1959), ed. R. S. Sylvester. A modernised English version was published as *Two Early Tudor Lives*, ed. R. S. Sylvester and D. P. Harding (New Haven and London, 1962), which is the edition used throughout this book for ease of quotation in modern English. S. M. Jack wrote the entry for Wolsey in the *Oxford Dictionary of National Biography* (*ODNB* online) in 2004, revised in 2012. The most extensive account of Wolsey's public career is P. Gwyn's *The King's Cardinal: The Rise and Fall of Thomas Wolsey* (London, 1990). The collection of essays edited by S. J. Gunn, and P. G. Lindley, *Cardinal Wolsey: Church, State and Art* (Cambridge, 1991) covers very many aspects of Wolsey's administration as Chancellor and legate and his artistic patronage. See the Introduction for mention of Richard Fiddes's eighteenth-century *The Life of Cardinal Wolsey* and reference to accounts by Pollard and Elton, and more recent treatments by Stella Fletcher (London, 2009) and David Matusiak (Stroud, 2014).

For two recent appraisals of literary and other representations of Wolsey since his death, see J. Patrick Hornbeck II, *Remembering Wolsey: A History of Commemorations and Representations* (New York, 2019) and G. Schwartz-Leeper, *From Princes to Pages: The Literary Lives of Cardinal Wolsey, Tudor England's "Other King"* (Leiden, 2016). For brief discussions of Wolsey on film and television, see G. Richardson, 'Anne of a Thousand Days' in S. Doran and T. Freeman (eds), *Tudors and Stuarts on Film: Historical Perspectives* (Basingstoke, 2009), pp. 60–75 and 'A Cardboard Crown: Kingship in *The Tudors*', in W. Robison (ed.), *History, Fiction, and The Tudors. Queenship and Power* (New York, 2016), pp. 179–94.

D. Starkey's, *Henry: Virtuous Prince* (London, 2008) is very useful on the character and formation of the young Henry VIII in the years before Wolsey entered his service. See also G. Richardson, 'Boys and Their Toys: Kingship, Masculinity and Material Culture in the Sixteenth Century' in S. McGlynn and E. Woodacre (eds), *The Image and Perception of Monarchy in Medieval and Early-Modern England* (London, 2014), pp. 183–206, for a fuller discussion of young male monarchs and patriarchy. Wolsey features prominently in J. J. Scarisbrick's biography, *Henry VIII*, and he makes perceptive remarks about Wolsey's relationship with the king. Scarisbrick sees Wolsey's effort at peace-making as genuine and more ideologically based than does Gwyn. The book also offers what is still the fullest exposition of the canon law of the annulment case, although it has its critics. D. MacCulloch, *Thomas Cromwell: A Life* (London, 2018) demonstrates how much Wolsey depended upon Cromwell in his last years, how the latter's work for the cardinal led to his entry into royal service and how long-lasting was Cromwell's sense of loyalty to Wolsey, even if his support of some evangelicals would have alarmed his master. E. Ives, *The Life and Death of Anne Boleyn* (Oxford, 2004), pays due attention to Wolsey and his relations with Anne and argues that she did play a leading role in the downfall of the cardinal. D. Starkey, *Six Wives: The Queens of Henry VIII* (London, 2003) gives engaging attention to Henry's relationship with Katherine, to Anne's rise and her influence against Wolsey and to Wolsey's role in the annulment case. G. Mattingly, *Catherine of Aragon* (London, 1942) is still a gripping account of the queen's

304   *Suggestions for further reading*

tragic life. The online *Oxford Dictionary of National Biography* provides information on virtually all those significant in Wolsey's administration and the Church at the time, including prominent members of the nobility and gentry, the royal secretaries, Archbishop Warham and the other bishops. See G. Walker, *John Skelton and the Politics of the 1520s* (Cambridge, 1988) for a reappraisal of Skelton's poetry and his satires of Wolsey.

Politics, government and the law

J. Guy's introduction to sixteenth-century government *Tudor England* (Oxford, 1988) remains useful, as does J. Guy (ed.), *The Tudor Monarchy* (London, 1997). S. J. Gunn, *Early Tudor Government 1485–1558* (Basingstoke, 1995) provides an essential treatment of government in which Wolsey features prominently. See also S. Hindle, 'County Government in England', in R. Tittler and N. L. Jones (eds), *A Companion to Tudor Britain* (London, 1994). S. G. Ellis, *Tudor Frontiers and Noble Power: The Making of the British State* (Oxford 1995) deals with the limits of state formation which Wolsey had to contend. Further insight into government and administration is offered in the collection edited by D. MacCulloch, *The Reign of Henry VIII: Politics, Policy and Piety* (London, 1995), including Richard Hoyle's essay, 'War and Public Finance', pp. 75–99. G. Bernard (ed.), *The Tudor Nobility* (Manchester 1992) and his *Power and Politics in Tudor England* (Aldershot, 2000) look at the role of the nobility particularly. See also H. Miller, *Henry VIII and the English Nobility* (Oxford, 1986).

On Wolsey's role as Lord Chancellor and his administration more generally, the seminal work is J. Guy's *The Cardinal's Court: The Impact of Thomas Wolsey on Star Chamber* (Totowa, NJ, 1977), to be read in conjunction with extensive relevant sections in Gwyn's *The King's Cardinal*. On the royal court and council, see J. Guy, 'Thomas Wolsey, Thomas Cromwell and the Reform of Henrician Government', in MacCulloch (ed.), *The Reign of Henry VIII*, pp. 35–57. D. Starkey, 'Representation through Intimacy: A Study in the Symbolism of Monarchy and Court Office in Early-Modern England', in J. Guy (ed.), *The Tudor Monarchy*, offers a good account of Starkey's important work on the privy chamber. This work permeates his *The Reign of Henry VIII: Personality and Politics* (London, 1991) and *Six*

Wives mentioned previously. On the debate surrounding the 1519 'expulsion of the minions' episode, see G. Richardson, 'The Privy Chamber of Henry VIII and Anglo-French Relations 1515–1520', *The Court Historian* 4 (2) (1999): 119–40. For Buckingham, see C. Rawcliffe, *The Staffords, Earls of Stafford and Dukes of Buckingham, 1394–1521* (Cambridge, 1978). On the issue of court faction and Wolsey, see E. Ives, 'The Fall of Wolsey', in Gunn and Lindley, pp. 286–315, but this should be read in conjunction with G. Bernard, 'The Fall of Wolsey Reconsidered', *Journal of British Studies* 35 (3) (July 1996): 277–310.

On important aspects of Wolsey's administration and political patronage, see S. G. Ellis, 'A Border Baron and the Tudor State: The Rise and Fall of Lord Dacre of the North', *The Historical Journal* 35 (2) (1992): 253–77. See also N. Lewycky, 'Cardinal Thomas Wolsey and the City of York, 1514–1529', *Northern History* 46 (1): 43–60 and her 'Serving God and King: Cardinal Thomas Wolsey's Patronage Networks and Early Tudor Government, 1514–1529, with Special Reference to the Archdiocese of York' (Unpublished University of York PhD dissertation, 2009). For Wolsey and the West Country, see S. Lambe, '"Towards God religious, towards us most faithful": The Paulet Family and the Gentry of Early Tudor Somerset 1485–1547' (Unpublished University of Surrey PhD thesis, 2016), pp. 64–6. On the 'Amicable Grant' and the limits of Wolsey's power, see G. Bernard, *War, Taxation and Rebellion in Early Tudor England: Henry VIII, Wolsey and the Amicable Grant of 1525* (London, 1986), and R. L. Woods, 'Politics and Precedent: Wolsey's Parliament of 1523', *Huntingdon Library Quarterly*, 40 (4) (August 1977): 297–312.

Foreign policy

For the international context of European monarchy with which Wolsey had to deal, see G. Richardson, *Renaissance Monarchy: The Reigns of Henry VIII, Francis I and Charles V* (London, 2002). Scarisbrick's *Henry VIII* deals extensively with Wolsey's efforts on Henry's behalf internationally and his attitude to war and peace. R. J. Knecht's *Renaissance Warrior and Patron: The Reign of Francis I* (Cambridge, 1994) remains the fullest account of the French monarch with whom Wolsey dealt extensively on Henry's behalf.

306   *Suggestions for further reading*

G. Parker, *Emperor: A New Life of Charles V* (New Haven and London, 2019) is the same for the emperor whose priorities often clashed with those of Henry and Wolsey.

G. Richardson, *The Field of Cloth of Gold* (New Haven and London, 2013) discusses Wolsey's role in that event in 1520 and his efforts to promote Anglo–French peace until his fall. See also Richardson's 'Eternal Peace, Occasional War: Anglo French Relations under Henry VIII', in S. Doran and G. Richardson (eds), *Tudor England and Its Neighbours* (London, 2005) and also D. Grummit (ed.), *The English Experience in France c.1450–1558* (Aldershot, 2002). On the significance of Wolsey's legacy in Anglo–French relations, see Richardson's 'The French Connection: Francis I and England's Break with Rome', in G. Richardson, *'The Contending Kingdoms': France and England, 1520–1700* (Aldershot, 2008). On Henry's first war in France which Wolsey organised, see C. G. Cruickshank, *Army Royal, Henry VIII's Invasion of France 1513* (Oxford, 1969). On Wolsey's role in mediating peace in 1521, see P. Gwyn, 'Wolsey's Foreign Policy: The Conferences at Calais and Bruges Reconsidered', *HJ* 23 (4) (1980): 755–72. For the second and final war against France during Wolsey's time, see S. J. Gunn, 'The Duke of Suffolk's March on Paris in 1523', *EHR* 101 (400) (1986): 596–634.

The Church, governance and reform

The governance of the Church and that of the state more generally were closely related during Wolsey's time when the king's authority and the relationship between secular and canonical jurisdictions was a perennial issue; see G. W. Bernard, *The King's Reformation: Henry VIII and the Remaking of the English Church* (New Haven and London, 2005). See also his *The Late Medieval English Church: Vitality and Vulnerability before the Break with Rome* (New Haven and London, 2013).

On the context for, and impact of, Wolsey's episcopal and monastic reform efforts, see P. Marshall, *Reformation England 1480–1642* (Bloomsbury, USA, 2003) and J. J. Scarisbrick, *The Reformation and the English People* (Oxford, 1984). On the episcopate, see A. A. Chibi, *Henry VIII's Bishops: Diplomats, Administrators, Scholars and Shepherds* (Cambridge, 2003). See also S. E. Lehmberg, *The*

Reformation of Cathedrals: Cathedrals in English Society, 1485–1603 (Princeton, 1988), M. Bowker, *The Diocese of Lincoln under John Longland 1521–1547* (Cambridge, 1981) and M. J. Dowling, *Fisher of Men: A Life of John Fisher, 1469–1535* (Basingstoke, 1999).

On Wolsey and his efforts against heresy, see J. Arnold, 'John Colet, preaching and reform at St Paul's' Cathedral, 1505–19', *Historical Research*, 76 (194) (November 2003): 450–68 and C. W. D'Alton, 'The Suppression of Lutheran Heretics in England, 1526–1529', *Journal of Ecclesiastical History* 54(2) (April 2005): 228–53 on the demarcation between reformist and heretical thought under Wolsey. C. A. Hatt, *English Works of John Fisher, Bishop of Rochester (1469–1535) Sermons and Other Writings 1520–1535* (Oxford, 2002) for the texts of Fisher's sermons in 1521 and 1526 and their contexts. On the structure and governance of the monastic orders, see D. K. Knowles, *The Religious Orders in England* (3 vols; Oxford, 1947–59) and also J. G. Clark, *The Religious Orders in Pre-Reformation England* (Woodbridge, 2002). Cromwell's role in Wolsey's dissolution of monasteries is traced meticulously in P. J. Ward, 'The Origins of Thomas Cromwell's Public Career: Service under Cardinal Wolsey and Henry VIII, 1524–30' (Unpublished University of London PhD dissertation, 1999).

Relations with the papacy and the annulment case

For England's relations with the papacy and Wolsey's dealings with three successive pontiffs, see W. Wilkie, *The Cardinal Protectors of England: Rome and the Tudors before the Reformation* (Cambridge, 1974) and P. Partner, *The Pope's Men: The Papal Civil Service in the Renaissance* (Oxford, 1990). P. D. Clarke and M. Questier, *Papal Authority and the Limits of the Law in Tudor England, Camden Miscellany* XXXXVI, Camden Fifth Series, 48 (London, 2015) discusses the exact nature of Wolsey's legatine power and its consequences. W. Rockett, 'Wolsey, More, and the Unity of Christendom', *Sixteenth Century Journal* 35 (1) (2004): 133–53; J. Gairdner, 'New Lights on the Divorce of Henry VIII' *EHR* 11 (44) (October 1896): 673–702; 'New Lights on the Divorce of Henry VIII (Continued)' *EHR* 12 (46) (April 1897): 237–53; J. Sharkey, 'Between King and Pope: Thomas Wolsey and the Knight Mission', *Historical Research* 84 (224) (May 2011): 236–48; M. Dowling, 'Humanist

308   *Suggestions for further reading*

Support for Katherine of Aragon', *Bulletin of the Institute of Historical Research* 57 (135) (1984): 46–55. On the annulment and Wolsey's fall, see E. Ives, 'The Fall of Wolsey', in Gunn and Lindley, pp. 286–315; but see also G. Bernard, 'The Fall of Wolsey Reconsidered', *Journal of British Studies* 35 (3) (July 1996): 277–310 and L. Gardiner, 'Further News of Cardinal Wolsey's End, November–December 1530', *Bulletin of the Institute of Historical Research*, 57 (1984): 99–107.

Cultural patronage

On the cultural context of Henry VIII's reign and Wolsey's contribution, see D. Starkey (ed.), *Henry VIII: A European Court in England* (London, 1991) and S. Doran (ed.), *Henry VIII: Man and Monarch*, British Library Exhibition Catalogue (London, 2009).

On Wolsey's architectural patronage, see H. M. Colvin (ed.), *The History of the King's Works* (6 vols; London, 1933–82) and S. Thurley, *The Royal Palaces of Tudor England: Architecture and Court Life (1460–1547)* (New Haven and London, 1993). See also his *Hampton Court* (New Haven and London, 2003) and a jointly edited collection *Whitehall Palace: An Architectural History of the Royal Apartments 1240–1698* (New Haven and London, 2008).

The majority of the essays in Gunn and Lindley's *Cardinal Wolsey: Church, State and Art* (cited previously) are concerned with Wolsey's intellectual and material patronage and provide invaluable insights. T. Campbell's *Henry VIII and the Art of Majesty: Tapestries at the Tudor Court* (New Haven and London, 2008) has a useful chapter on the early court, including Wolsey. On Wolsey's books, see J. Carley, 'Thomas Wolsey's Epistle and Gospel Lectionaries: Unanswered Questions and New Hypotheses', *Bodleian Library Record* (August 2016): 43–59 and *The Books of King Henry VIII and His Wives* (London, 2004), which notes how many of Wolsey's books ended up in the royal collection. For the illuminated Gospel and Epistles lectionaries themselves, see www.wolseymanuscripts. ac.uk. See also J. Willoughby, 'Thomas Wolsey and the Books of Cardinal College, Oxford', *Bodleian Library Record* (October 2015): 114–34.

Index

Adrian VI, Pope (Adrian of Utrecht) 130, 135

Agostini, Agostino, physician to Wolsey 159, 271–2, 276, 279

Allen, Dr John, canon of Lincoln Cathedral 141–2

Almoner 139; royal 23, 25, 34, 36, 139; *see also* Wolsey, Cardinal Thomas

Amadas, Robert, goldsmith 176–7, 188, 297

Amboise Georges, Cardinal of 154, 170–1, 174, 209

'Amicable Grant' 103–7, 200, 211, 295

Amiens 119, 177, 186, 192, 209–10, 212, 228; *see also* Peace, Treaty of Westminster (1527)

Aragon, kingdom, king of: Katherine of (*see* Charles V, king of Aragon; Ferdinand, king of Aragon)

Ardres 62, 64, 65, 67

Arthur, prince of Wales 223, 226, 240

Bainbridge, Christopher, Archbishop of York 37, 46, 51, 118–21, 139, 173

Barcelona (treaty of, 1529) 243

Barlow, John, chaplain and messenger 232–4

Barnes, Robert of Cambridge Austin Friars 145–8, 150

Battle(s) of: Marignano (1515) 50; Pavia (1525) 104, 170, 200, 274; The Spurs (1513) 44

Beaufort, Henry, bishop of Winchester 117–18

Beaufort, Lady Margaret, mother of Henry VII 147, 150

Bibbiena, Cardinal of *see* Dovizi, Bernardo

Bilney, Thomas 147, 150

Birchenshawe, John, abbot of St Werburgh 140

Blackfriars, trial at, 1529 *see* Henry VIII, king of England, The king's 'Great Matter'

Blythe, Richard, bishop of Coventry and Lichfield 140–1

Boisy, Adrien, cardinal de *see* Gouffier, Adrien de, Cardinal de Boisy

Boleyn, Anne later queen of England 3, 5, 9, 11, 92, 102, 109, 110, 112, 157, 168, 208, 220, 230, 232, 236, 241–2, 245, 253–5, 257–8, 261, 268–71, 274, 292;

Boleyn, Sir Thomas, Earl of Wiltshire, father of Anne 3, 61, 97, 208, 227, 232, 245, 254, 256,

258, 267, 275, 292, 298; Mary, sister of Anne 109

Boucq, Jacques de, Flemish herald 39, 174

Bourbon, Charles, duke of Bourbon-Montpensier 64, 199–200, 208

Brandon, Charles, earl of Lincoln and duke of Suffolk 29, 35, 36, 47, 48–9, 54, 67, 91, 93, 106, 199, 227, 242–3, 247, 256, 259, 270

Brereton, Sir William 101–2

Bridewell, palace of 23, 161–2, 188, 245, 262

Bridge Court, Battersea 162

Brinon, Jean 201

Browne, Sir Anthony 97

Bruges, city and (treaty of 1521) 68, 129, 196–7, 215

Bryan, Sir Francis 96, 160, 240, 241–2, 258, 272–3, 276–9, 291

Buckingham, duke of *see* Stafford, Edward

Calais, and Pale of Calais 20, 34, 57, 62–3, 68, 69, 97, 98, 119, 121, 193, 195, 276; Conference at (1521) 129, 196–7, 199

Cambrai, treaties of (1517) and (1529) 'Peace of the Ladies' 55, 246–9, 253, 258, 272, 275, 277

Cambridge, town and university 25, 143, 145, 147–8, 158, 160, 162, 180, 181

Campeggio, Cardinal Lorenzo (Laurentius) papal legate, titular bishop of Salisbury 55, 109, 116, 121–4, 127, 135–6, 138, 168, 184, 237–8, 241, 243, 245, 247, 254–5, 257

Campion, Edmund 6

Canterbury, Archbishop: Court of arches 116; town, and abbey of

Saint Augustine 63, 141, 187, 198, 237, 239; *see also* Warham, William

Capon, Dr William, Dean of St Mary's, Ipswich 158, 269

Cardinal College, now Christ Church, Oxford 13, 38, 54, 124, 139–44, 147–8, 150, 175, 177, 179, 181–4, 186, 269

Cardinal-Protectors of England 37, 119–21

Carey, Dame Eleanor and her brother William 109

Casali, Gregorio English resident ambassador in Rome 227, 229, 234–8, 246, 248

Castellesi, Adriano, Cardinal 4, 29, 120–1, 138

Cavendish, George, gentleman usher, biographer of Wolsey 1, 5, 6, 7, 10, 14, 16, 17, 20, 21, 22, 30, 31, 42, 54, 73, 79, 80, 88, 94, 115, 157–8, 165, 173, 176, 192, 213, 219, 229, 244–5, 247, 252–6, 260, 265–9, 271, 282, 288–91, 300

Cawood Castle or House, near York 175, 177, 269–71, 278, 259–60, 290

Chancellor, Lord, Chancery 7, 9, 26, 64, 74, 75–81, 86, 88, 90, 94, 104, 111, 219; *see also* Wolsey, Cardinal Thomas

Chapuys, Eustace, Imperial ambassador 3, 10, 254, 256–8, 272–6, 279

Charles V, king of Aragon, and Holy Roman Emperor 11, 21, 35, 55, 57, 60, 61, 63, 65–6, 68, 69, 70, 91, 98, 103, 124, 129–30, 193–5, 200–5; his sister Eleanor 206, 209, 214, 221–6, 243, 245–6, 254, 256, 273–4, 294

Charles VII, king of France 27, 194

Chester, County Palatinate of, Chesire 87, 101, 140

Chichele, Henry, Archbishop of Canterbury 117

Christ Church, Oxford *see* Cardinal College

Church, in England 2, 4, 5, 9, 12–13, 100, 121, 149–51, 155, 249, 252, 257, 261–4, 267, 280–2, 288, 295–6; Bishops/ prelates, dioceses, clergy, reform of 125–8, 136–40; 'Universal' 10, 29, 116–7, 228, 249, 279–81; *see also* monasticism, religious orders, reform, dissolutions

Claude de France, queen of France 62, 206

Clement VII, Pope (Giulio de' Medici) 120–1, 125, 128, 129, 135–7, 138, 149, 200, 208, 212, 214, 215, 225, 227–34, 237, 239, 246, 249, 263, 273, 277–8, 288

Clements, John, lecturer in classics 182–3

Clerk, John, royal secretary, ambassador, Bishop of Bath and Wells 26, 95, 118, 129, 135, 136, 146, 204

Clerk, John, student at Cardinal College 147–8

Cognac, League of (1526) 205, 207–9, 214, 215

Colet, John dean of St Paul's Cathedral 18, 53, 84, 180

Coligny, Gaspard de, seigneur de Châtillon 64

common law, common law lawyers 81–5

Compiègne 119, 213, 228, 232

Constantinople 55, 184

Corpus Christi College, Oxford 21, 180

Council in the North 82, 102

Council *see* Royal council, councillors

courts, judicial: Court of Requests 81, 82, 86; *see also* King's Bench, Court of

courts, royal *see* Royal Court

Creighton, Mandell, biographer of Wolsey 7, 16

Cromwell, Thomas, later Earl of Essex 6, 8, 102, 106, 139, 143–4, 148, 160, 172, 182, 261, 265–7, 270, 279, 290, 293, 294

Croy, Guillaume de, marquis of Aerschot 68

Dacre, Lord of the North 85, 102

Darcy, Thomas, Lord 256, 264–5

Daubeney, Giles, Lord 101, 163–5

Daundy, Joan Wolsey's mother 17

Deane, William, Archbishop of Canterbury 28

Denys, Thomas, Wolsey's chamberlain 158

De Praet, imperial ambassador in England 88

Docwra, Thomas, Prior of the Knights of Saint John 174

Doria, Andrea and Filipino, mercenary admirals 215–16

Dover, town and port 63, 121, 198, 239, 275, 279

Dovizi, Bernardo, Cardinal da Bibbiena 122–4

Du Bellay, Jean, bishop of Bayonne, French ambassador in England 168, 170, 212, 242, 244, 246, 256, 257–8, 275

Duprat, Antoine, archbishop of Sens, cardinal, chancellor of France 119

Durham, Bishopric of, Durham Place 34, 67, 155, 163, 253; *see also* Ruthall, Thomas

East Anglia 104, 106, 137, 142, 144, 148, 157, 215
Edward III, king of England 27, 91, 212
Edward IV, king of England 43, 91, 107, 141
Egerton, Sir Ralf 101
Elizabeth I, queen of England 6
Eltham, palace of: *Ordinances* of (1526) 106–9, 168, 203, 204
enclosures, Wolsey's action against 85–8
Erasmus of Rotterdam 25, 58, 70, 123–4, 126, 139, 145, 154–5, 180, 182, 183
Esher, Wolsey's manor house at 170, 175, 262, 267
Etaples, (treaty of, 1492) 27
Evil May Day (1517) 83

Faryfax, Robert, composer and musician 186–7
Ferdinand, king of Aragon 27, 28, 43, 46, 50, 202
Fiddes, Richard, biographer of Wolsey 6, 9, 16
Field of Cloth of Gold 11, 61–8, 70, 129, 157–8, 170, 173, 177, 192–4, 196, 208, 209, 211, 212; *Field of Cloth of Gold, The*, painting at Hampton Court Palace 66
Fisher, John, bishop of Rochester 36, 126, 134, 136, 139, 145, 146, 192–3, 224, 263–4, 280–1, 288
Fitzjames, Richard, bishop of London 130–1
Fitzroy, Henry, duke of Richmond 102
Fitzwilliam, William, Sir, (later 1st earl of Southampton) 158, 160, 203–4, 206, 266
Foix, Odet de, seigneur de Lautrec 199, 215

Foxe, Edward, English ambassador in Rome 236, 248, 236–8, 248
Foxe, John, martyrologist 5, 7, 8, 147
Fox, Richard, bishop of Winchester 21, 29, 30, 31, 33, 34, 44, 76, 124, 180
France 33–4, 122, 127, 134, 136, 138, 199, 200, 205, 209, 211, 214, 293; Relations with, commercial, cultural 42, 46, 49, 54, 55, 58, 60, 83, 98–9, 107, 108, 186–7, 199 (*see also* Peace)
Francis I, earl of Angoulême, and king of France 11, 33, 47, 48, 50, 54, 55, 56, 57, 59, 60, 63, 68, 70, 91, 96–8, 104, 120, 122, 156, 170, 176, 177, 192–4, 198, 200, 201, 204, 206–7, 221, 226, 242–3, 272, 274–7, 294
François the dauphin, son of Francis I 56, 58, 65, 69, 193, 202, 206, 207, 211, 215, 249

Gambara, Umberto, papal nuncio to England 53, 229, 234, 236
Gardiner, Stephen, secretary (later Bishop of Winchester) 37, 95, 160–1, 209, 236–9, 248, 253–4, 269, 277, 293
Garrett, Thomas, student of Cardinal College 147–8
Garter, Order of 23, 75, 211, 212, 214; *see also* Saint George's, Chapel Windsor castle
Gascoigne, Sir William 101–2, 103, 159, 260
gentilshommes de la chambre see Royal court
Gentlemen of the king's Privy Chamber *see* Royal court
Germany *see* Holy Roman Empire
Ghinucci, Girolamo, titular bishop of Worcester 109, 227, 229

Index 313

Gigli, Giovanni, titular bishop of Worcester 119; Silvestro, titular bishop of Worcester 37, 120–1, 128, 138

Giustinian, Sebastian, Venetian ambassador to England 10, 16, 55, 84, 88, 96–7, 155, 175, 176, 179

Gouffier, Adrien de, Cardinal de Boisy 67, 124

Gostwick (later Sir) John 159–60

Grafton, Northamptonshire 255–6, 257, 260

Grammont, Gabriel, cardinal de, bishop of Tarbes 206, 227

'Great Matter' the king's *see* Henry VIII, king of England

Great Seal of England 74, 75–6, 99, 177, 202, 259, 262, 292

Greenwich, Palace 38, 49, 59, 88, 178, 198, 208, 212, 221, 237, 262, 266, 292

Gresham, Richard, merchant 173–4

Grey, Thomas, marquis of Dorset 19, 20, 66, 84, 106, 201

Grocyn, William, scholar 18

Guildford, Sir Henry, Comptroller of the royal household 66, 178

Guînes 62, 64, 65, 66, 67

Habsburg, house of: Charles of, Holy Roman Emperor (*see* Charles V, king of Aragon); Maximilian of (*see* Maximilian I, Holy Roman Emperor)

Hales, Christopher, attorney-general 257

Hall, Edward, MP and author of 'Hall's Chronicle' 4, 5, 6, 7, 11, 14, 28, 31, 92, 93, 95, 105, 107, 117, 121, 133–4, 175, 244, 247, 263, 270, 279

Hampton Court Palace 13, 39–40, 65, 95, 163–8, 170, 174, 175, 183–8, 197, 198, 205, 213, 236, 266, 297, 300

Hanseatic League, 'Steelyard', London 145–6

Hart, Percival gentleman 97

Hayes, Cornelius, goldsmith 177–8

Heneage, Thomas, gentleman usher 160

Henry VII, king of England 4, 20, 21, 22, 27, 28, 43, 79, 84, 87, 130, 141, 186, 223

Henry VIII, king of England 1–2, 11, 14, 22, 36, 38, 44, 48–9, 52, 53, 58, 63, 67–70, 75, 84, 88, 89–90, 93, 94–5, 105, 107, 110–11, 197, 199, 201, 202; Blackfriars, trial at 1529 225, 244, 247; 'Break with Rome', beginning of 280–2; 'Defender of the Faith' 128–34, 143, 249; The king's 'Great Matter' 6, 7, 9, 28, 168, 206, 208, 210, 219–30, 231–5, 238–42, 248, 254, 258–9, 263, 267, 275, 277–81, 289–92, 297–303, 307–8; tomb project 172–3, 187

Henry, Prince of England, son of Henry VIII 28

heresy, Wolsey and *see* Luther, Martin, Wolsey and Lutheran heresy

Holbein, Hans, the Younger, painter 171, 178–80, 189

Holinshed, Raphael, chronicler 6

Holland, William, goldsmith 175

Holy Roman Empire, Emperor, Electors of, lands of 55, 56–7, 60, 61, 69, 96; *see also* Charles V, king of Aragon; Maximilian I, Holy Roman Emperor

hostages, French, for the 1518 treaty of London *see* Universal Peace

314   *Index*

Howard, house of: Edward, Lord
Admiral 34; Thomas, earl of Surrey
and 2nd duke of Norfolk (d, 1524)
29, 35, 37, 45, 47, 54, 92, 97,
106; Thomas, earl of Surrey, and
3rd duke of Norfolk 3, 35, 93, 242,
256, 258–9, 265, 271, 273–5,
279, 291; Thomas, brother of
Edward 34
Hunne, Richard, 'Hunne's Case'
130–2, 261

illuminated manuscripts/books *see*
Wolsey, Cardinal Thomas, books
and manuscripts
Imperial *see* Holy Roman Empire
Ipswich 13, 16–17; *see also* Saint
Mary's College, Ipswich
Isabella, queen of Castile 240

James IV, king of Scotland 20, 21,
34, 50, 65
Jerningham, Sir Richard, English
ambassador in France 193, 203
Jewel House, the Royal 177–8
Jordan, Dame Isabel of Wilton
Priory 109
jousts, tilting *see* tournament
Julius II, Pope (Giuliano della
Rovere) 28, 29, 33, 42, 120,
222–3, 226–31
Justices and Commissions of the
Peace 81, 82, 100, 211

Katherine of Aragon, queen of
England, wife of Henry VIII 2,
6, 20, 21, 22, 28, 29, 31, 63, 67,
134, 145, 166, 206; annulment
case 220–3, 226–7, 230–1, 236,
239–40, 243–5, 248, 253, 284
Kidderminster, Richard, abbot of
Winchcombe 131–2, 261

King's Bench, Court of 77, 79, 131,
257; *see also* courts, judicial
Kingston, Sir William, Constable of
the Tower 282–5
Kratzer, Niklaus, astronomer 208
Keane, Charles, actor 6
Knight, William, English ambassador
to Rome 228, 229–34, 245
Knights of Saint John of Jerusalem
23, 163, 174

La Bastie, French ambassador *see* La
Vernade
La Guiche, Pierre de, French
ambassador 3
La Marck, Robert II, duke of
Boullion 195
Larke, Joan or Jane, Wolsey's partner
25–6, 141; Thomas, brother to
Joan 25, 158
Latimer, Hugh, chaplain to
Cambridge University 147, 150
Lautrec, Marshal of France *see* Foix,
Odet de
Lavenham, Suffolk 104
La Vernade, de Olivier, seigneur de
La Bastie, French ambassador
61, 96
Legate, legatine authority *see* Wolsey,
Cardinal Thomas
Leicester, abbey and town 283–5
Leo X, Pope (Giovanni de' Medici)
34, 36, 37, 42, 43, 44, 50, 52, 55,
56, 69, 75, 118, 120, 123–4, 128,
131, 149, 194–7, 247
Lilgrave, William, Somerset 19
Limington 19–20, 101
Lincoln 143, 173; *see also* Longland,
John, bishop of Lincoln; Wolsey,
Cardinal Thomas
loans, forced 103–7; *see also* 'Amicable
Grant'

Index 315

London 53, 83, 92, 93, 94, 99, 102, 103, 105, 128, 150, 166, 176, 198, 215; Tower of 260, 282, 289, 290, 291; (1514 treaty of) (*see* Peace); (1518 treaty of) (*see* Peace, Universal Peace)

London, Dr John, Warden of New College, Oxford 147–8

Longland, John, bishop of Lincoln 137–40, 142, 220

Louis XII, king of France 29, 33, 43, 44, 46, 47, 49, 50, 70, 174, 194, 215, 220

Louise of Savoy, mother of Francis I 65, 67, 139, 177, 201, 202, 246, 248

Low Countries *see* Netherlands

Luther, Martin, Wolsey and Lutheran heresy 128, 145–8, 150, 183

Lydd, Kent 20

Madeleine de France, daughter of Francis I 193

Madrid, treaty of, (1526) 202–4, 249, 277

Magdalen College, Oxford 18, 19, 79, 180, 184

Maiano, Giovanni da, Florentine sculptor 170–2

Manuel, Juan, Imperial ambassador in Rome 68, 69

Marguerite of Angoulême, queen of Navarre, sister of Francis I 239

Marguerite of Savoy (of Austria), Regent of the Netherlands 215, 246

Marignano *see under* Battle(s) of

Marrney, Sir Henry 93

Martin V, Pope (Oddone Colonna) 117

Mary [Tudor], princess of England, daughter of Henry VIII 5, 56, 58, 65, 82, 90, 166, 183, 193, 207, 222, 284

Mary [Tudor], queen of France, duchess of Suffolk, sister of Henry VIII 21, 35, 45–6, 47–9, 69

Maximilian I, Holy Roman Emperor 21, 27, 32, 43, 50, 55, 57, 60, 121

Medici, Giovanni de' *see* Clement VII, Pope; Leo X, Pope

Mendoza, Inigo de, Imperial ambassador in England 206–7, 241

Milan, duchy of 50–1, 69, 194–9, 205, 275–6, 283; *see also* Sforza, Massimiliano, duke of Milan

'minions', favourites of Henry VIII *see* Gentlemen of the King's Privy Chamber

monasticism, religious orders, reform, dissolutions 117, 123–4, 126–30, 138–44, 150

Montmorency, Anne de, seigneur de La Rochepot 26, 213–14

More, Sir Thomas, secretary, councillor, Lord Chancellor 14, 79, 87, 95, 126, 128, 178, 183, 209, 246, 252, 259, 262, 288

More, The, Wolsey's residence in Hertfordshire 95, 169–70, 253; (treaty of, 1525) (*see* Peace)

Morris, Christopher 'Gunner', messenger 229–31

Morton, Cardinal John, Archbishop of Canterbury 78, 118–19, 127, 130, 149, 154, 164, 293

Nanfan, Sir Richard, Lieutenant of Calais 20, 21, 278

Naples, kingdom, kings, city of 194, 215, 236, 239, 242

Neufville, Nicholas de, French ambassador in England 45

Neville, Thomas 95

Norfolk, dukes of *see* Howard

316　*Index*

Norris, Henry, Groom of the Stool
　255–6, 260–1, 281
Northumberland, earls of *see* Percy,
　Henry
Noyon, (treaty of, 1516) 194

Order of the Garter *see* Garter, Order of
Order of Saint Michael *see* Saint
　Michael, Order of
Orléans, house of: Henri d' duke of,
　son of Francis I, (later Henri II
　of France) 195; Louis d' duke of
　Longueville 44
Ottoman Empire and rulers 55, 56,
　70, 205, 277
Oxford University x, xi, 6, 15, 18–19,
　21, 36, 38, 139, 140–2, 145,
　147–8, 166, 180–2, 182–3; *see also*
　Cardinal College, Christ Church

Pace, Richard, royal secretary 58, 90,
　95, 99, 118, 129–30
Page, Sir Richard 103
papacy, papal 8, 51, 52, 55, 65,
　68, 69, 70, 205, 212, 214, 219,
　228, 272–3, 276–7, 280–2; bulls
　and dispensations, (1504) 221,
　240–1; 'breve/brief', Spanish brief
　224–5, 240–2; Curia, Consistory
　and Rota 28, 117–23, 124,
　135–8, 139, 142, 206, 229, 235,
　246, 263; requests for (1527–9)
　231–2, 235–6, 237–9, 255; *see also*
　Clement VII, Pope; Julius II, Pope;
　Leo X, Pope
Paris 26, 33, 59, 122, 156, 176, 199,
　206, 239
Parliament of England 2, 77, 82–3,
　103–6, 256–7, 259–60, 262–3
Passano, Jean Joachim de, seigneur de
　Vaux, French ambassador 200–1,
　272–4, 277–9

Paulet, Sir Amias 20, 101
Pavia *see* Battle(s) of
peace, peace-making, ideals of 9, 11,
　57, 58, 59, 70, 75; Amiens (treaty
　of, 1527) (*see* peace, 'Eternal
　Peace'); Anglo-French 43, 44, 45,
　47, 92, 175–6, 186, 193, 196,
　202, 204, 206–8, 211–4, 221,
　226, 239, 275; 'Eternal Peace'
　(treaty of, 1527) 169, 175–6, 186.
　205, 207, 209–10, 226; French
　hostages, for the Universal Peace
　60, 61, 91, 96; Treaty of London,
　(1514) 45, 51, 207; Treaty of
　London (1518) (*see* Universal
　Peace); Treaty of The More (1525)
　201–3, 206–7, 272; Treaty of
　Westminster (1527) 207–8, 221;
　Universal Peace (treaty of, 1518)
　55, 56, 57, 59, 70–1, 96, 192,
　194–6, 247
Pius III, Pope (Francesco
　Piccolomini) 119–20
Percy, Henry, 4th and 5th earls of
　Northumberland 67, 58, 85, 102,
　157, 175, 270–1, 282–3
Perreál Jean, French court painter 45
Pollard, A.F., biographer of Wolsey 7,
　8, 10, 16, 115, 133, 293
popes *see* individual names; papacy,
　papal
praemunire charge of, controversies
　over 130–2, 256–7, 260–2, 264–5,
　268, 280
Privy Council *see* Royal Council
Privy Seal, Keeper of 76, 136
Pucci, Cardinal, papal datary
　234–5
Pygot, Thomas 84; Richard,
　composer and musician 186
Pynson, Richard, royal printer
　41n33, 58

Redman, Henry mason 162
Richard II, king of England 100
Richard III king of England 106, 118, 285
Richmond, Palace, Park 38, 168, 170, 232, 268, 272, 285
Rome 37, 51, 52, 66, 69–70, 208, 209, 215, 224, 226, 235, 239, 249; sack of 225; *see also* papacy, papal
Rotterdam, Erasmus of *see* Erasmus of Rotterdam
Rovezzano, Benedetto da, sculptor 172–3, 267
Royal Council, councillors 29, 31, 32, 66, 74, 75–6, 82, 87, 88, 94, 97, 107; *see also* Star Chamber
Royal Court/household, courtiers, entourages, household officers 98, 100, 106–9, 161; Gentlemen of the King's Privy Chamber, minions 96–8, 102, 108–9, 203, 204; *gentilshommes de la chambre du roi* 59, 60
Russell, Sir John 266
Ruthall, Thomas, bishop of Durham 99, 136, 138, 174

Sacheverell, Sir Richard 84
Sadler, Ralph, Cromwell's servant 266
Saint Alban's, abbey of *see* Wolsey, Cardinal Thomas
Saint Frideswide's Priory, Oxford 142–3, 180–1
Saint George 34, 168; Chapel of, Windsor Castle 23, 171, 172; *see also* Garter, Order of the
Saint-Germain-en-Laye, château of 193
Saint Mary's College, Ipswich 13, 124, 142–4, 150, 175, 177, 182–3
Saint Michael, Order of 211–12

Saint Paul's Cathedral, Churchyard/ Preaching Place 128–9, 133, 139, 146, 172, 186, 212–13
Sandys, Sir William, (later Baron) 57
Savorgnano, Mario, Venetian ambassador 162, 176
Scotland 21, 34, 50, 65, 63, 85, 137, 276; *see also* James IV of Scotland
secretaries, royal *see* Clerk, Gardiner, More, Pace
Sforza, Massimiliano, duke of Milan 50, 205
Shakespeare, William 4, 117
Shelley, Sir William 266–7, 284
Skelton, John, poet 3, 5, 26, 86, 91, 99, 134, 150, 164, 179, 265
Smith, Sir Thomas, Elizabethan commentator 80, 85
Smith, William, bishop of Lincoln 36, 173
Somerset, Charles (born Beaufort) earl of Worcester 33
Spain: 'Spurs' (*see* Battle(s) of); *see* Charles V, king of Aragon; Ferdinand, king of Aragon
Stafford, Edward, duke of Buckingham 6, 37, 67; fall of 91–4, 106, 291
Standish, Henry, Franciscan, Bishop of St Asaph 131–2, 281
Star Chamber, royal council as 78, 84, 85, 88, 93, 106, 211
Strong, Sampson, artist 38
Stubbs, Lawrence, Wolsey's almoner and building supervisor 158, 164
Suffolk 13, 104; De la Pole, dukes of 75; duchess of (*see* Mary [Tudor], queen of France, duchess of Suffolk, sister of Henry VIII); duke of (*see* Brandon, Charles); Ufford, earls of 75
Swiss confederation, mercenaries 44, 50, 54, 205

318 *Index*

Talbot, George, earl of Shrewsbury 34, 269, 272
Taverner, John composer and musician 186
Taylor, Dr John, ambassador in France, dean of the Chapel Royal 26, 156, 203–5
taxation, levies, subsidies 82–3, 103–6, 118, 157, 295; *see also* Amicable Grant
Thames, river, riverside 23, 37, 38, 88, 122, 160, 161–3, 168
Tittenhanger 253
Torrigiano, Pietro, Florentine sculptor 170–2, 188
Tournai, city of, bishopric of 35, 36, 37, 47, 49, 56, 60, 65, 121, 173, 197
tournaments 2, 58, 61, 66
Trinity College, Cambridge 143
Tunstall, Cuthbert, bishop of London 136, 139, 146–8, 209, 278, 246
Turks *see* Ottomans
Twisleton, John, goldsmith 188
Tyndale, William 3, 4, 145, 47, 226

Universal Peace (Treaty of, 1518) *see* Peace
Urban II, Pope 55

Vaux, seigner de *see* Passano, Jean Joachim
Venice, Venetians, ambassadors 46, 49, 50, 51, 55, 64, 84, 88, 96, 155, 162, 175, 184; *see also* Giustinian
Vergil, Polydore, papal collector and author 4, 17, 25, 29, 30–2, 36, 51, 54, 91, 94, 95, 111, 133–4, 226
Victoria and Albert Museum 174
Vivez, Juan, humanist scholar 183

Wales, Council of the Marches in, dioceses of 82, 87, 100, 137

Wallop, John, English ambassador 205
Walpole, Horace, of Strawberry Hill 7, 54
Walsh, Sir Walter, Gentlemen of the Privy Chamber 270–1
Walsingham, Norfolk, Shrine of Our Lady 24, 145, 160, 165
Warham, William, Archbishop of Canterbury 12, 20, 53, 75, 76, 77, 132–4, 137, 138, 178, 293
Warren, Richard, gentleman usher to Wolsey 62, 158
Waynflete, William *see* Magdalen College, Oxford
West, Nicholas, bishop of Ely 106, 136
Westminster, city of 53, 102, 124, 166, 292; Abbey 53, 162; Palace, Hall of 27, 37, 38, 50, 78, 79, 83, 85, 88, 94, 95, 100, 111, 163, 256; (treaty of, 1527) (*see* Peace)
Whitehall, palace *see* York Place, Westminster
Wilton, Priory, abbess of 109, 140; *see also* Carey, Dame Eleanor and her brother William
Winchester, bishop of 21, 35, 155, 170, 253, 267–9, 278; York, dean and archbishop of 1, 12, 16, 24, 34, 37, 45, 70, 75, 102, 116, 133–4, 137, 155, 157, 267–8, 278–80; *see also* Fox Richard; Gardiner, Stephen
Windsor, Sir Andrew 84
Windsor, town and castle 38; (treaty of, 1522) 198; *see also* Saint George's Chapel, Windsor
Wingfield, Sir Richard, ambassador in France 61, 65, 176, 193, 203
Wolsey, Cardinal Thomas: almoner and councillor to Henry VIII 23, 27, 29, 36, 74–6; appearance, likeness, portraits, portrayals

38–9, 174, 178–9; arms, coat of arms, motto 24, 52, 171, 177, 178, 184; arrest and death 282–5; Artistic, architectural, patronage 35, 296–7; Bath and Wells, bishop of 121–2, 155; birth, background and childhood family 16–17; books and manuscripts 183–5; building and renovation works 161, 162–3, 164–70; Cardinal, cardinalate 51, 52, 63, 66, 74, 214 (cardinal spider 168); cat or cats 168, 298; Chancellor and Chancery 7, 9, 23, 24, 26, 64, 74–9, 94, 100, 111, 132, 141, 214, 257–8, 294–5; chaplain to William Deane and to Henry VII 28, 79; character, personality 111; children, Dorothy, and Thomas Wynter 26, 156 (*see also* Larke, Joan); ecclesiastical 132–4, 136, 142, 149, 154–6, 163, 167–8, 173, 176, 183, 247; French pension 50, 201, 272; glass, stained glass 167–9; 'Great Matter' 6, 7, 9, 28, 168, 206, 208, 210, 219–30, 231–5, 238–42, 248, 254, 258, 263, 267, 275, 277–81, 289–92, 297–303, 307–8; hat or 'galero' 1, 6, 53, 54, 64, 75, 115, 122, 177, 184, 298; health, illness 165–6, 283–5; Household 155, 158–61, 165 (Chapel in his household 24, 158–9, 167–8, 186–7; Gentlemen ushers 160 (*see also* Cavendish, George; Heneage, Thomas; Warren, Richard); Horses and hunting 159, 213); Lincoln, dean and bishop of 22, 23, 35, 37; music and choirs 186–7; ordination, priesthood 19, 24, 25, 229; Papacy, candidatures for, relations with 129–30, 135,

219, 241; papal *legate a latere*, powers, dispensations, conferences 1, 2, 7, 9, 51, 52, 55, 64, 67, 74–5, 100, 115–18, 129, 132–6, 135–6, 155, 194, 220, 225, 228, 235, 258, 295–6; plate, goldsmiths work 175–8; relationship with Henry 89–90, 94–5, 110–12, 167, 177–8, 188–9, 206–7, 224–5, 228–30, 233, 255–5, 259–61, 264–5, 266–9, 278–80, 281–5, 297–8; schooling and university education at Magdalen College, Oxford 18–19; St Alban's, abbot of 155, 169, 177, 267, 269, 278; tapestry and hangings, textiles 162–3, 173–5; tomb project 171–3, 179, 297, 300; Tournai, bishop of 201

Wolsey, Robert, father of Thomas 16–17

Worcester, bishops of 37, 109, 119, 121, 128, 136, 147, 227; earl of (*see* Somerset, Charles); *see also* Ghinucci, Girolamo; Gigli, Giovanni

Wriothesely, Thomas, Garter King of Arms 75

Wykeham, William of, founder of New College, Oxford 180

York, Archbishopric of 46, 102–3, 115, 116, 133–4, 137, 157, 173, 267–8; *see also* Bainbridge, Christopher; Wolsey, Cardinal Thomas

York, City of 102–3, 170, 269–70

York Place, Westminster 13, 37, 88, 94, 155, 158, 161–3, 164, 169, 171–7, 183, 188, 197, 198, 221, 245, 256, 259, 266–8

Younge, Sir John Master of the Rolls 174

Taylor & Francis eBooks

www.taylorfrancis.com

A single destination for eBooks from Taylor & Francis
with increased functionality and an improved user
experience to meet the needs of our customers.

90,000+ eBooks of award-winning academic content in
Humanities, Social Science, Science, Technology, Engineering,
and Medical written by a global network of editors and authors.

TAYLOR & FRANCIS EBOOKS OFFERS:

A streamlined
experience for
our library
customers

A single point
of discovery
for all of our
eBook content

Improved
search and
discovery of
content at both
book and
chapter level

REQUEST A FREE TRIAL
support@taylorfrancis.com